More HOW TO DRAW MANGA

Vol. 3

Enhancing a Character's Sense of Presence

MORE HOW TO DRAW MANGA Vol. 3: Enhancing a Character's Sense of Presence
by Hikaru Hayashi, Rio Yagizawa/ Go Office

This book was first designed and published by Graphic-sha Publishing Co., Ltd. in Japan in 2003.
This English edition was published by Graphic-sha Publishing Co., Ltd. in Japan in 2004.

Artwork and Production: Kazuaki Morita, Yumiko Deguchi, Hiroko Shioda, Akira Gokita, Haruto, Kozue Onishi, Ushio, Kei Asagi, Ru'u, Mayumi Tomaru, Kento Shimazaki, Rio Yagizawa

Production Assistant: Takumi Takahashi, Kozue Onishi, Haruki Takahashi
Production Support: Julie Asakura
Cover Artwork: Kazuaki Morita
English Main Title Logo Design: Hideyuki Amemura
Composition and Text: Hikaru Hayashi, Rio Yagizawa (Go Office)
Article Contributor : Yoshihiro Yonezawa
Reference Photography: Go Office
English Edition Layout: Shinichi Ishioka
English Translation Management: Língua fránca, Inc. (an3y-skmt@asahi-net.or.jp)
Planning Editor: Motofumi Nakanishi (Graphic-sha Publishing Co., Ltd.)
Foreign Language Edition Project Coordinator: Kumiko Sakamoto (Graphic-sha Publishing Co., Ltd.)

Distributor:
Japan Publications Trading Co., Ltd.
1-2-1 Sarugaku-cho, Chiyoda-ku, Tokyo, 101-0064
Telephone: +81(0)3-3292-3751 Fax: +81(0)3-3292-0410
E-mail: jpt@jptco.co.jp
URL: http://www.jptco.co.jp/

First printing: August 2004

ISBN 4-7661-1484-1
Printed and bound in China

More HOW TO DRAW MANGA

Vol. 3

Enhancing a Character's Sense of Presence

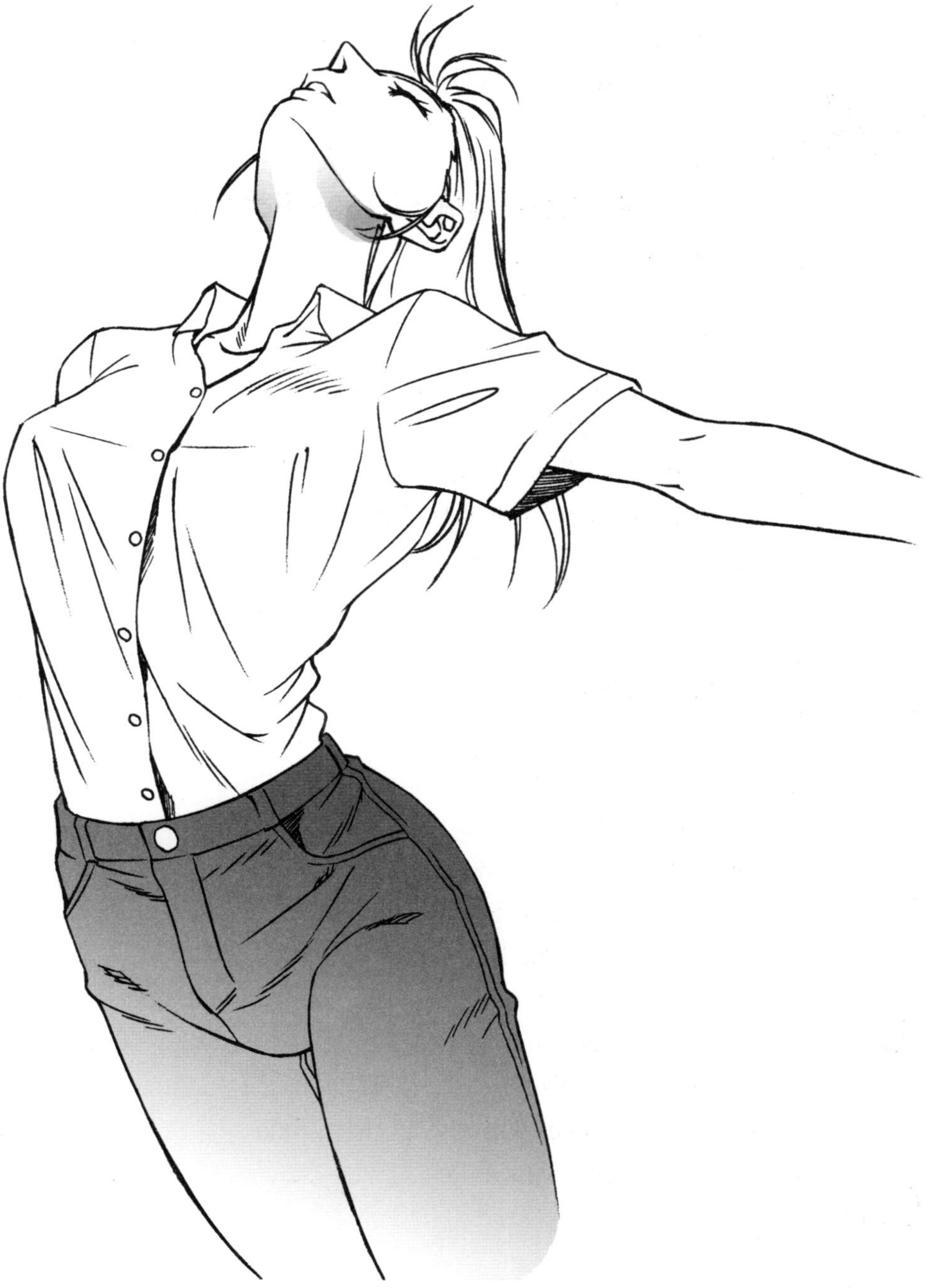

Table of Contents

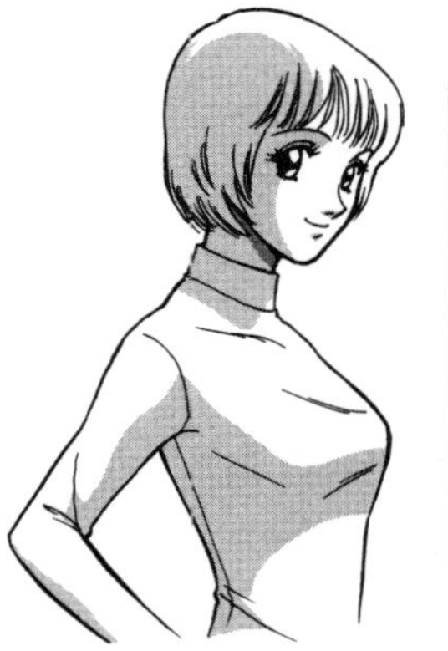

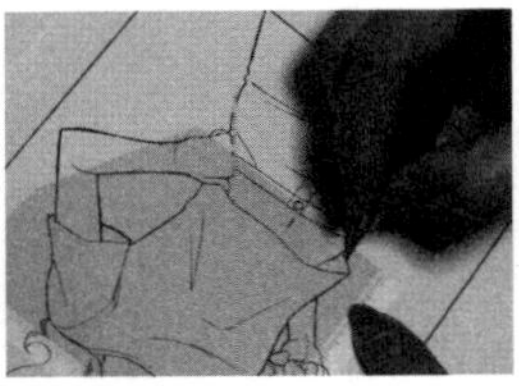

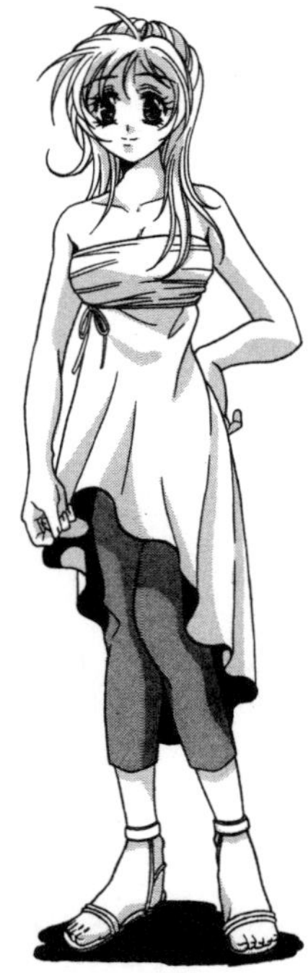

Chapter 1
The Importance of Tone Work

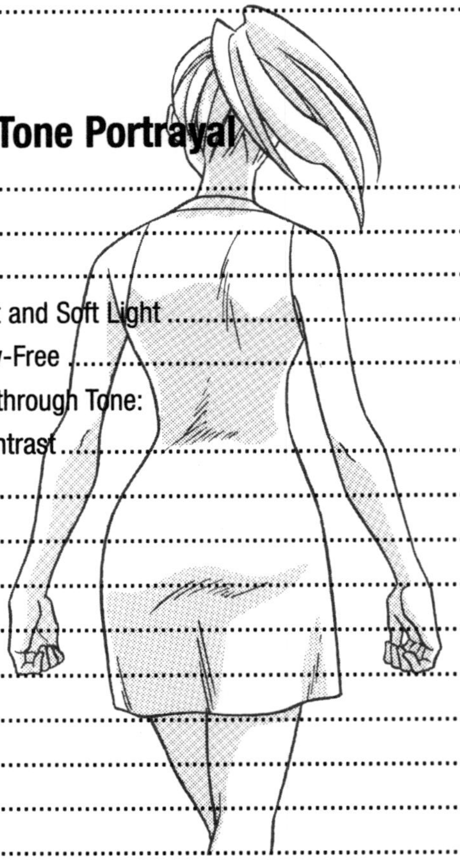

Chapter 2
Character Shading and Tone Portrayal

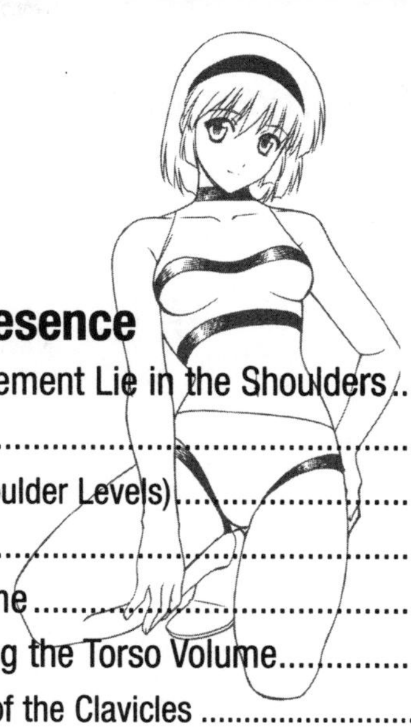

Chapter 3
Movement with a Sense of Presence

Chapter 4
More *Manga*

Objectives of this Book

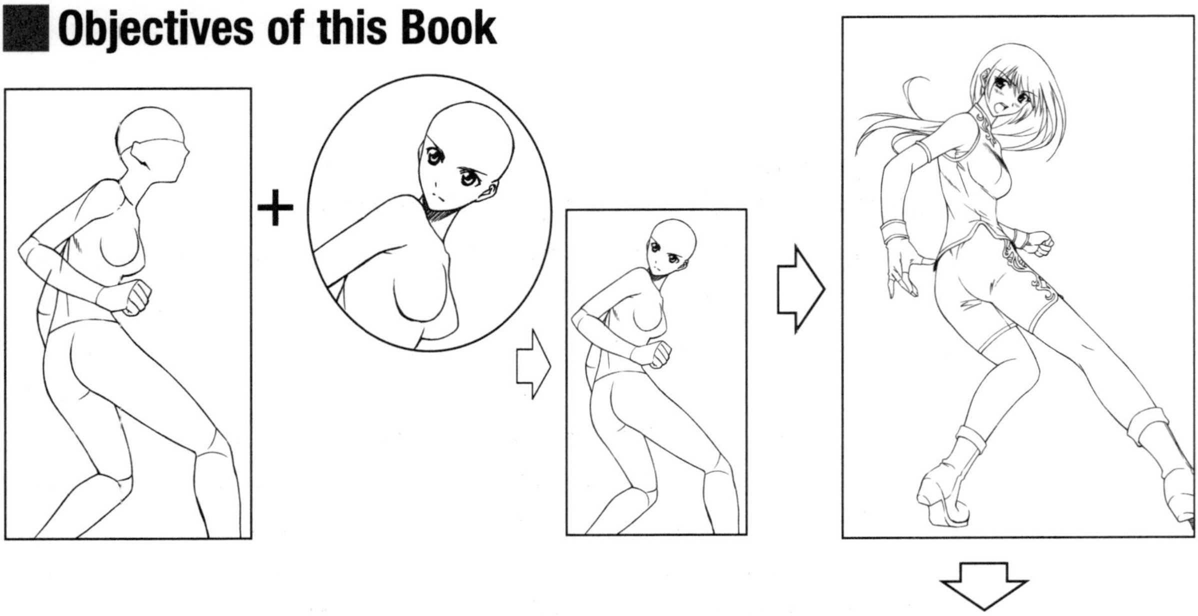

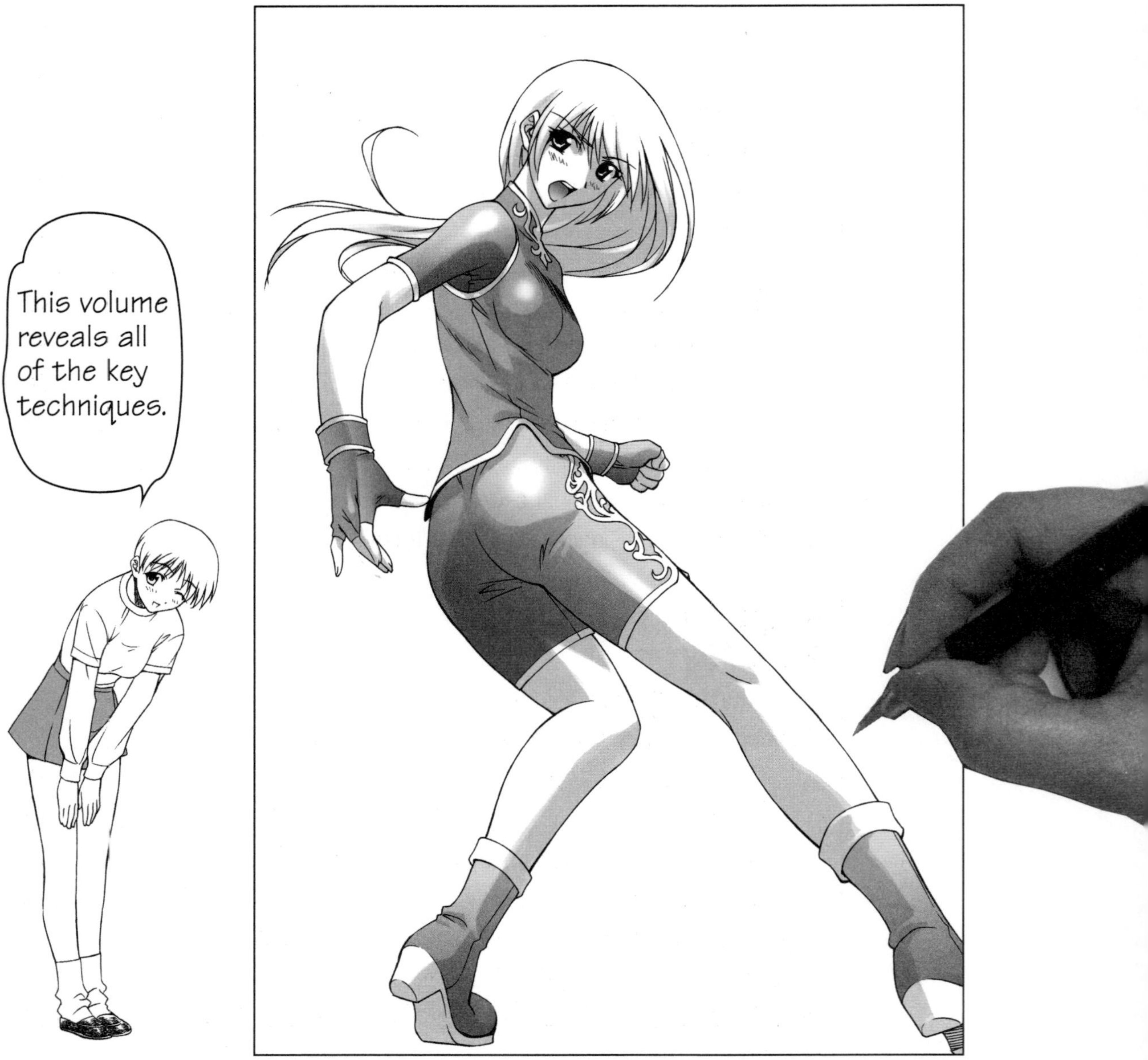

Chapter 1

The Importance of Tone Work

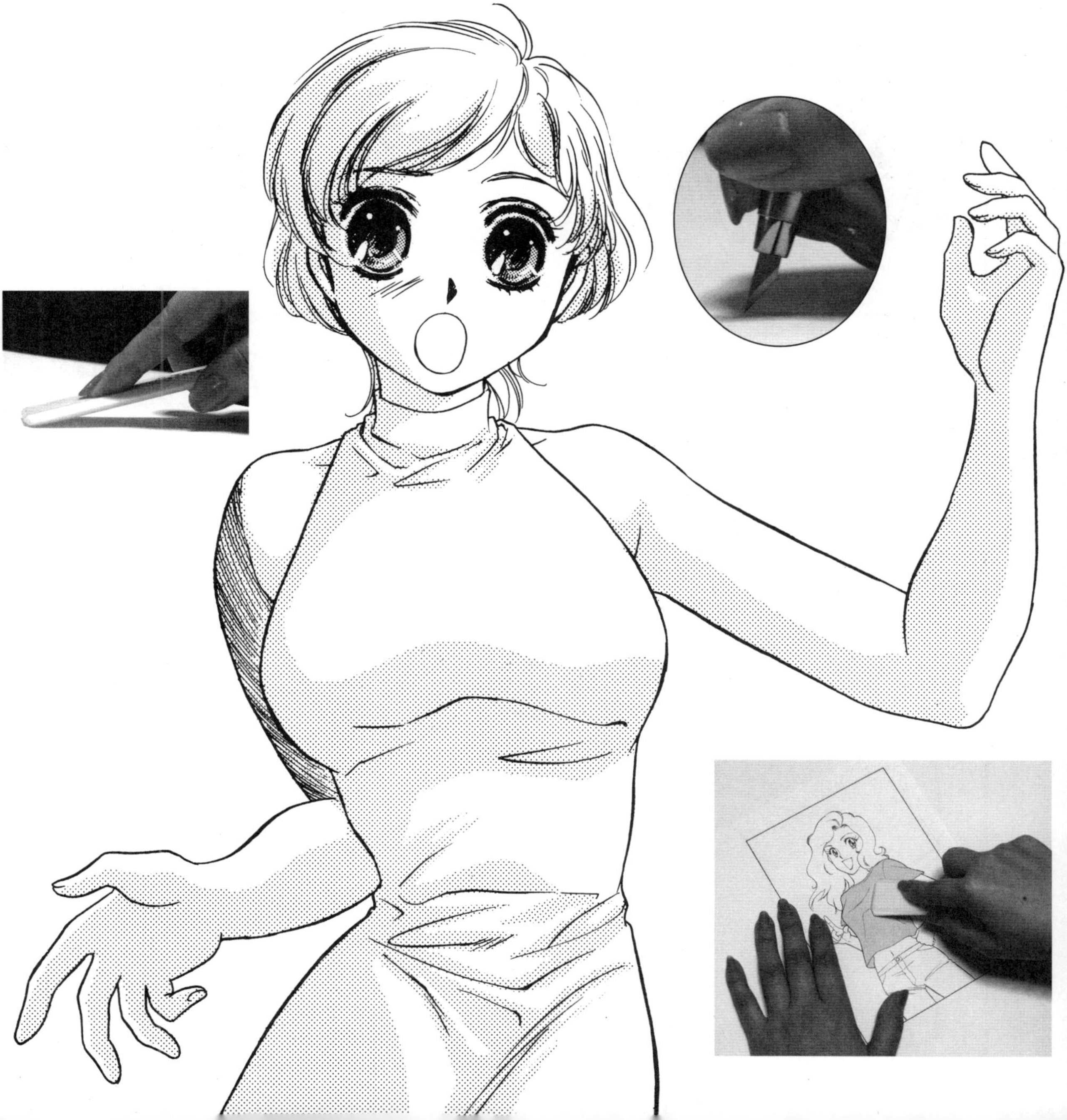

Tones Attached to Characters Serve 2 Purposes —Shading and Color—

Shading

Shading is a technique used to evoke a sense of 3-dimensionality when added to the face or figure. It is primarily used in key panels or shots.

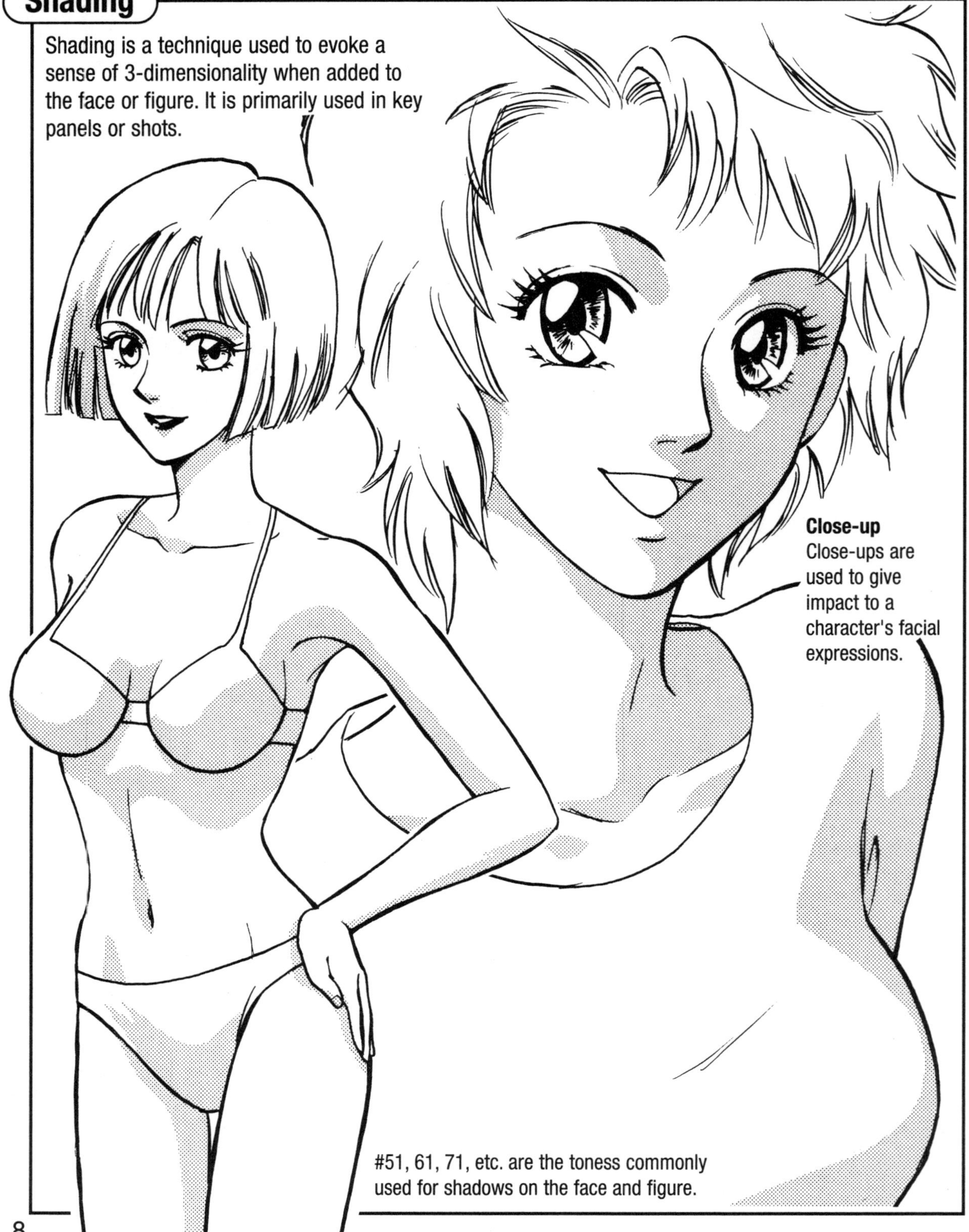

Close-up
Close-ups are used to give impact to a character's facial expressions.

#51, 61, 71, etc. are the toness commonly used for shadows on the face and figure.

Color

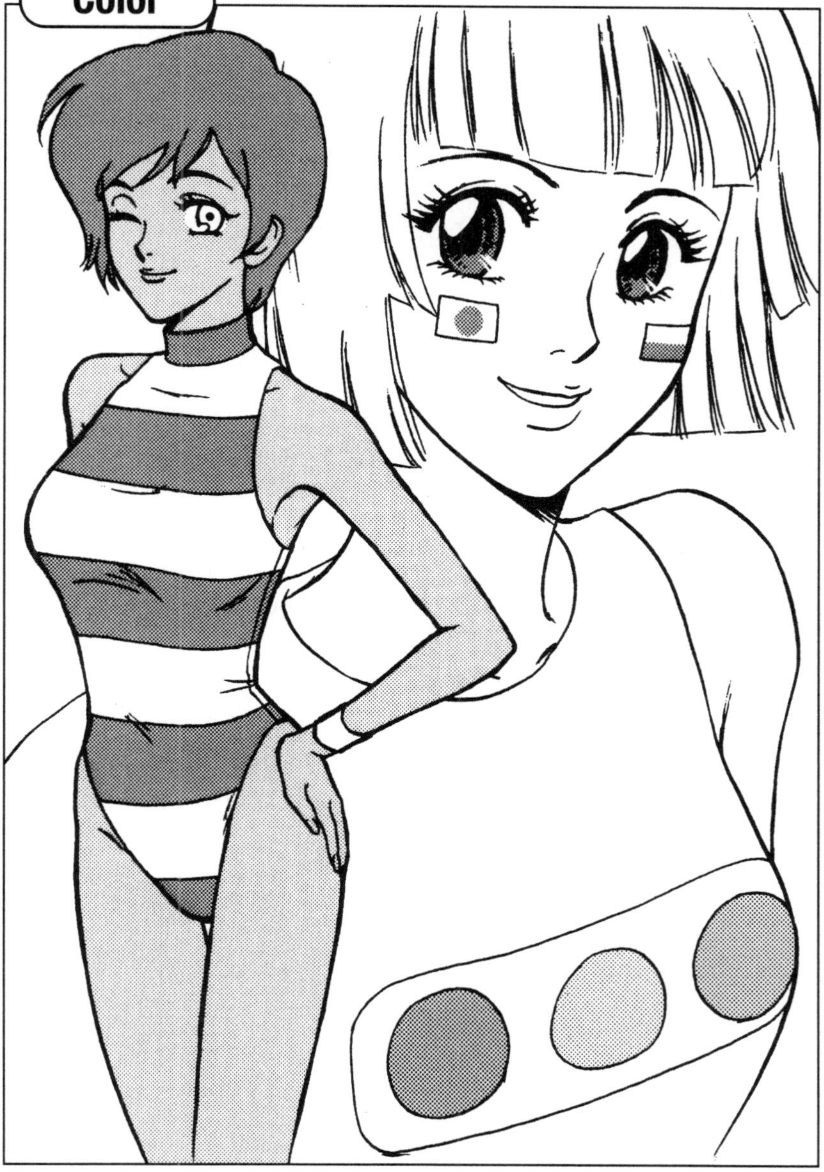

Colors are portrayed by contrasting values of black, white, and grey, distinguishing lighter values from darker ones.

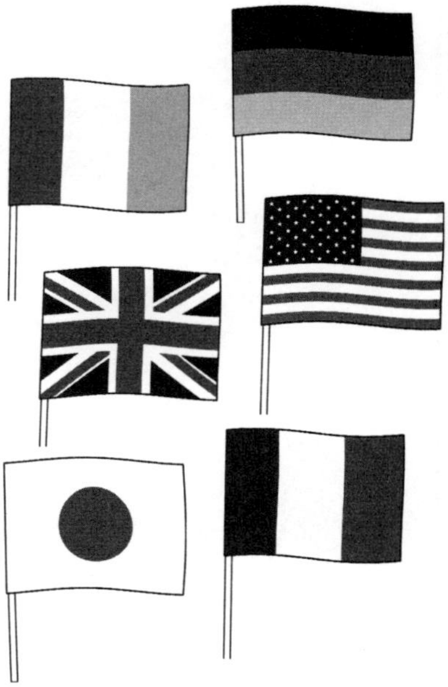

Tone Guides for Portraying Color

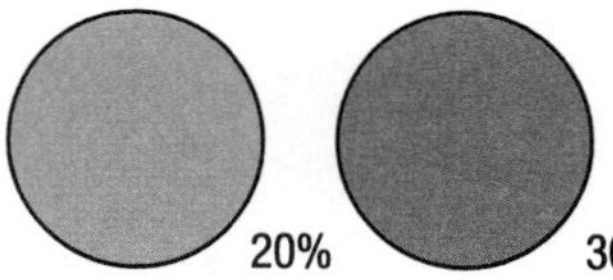

20% 30%

Darker values are often used to portray red or blue.

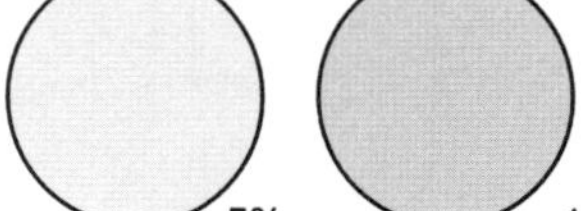

5% 10%

Lighter values are commonly used to portray yellow or pink.

Ref. Fig.:
Tone Used for Both Shading and Color

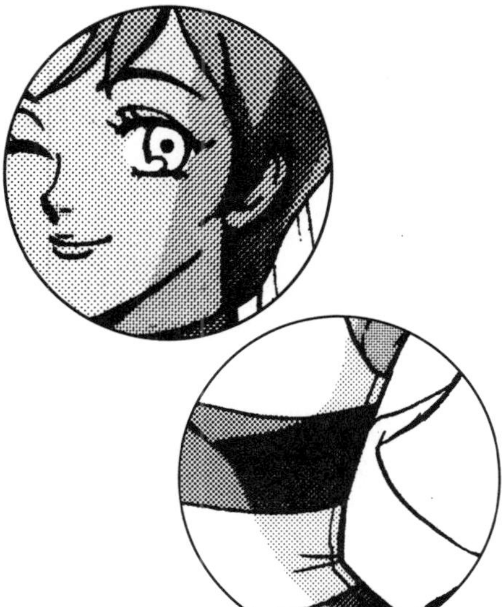

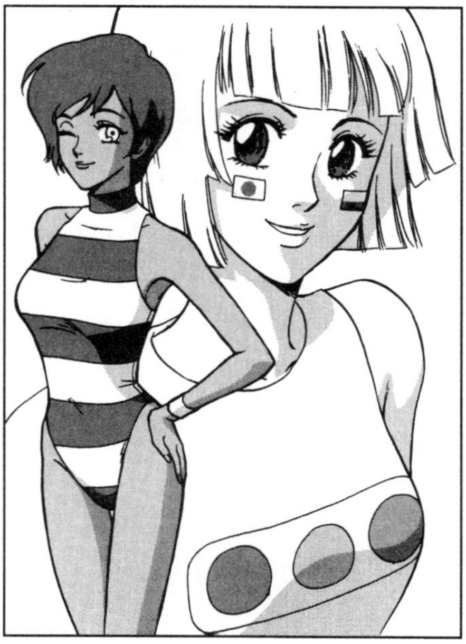

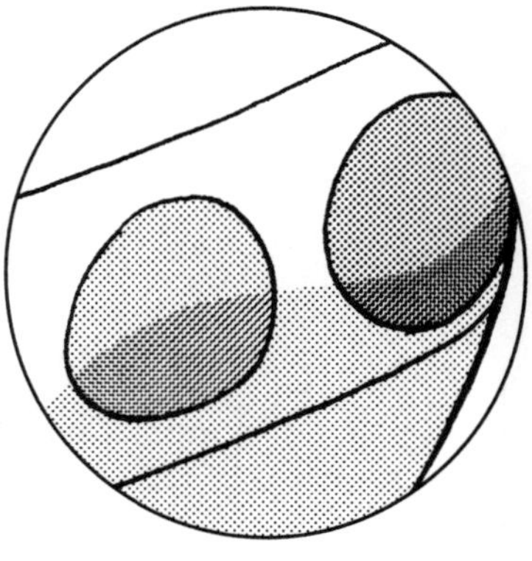

- The same tone is attached in layers to portray shadow.
- This technique, which creates a look common to anime, works well with close-ups and with illustration-style artwork.

7 Panelization Styles Used to Enhance the Character's Sense of Presence

—7 Standard Panelization Styles—

While *manga* artists seem to draw faces in countless different sizes, in truth they use only 7. Once you are able to distinguish properly these 7 different panelization styles you will finally achieve success in enhancing your characters' senses of presence.

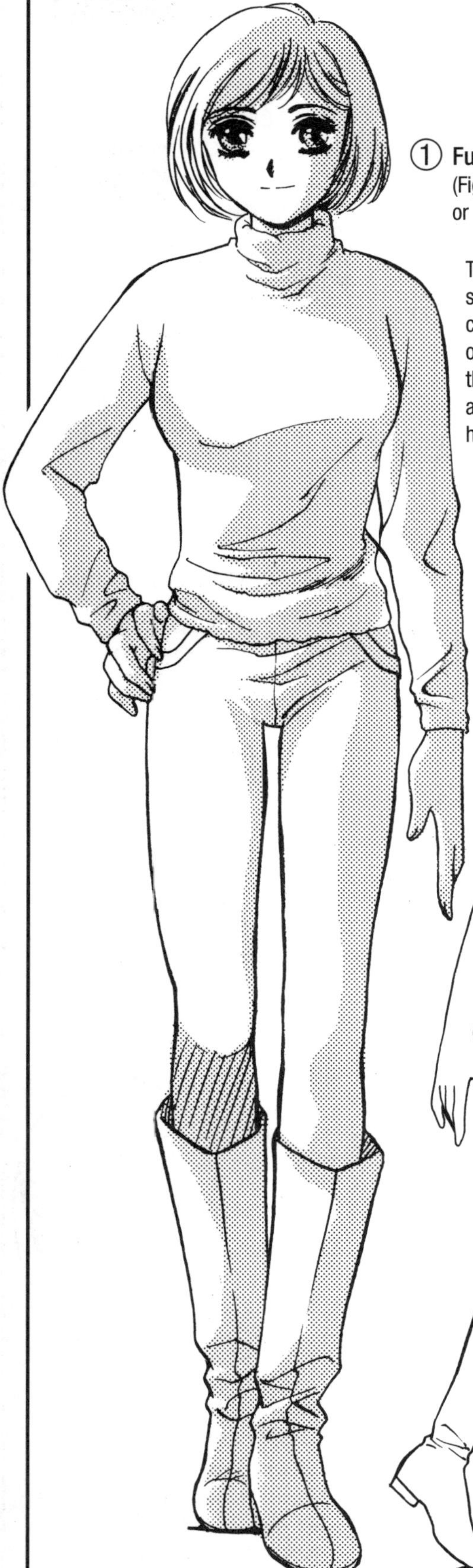

① Full Figure: Large
(Fig. height approx. 22 cm or 8 5/8")

This is an impressive shot, used when the character is making his or her appearance on the scene. The head is about 3 cm (1 1/8") in height.

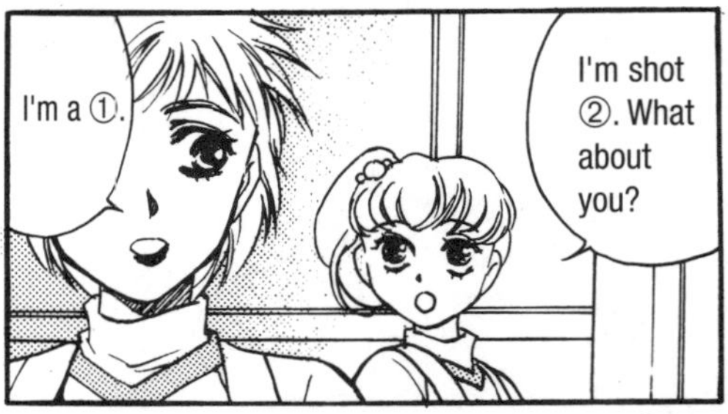

Here we see a cut using faces' sizes used with ① and ②. Bust shots like these are often used with conversation scenes. The faces appear at various sizes, according to the facial expression or dimensions of the face within the panel.

② Full Figure: Medium
(Fig. height approx. 14 cm or 5 1/2")

This height is used for showing the character's full figure. This height is still considered on the large size for dramatic portrayal. The facial shadows are optional. The figure below shows a character of the same height seated.

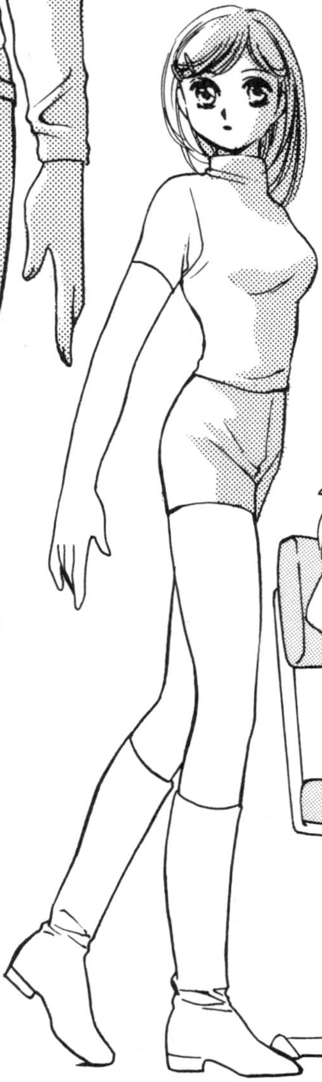

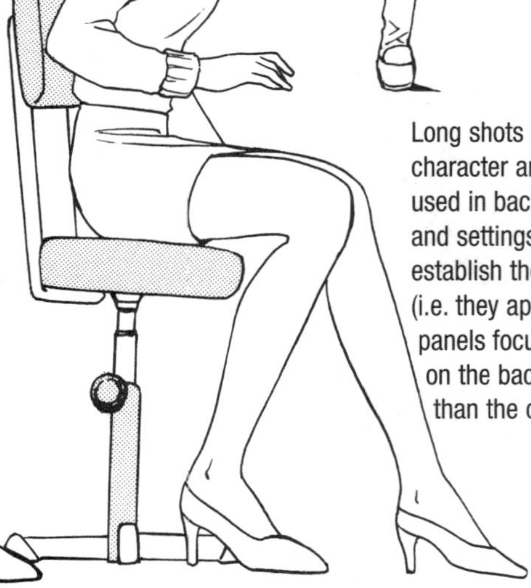

③ Long Shot: Large
(Fig. height approx. 7 cm or 2 3/4")

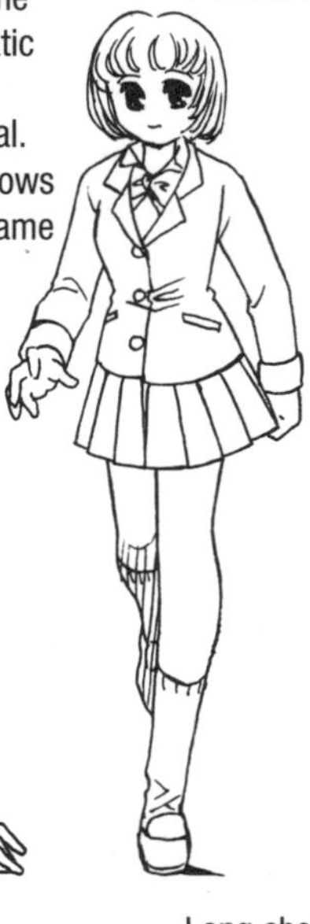

④ Long Shot: Mid-length
(Fig. height approx. 4 cm or 1 1/2")

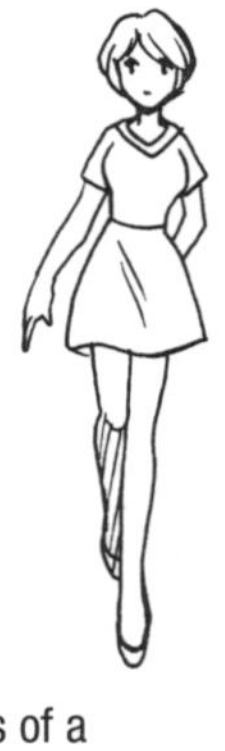

Long shots of a character are primarily used in backgrounds and settings in order to establish the scene. (i.e. they appear in panels focusing more on the background than the character.)

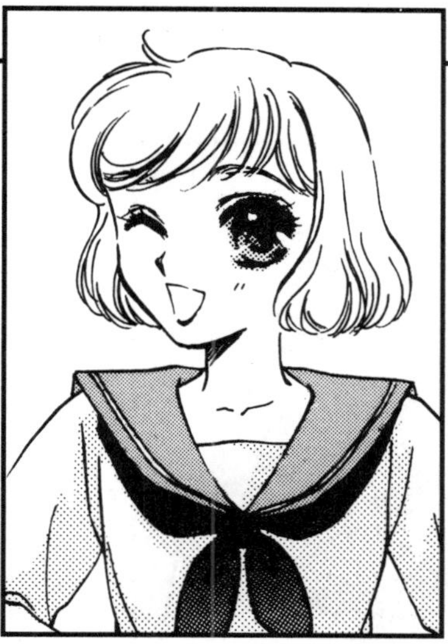

Bust Shot
This is the bust of the large full figure described earlier. It is the most frequently used shot of a character used in *manga*. Use of tone on the face is optional. Shadows on the figure are effective.

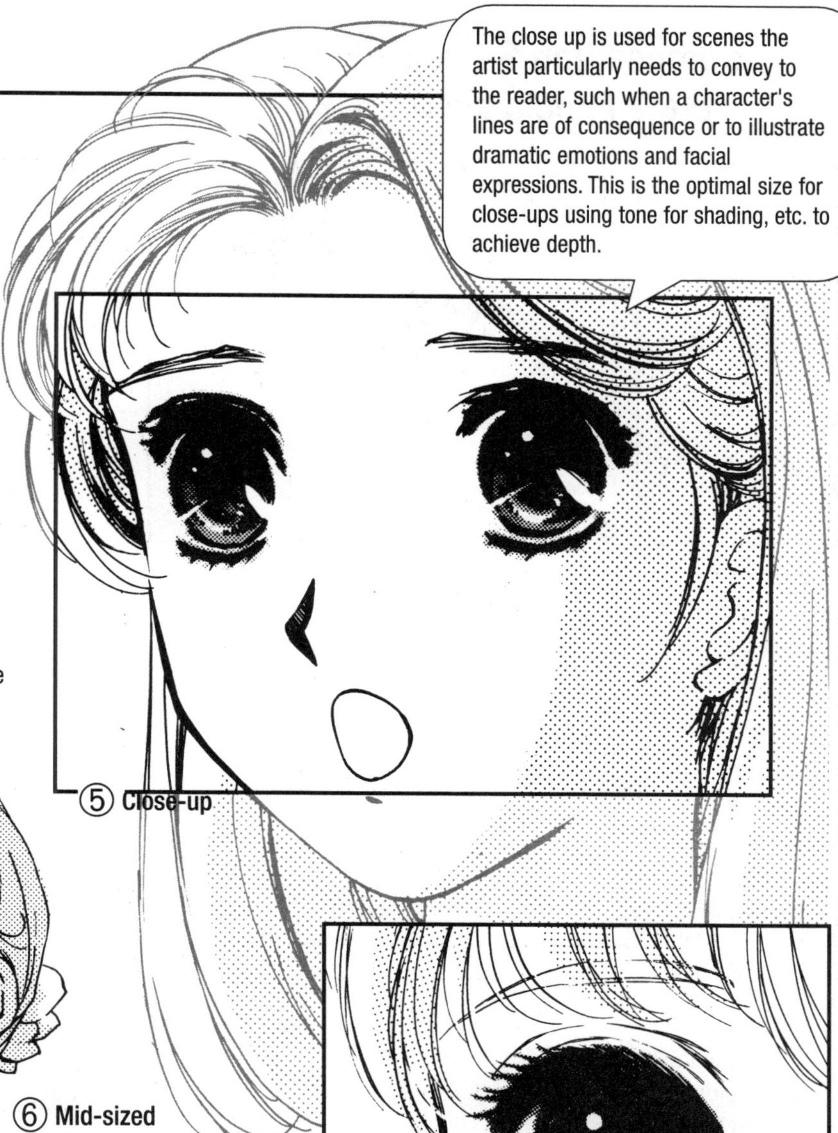

⑤ Close-up

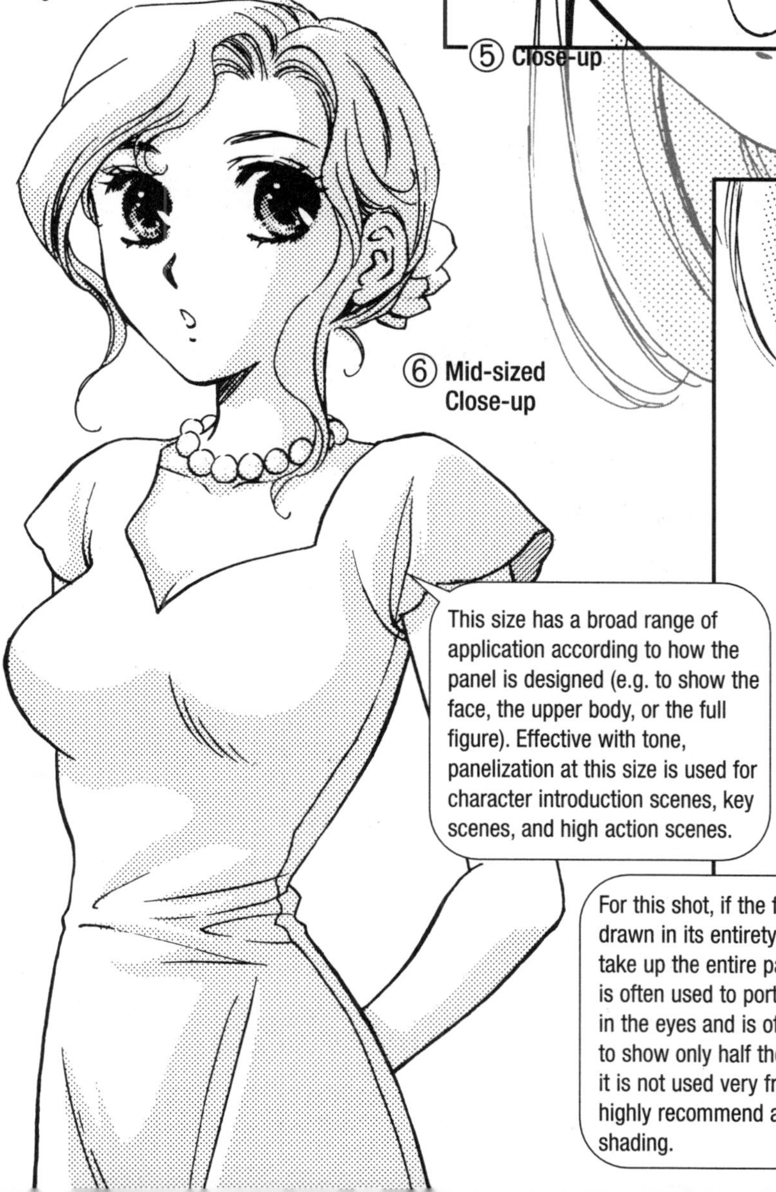

⑥ Mid-sized Close-up

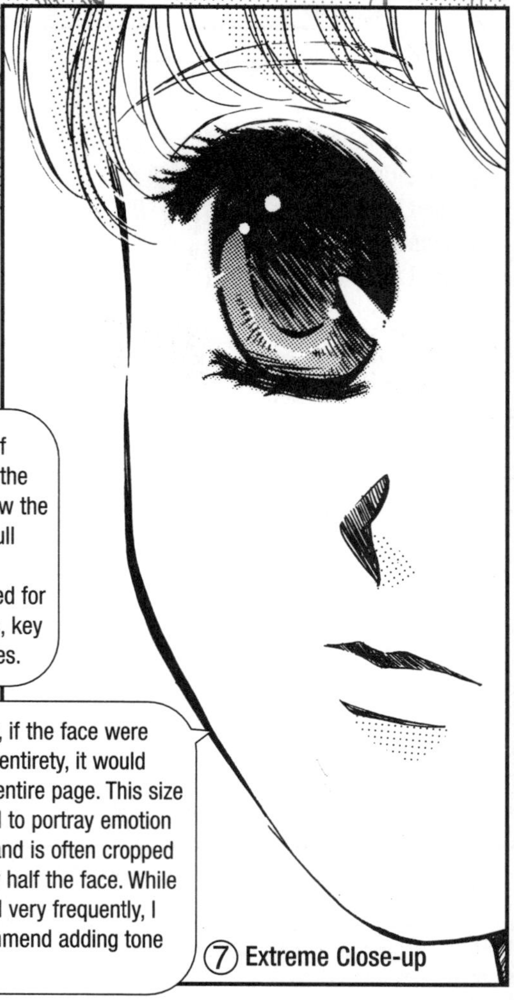

⑦ Extreme Close-up

Composition Samples Using the 7 Panelization Styles

Use tone for uniforms and other areas where the color is predetermined. As shadows are added when the face or figure size is large, the tone gives tonal balance, drawing out the character.

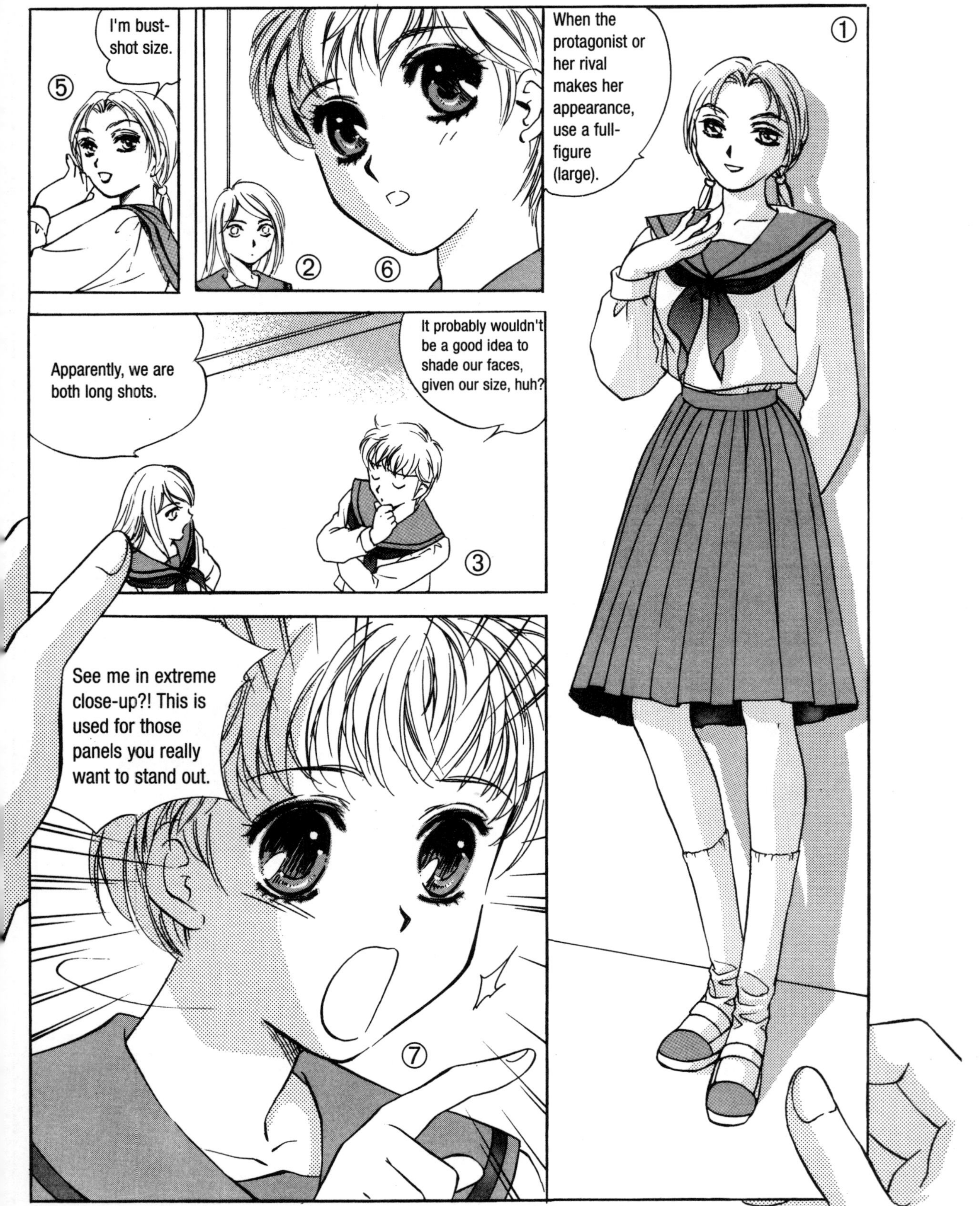

① Full figure (large): Tone added for shadows on the face and figure and for the uniform's colors ② Full figure (medium and larger): Tone added only for shadows on the face and for the uniform's colors ③ Long shot (large): Tone added only for the uniform's colors ⑤ Bust shot: Tone added only for the uniform's colors ⑥ Close-up (mid-sized): The face is cropped, and tone is added for shadows in the face and the uniform's colors ⑦ Close-up: Tone added for shadows in the face and the uniform's colors Note: Actual size of drawing approx. 1.2 times (120%) that shown in figure.

3 Panelization Styles Suited toward Shading

Adding shadows to the face and figure are more effective when used with the following 3 panelization styles.

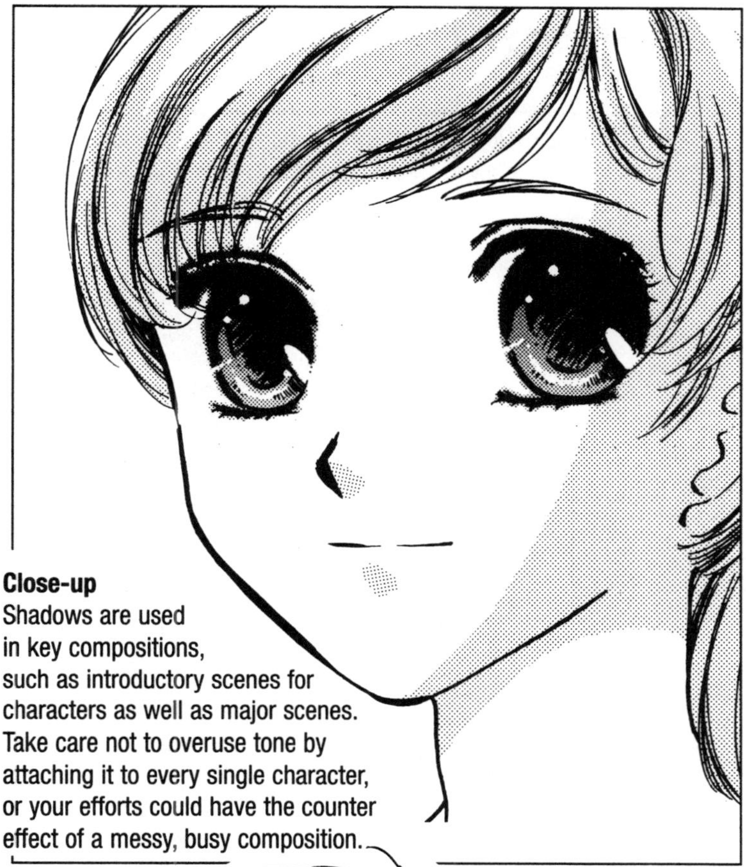

Close-up
Shadows are used in key compositions, such as introductory scenes for characters as well as major scenes. Take care not to overuse tone by attaching it to every single character, or your efforts could have the counter effect of a messy, busy composition.

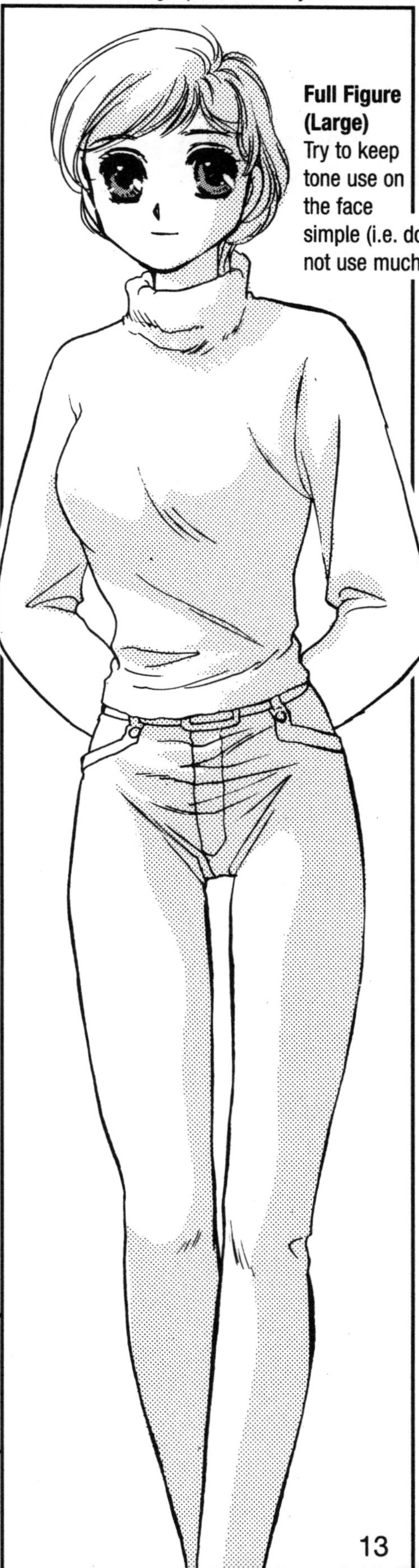

Full Figure (Large)
Try to keep tone use on the face simple (i.e. do not use much).

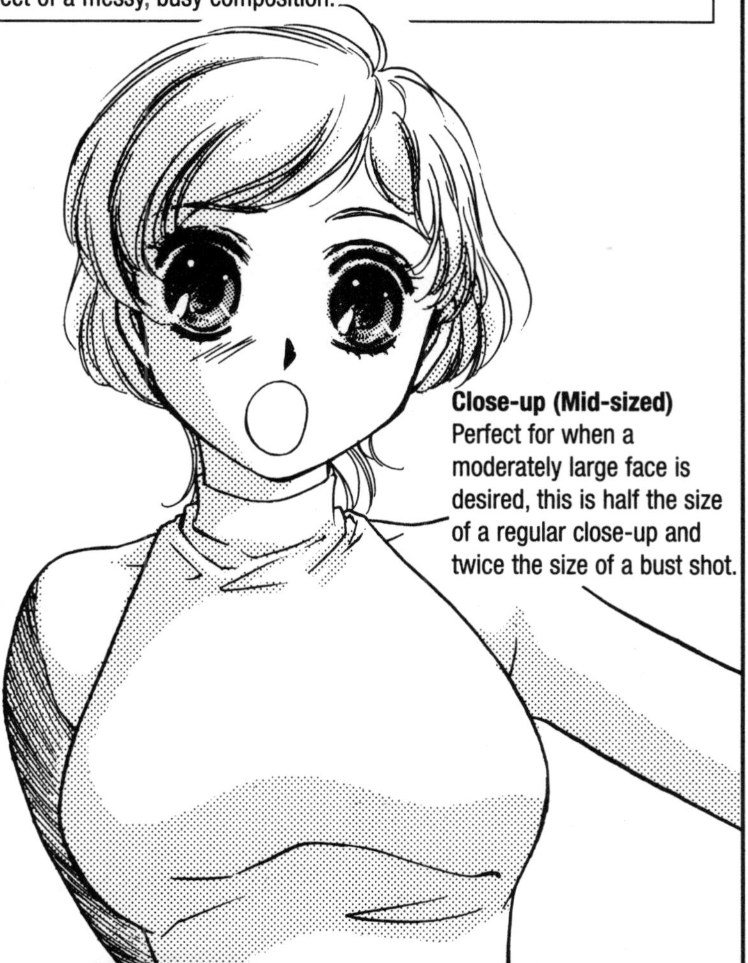

Close-up (Mid-sized)
Perfect for when a moderately large face is desired, this is half the size of a regular close-up and twice the size of a bust shot.

The Fundamentals of Light and Shadow

Average Light

Since volume is portrayed using light and shadow, use shadow to create a sense of 3-dimensionality.

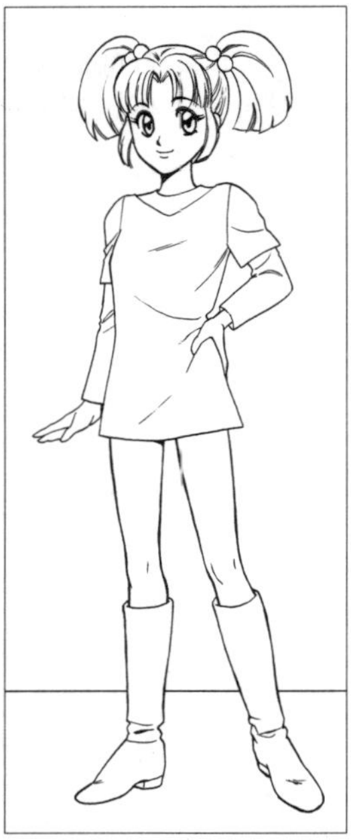

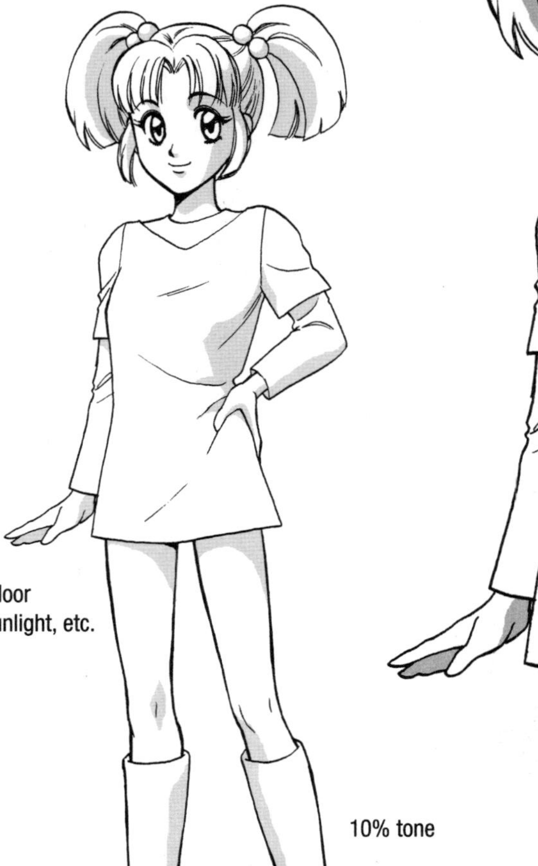

Normal indoor lighting, sunlight, etc.

10% tone

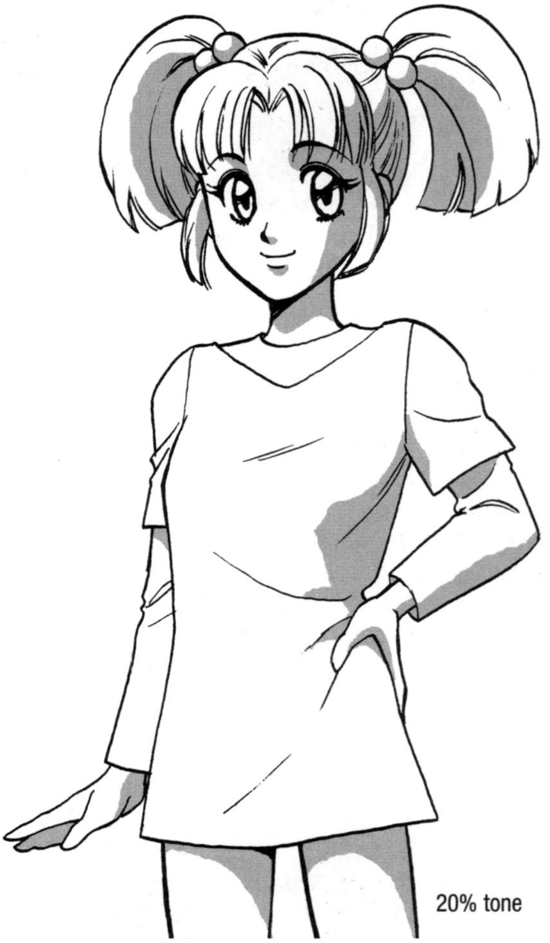

20% tone

Light Source

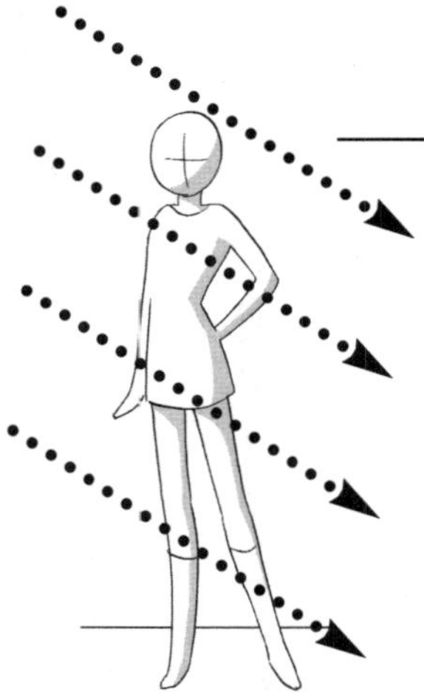

Here, the rays of light following parallel lines are referred to as "directional light."

While film and paintings require minute direction in terms of the light source's position or the placement of lighting, its intensity, number of lights/light sources, etc., in *manga* only the position of the light source need be decided (e.g. whether to place it to the character's upper left or right side, etc.).

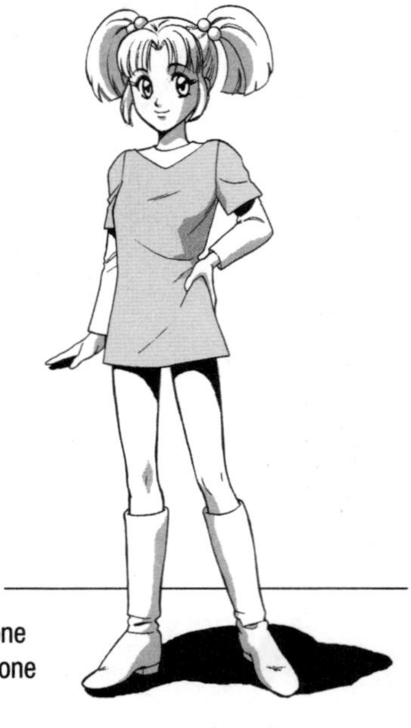

Clothing: 10% tone
Shadows: 20% tone

Special Lighting Effects

The spotlight is the most well known "light ray." In contrast to the Sun, which is a directional light source, the spotlight is also referred to as a point light source.

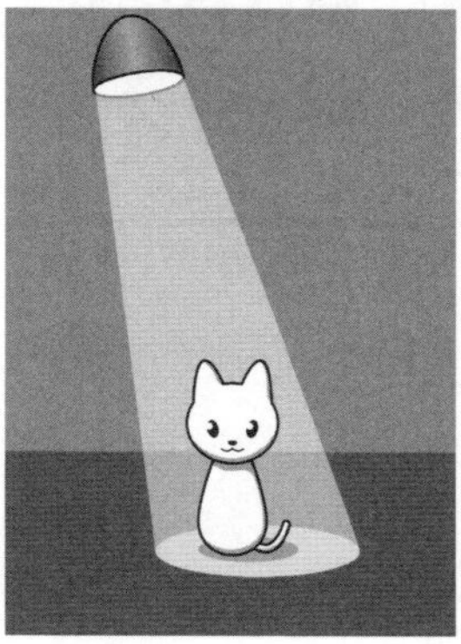

Spotlight

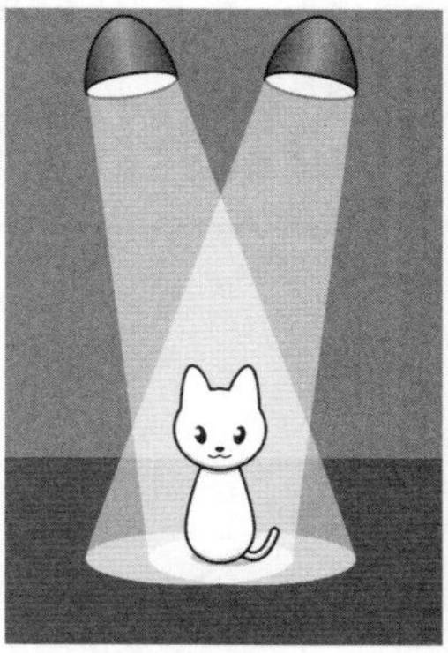

Double spotlight

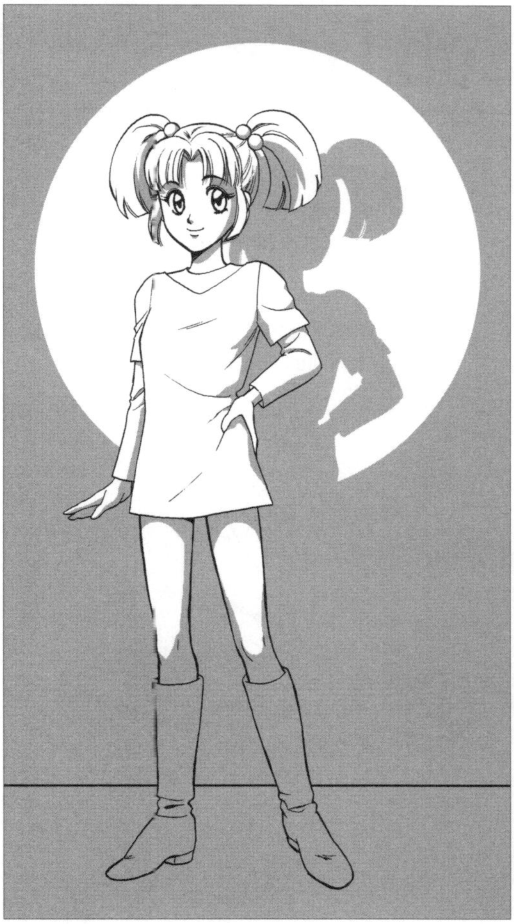

Spotlight

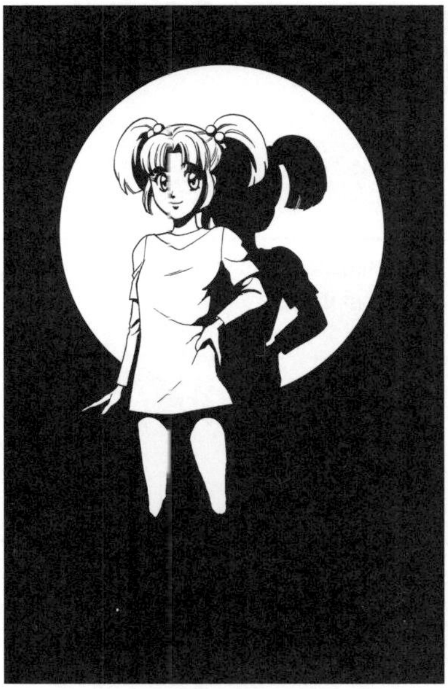

Because the light off a spotlight tends to be intense, use solid black ink instead of tone to produce a dramatic effect.

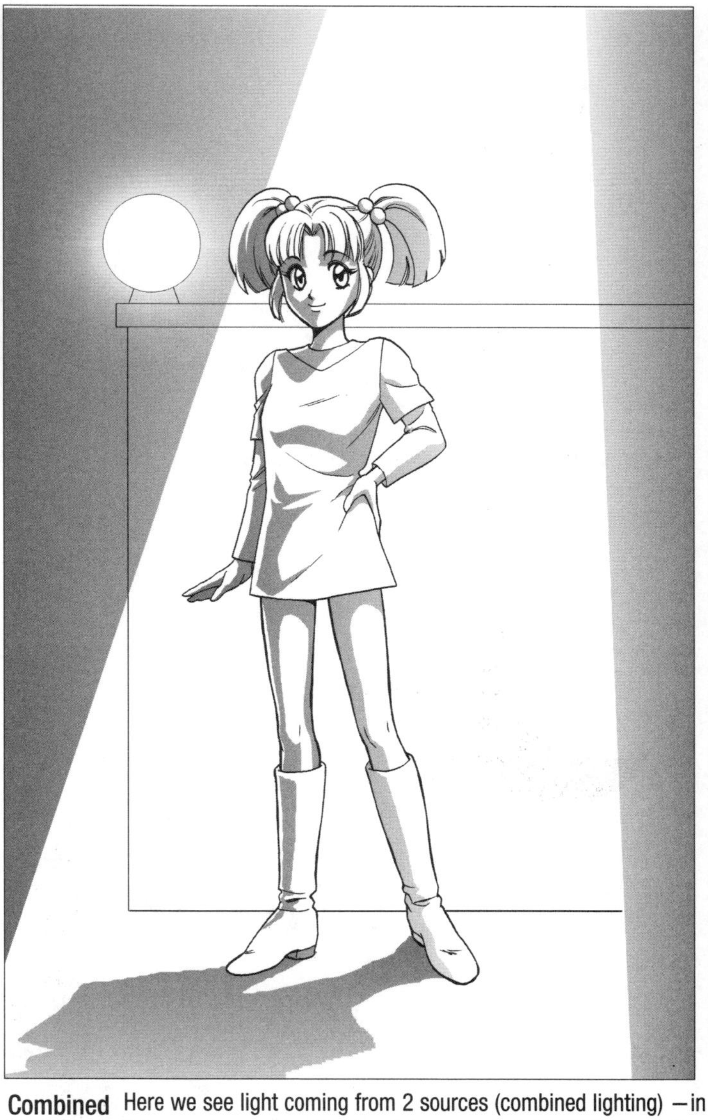

Combined Lighting Here we see light coming from 2 sources (combined lighting) —in this case from a streetlight and from a gate light. While in reality, most lighting is combined, in *manga* convention leans toward point sources or spotlights. Combined lighting is used when seeking an out-of-the-ordinary mode of portrayal or effect.

3 Types of Shadows Connected to Light: Standard, Bright, and Soft Light

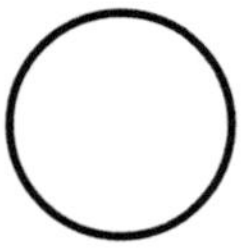

Without Shadow

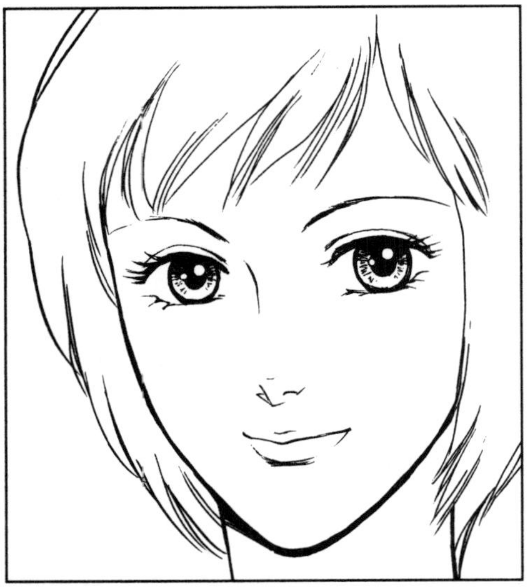

While this style appears clean, it makes for an overly simplistic image up close.

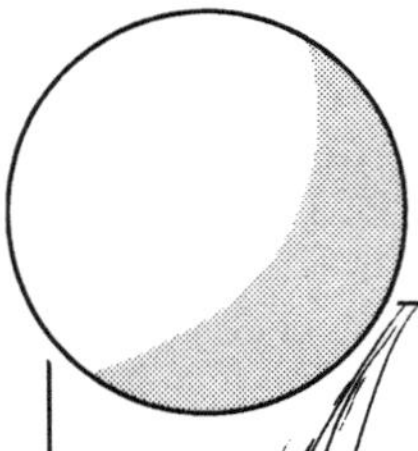

Shape with Standard Lighting
Typically rendered in grey

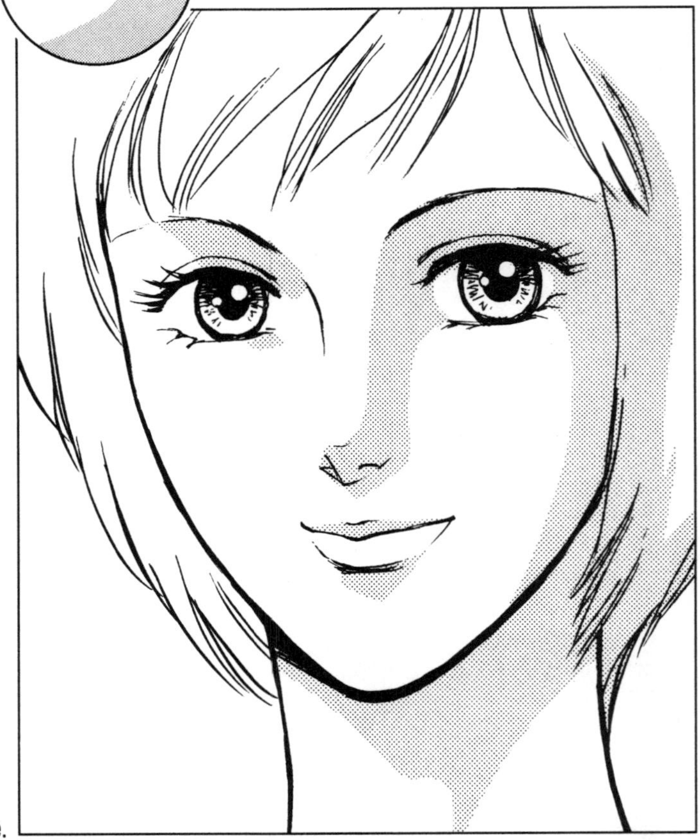

This is extremely common shading and works well for outdoors and indoors alike.

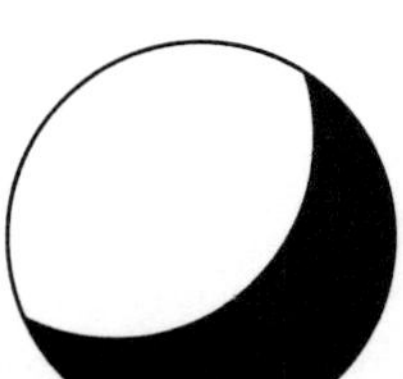

Bright Lighting
Use black or a dark gradation tone.

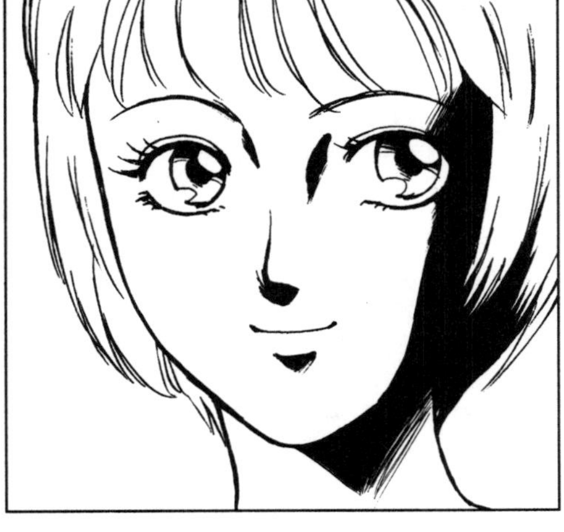

Shadows rendered in black

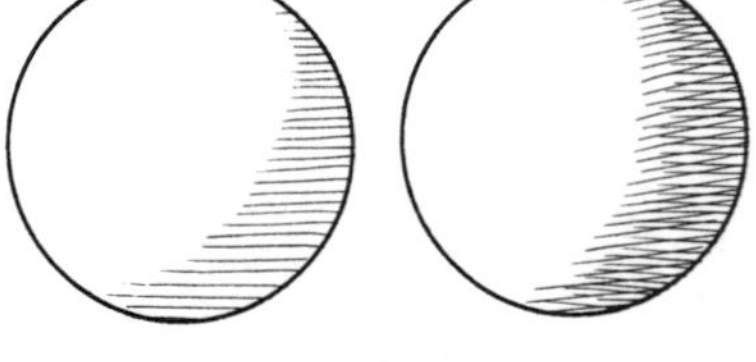

Shadows rendering in hatching and crosshatching

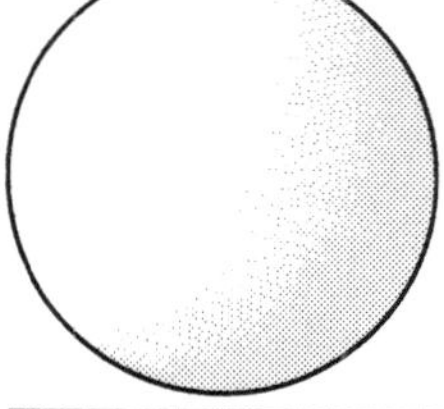

Soft Lighting
Use tone with fine dots or a light value (shade).

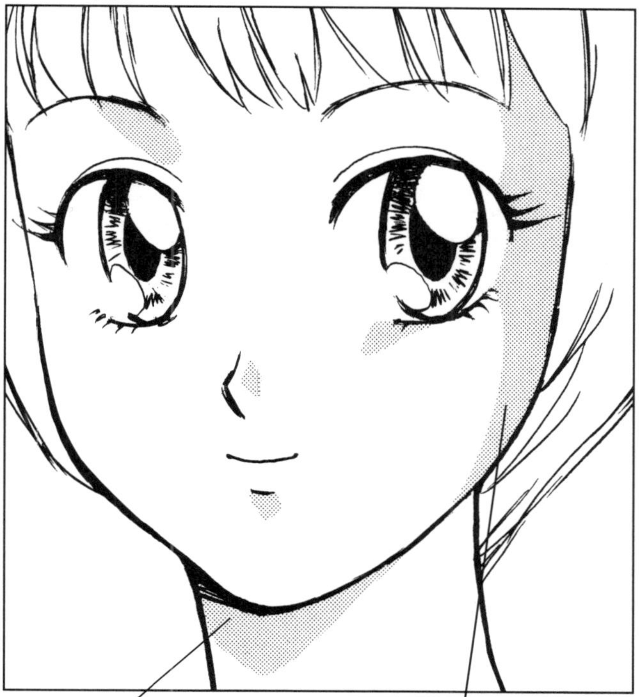

The trick is to keep the neck shadow light.

Use #71, fine-dot tone.

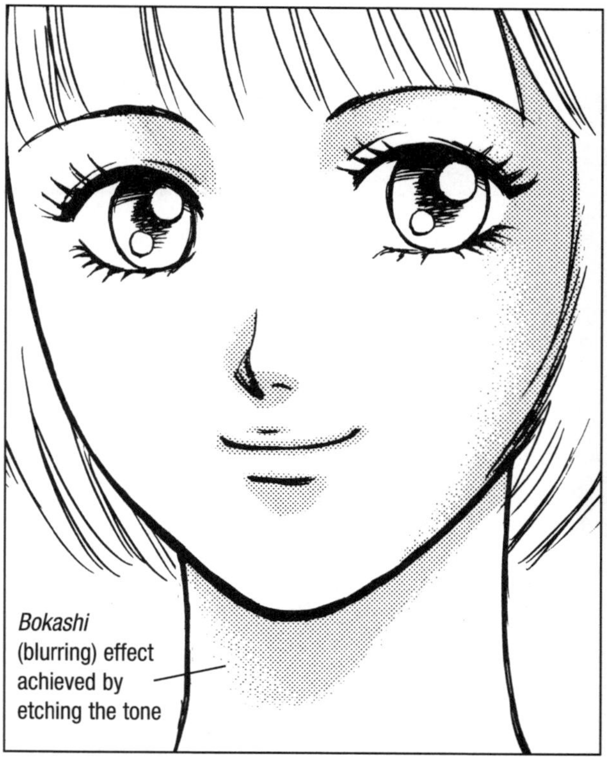

Bokashi (blurring) effect achieved by etching the tone

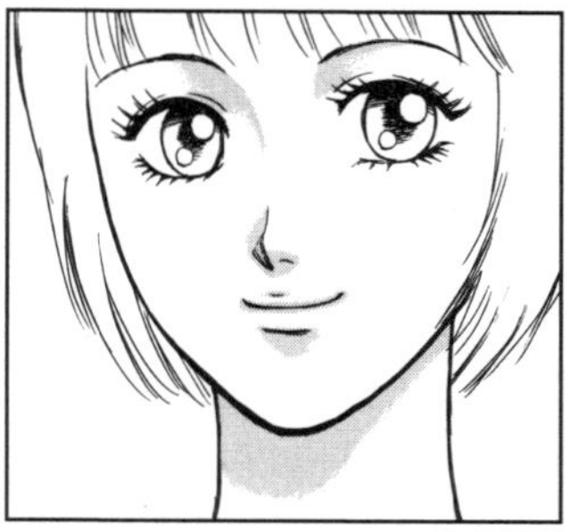

Tone unetched: The small area occupied by the shadow suggests "soft lighting."

Adding Solid Blacks to Boost the Sense of Presence

Good

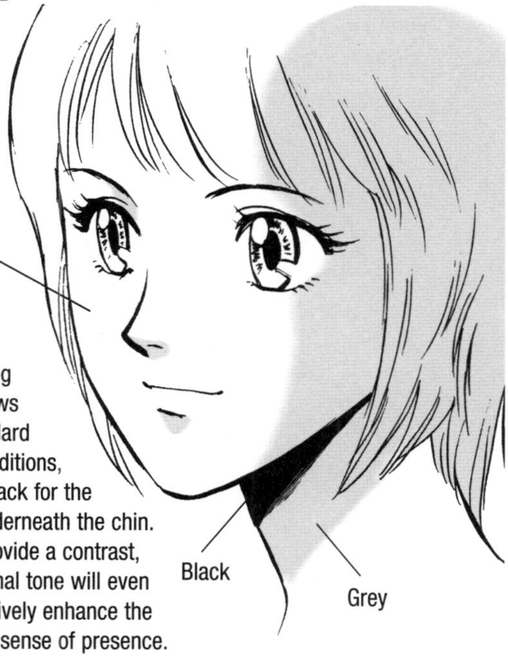

When adding grey shadows under standard lighting conditions, use solid black for the shadow underneath the chin. This will provide a contrast, and additional tone will even more effectively enhance the character's sense of presence.

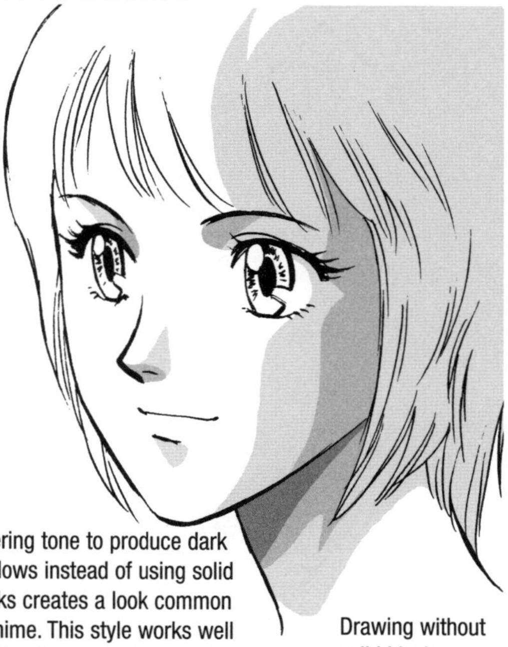

Layering tone to produce dark shadows instead of using solid blacks creates a look common to anime. This style works well with illustration-style artwork.

Drawing without solid blacks

The Shading Process

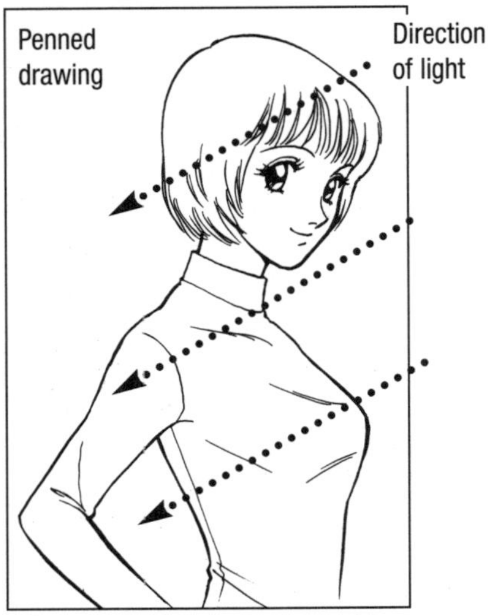

① **Determine the light source.**

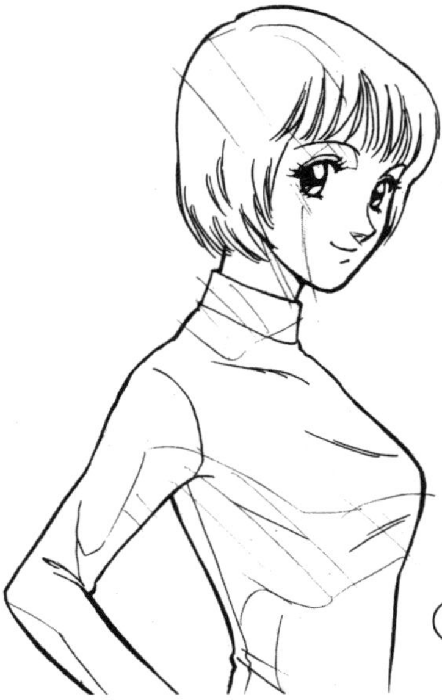

② **Plot the shadows.**
Use a non-photo blue or yellow pencil to jot down the shadows.

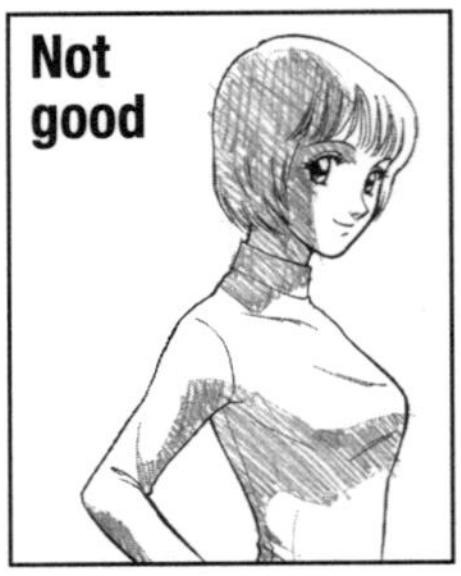

The plotted shadows will simply serve as guidelines for where to attach tone, so avoid filling them in.

Spotting Blacks

Fill in any solid blacks before attaching tone. Standard practice dictates adding blacks under the jaw line and underarm.

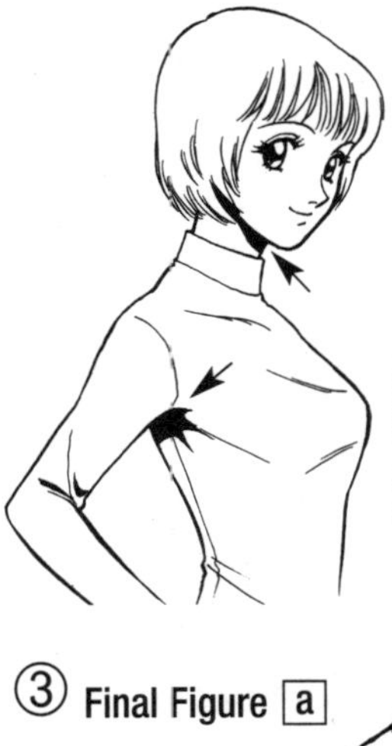

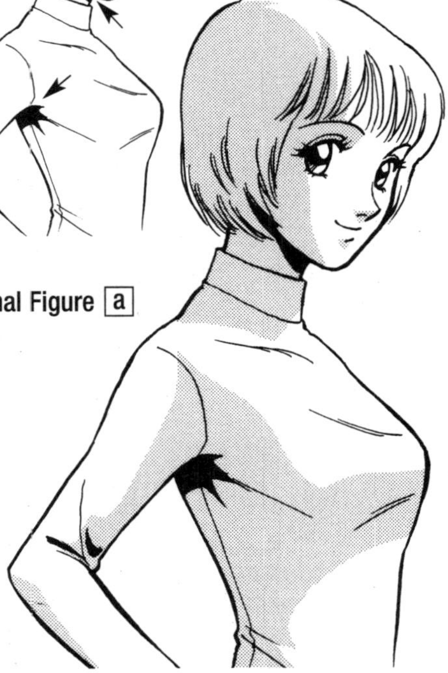

③ **Final Figure** a

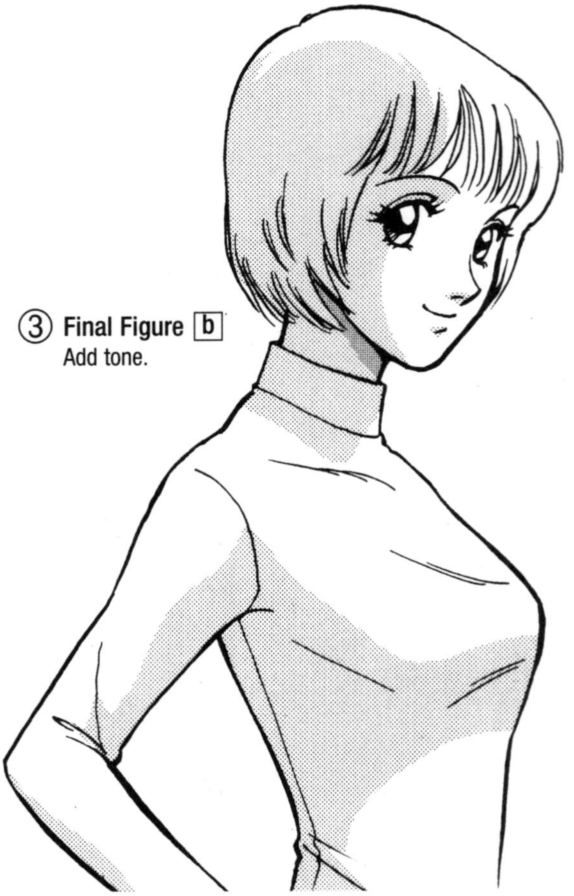

③ **Final Figure** b
Add tone.

Lead markings of non-photo blue and yellow pencils disappear when the drawing is put into print form or photocopied, so they are frequently used tools. A mechanical pencil may be used instead, provided that the lead color is light blue or yellow.

Sample Shading

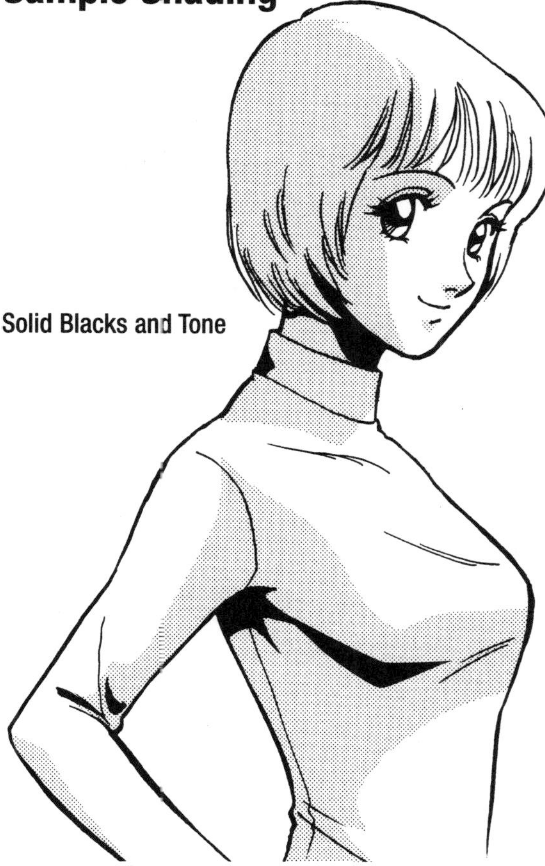

Solid Blacks and Tone

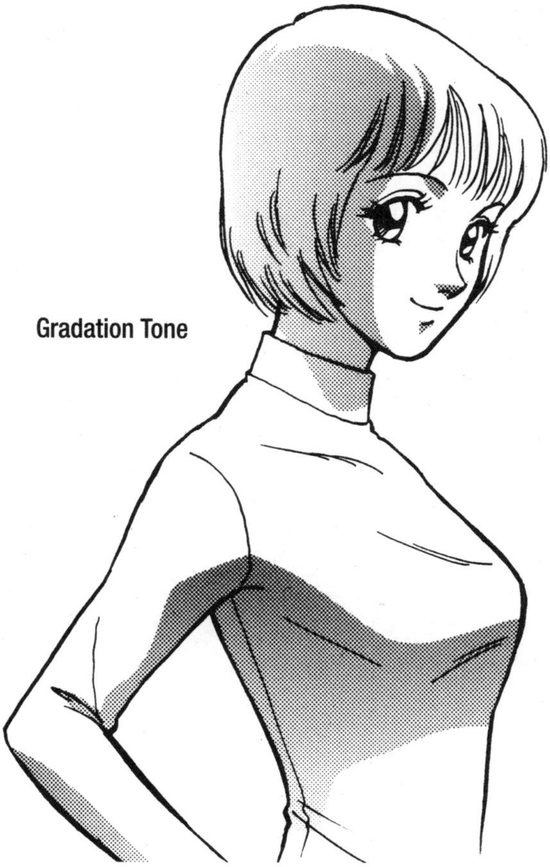

Gradation Tone

Hatched Shadows

This method, popular amongst realism *manga*, consists of filling in the shadows with solid black instead of attaching tone.

The trick is to ensure all of the hatched strokes are unidirectional, uniform, and fine.

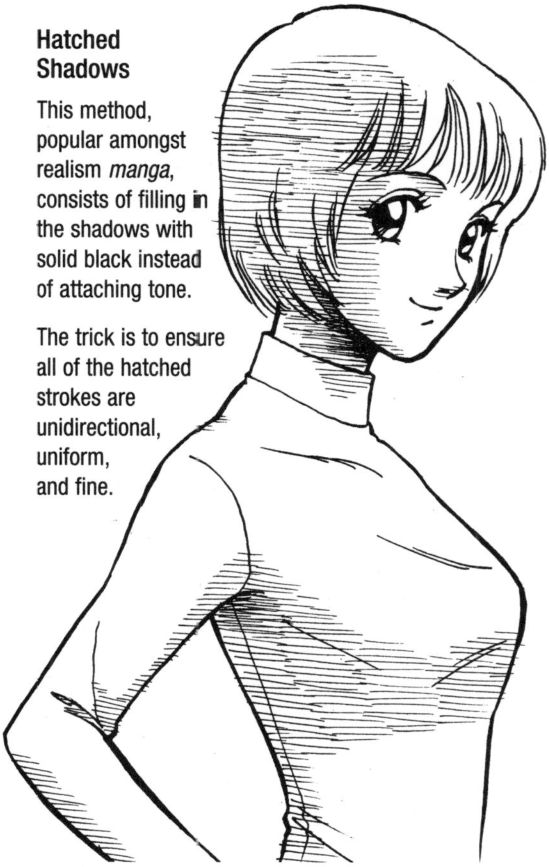

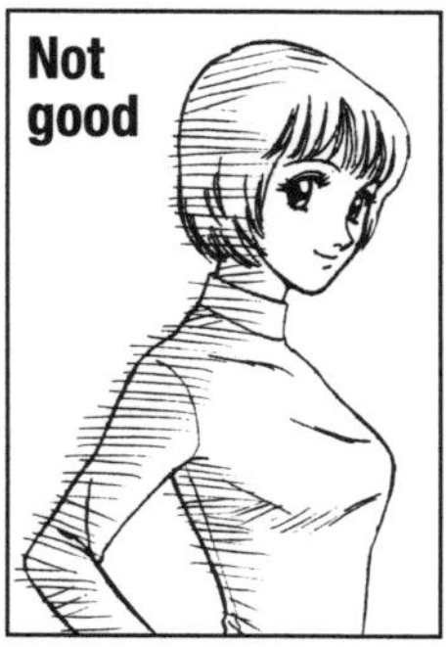

Not good

Take care when hatching that the strokes do not end up in different directions.

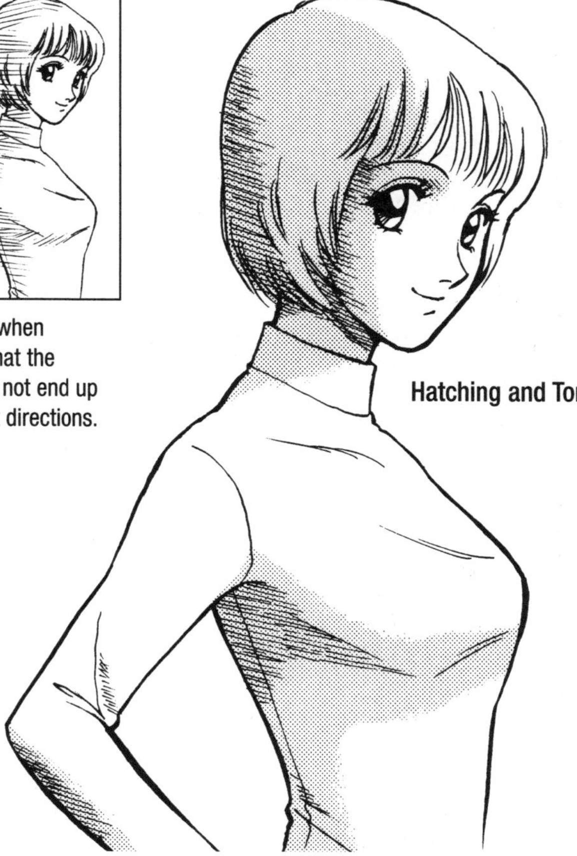

Hatching and Tone

The ABC's of Tone

• Composition created using solely 10% (saturation) tone

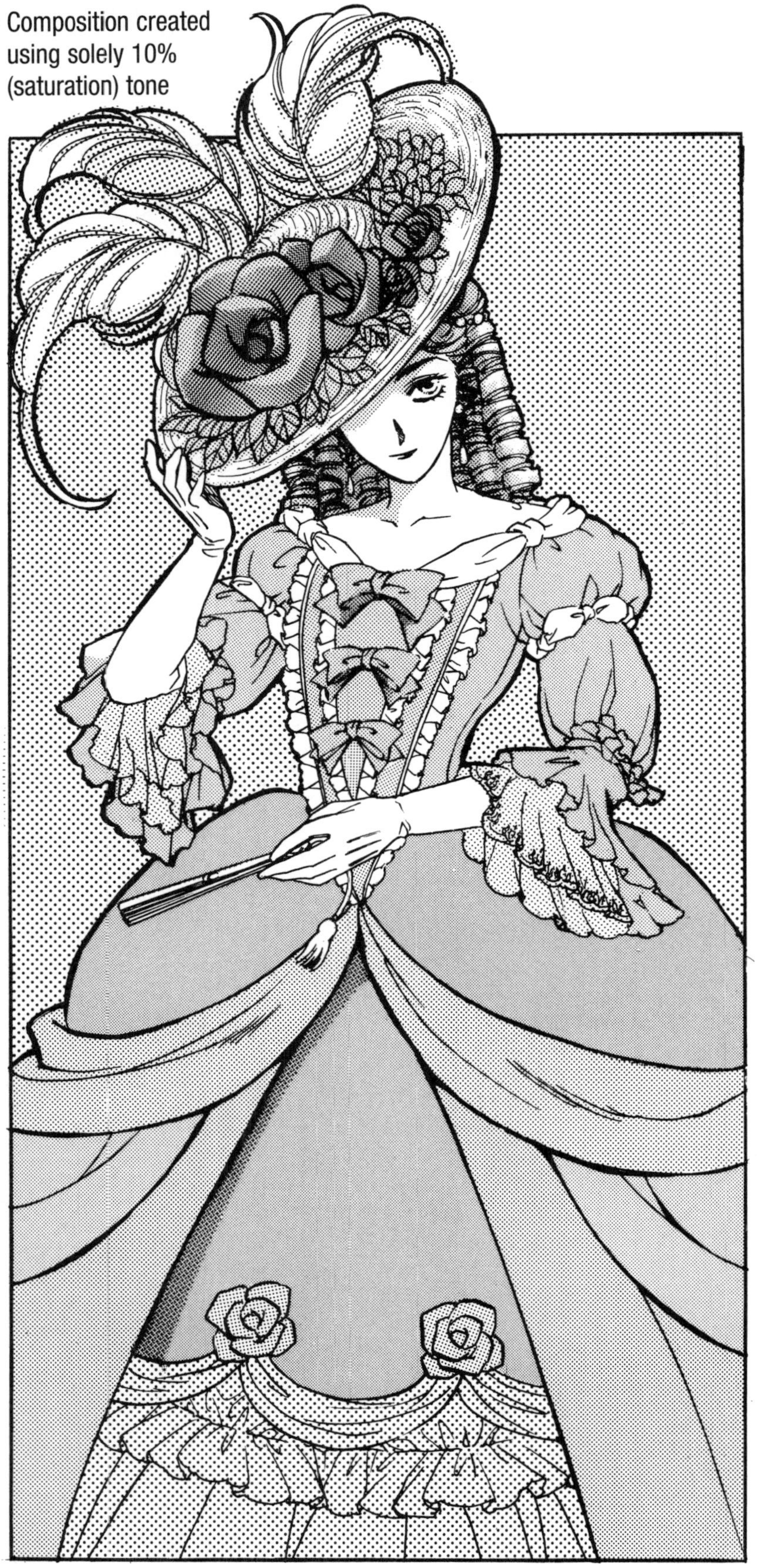

Figure created using tone of uniform saturation but with varying dot sizes

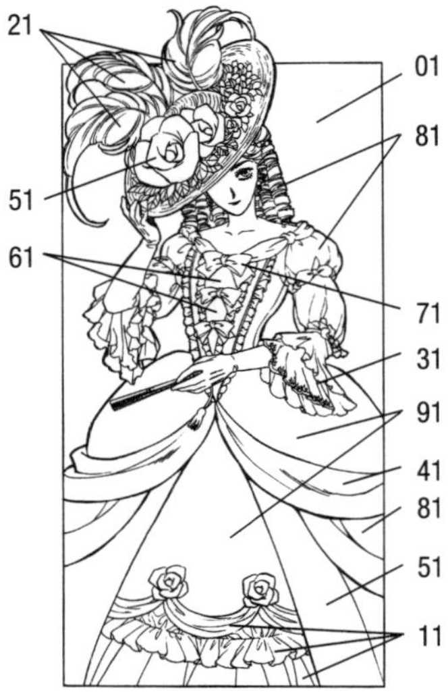

Nos. 11 to 91

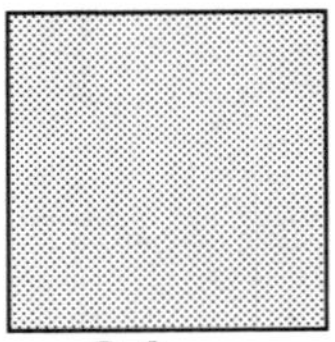

The most common form of tone, pictured here, is known as "dot tone."

61 ← The 1 refers to 10% saturation.

↑ The ten's place refers to the dots' size.

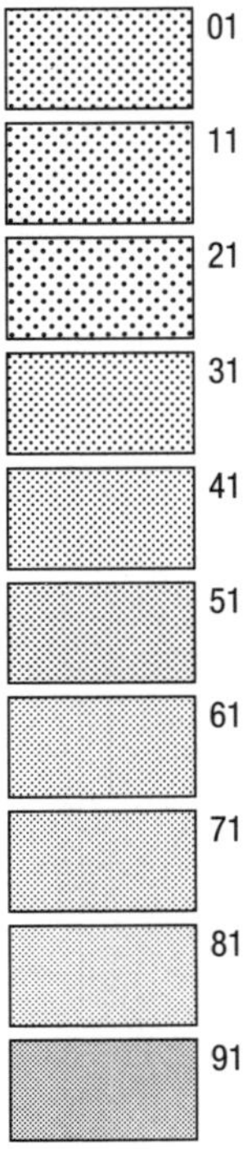

While each of these tones offer a different feel, we can see from their numbers that they are in fact all the same "saturation." The larger the figure in the ten's place, the smaller the dot size, and high numbers like 60, 70, and over have very tiny dots.

• Composition created using 10% to 90% (saturation) tone

This figure was created using tones solely of the 50s range. (i.e. all of the dots are the same size.)

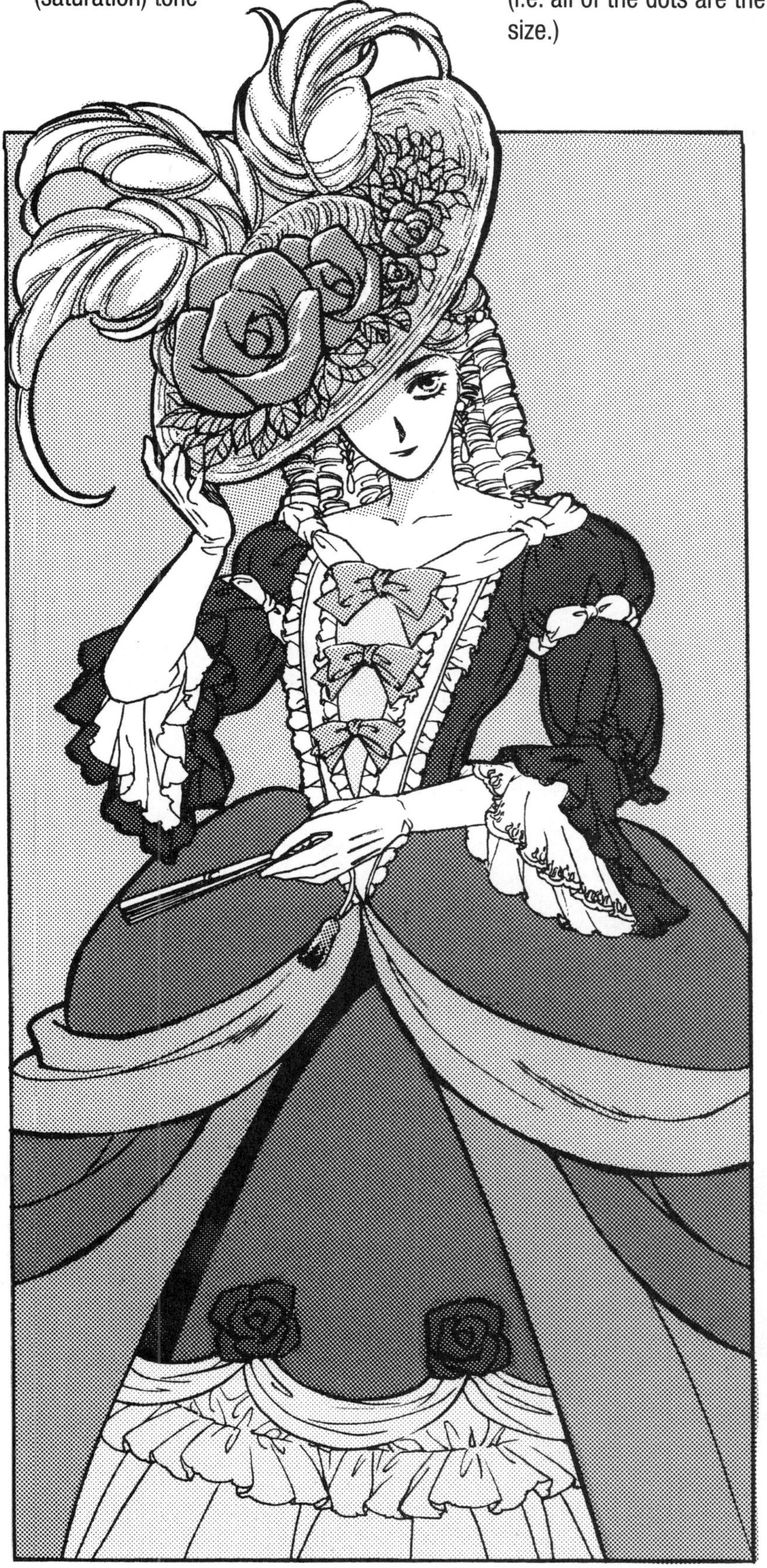

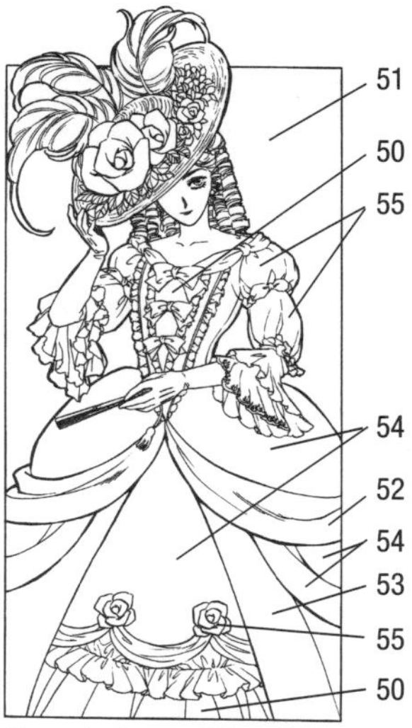

Tones between 50 and 55

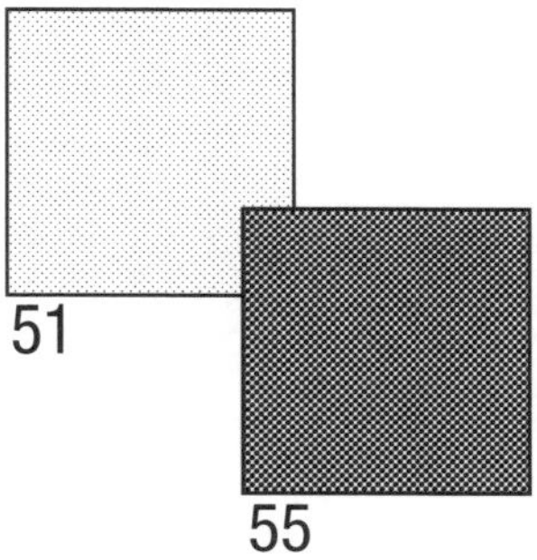

Tones with the same number in the ten's place have the same dot size. The difference lies in the density (saturation level).

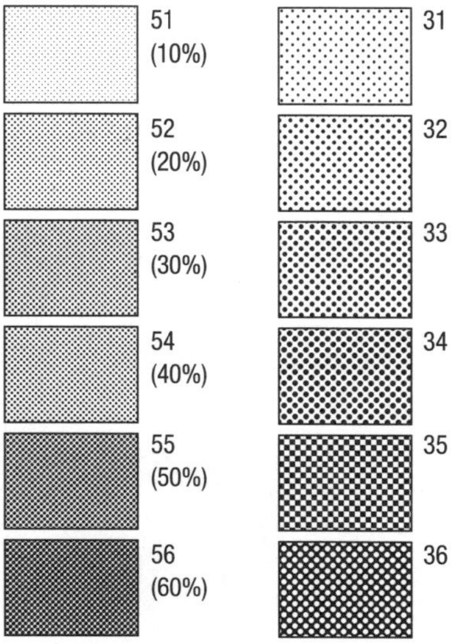

50s series tone
30s series tone

All tones used on these 2 pages are IC Screen. Slight differences do appear from brand to brand in dot size and in the spacing between dots, even when the tone numbers are identical.

Attaching Tone —Tools and the Process—

1 Getting Started (Before Attaching Tone)

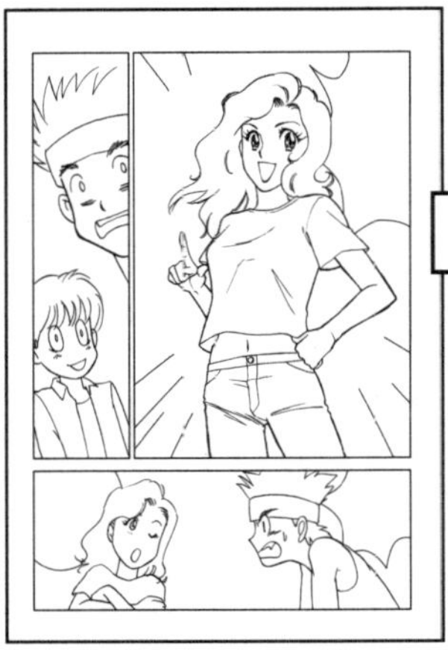

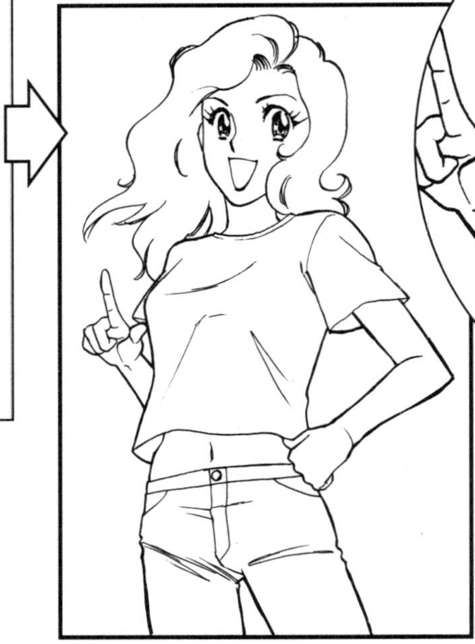

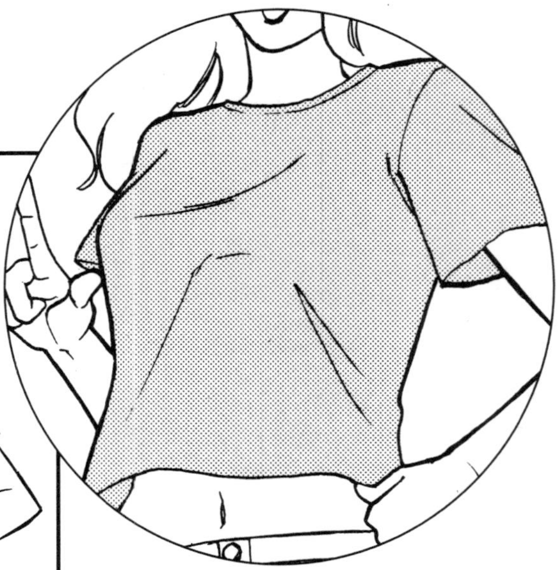

Attaching Dot Tone to a T-Shirt (IC-51 Used)

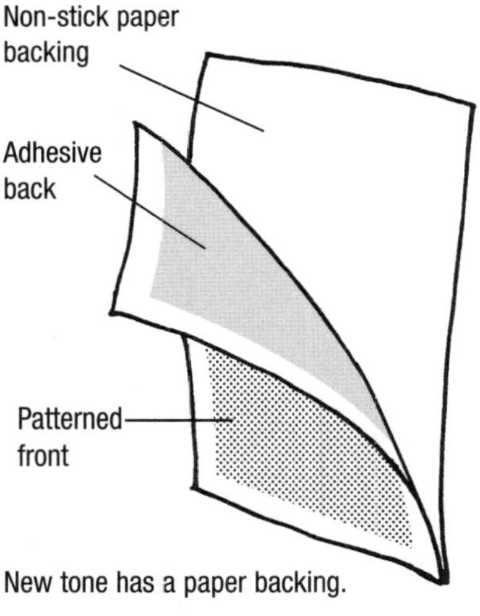

New tone has a paper backing.

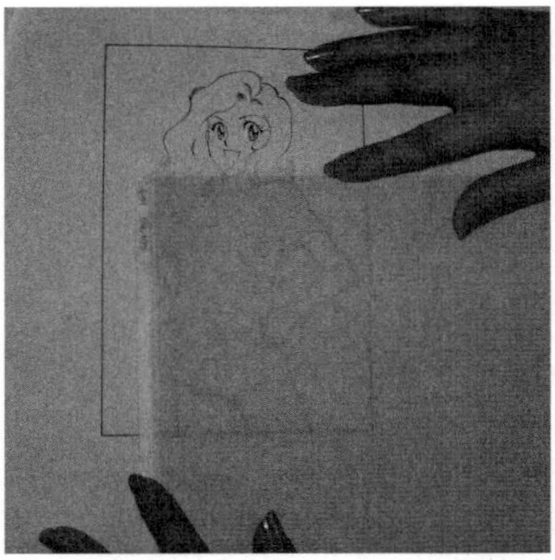

① Lay the tone with the backing attached over the panel.

Matching up the Tone Size

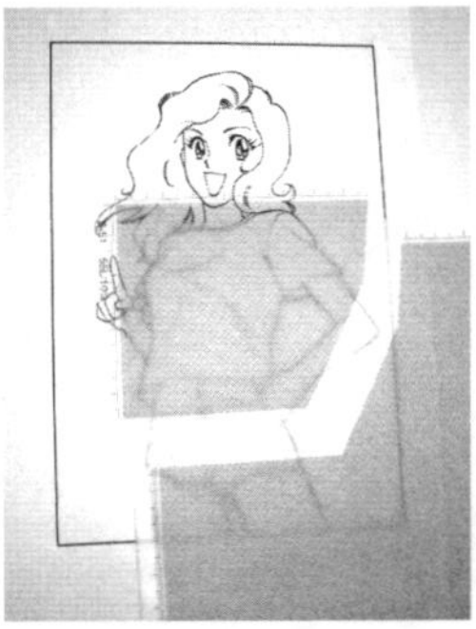

② Trim the tone to the desired size (cut it slightly on the large-side).

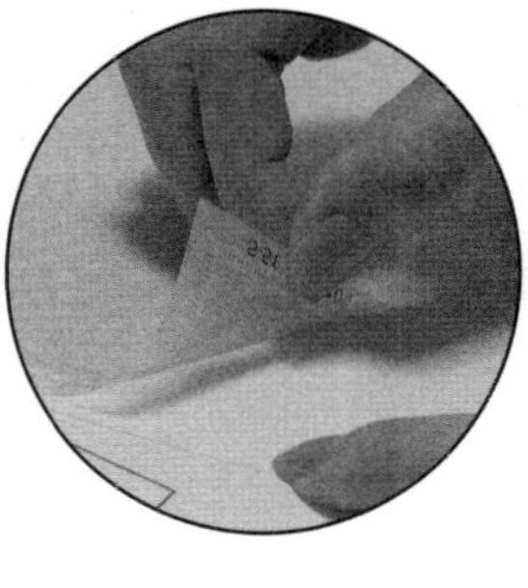

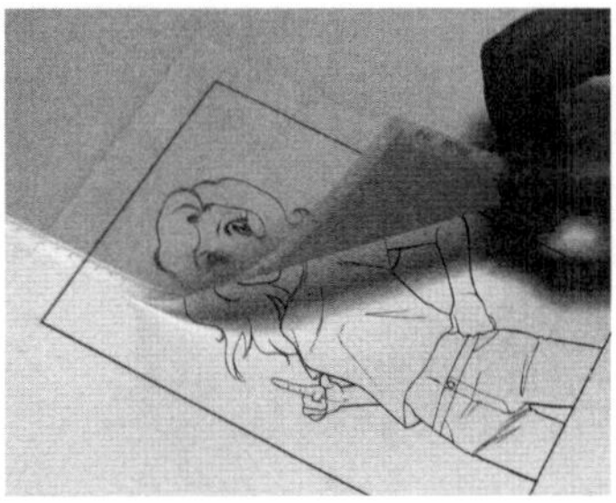

When attaching tone to the whole panel, some artists will slide the panel between the tone and its backing. Caution: the adhesive back of the tone does pick up specks easily.

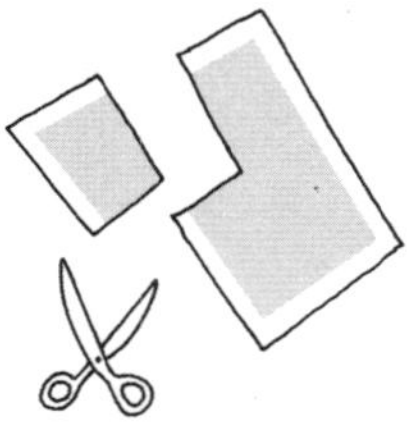

The tone may be trimmed with the backing still attached.

③ Place the tone on top of the panel and press lightly.

The key is to cover the entire target area.

Do not press down too hard on portions you plan on removing.

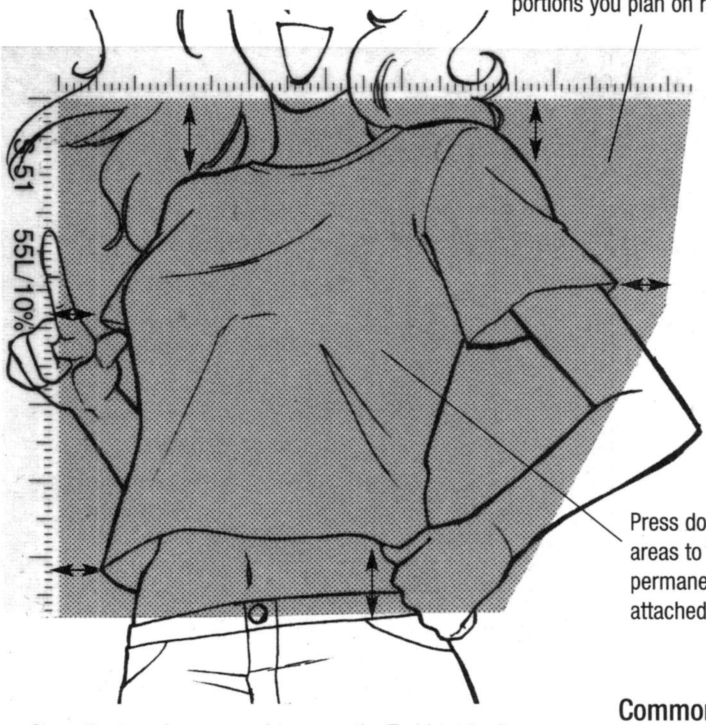

Press down on areas to be permanently attached.

Since the tone is supposed to cover the T-shirt, trim it to extend slightly over the target area in all directions. (Do not use the panel as your guide to trimming. Always remember that the target area is the area to which the tone will be attached.)

Points Concerning Tone Alignment

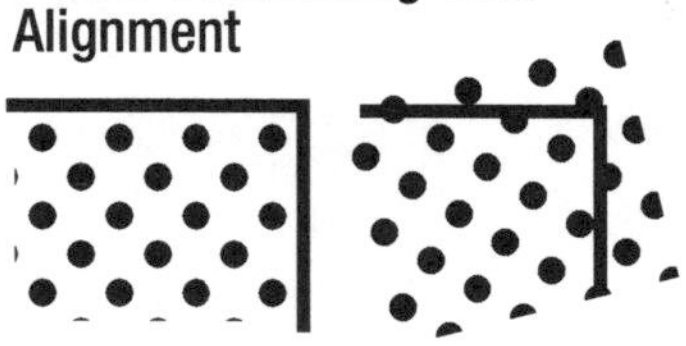

It is important that you align the tone squarely against the panel or drawing.

Except for when a particular effect is desired, tone is rarely attached at a skewed angle.

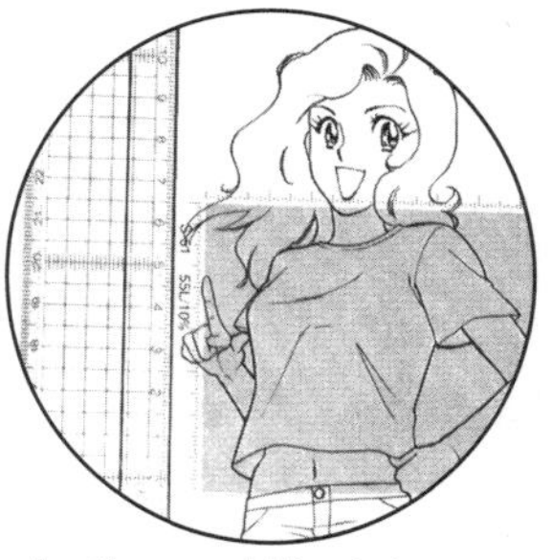

Another good idea is to check the alignment with a straightedge before pressing down on the tone.

Common Pitfalls

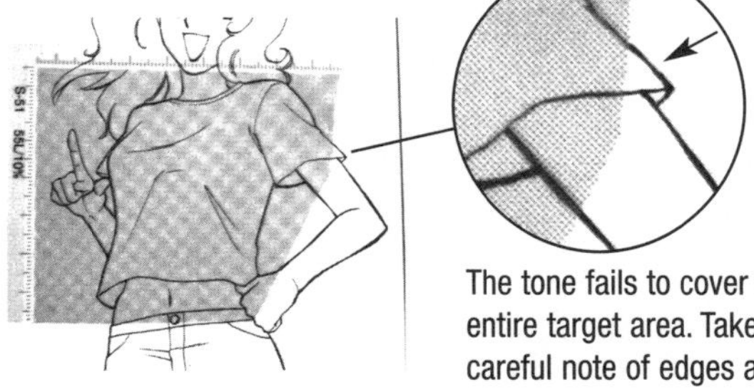

The tone fails to cover the entire target area. Take careful note of edges and corners.

Caution When matching the tone to the target:

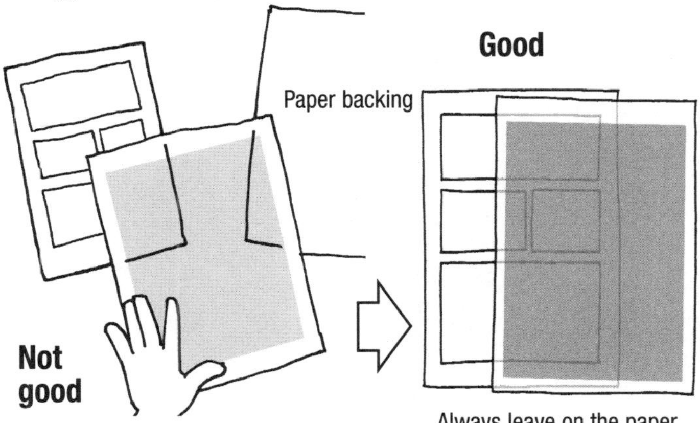

Absolutely never remove the paper backing from the entire tone when attaching tone to a small target area. (The adhesive back easily attracts dust and particles, which could ruin almost all of the tone.)

Always leave on the paper backing.

A Word on Soiled Tone

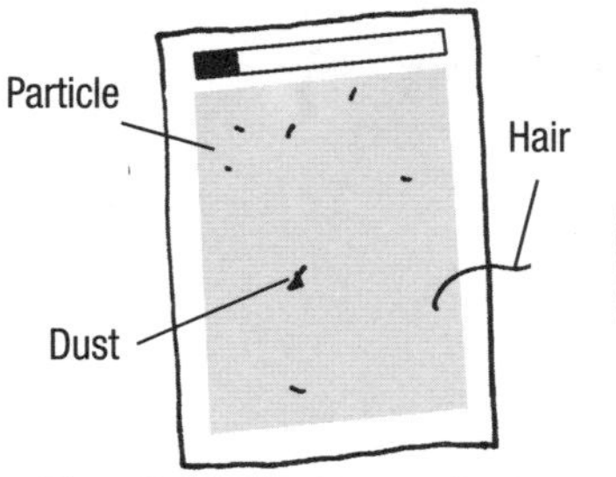

The adhesive backing easily attracts particles, and once the particles attach, they will not come off.

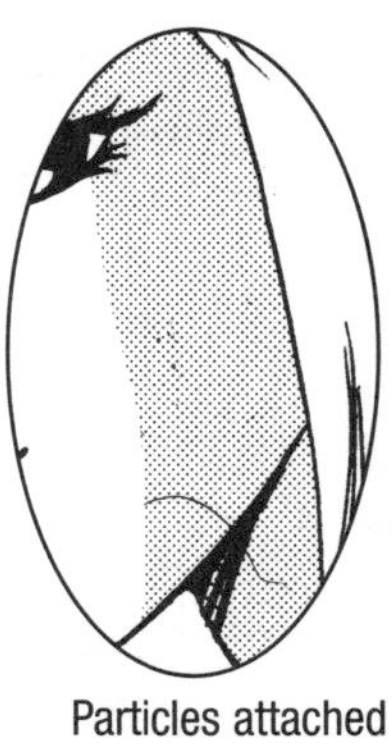

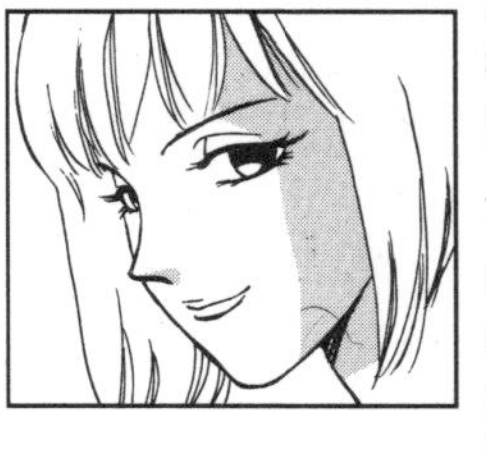

Particles attached to soiled tone will show up during the printing process.

The particles are still evident even after greatly reducing the image.

2 Trimming the Tone

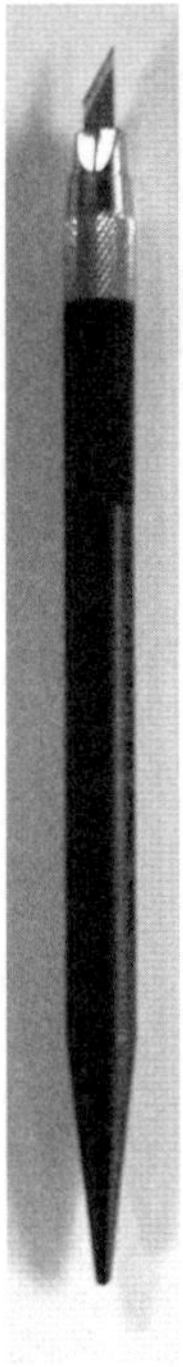

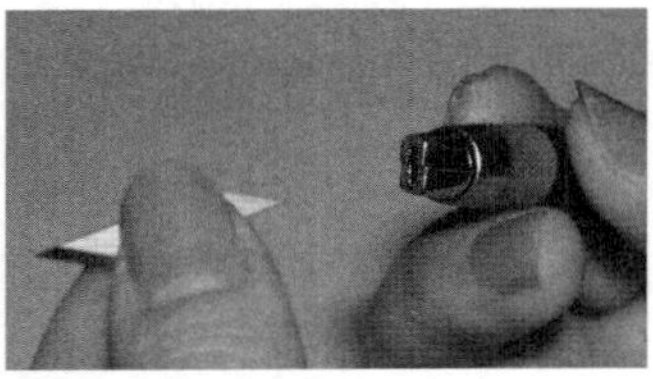

Replace the blades as they become dull.

Craft knives

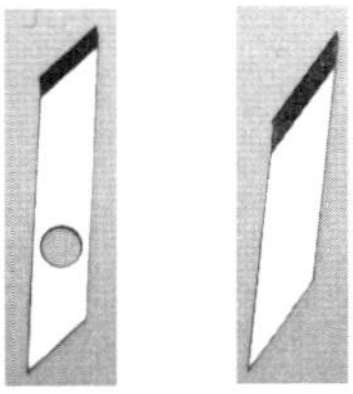

45° angle 60° angle

Blades with 60° angles do cut better, but they are sharp, so be careful when using them.

Good

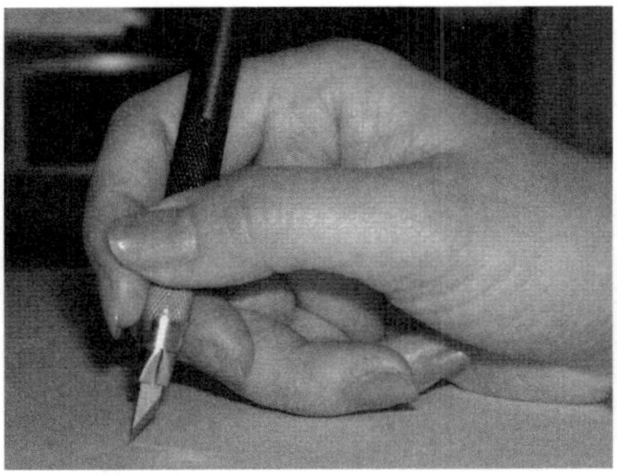

The knife is held similarly to a pencil, but more erectly.

Not good

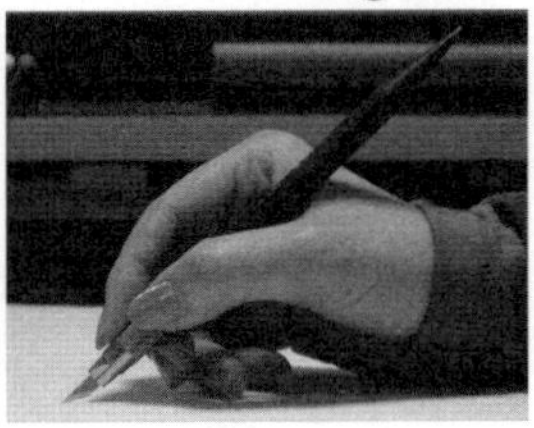

Good

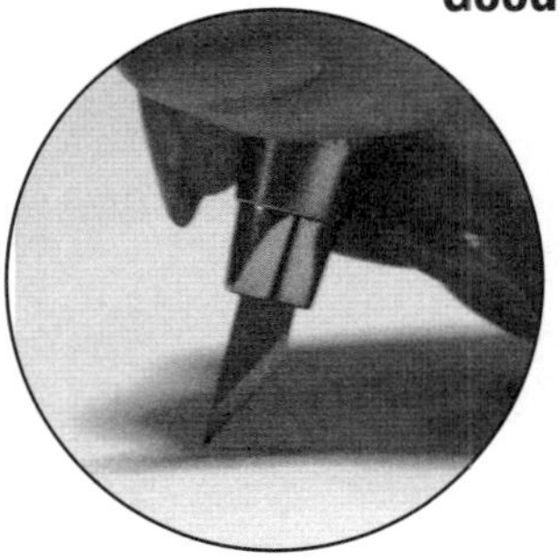

Not good

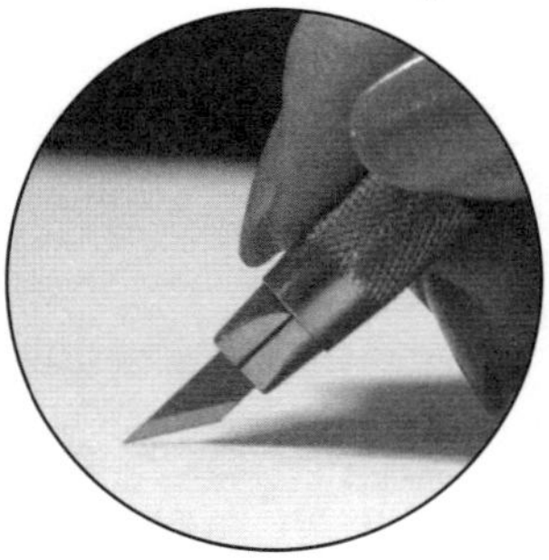

Hold the knife as upright as possible.

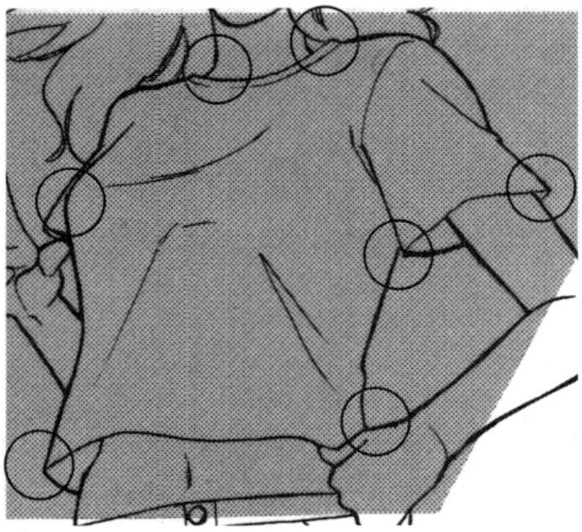

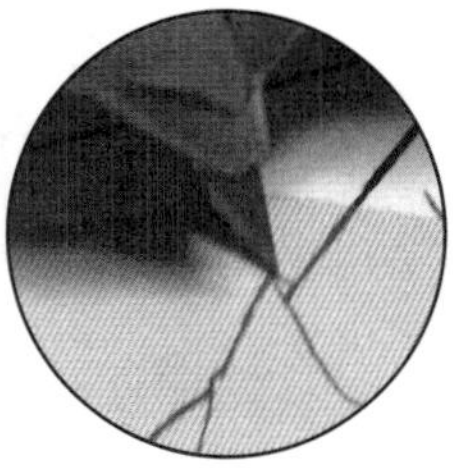

Take extra care with corners and areas where the knife direction changes, as they are often not fully cut.

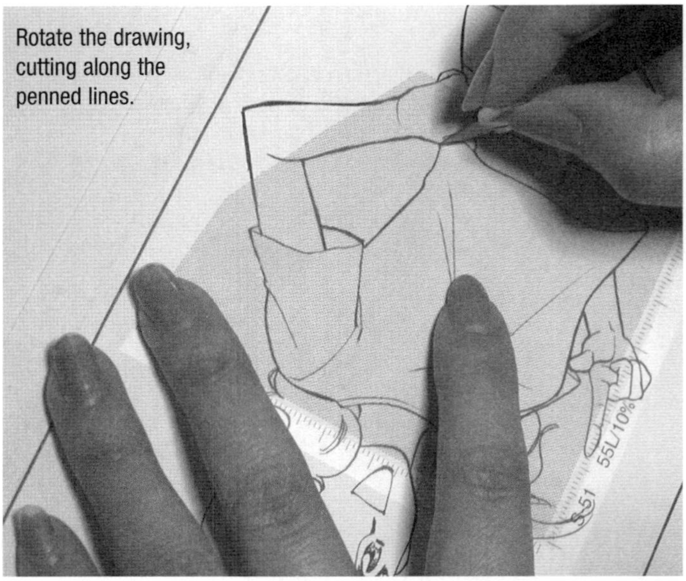

Rotate the drawing, cutting along the penned lines.

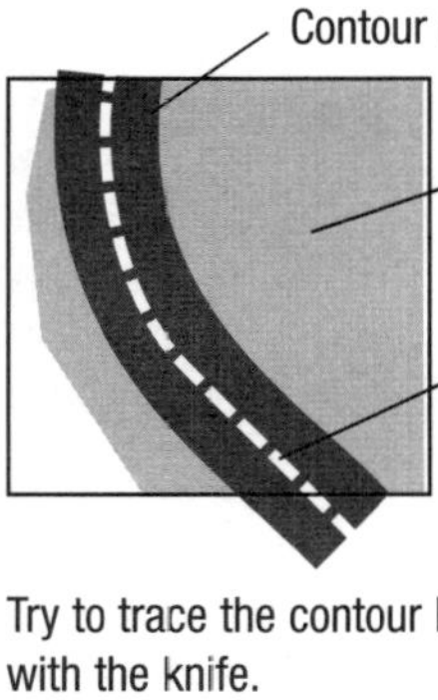

Try to trace the contour lines with the knife.

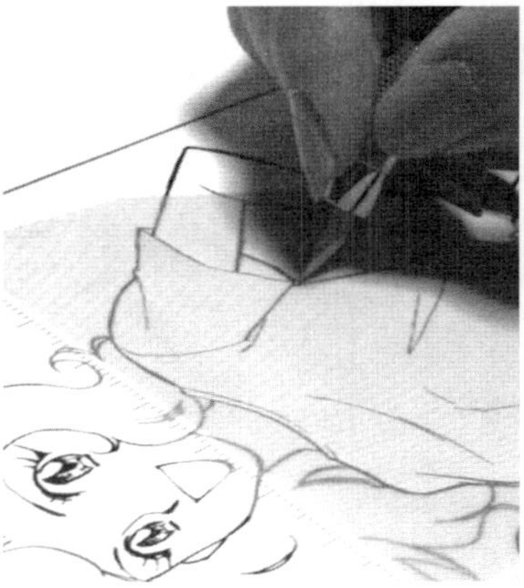

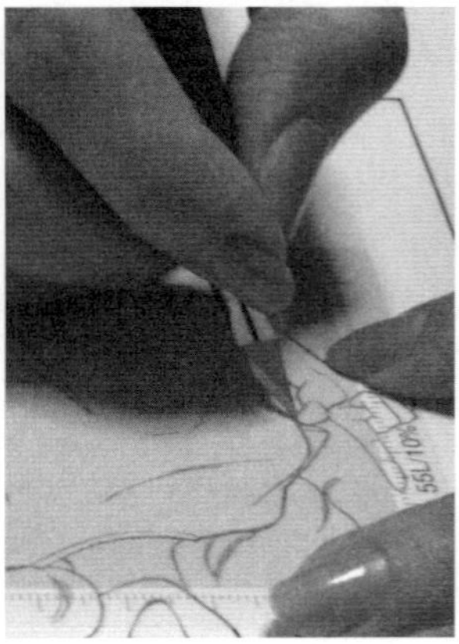

2 Removing the Tone

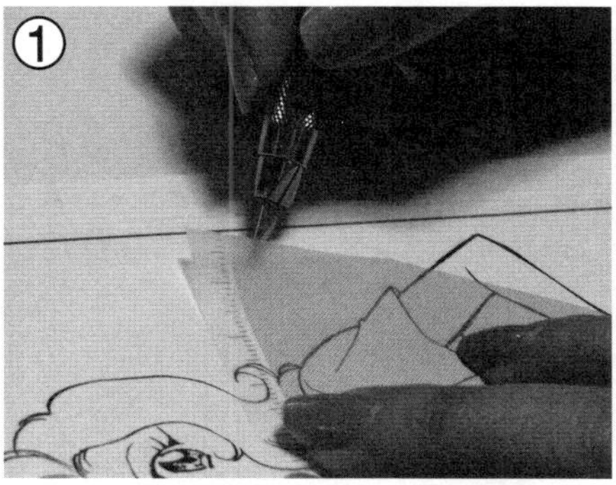

Holding down the tone, lift up an edge using the knife blade.

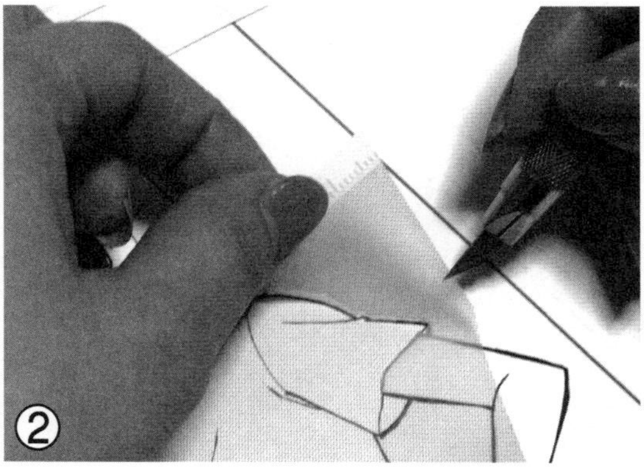

Lift up the edge.

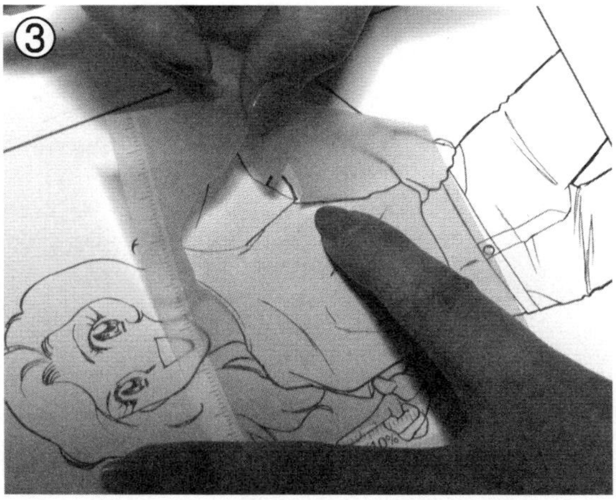

Remove the excess tone while holding down the target areas.

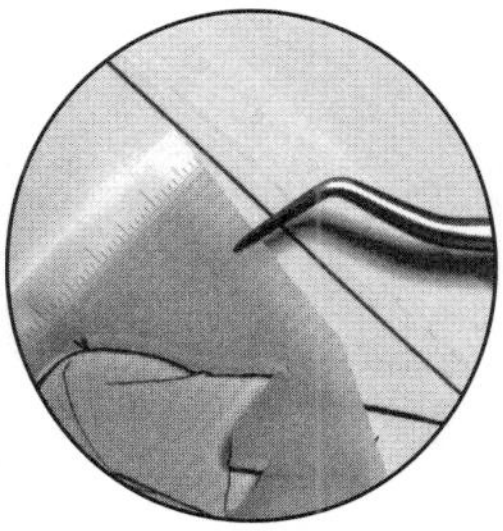

Tweezers may also be used.

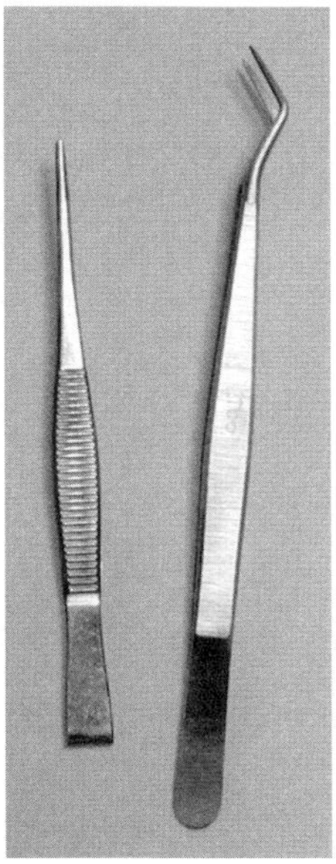

Since this prevents the adhesive back of the tone from directly touching anything, it protects the back from soiling. Once you have grown accustomed to this process, you will become more effective in handling your tone.

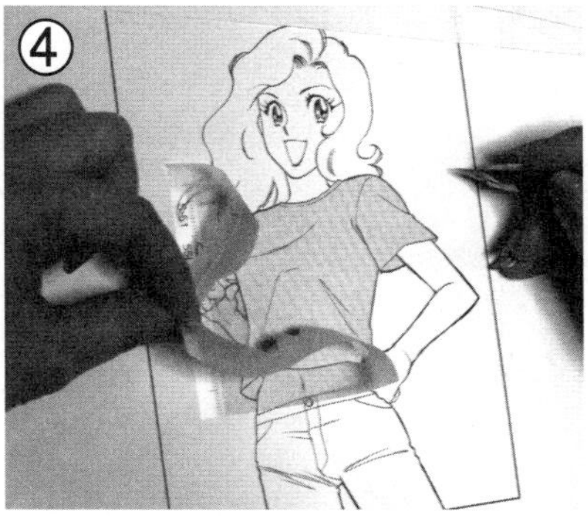

Removing the tone can be lots of fun if it has been cut properly.

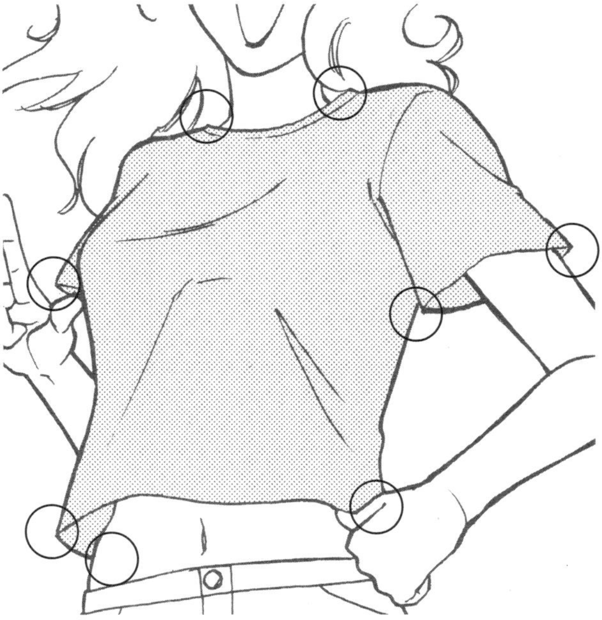

These points are peeled up easily. However, they are often not fully cut, so take extra care with corners or points where the knife direction changed when peeling off the tone.

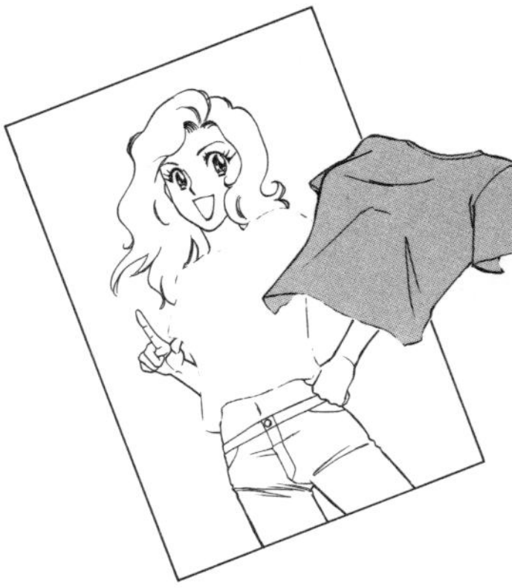

If you accidentally cut all the way through the drawing, reattach it by affixing cellophane tape to the back.

4 Rubbing the Tone

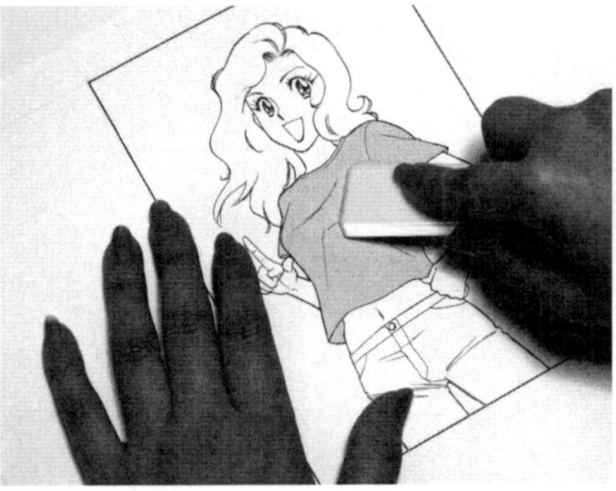

Tone Burnisher

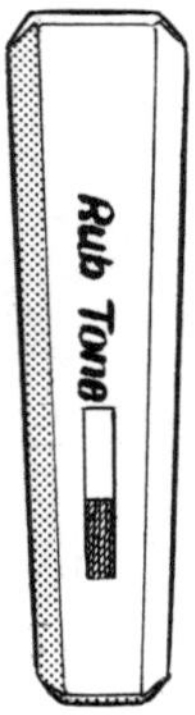

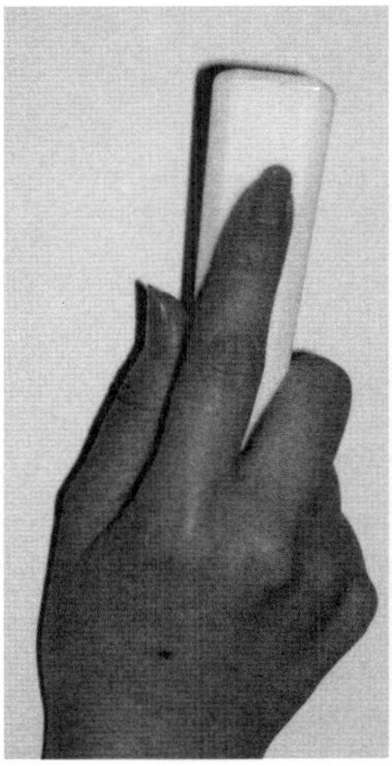

Correct way to hold the burnisher (Front)

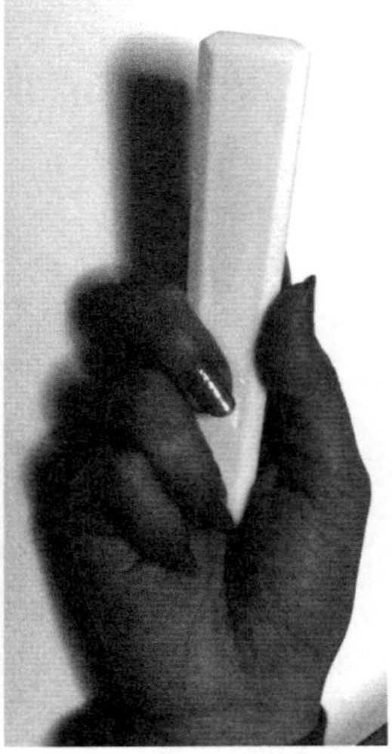

Back

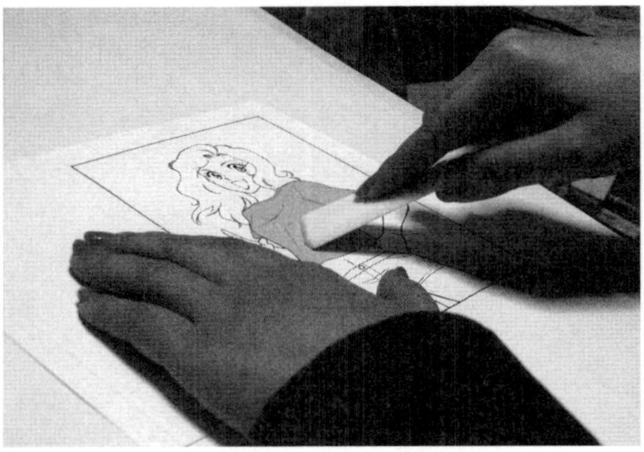

The burnisher ensures that the tone securely affixes to the drawing. Press the tone down on the drawing and rub with the burnisher to ensure it will not detach.

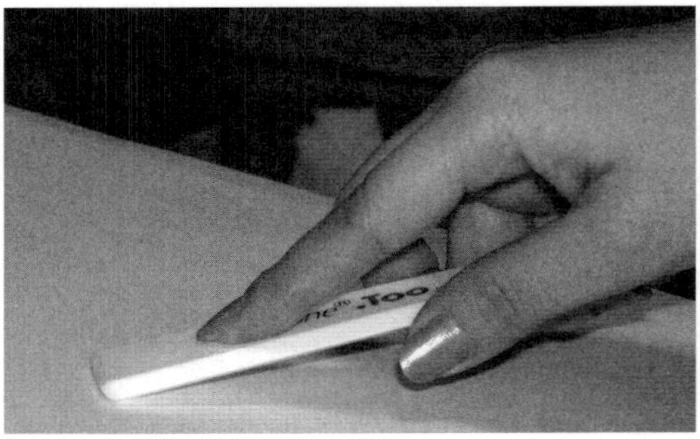

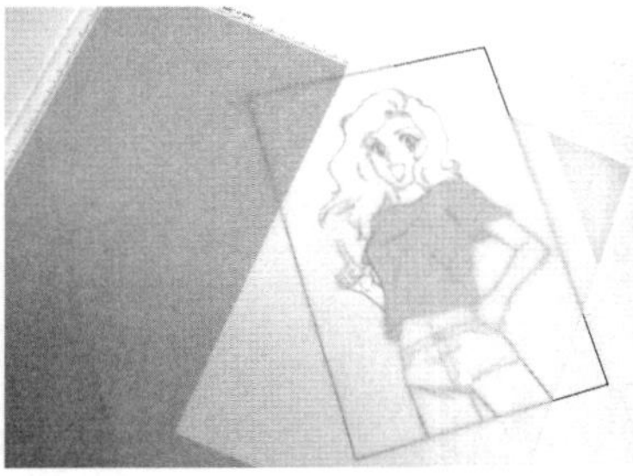

Lay the tone's paper backing or a sheet of photocopy paper over the tone and rub. There are rare occasions when rubbing directly the tone's surface that the tone rips or becomes damaged, so I recommend using a buffer paper to those who tend to press down hard.

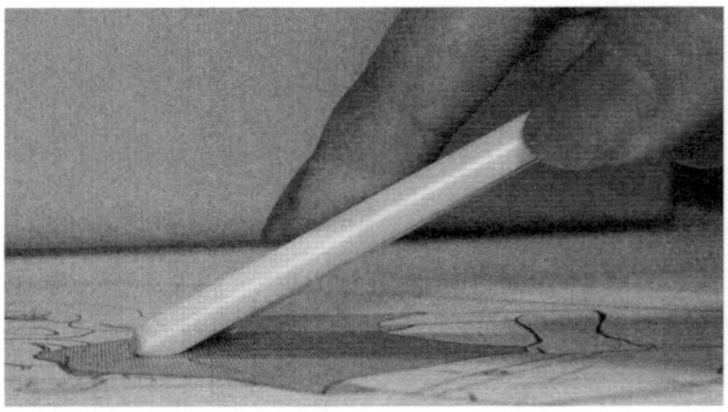

Hold the burnisher at a low angle with respect to the paper.

Rubbing Directions

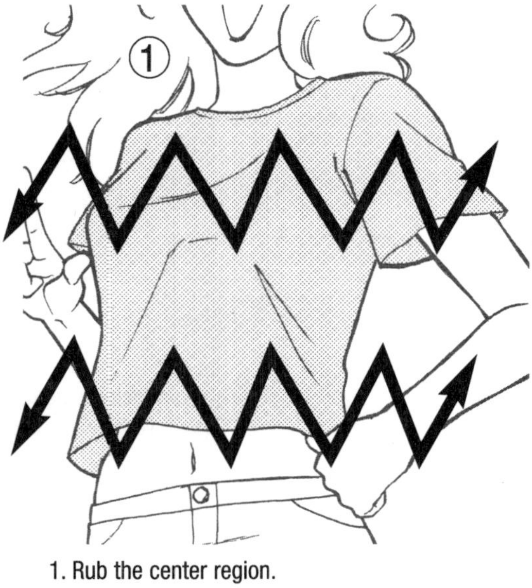

1. Rub the center region.

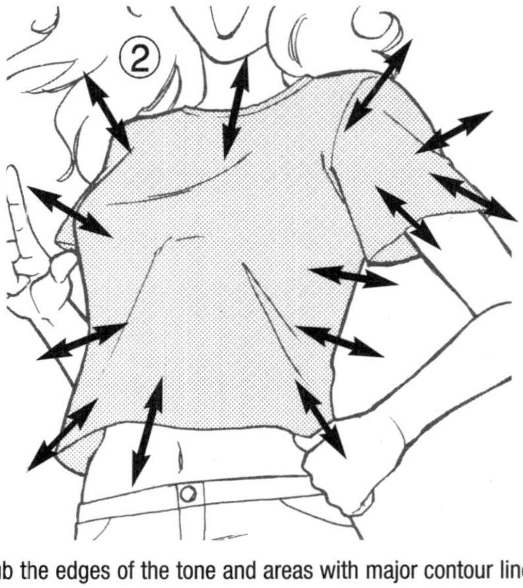

2. Rub the edges of the tone and areas with major contour lines.

Stylus

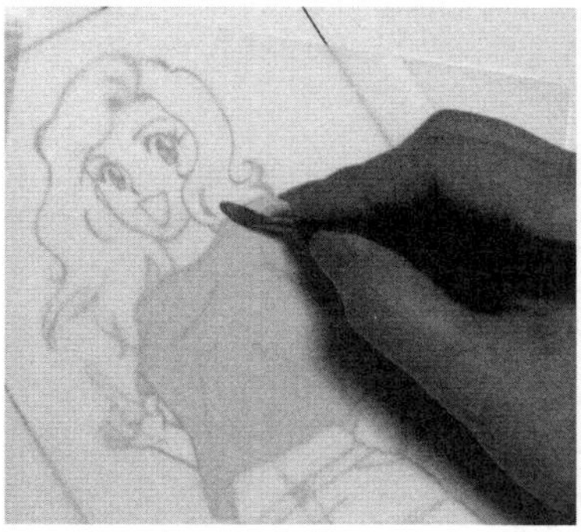

The burnisher-side of the stylus allows you to press down firmly; however, you also risk damaging the original drawing, so be sure to use a buffer sheet.

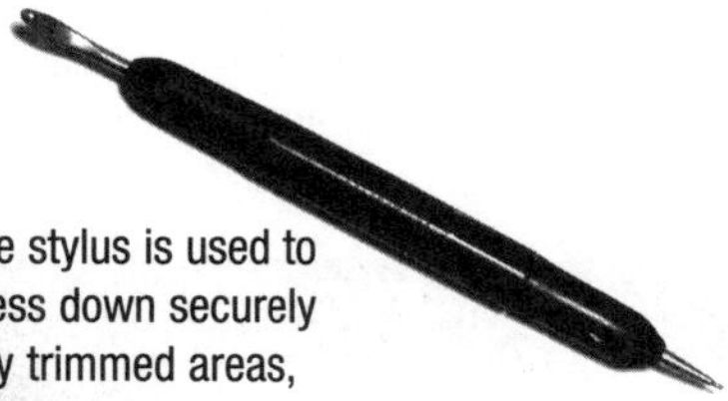

The stylus is used to press down securely tiny trimmed areas, corners, etc.

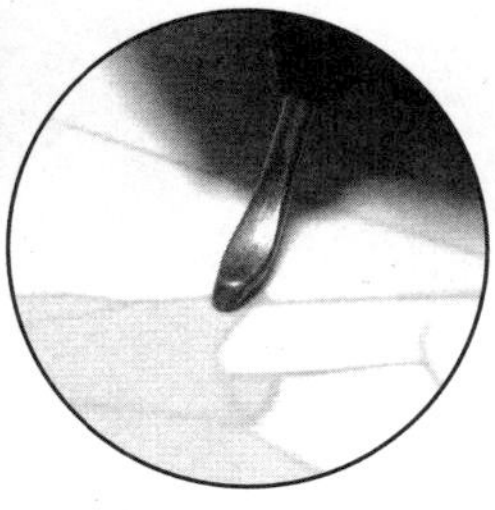

The stylus is used when adding the final touches, such as going over one extra time areas that detach easily.

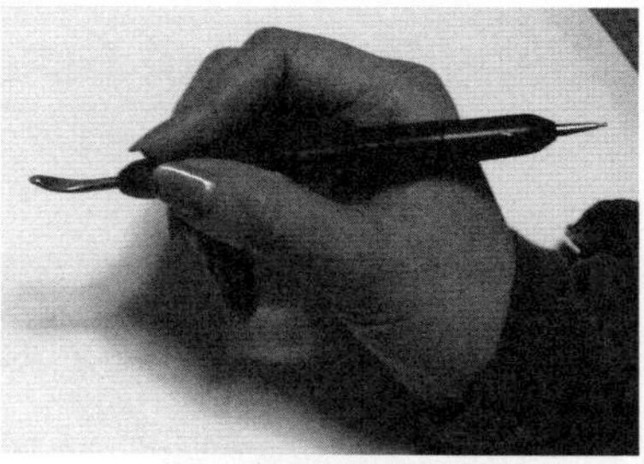

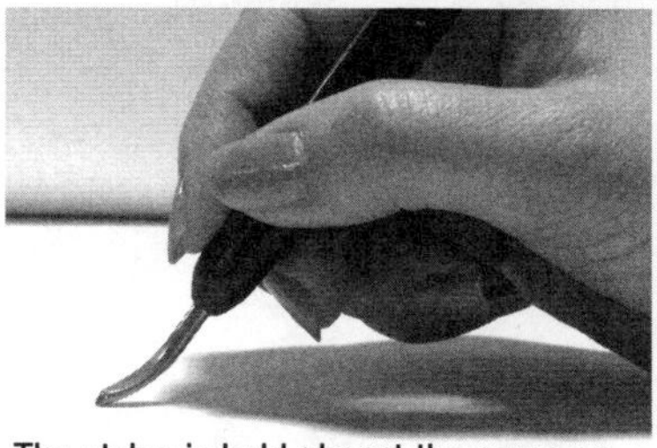

The stylus is held almost the same as a pencil.

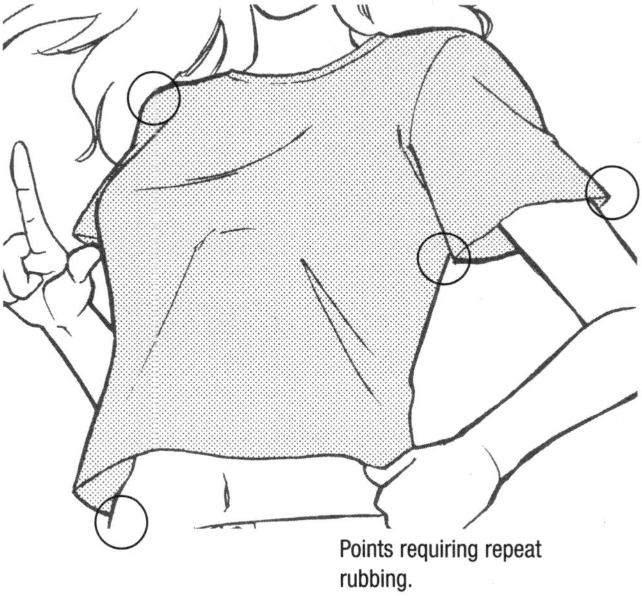

Points requiring repeat rubbing.

Good

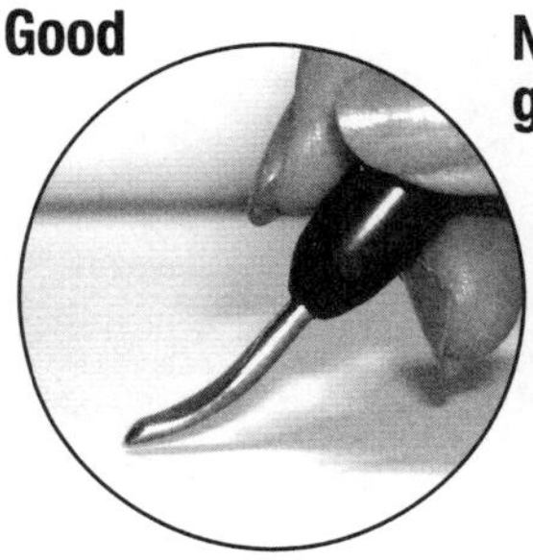

Hold the stylus at an angle close to the paper.

Not good

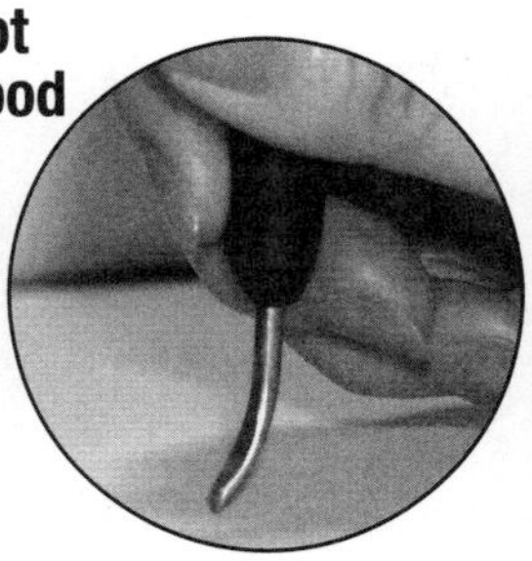

Here, the stylus is held too vertically.

Basic Knowledge in Removing Tone and Handling After Removal

1. Removing tone

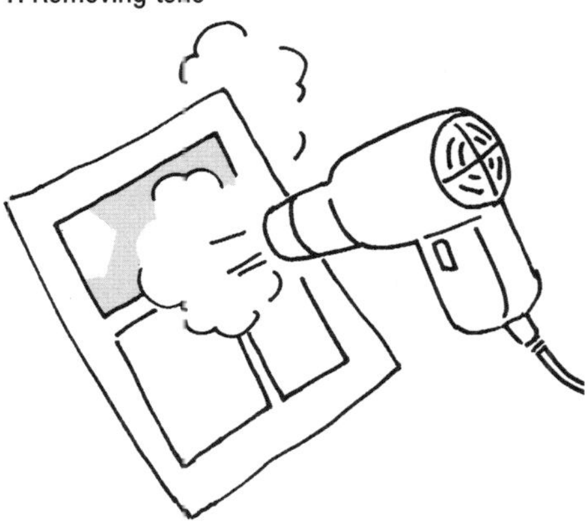

To remove tone that has been really securely attached, heat the tone lightly with a hairdryer.

2. After removal

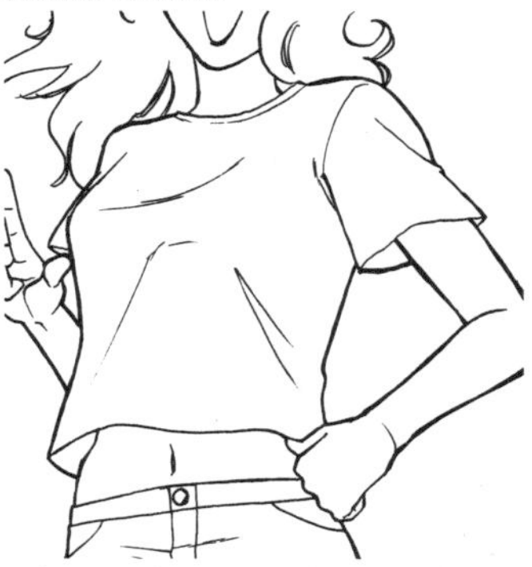

After the tone is removed, some glue will remain. This tends to collect dust and grime if left as is, plus it could become inadvertently stuck to drawings or other paper laid on top.

3. Removing residual glue

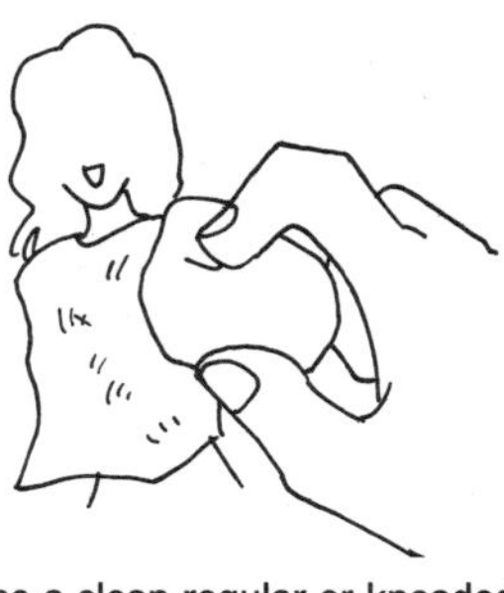

Use a clean regular or kneaded eraser to rub the residual glue off the drawing. Keep a kneaded eraser on hand specifically to use for any finishing touches needed by your tone work.

Sample Uses of Gradation Tone

Gradation tone generally comes in 2 types: dark gradation, which gradates from black to white, and light gradation, which gradates from grey to white. There is a diversity of gradation tones on the market, coming in varying widths, etc.

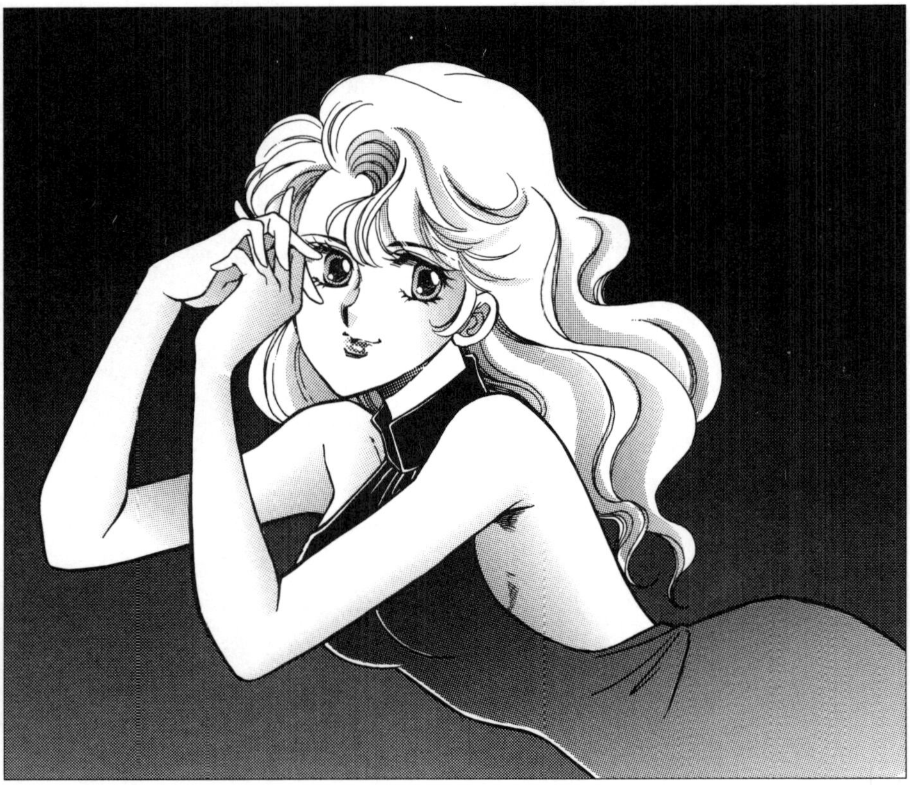

Gradation Tones

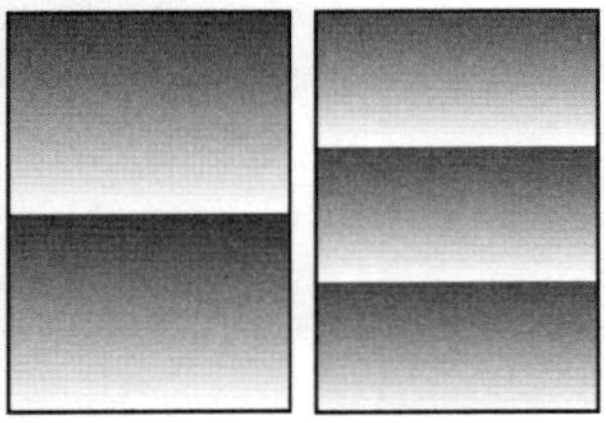

2-level (vertical) gradation | 3-level (vertical) gradation

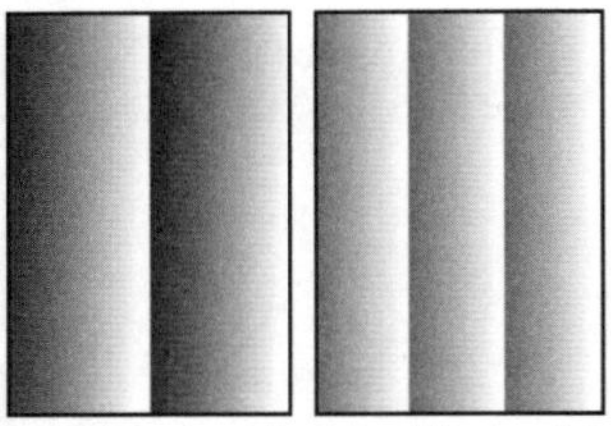

2-level (horizontal) gradation | 3-level (horizontal) gradation

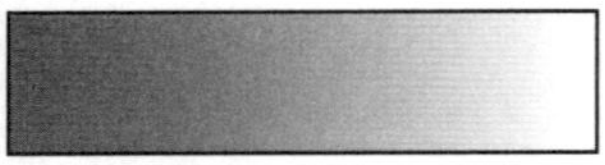

Light gradation

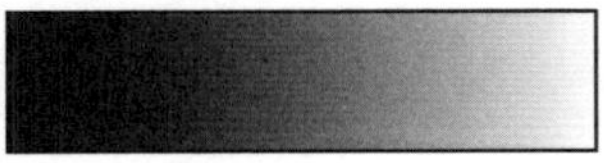

Dark gradation

Just what does that "L" mean at the end of the tone number?

The "L" is an abbreviation for "line," and it refers to the number of lines (rows) of dots. This acts as a guideline when layering tones.

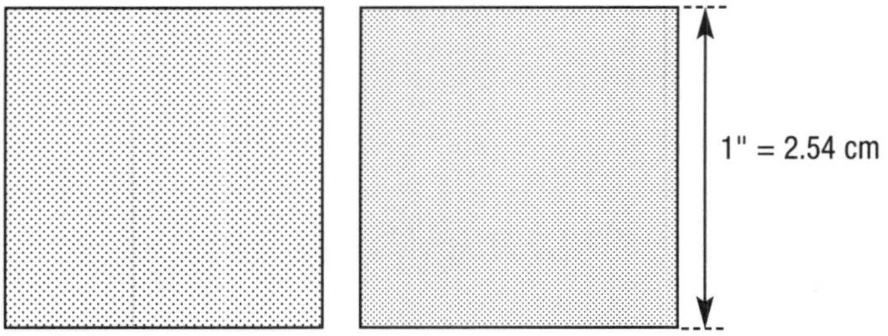

42.5L
1" = 2.54 cm
1 sq. in. contains 42.5 lines in all directions.

60L
1 sq. in. contains 60 lines in all directions.

Patterns, including a moiré effect, may appear when tones are overlapped.

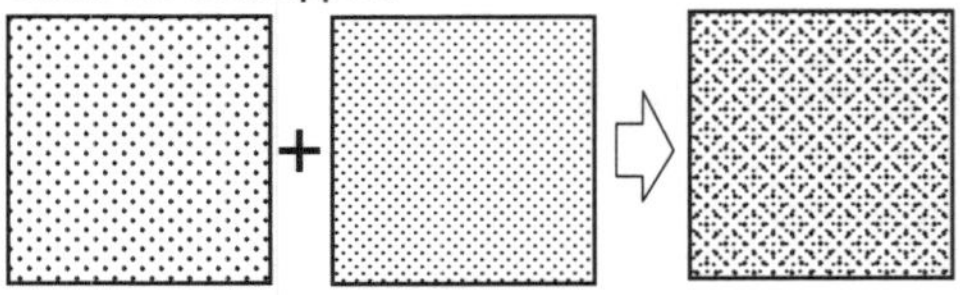

Although these are both 10% saturation, when overlapped, the different numbers of dot lines causes a pattern to form.

Layering to Darken the Tone without Creating a Pattern

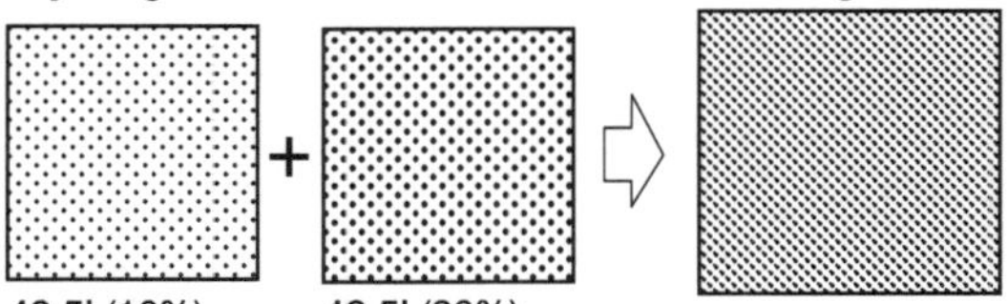

42.5L(10%) 42.5L(20%)

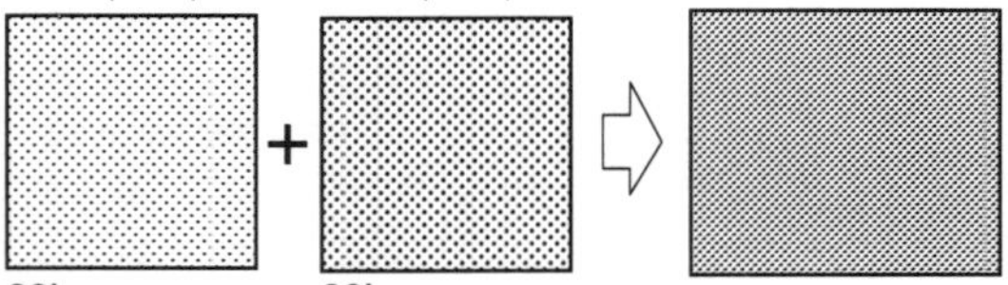

60L 60L

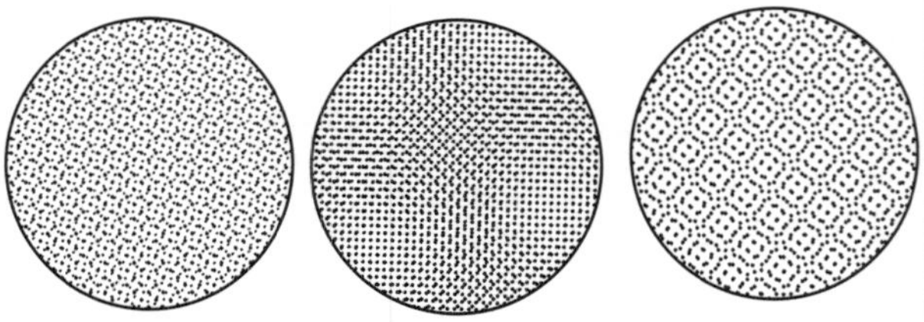

Overlapping tones with differing numbers of dot lines at various angles affects the appearance of the pattern formed.

A pattern can be created by layering tones with the same number of dot lines at an angle.

These patterns, including the moiré effect, may be used as print patterns.

Chapter 2

Character Shading and Tone Portrayal

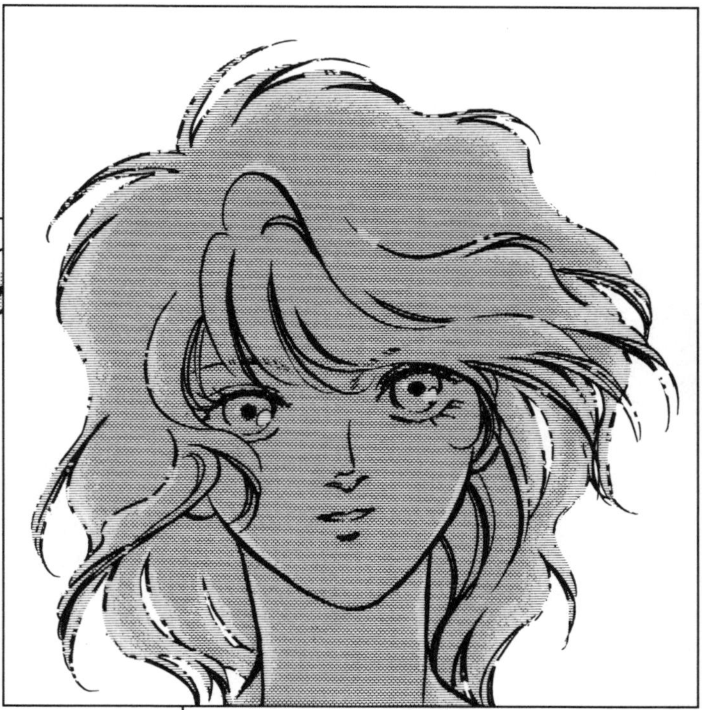

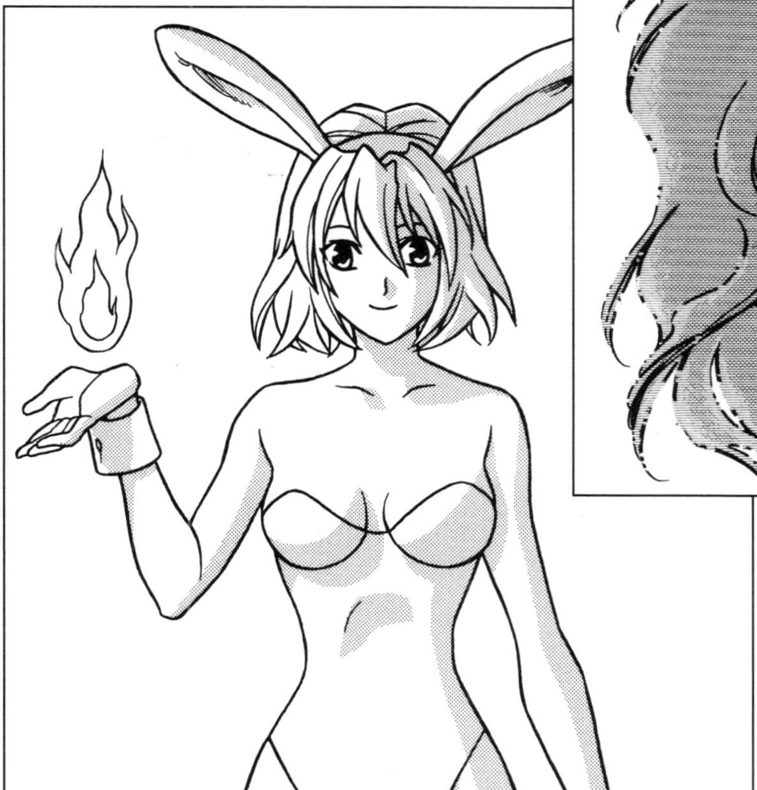

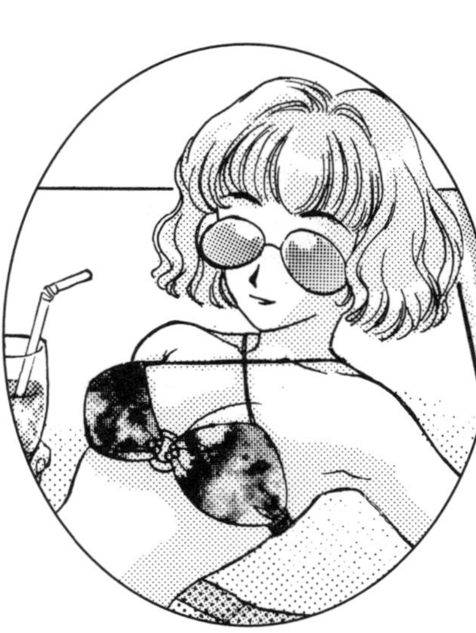

The ABC's of Facial Shadows

Shadows under the Chin

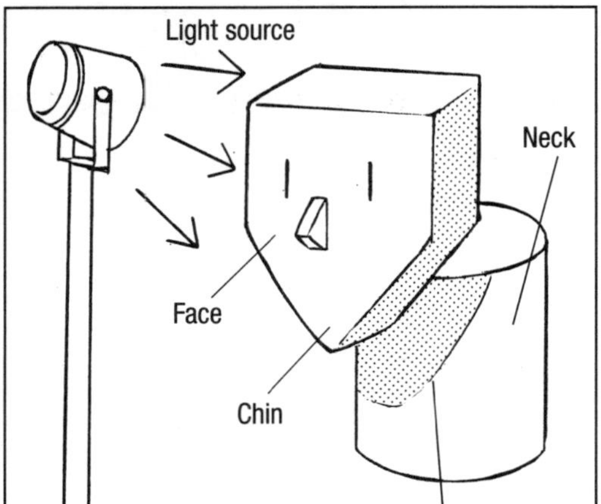

The neck is a cylinder, causing the shadow underneath the chin to have a curved contour.

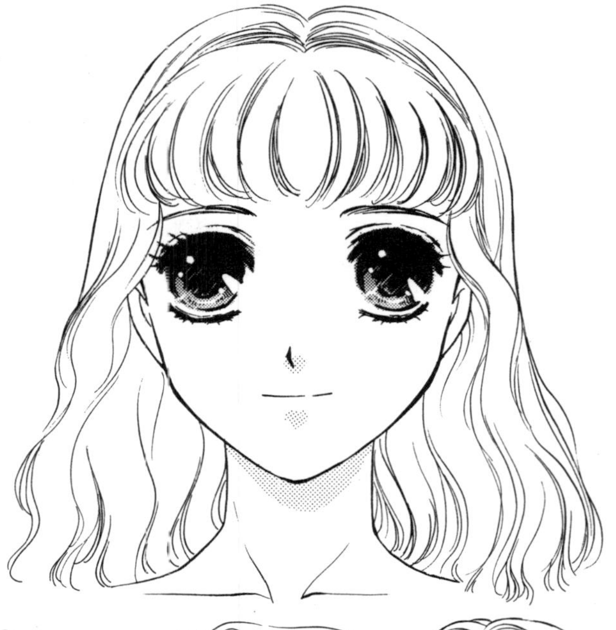

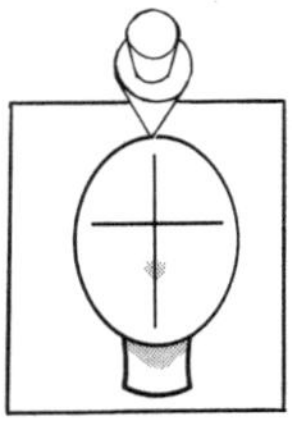

Straight on Light Source

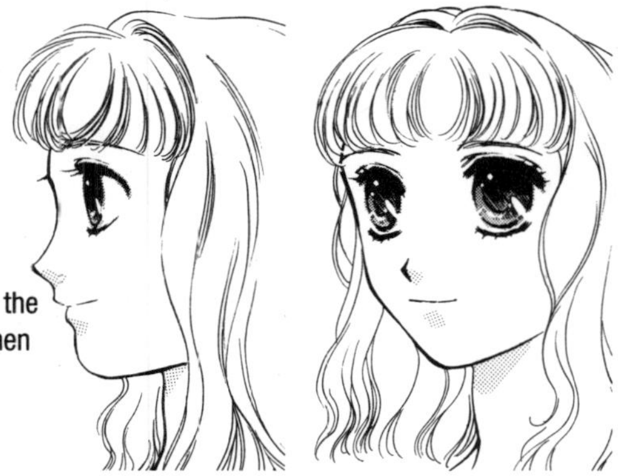

Shadows form under the nose and the chin when a light source shines from straight ahead.

Shadows also form underneath the lower lip and the bangs.

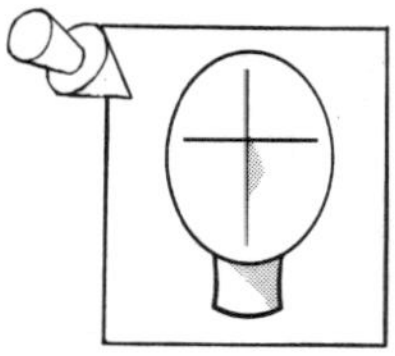

Front Left Light Source

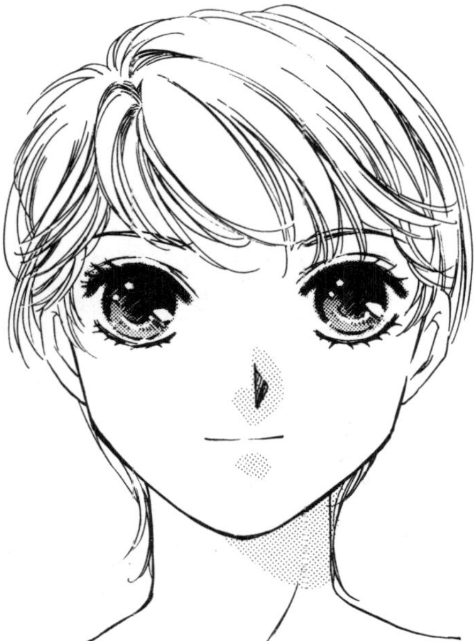

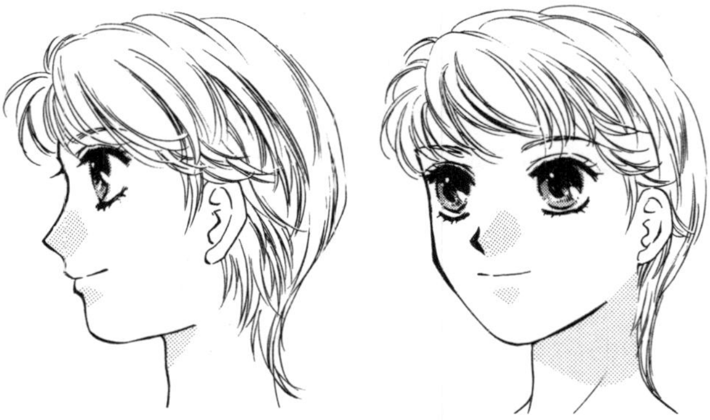

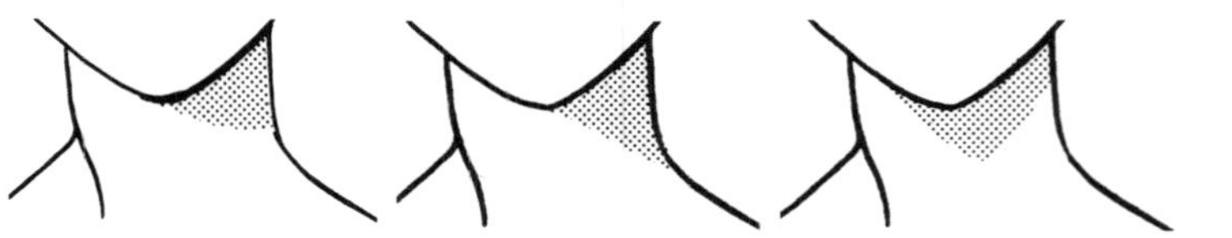

3 main types of shadows form underneath the chin. Use all of them at your discretion.

The Basics of Cheek Shadows

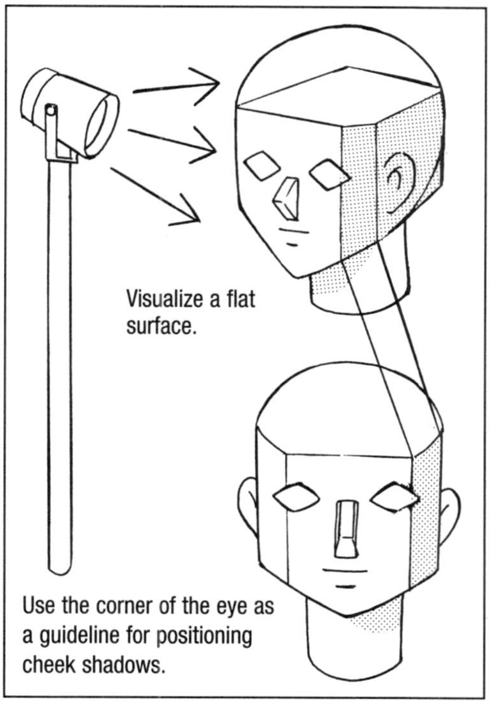

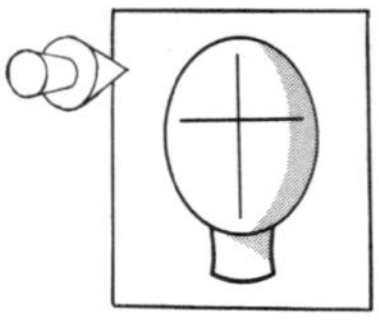

Front Left
Light Source

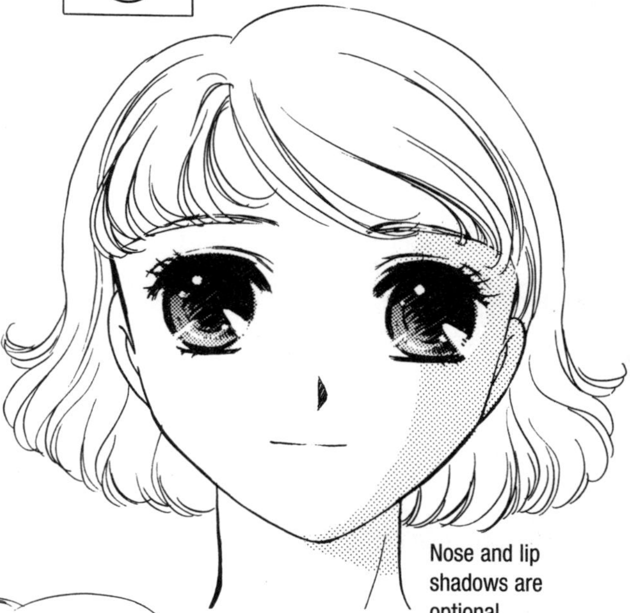

Nose and lip shadows are optional.

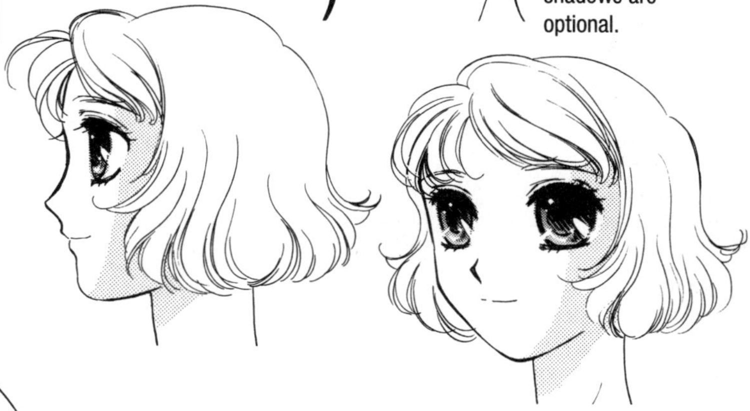

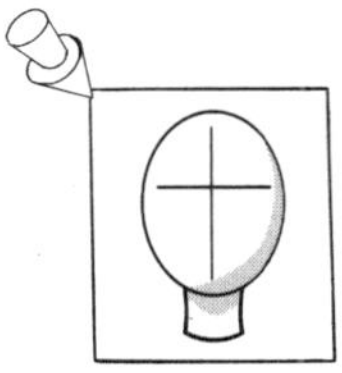

Upper Left
Light Source

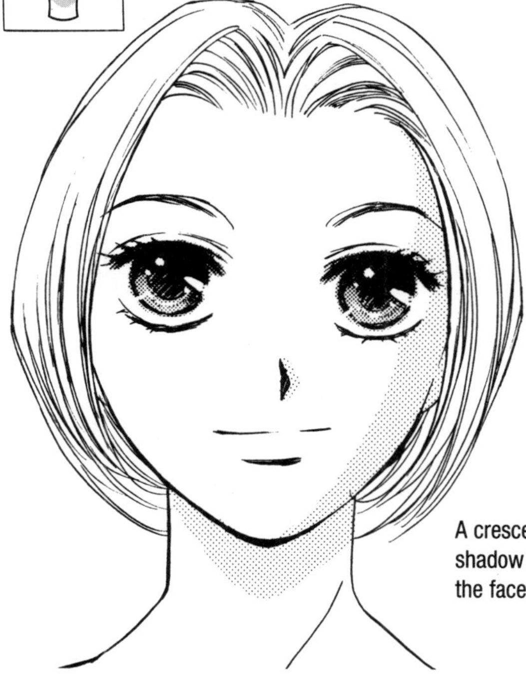

A crescent-shaped shadow forms on the face.

A shadow echoing the jaw line forms under the chin.

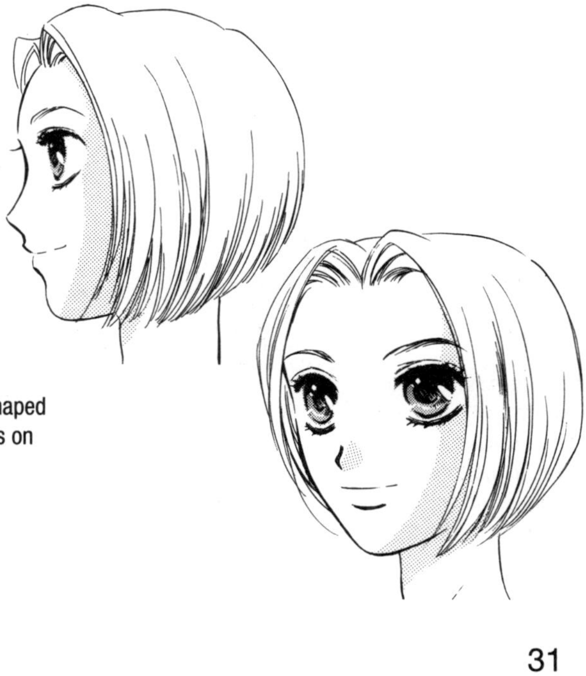

Dark and Light Shadows: Bright and Soft Light

A shadow's darkness depends on the intensity of the light source. Differences in the value used for a shadow varies according to the brightness of the lighting.

Bright Light

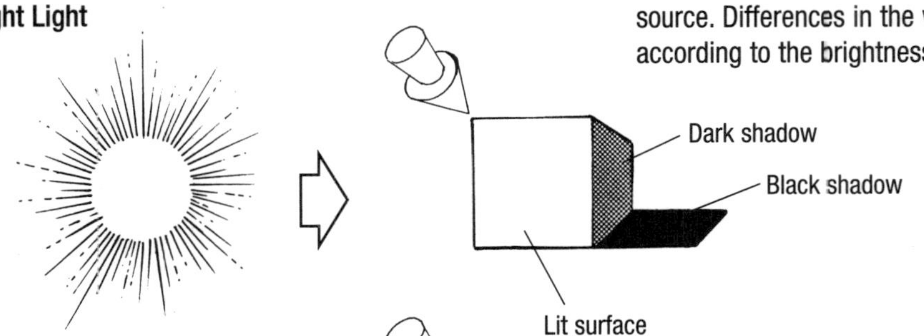

Soft Light

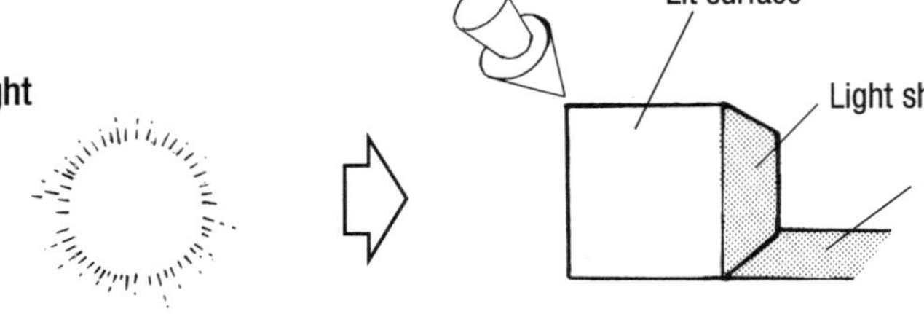

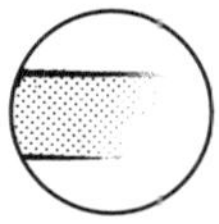

The shadow's edge may be blurred.

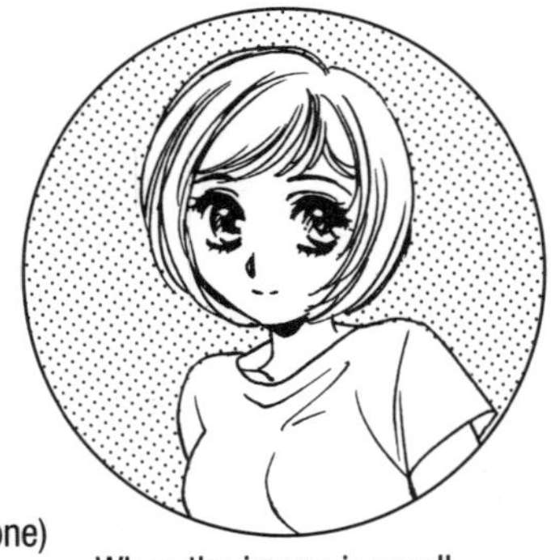

When the image is small, use a black shadow for underneath the chin, regardless of the light's brightness.

Common Modes of Rendering Shadow

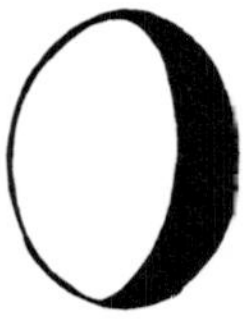

Shadows Rendered in Black

Use black shadows with spotlights or with bright, midsummer sunlight. Black shadows are used to create a striking impression or when seeking a specific effect.

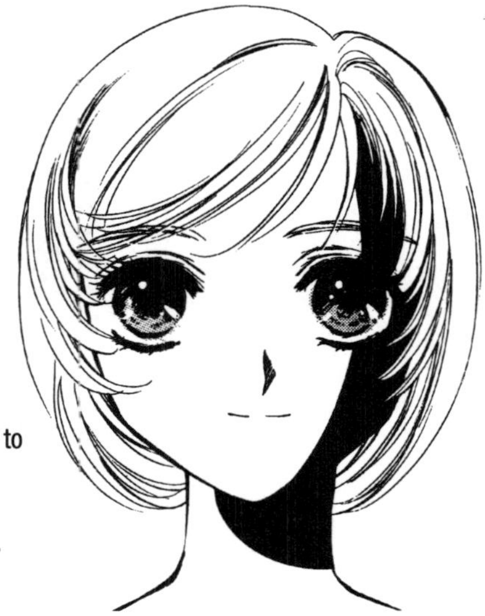

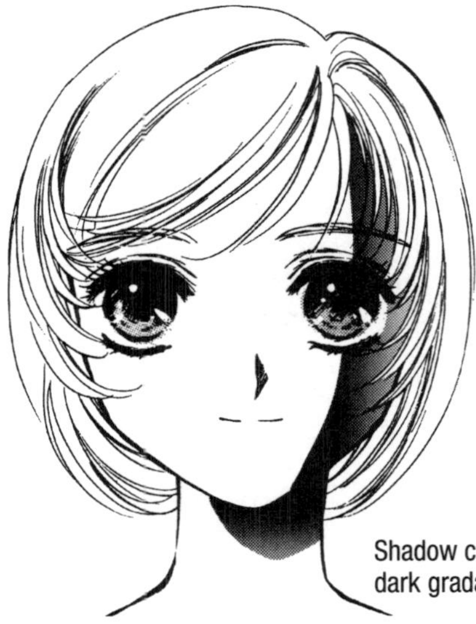

Shadow created with dark gradation tone

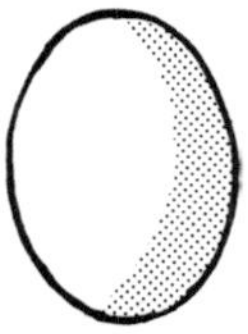

Shadows Rendered in Halftones

Halftone shadows are used to give the face 3-dimensionality and draw focus to the character, regardless of whether indoors or outdoors.

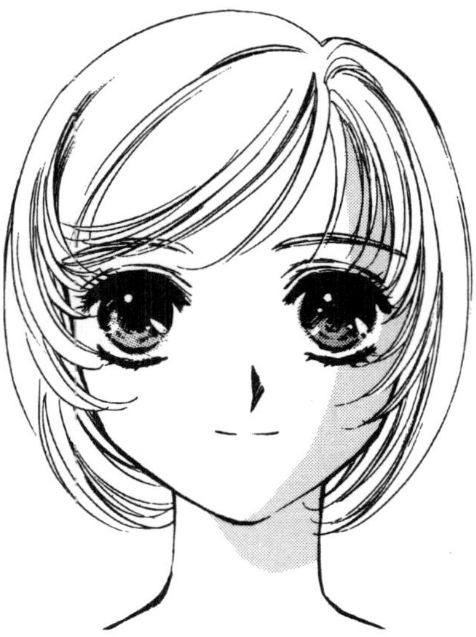

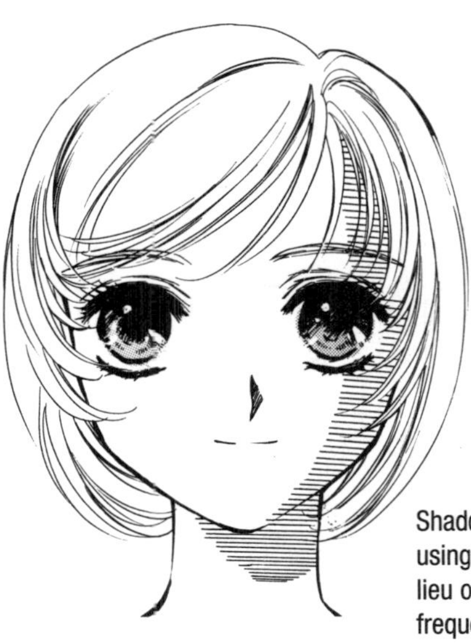

Shadows created using penned lines in lieu of tone appear frequently in realism *manga*.

Combination Shading Examples

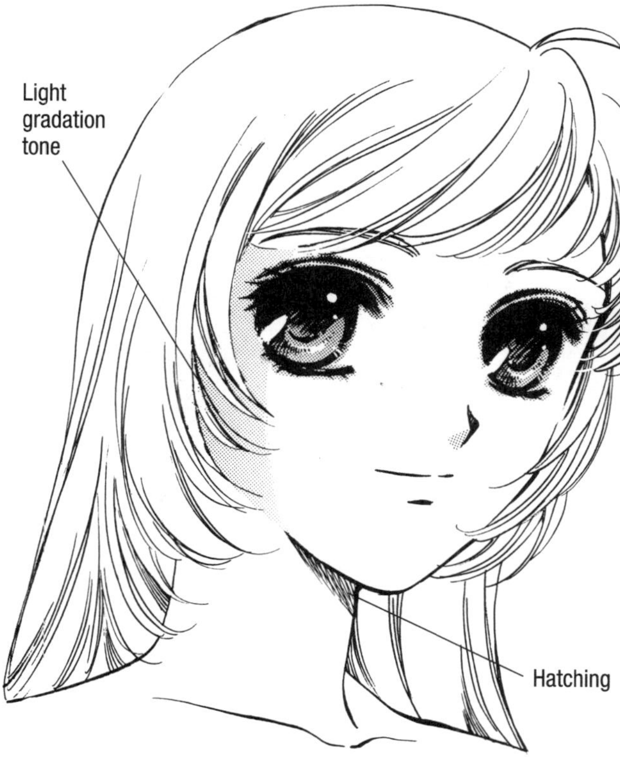

Light gradation tone is effective for recreating the texture of skin.

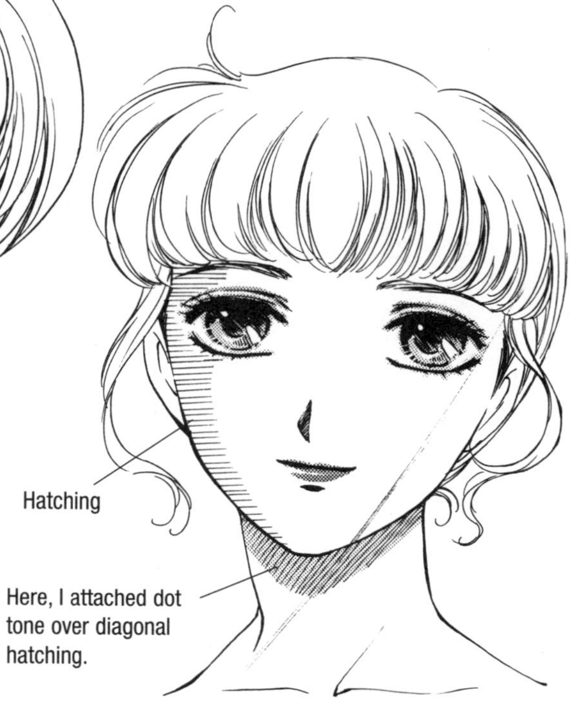

I created a sense of 3-dimensionality in the lips by attaching and etching standard dot tone.

Backlighting

Backlighting is when the light source is located in back of the subject. Shadow is added to the front of the subject's face, generating a dramatic mood.

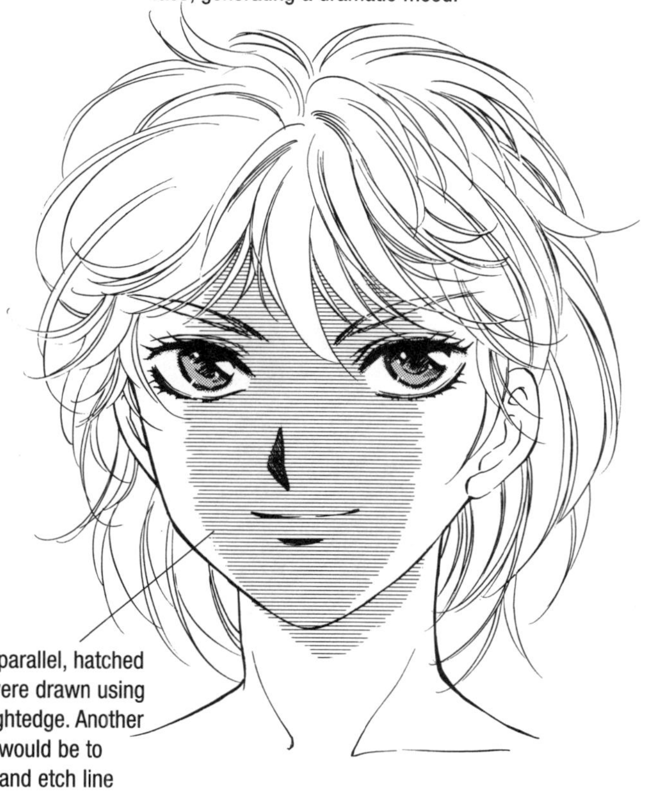

These parallel, hatched lines were drawn using a straightedge. Another option would be to attach and etch line tone.

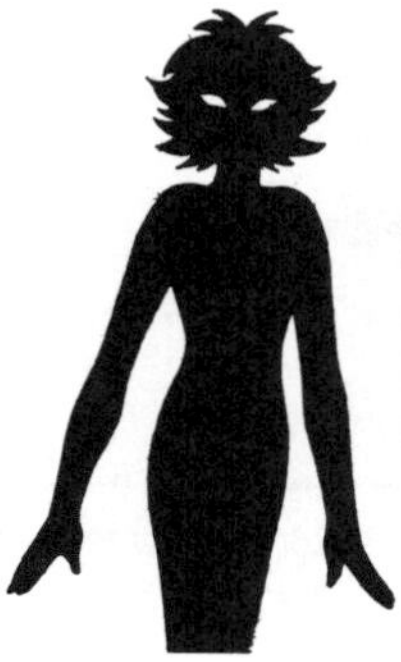

Filling in the figure with solid black creates a black silhouette. The key point here is that the eyes were left white.

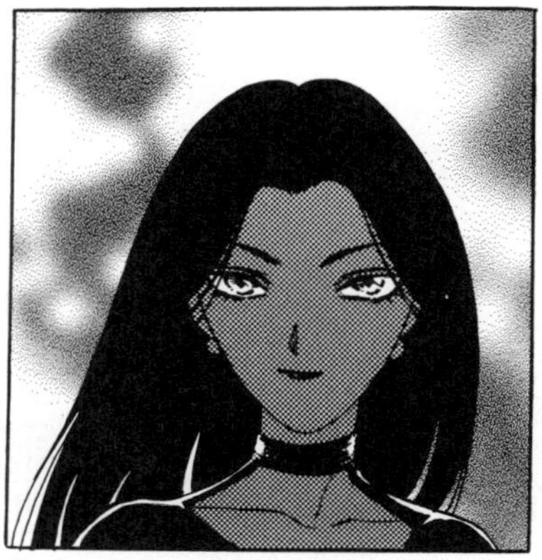

For this figure, tone was attached to the entire face but the eyes, left white. This treatment could be used to suggest flames burning behind the figure or other situations with low lighting.

When to Keep the Face Shadow-Free

Shadows do not work well on faces when the image is tiny. Use tone on clothing, hair, shoes, and other major colored areas. I limited the figures on this page to those that look better without shadows on their faces.

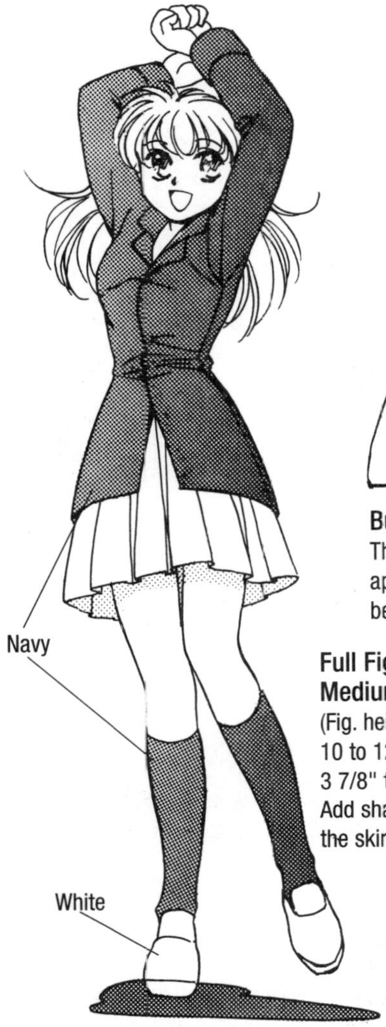

Full Figure: Medium
(Fig. height approx. 10 to 12 cm or 3 7/8" to 4 5/8")
Add shadows to the skirt, etc.

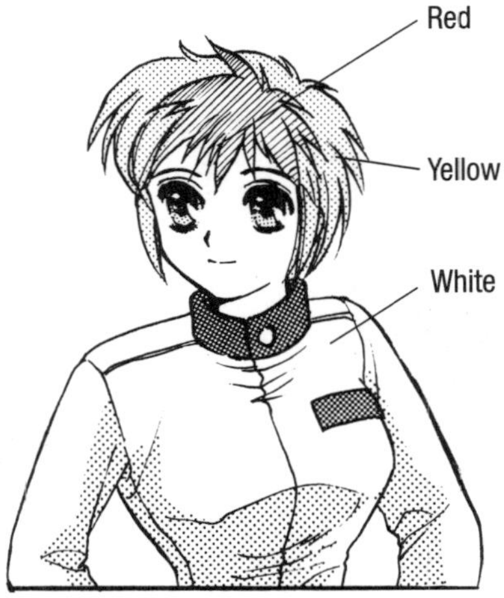

Bust Shot
The head (including hair) measures at approx. 3 cm. (1 1/8"). Shadows may be added to the body.

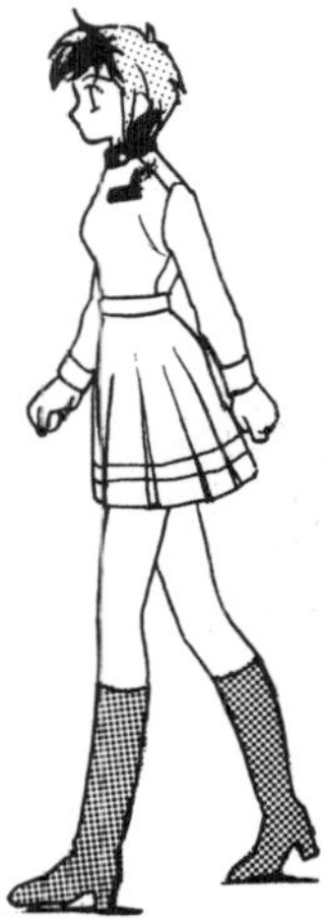

Long Shot: Large
Here, the figure is approx. 6 to 7 cm or 2 3/8" to 2 3/4" tall. For this size, I opted to render her "red" bangs using solid black in lieu of tone.

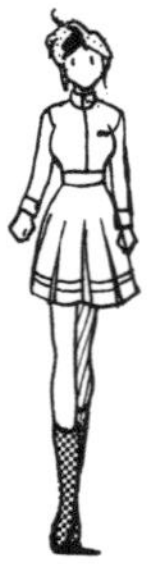

Standard Long Shot
This figure is approx. 3 to 4 cm or 1 1/8" to 1 1/2" tall. At this size, the facial features are barely discernible, and the face is virtually just an outline.

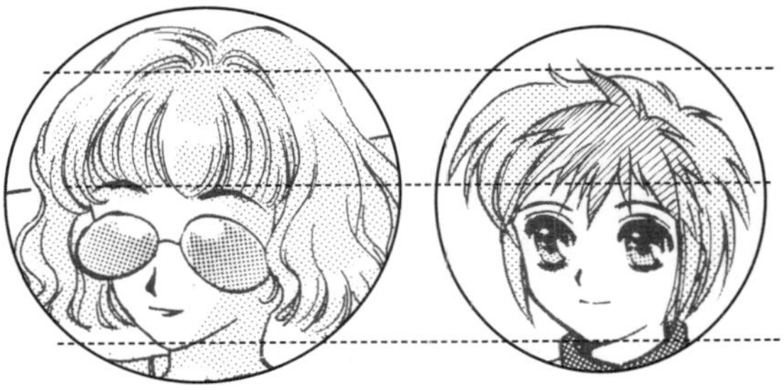

These are bust shot-sized head shots. While differences in hair volume make them appear to be extremely dissimilar in size, the facial features are the same size.

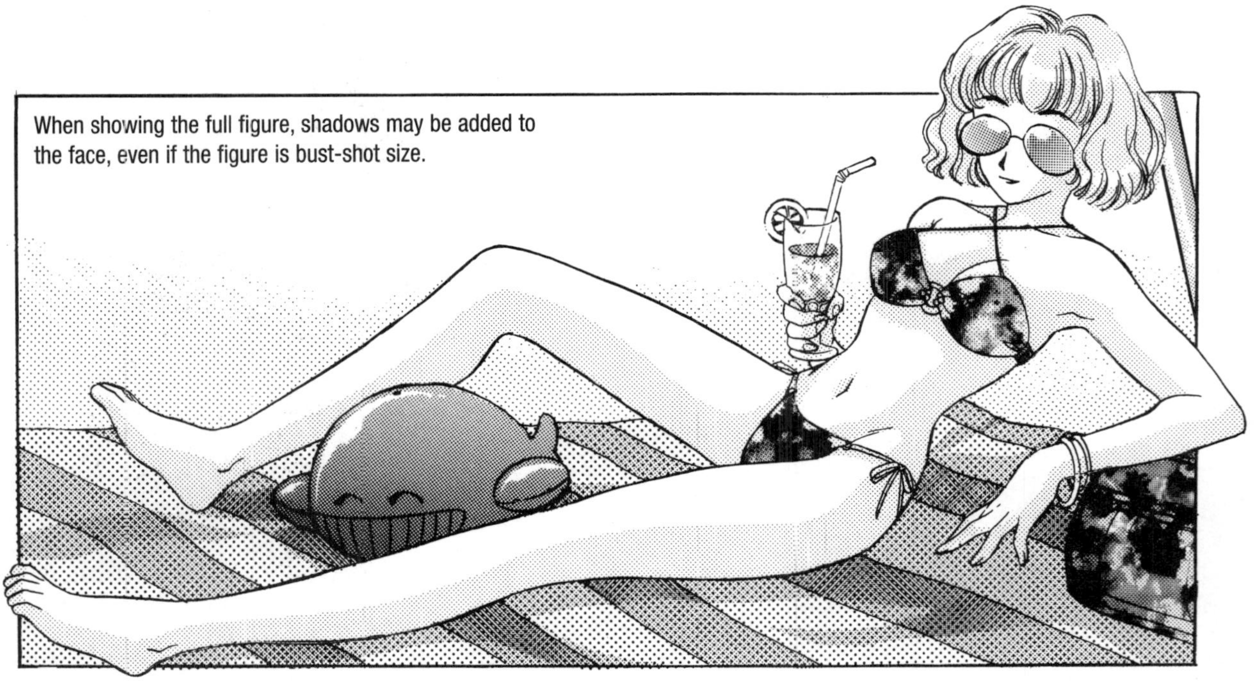

When showing the full figure, shadows may be added to the face, even if the figure is bust-shot size.

Figure 83% of original print size

Guidelines in Suggesting Color through Tone: Planning According to Value Contrast

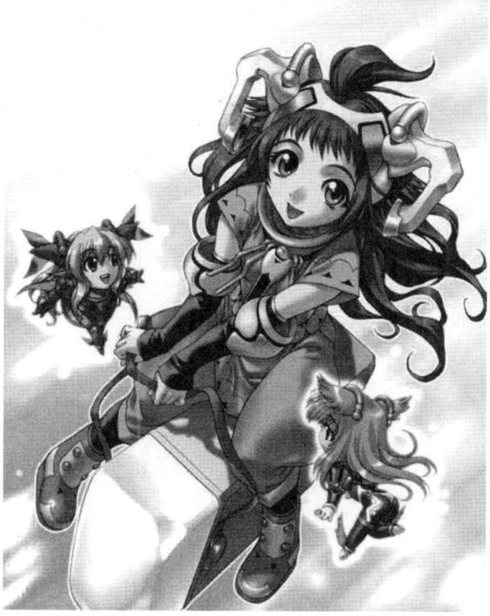

Here we see the cover illustration rendered in black and white (grey scale). Colored images are rendered using light and dark values when printed in black and white.

Tone Values and Corresponding Colors

Flesh tone shadows: 10%
Red & blue: 30 to 50%
Deep colors: Black (Solid) (Deep red or blue)
Pale colors: 10 to 20% (Pink or light blue)
Green: 20% (Use solid black for dark green) Light green: 10%
Yellow: 5 to 10%

Ref. Fig. **Rendering Hair Colors**

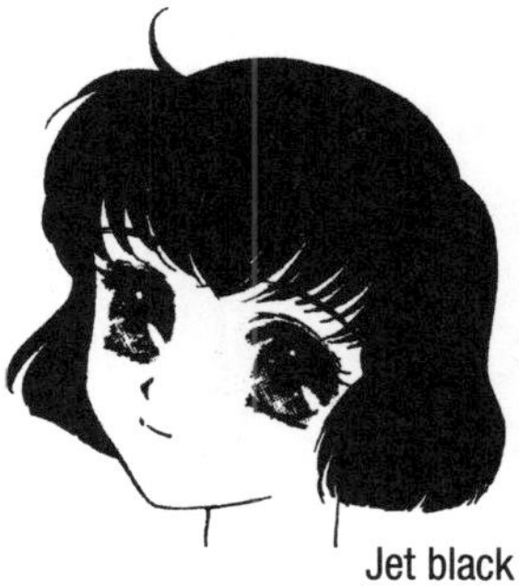

Jet black

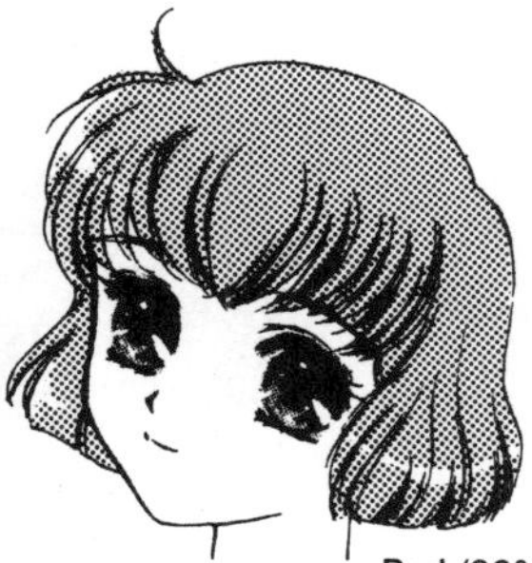

Red (30%)

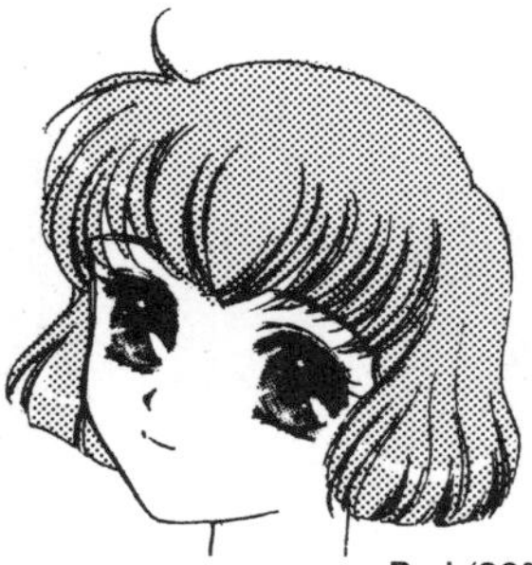

Red (20%)

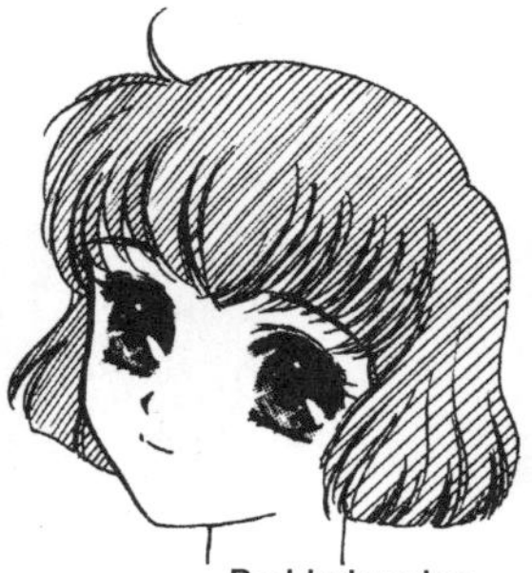

Red hair using diagonal hatching

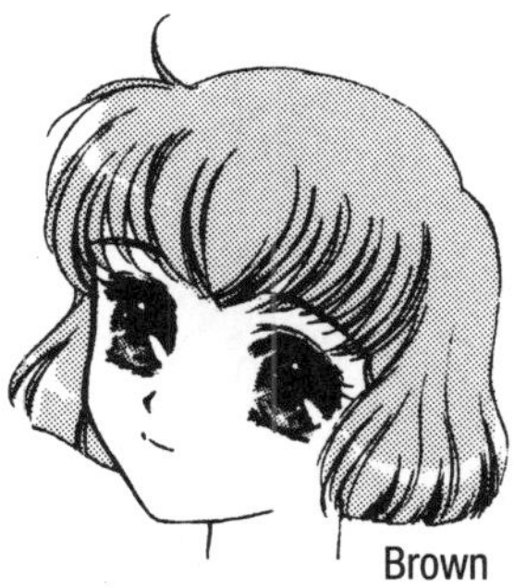

Brown

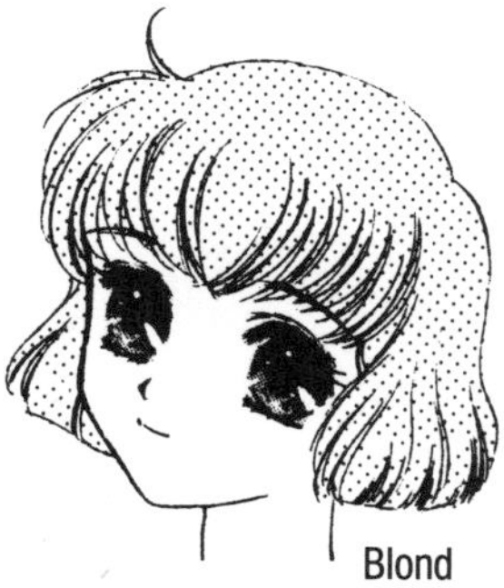

Blond

Different Colors Suggesting Using the Same Tone Value

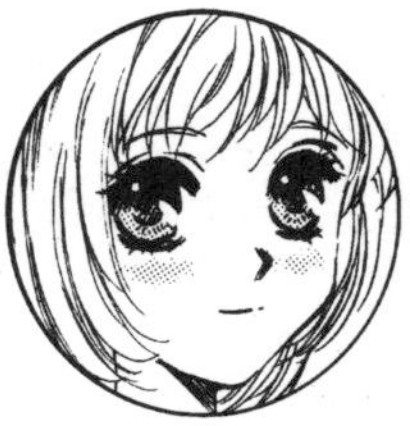

A flush to the cheeks

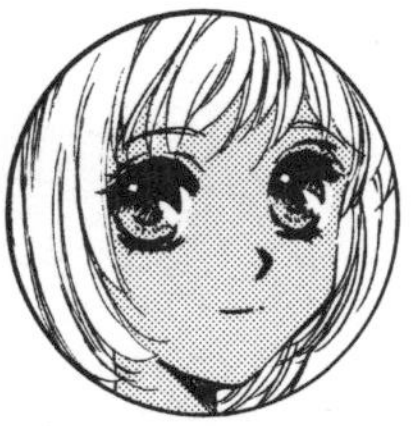

Suntan

Grey values are contrasted with black and shaded areas, creating the illusion of a color palette. (The same 10% tone was used for both figs.)

Eye Colors

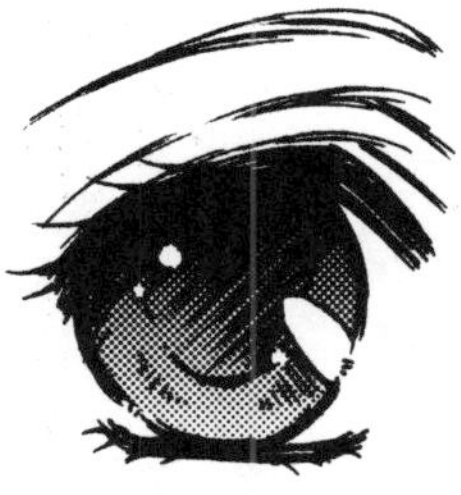

Dark brown

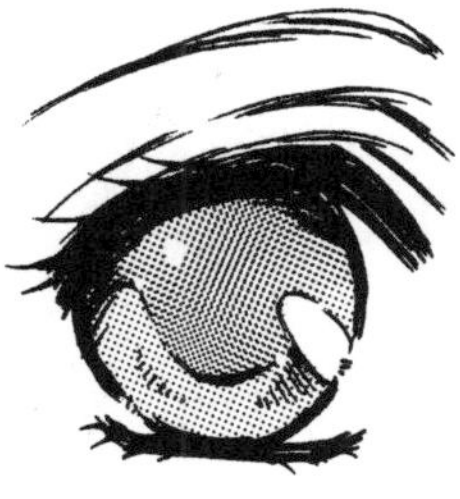

Blue

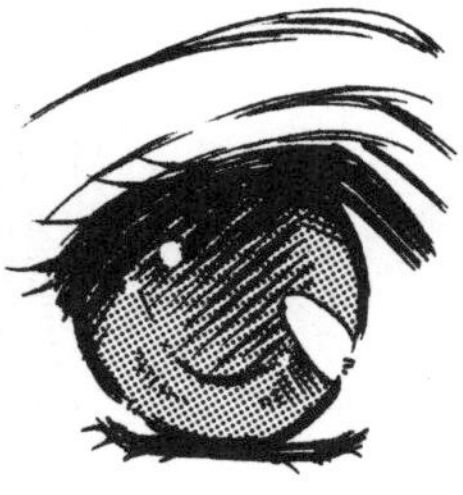

Red

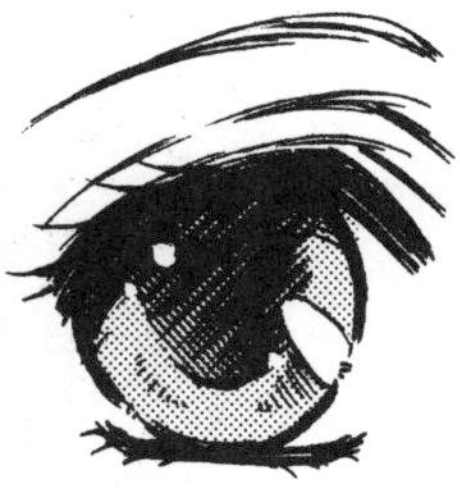

Violet

Common Facial Shadows

Let's look at the following 5 light-source positions: Front, right, side, low, and high

Front

a

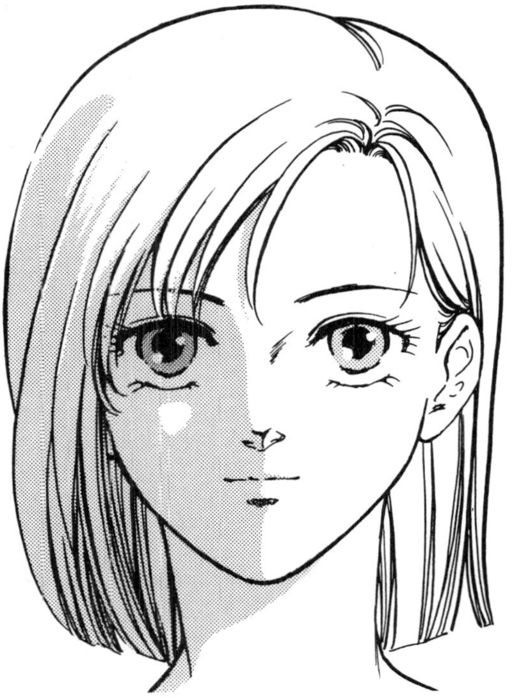

b

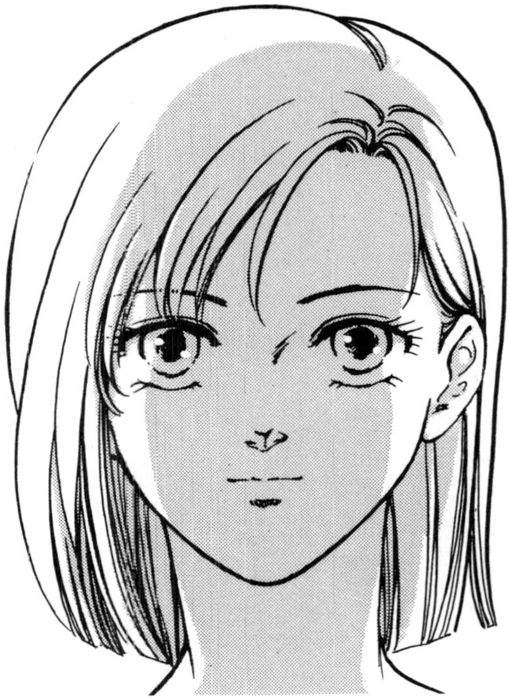

c

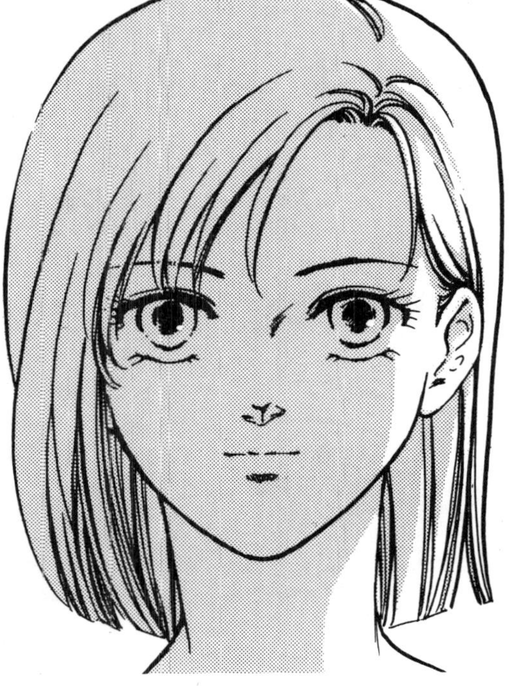

d

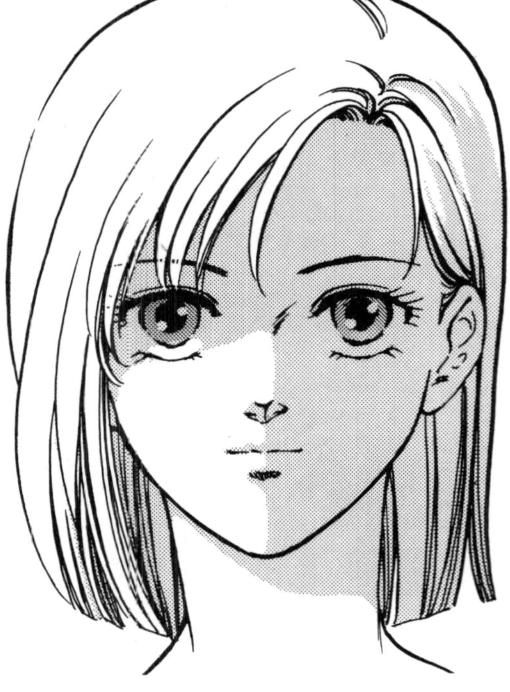

e

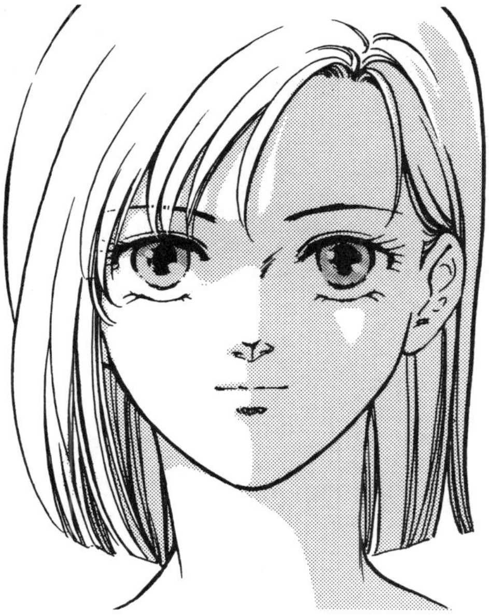

f

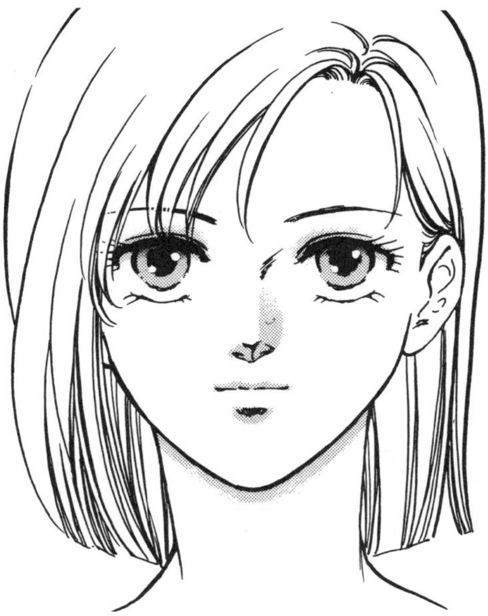

g

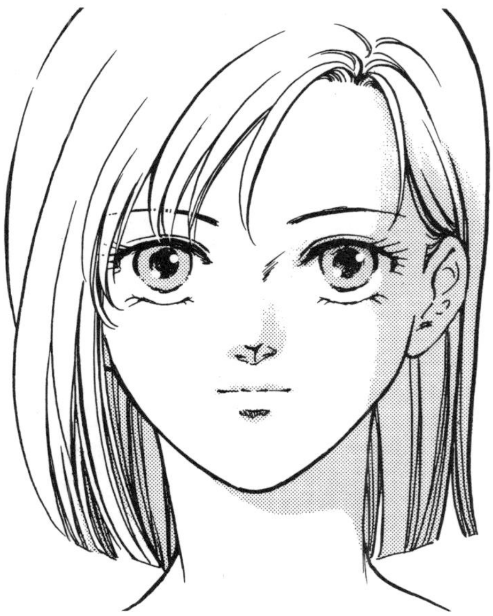

h

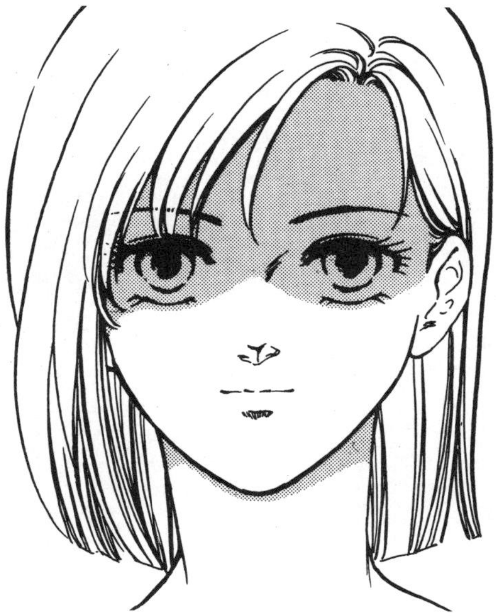

i

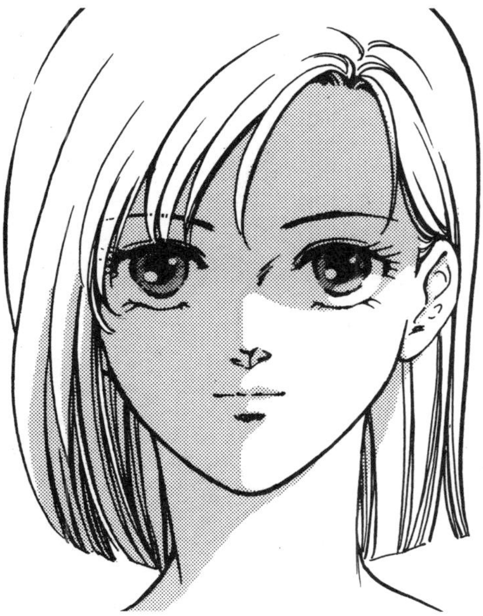

j

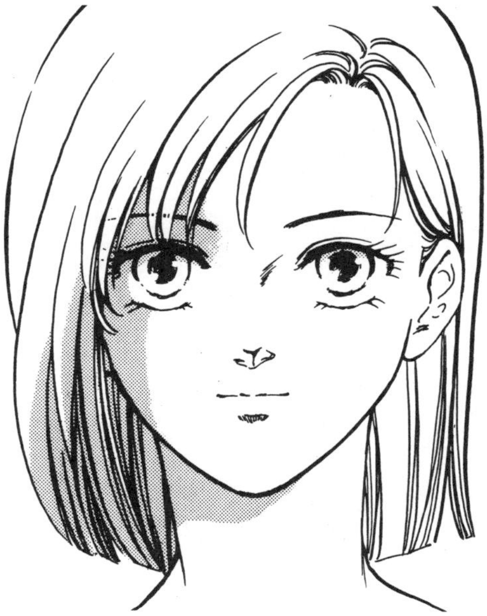

Practical Applications to Panels (Front View)

A broad range of facial shadows are created by modifying the angle of the face inside the panel or the way it is trimmed, or by switching the shadows from the right to the left side of the face, etc.

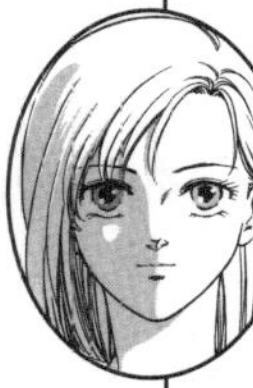

a

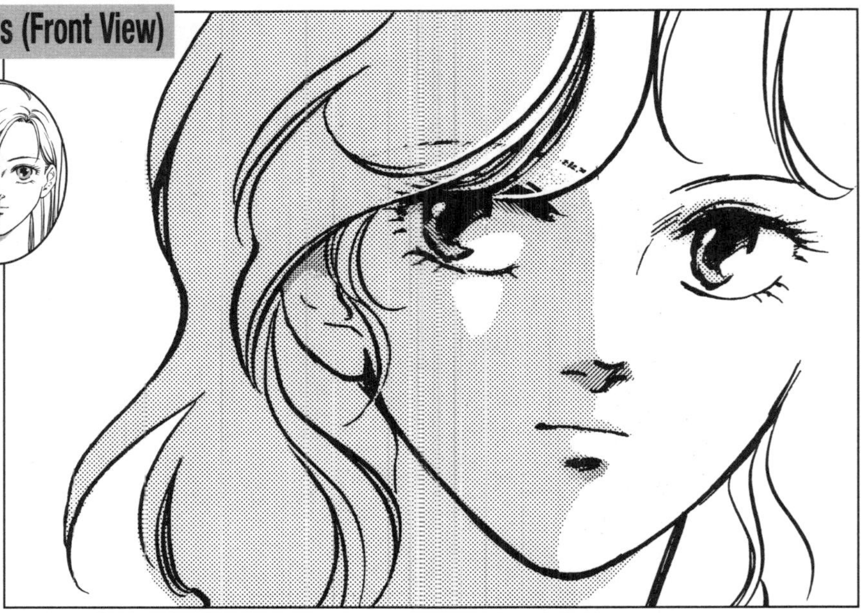

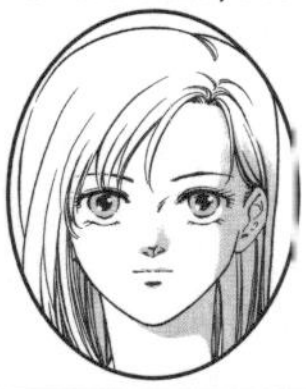

g

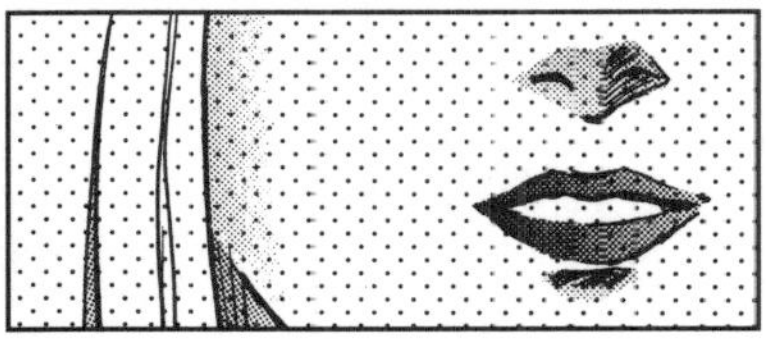

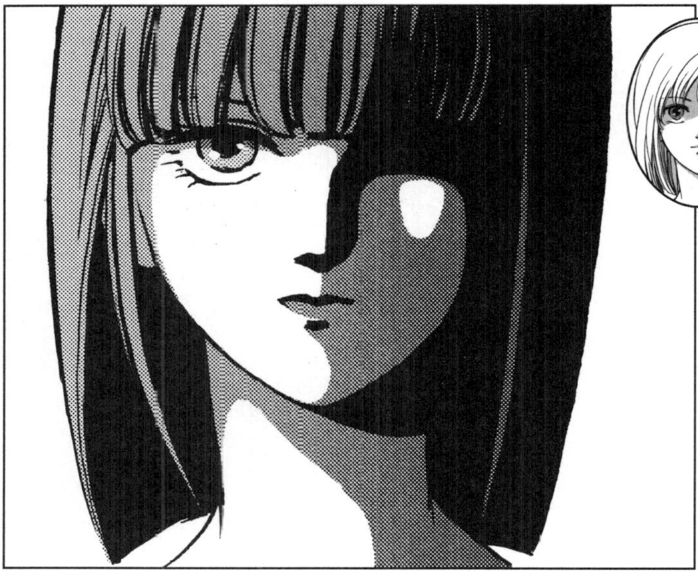

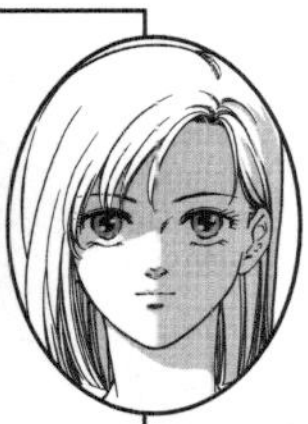

d

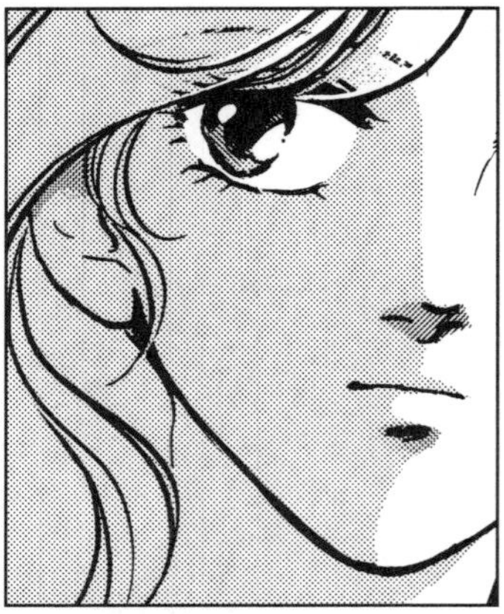

Here, no light is shown touching the face, and the tone was cut so as to leave the eye white.

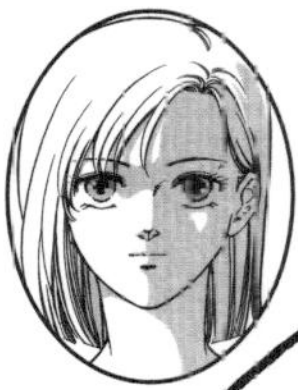

e

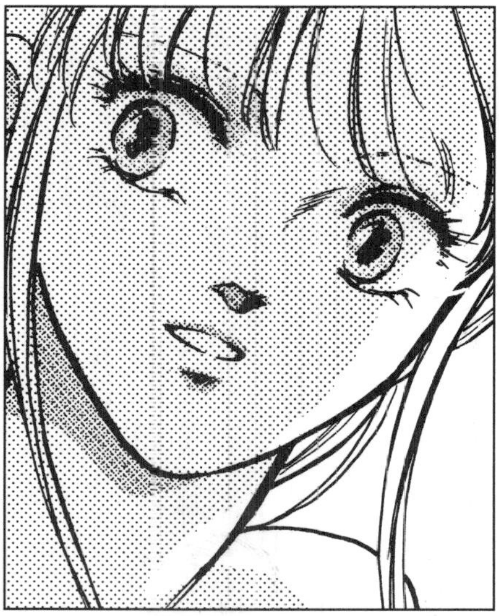

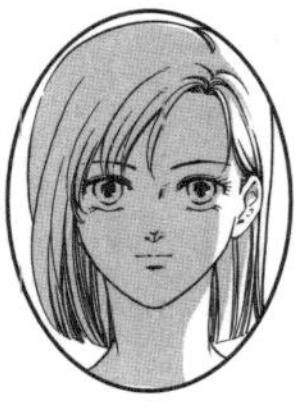

c

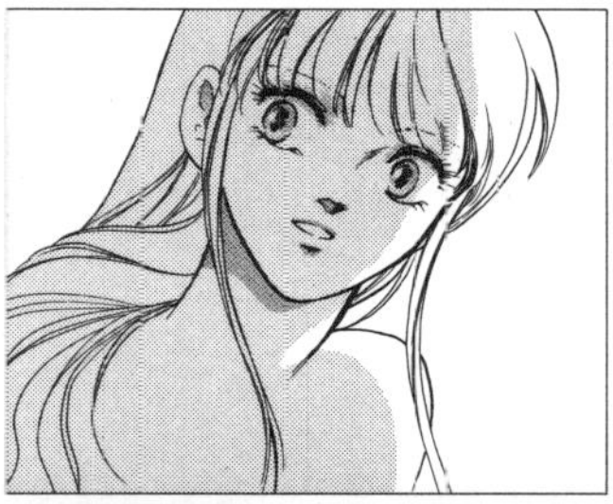

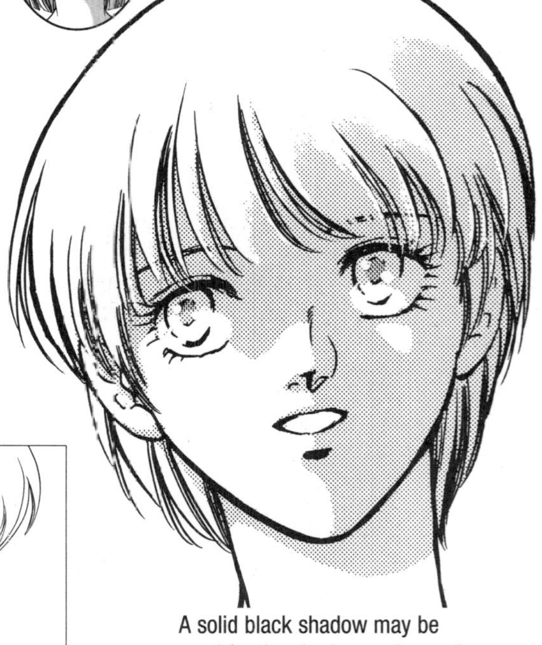

A solid black shadow may be used for the shadow underneath the chin in lieu of tone.

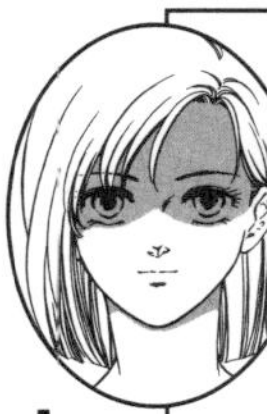

h

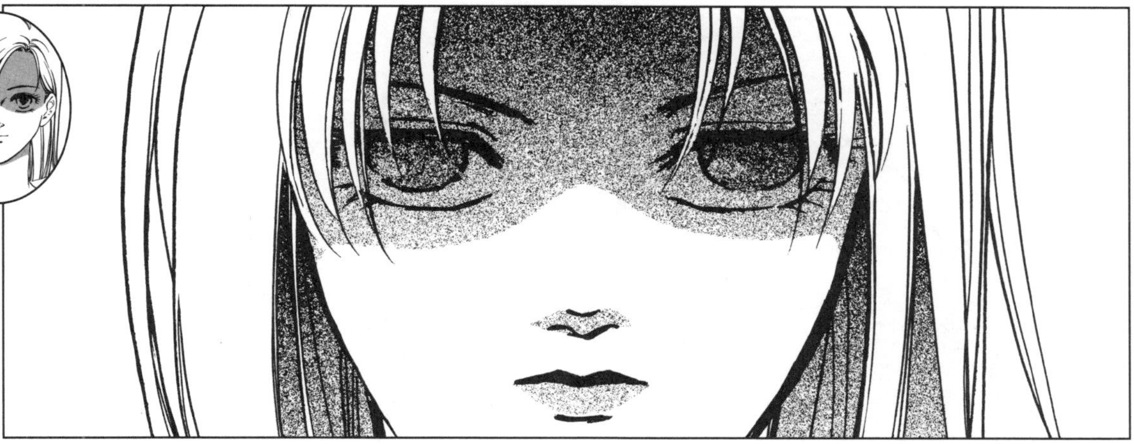

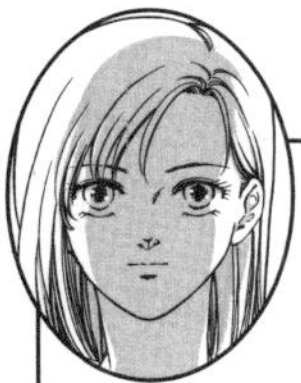

b

Here we see use of shadows formed from a backlight. Be conscious that the figure is backlit and use broken external contour lines to create the illusion of glowing light.

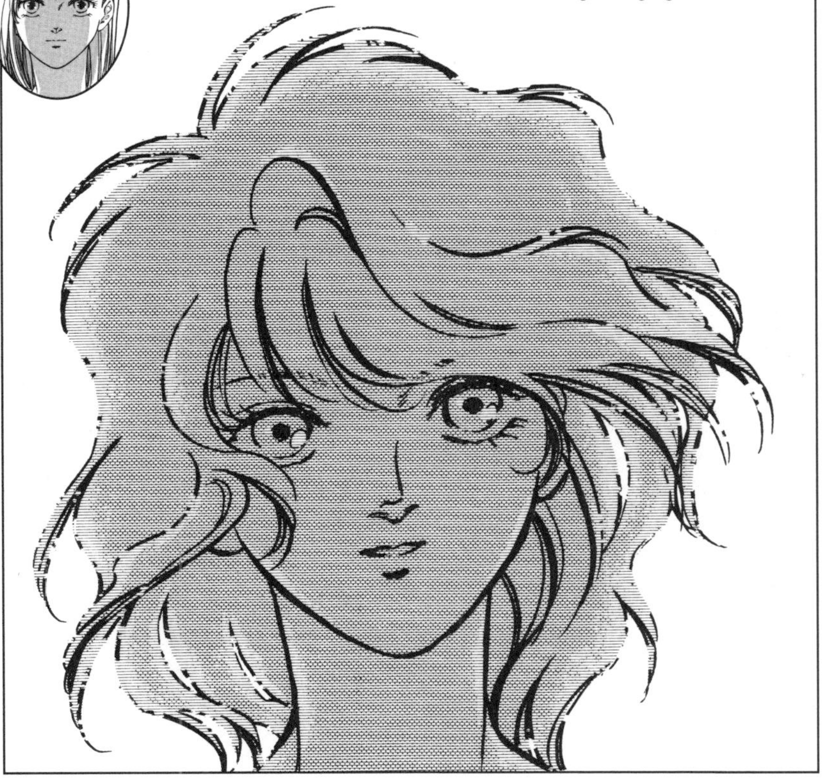

The mood of the image changes depending on the tone value and pattern used. Solid black may be used instead of tone.

Below is an image created using j-type facial shadows as a point of departure. I omitted the cheek shadow and added shadows underneath the nose and to the lips.

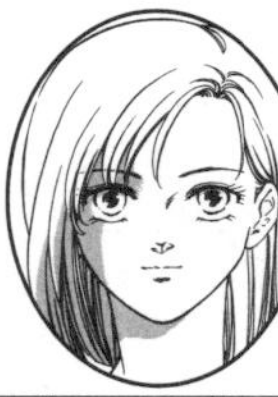

j

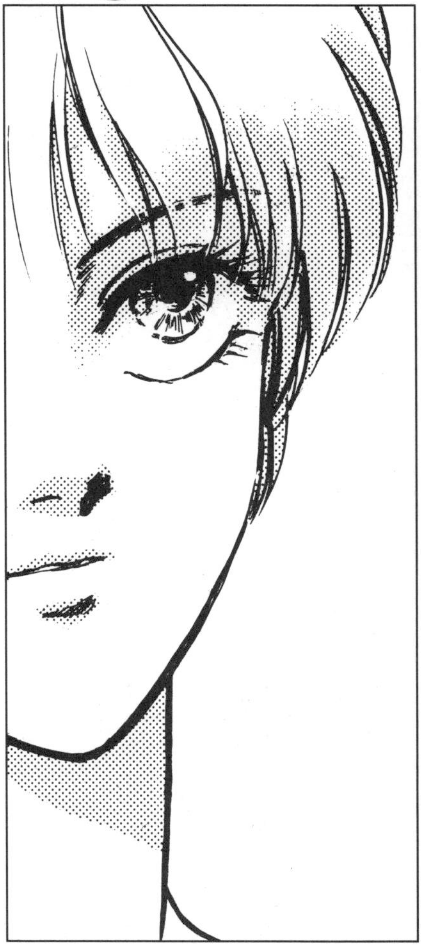

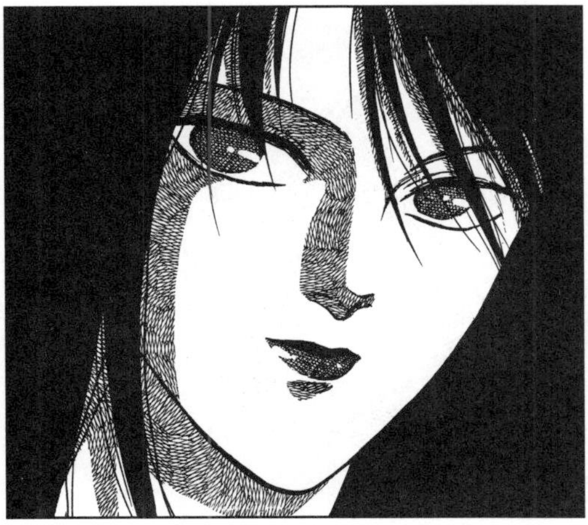

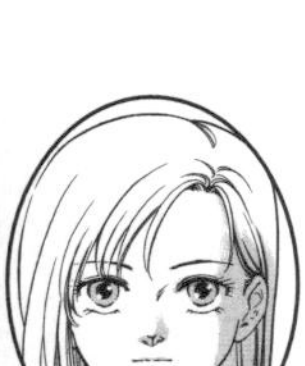

g

These are essentially g-type shadows. Depending on how prominent the facial features, shadows may be added underneath the brows and eye sockets.

3/4 View

a

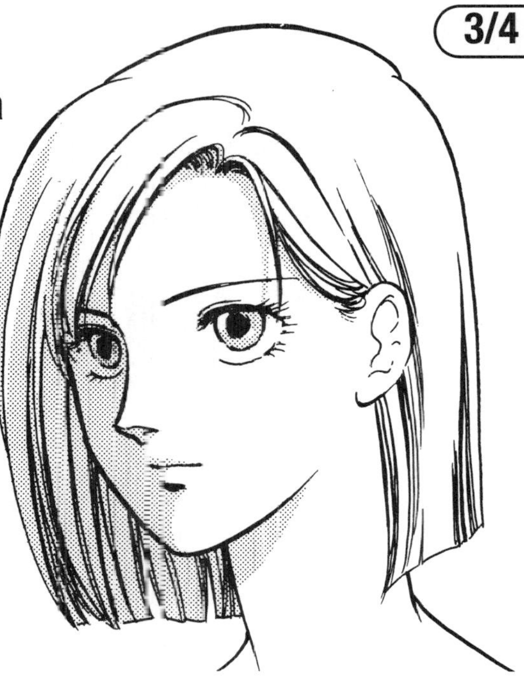

b

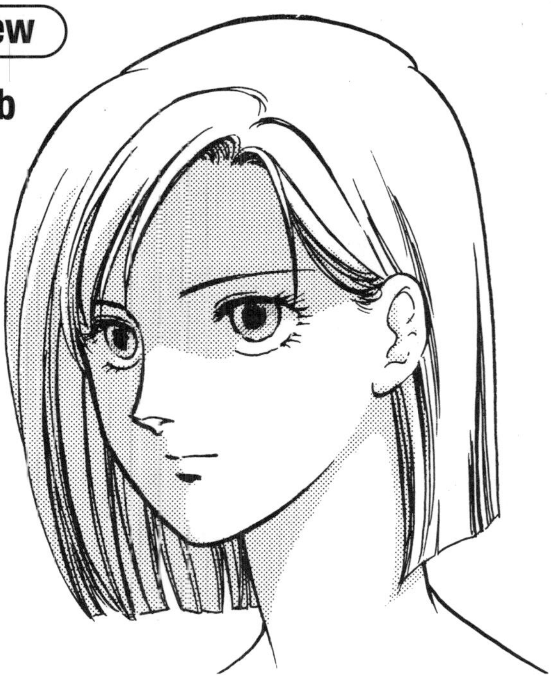

c

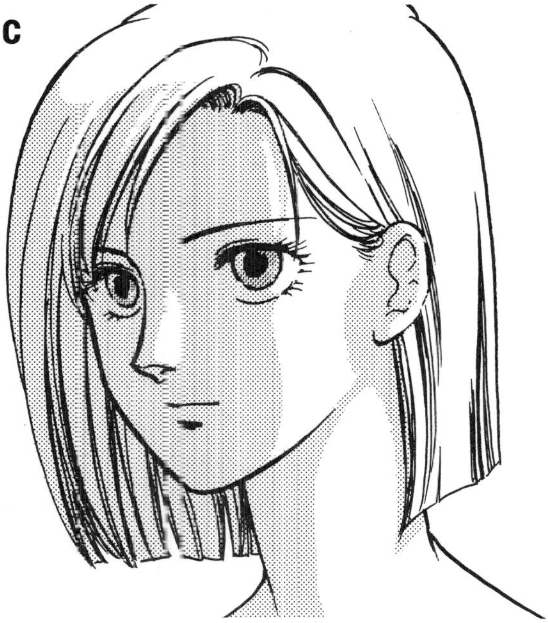

d

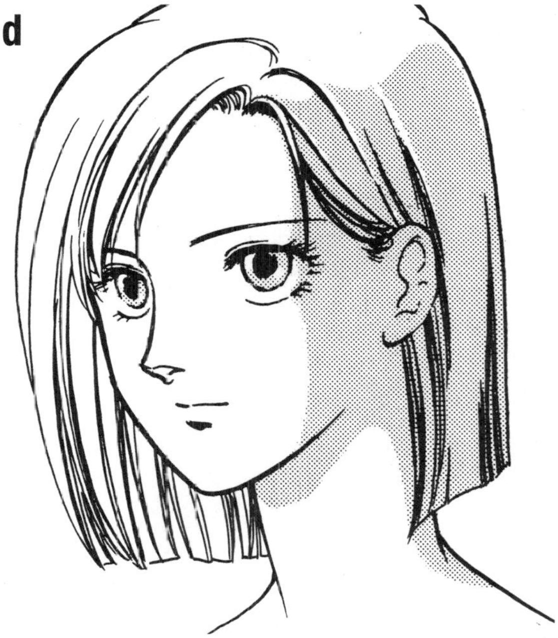

e

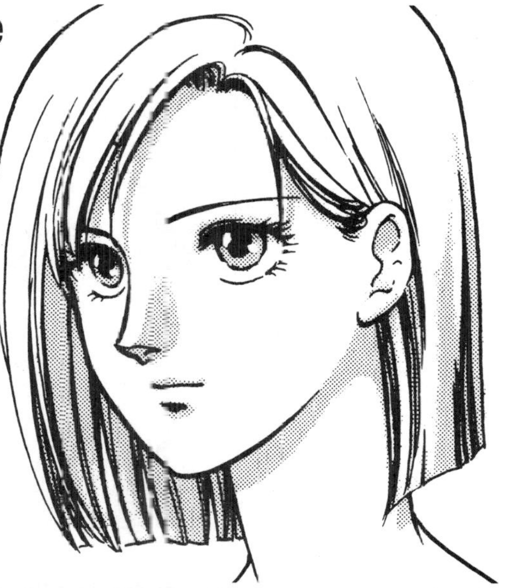

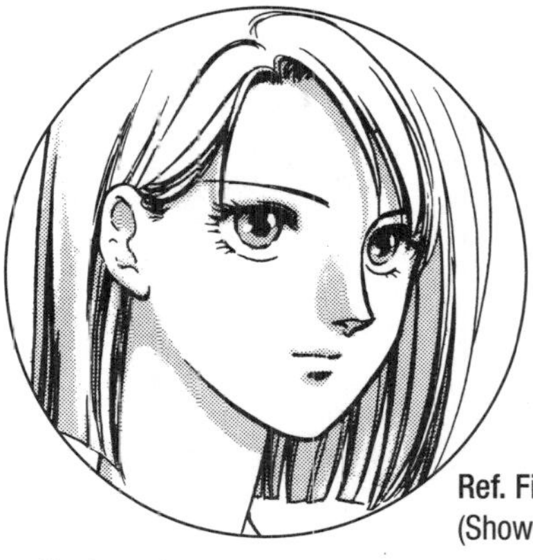

Ref. Fig. e
(Shown facing left)

Shadows form in basically the same manner, whether the figure faces right or left.

Rendering the Hair

Solid Black

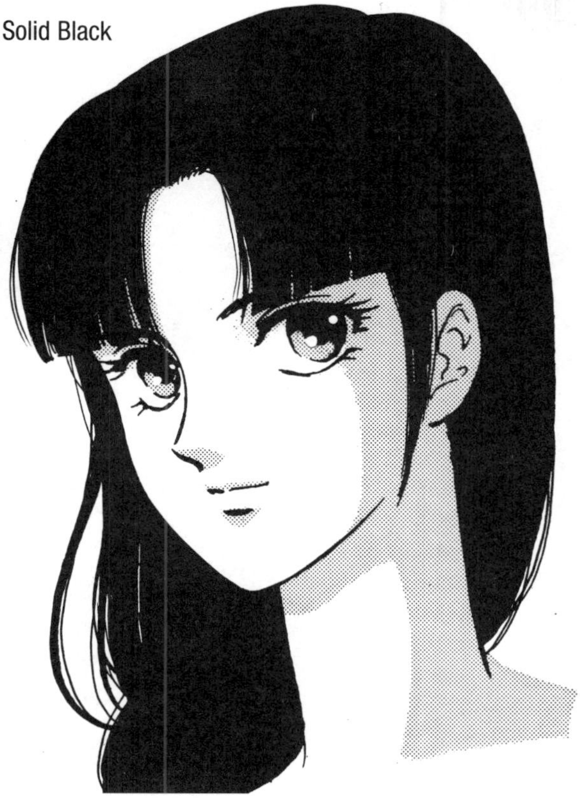

Black with Highlights

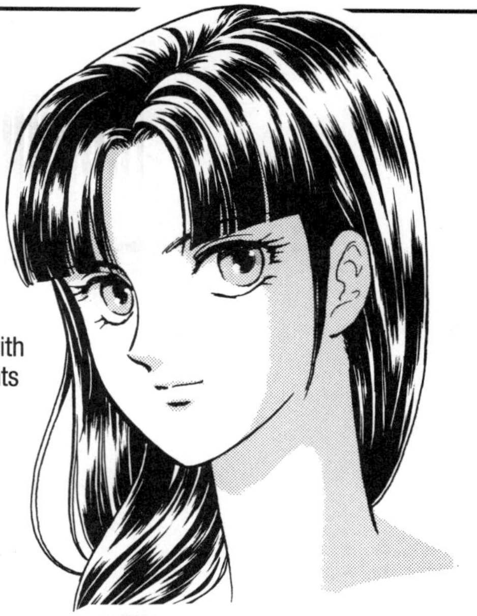

Tone used for shadows (in areas opposite the light source)

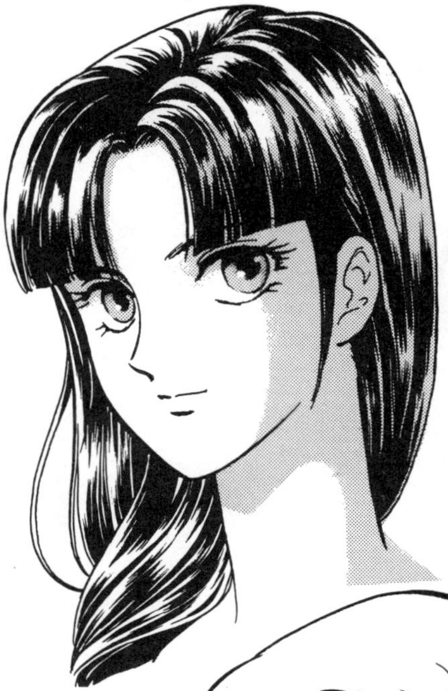

Gradation Tone

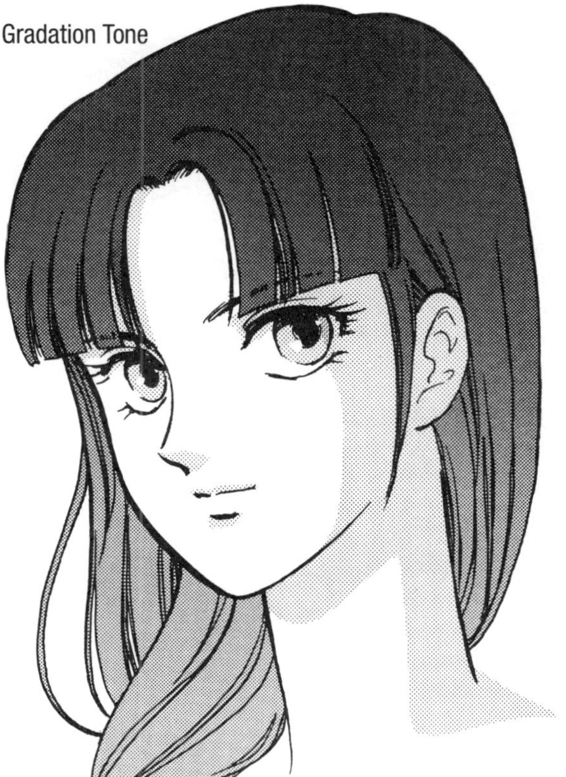

Highlights (areas touched by light) expanded

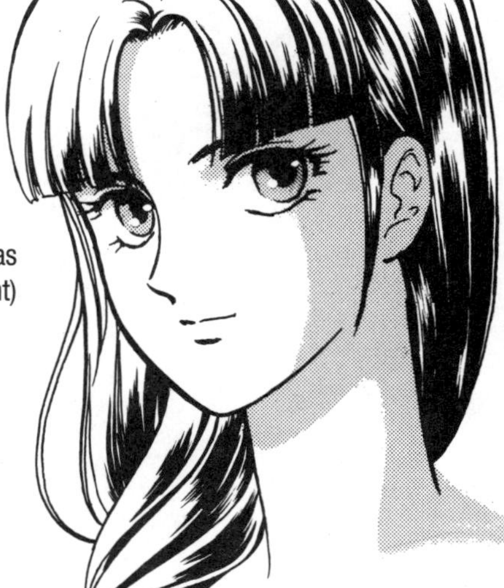

Practical Applications to Panels (3/4 View)

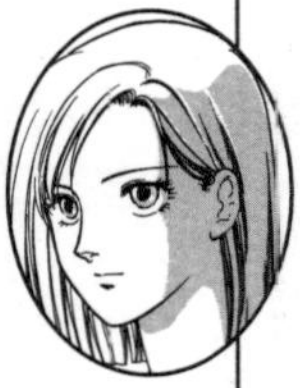

d

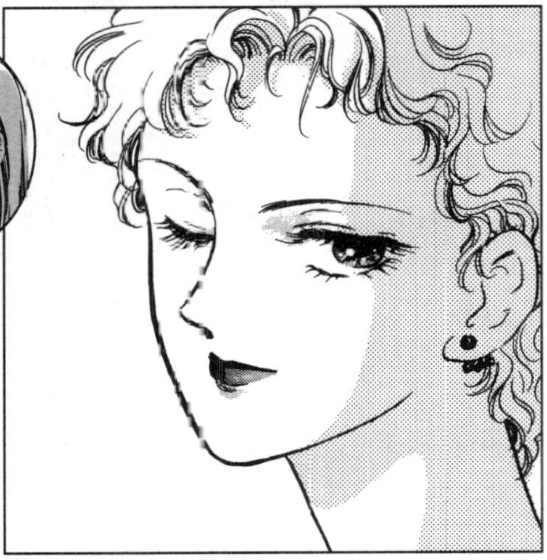

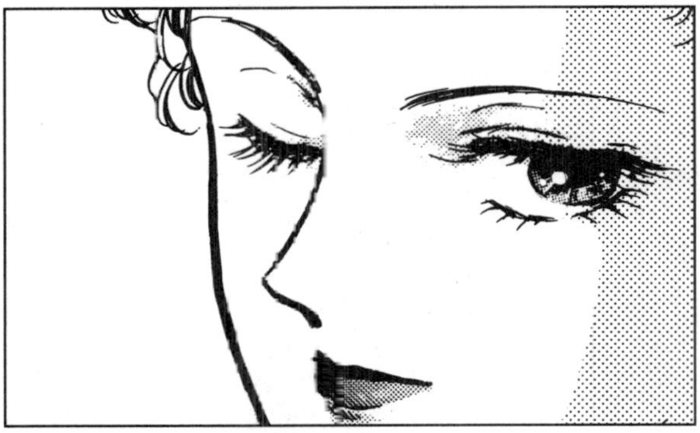

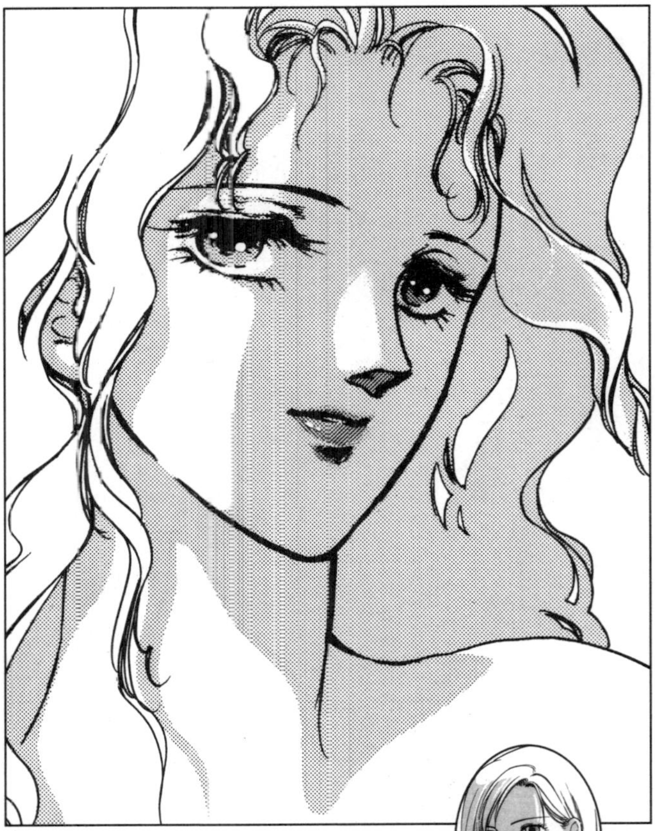

d-type shadows also work well in close-ups.
Shadows may be added to the eyes.

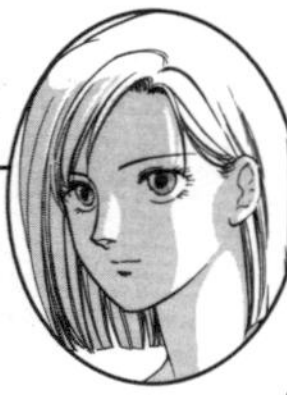

c

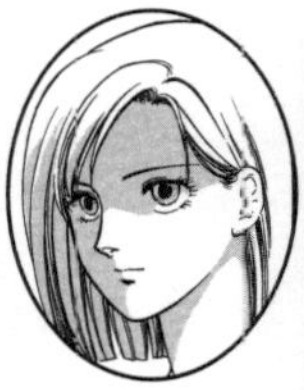

b

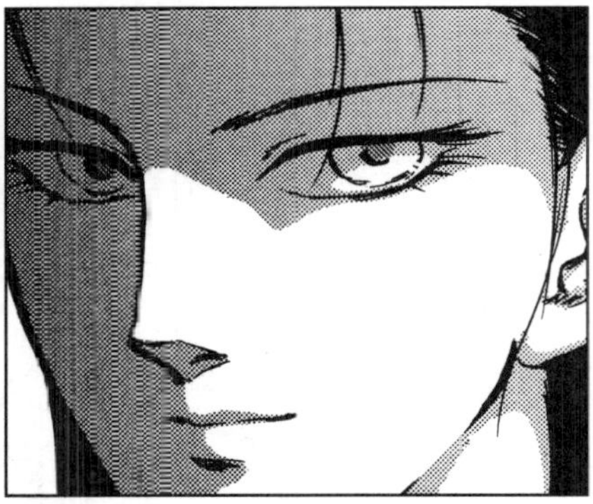

Here we see an image using b-type shadows. Use shadows with sharp angles with long faces. Gently curving shadows work well with more typical faces as seen below.

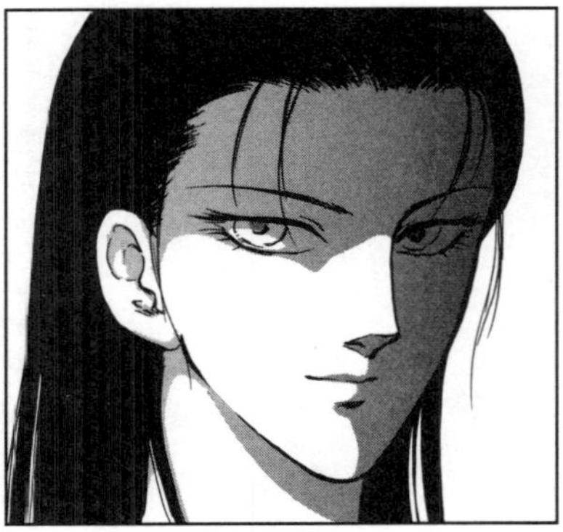

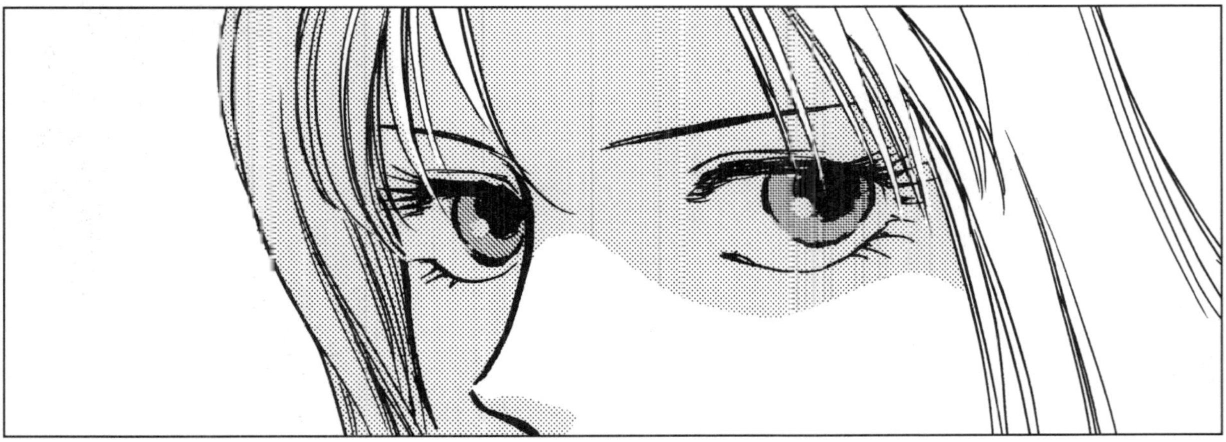

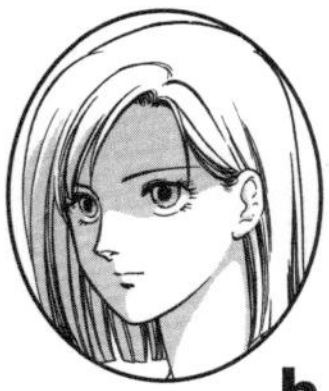

b

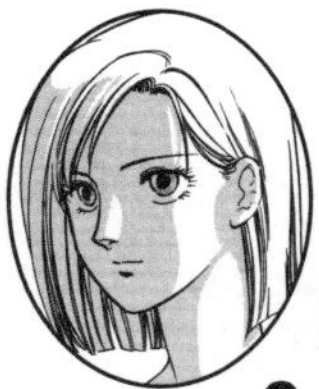

c

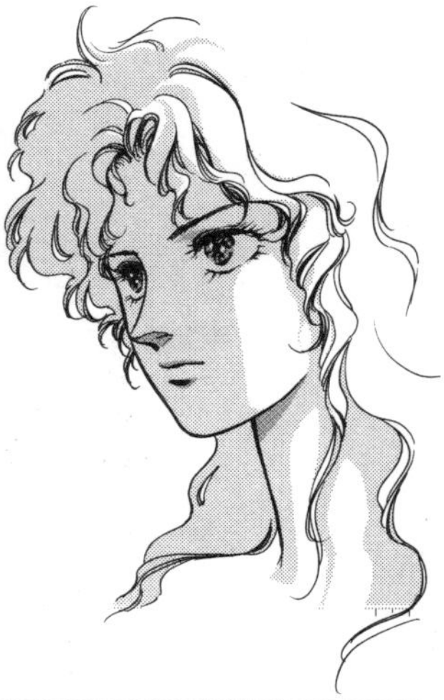

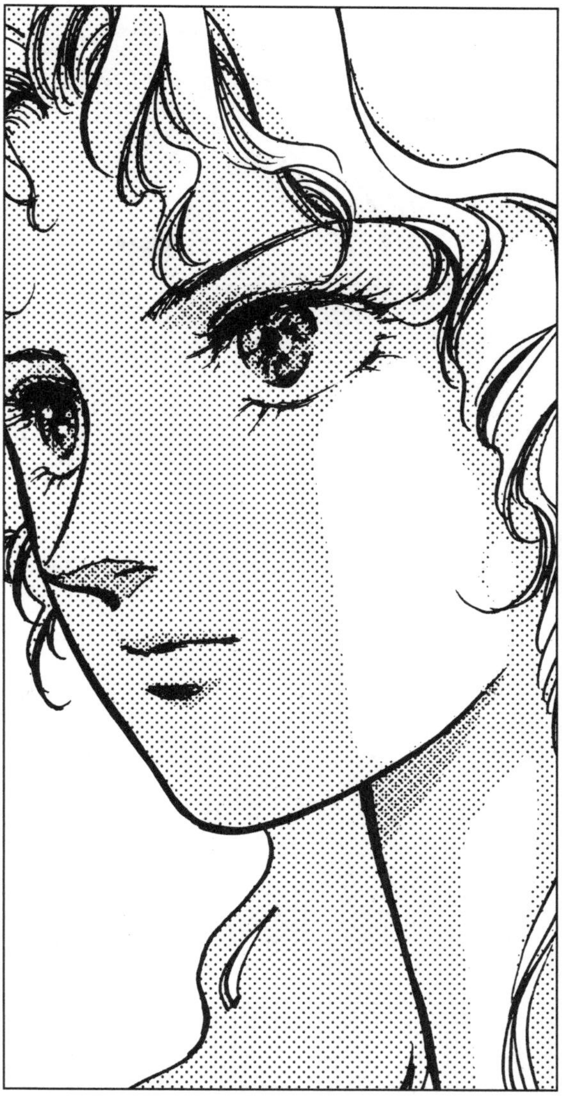

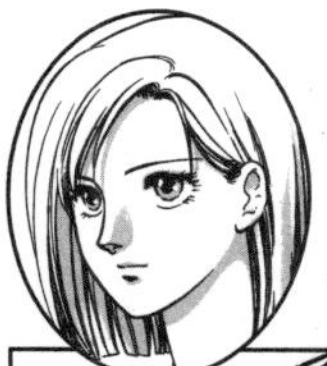

e

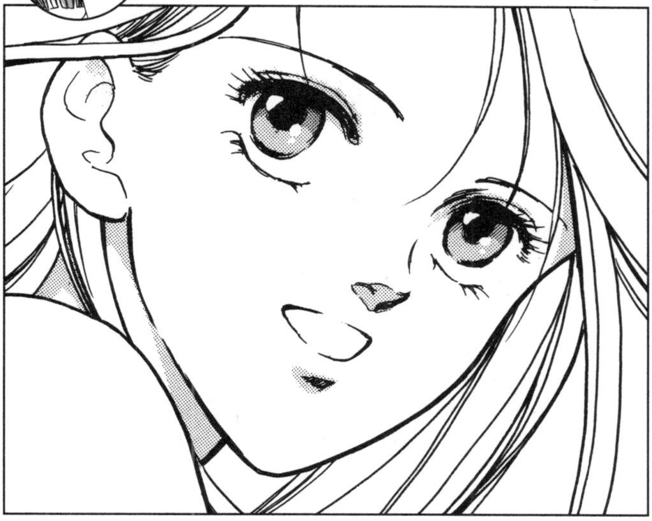

e-types have the fewest shadows, with shading solely located at the hair, the nose, and the chin. This works well with clean, cheerful compositions.

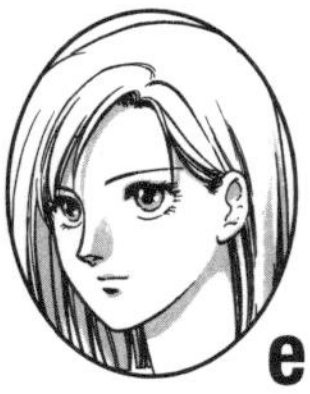

e

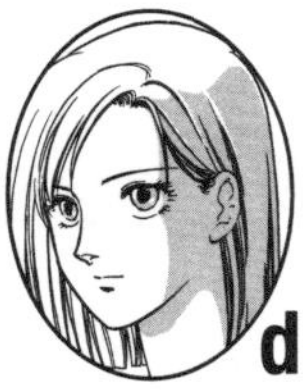

d

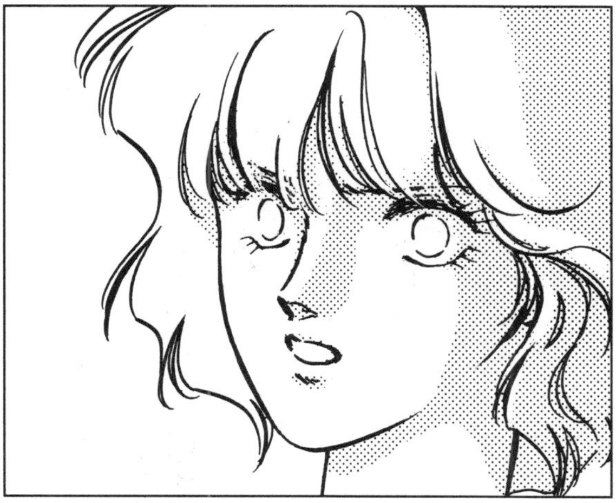

This combination of e and d shadows can be used to accentuate a particular mood.

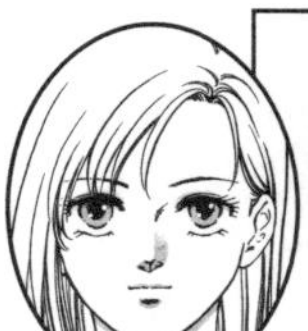

Front

f

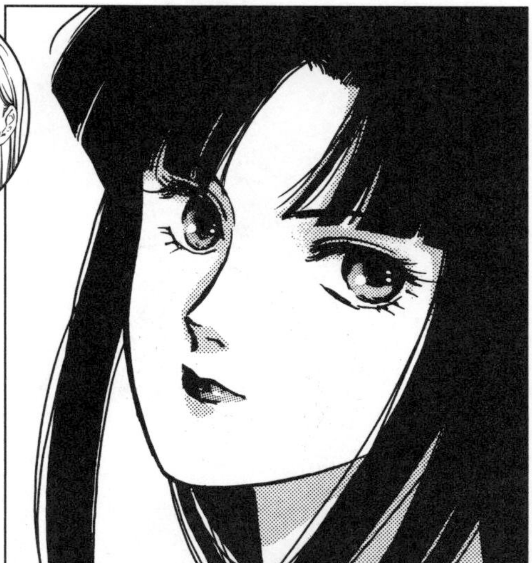

Forward facing figure using f-type shadows

Profile

a

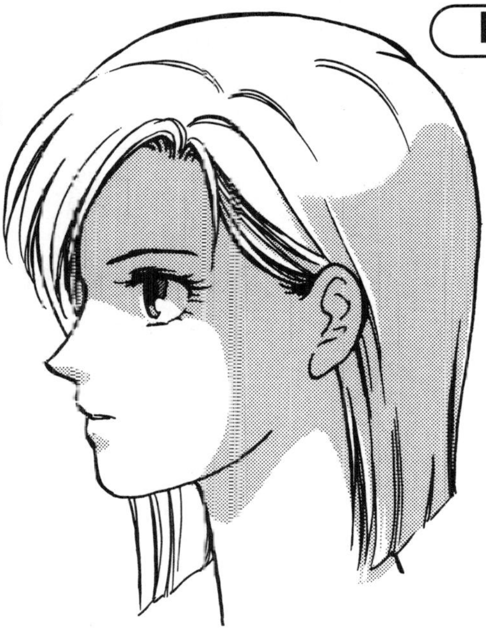

b

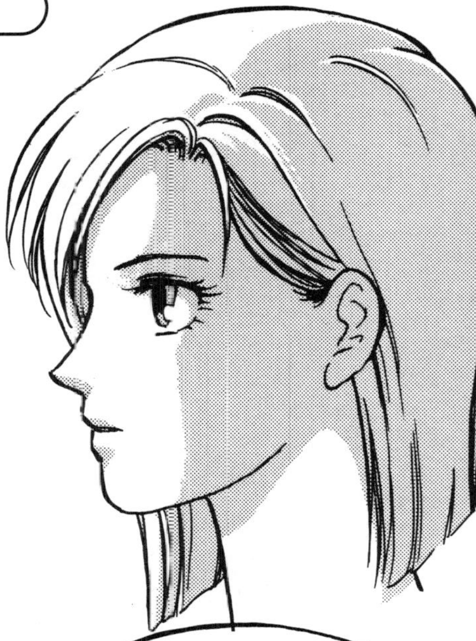

c

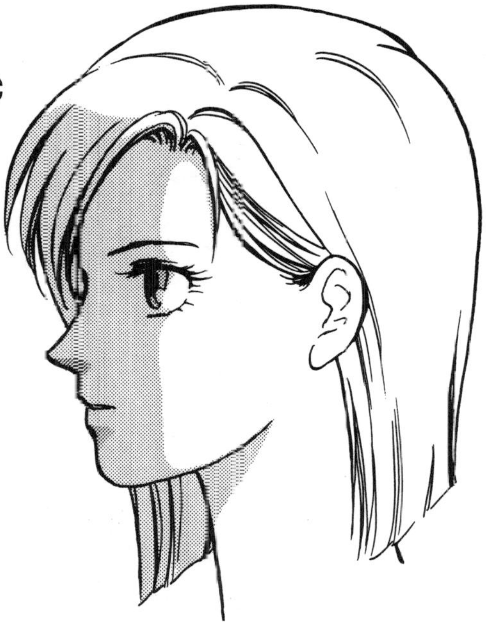

d

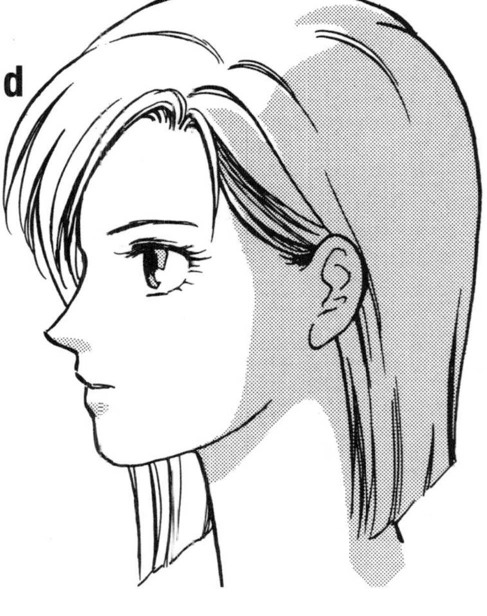

e

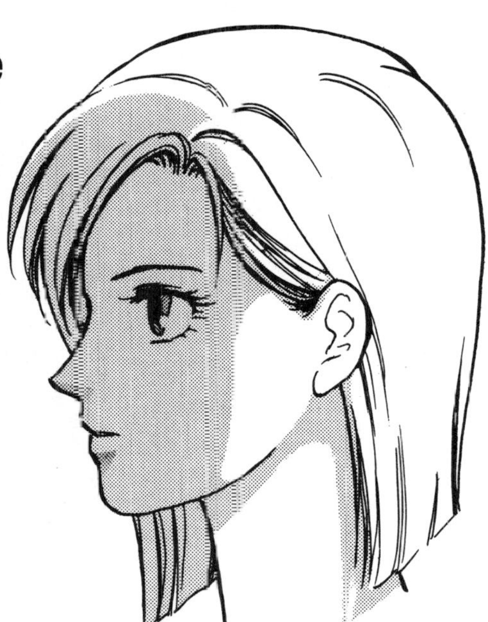

f

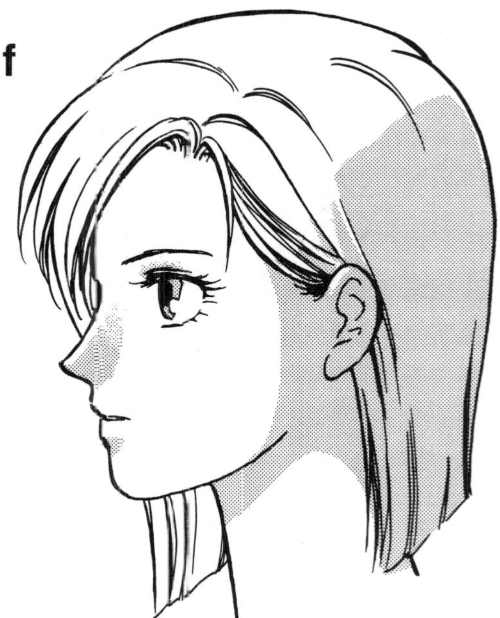

Practical Applications to Panels (Profile)

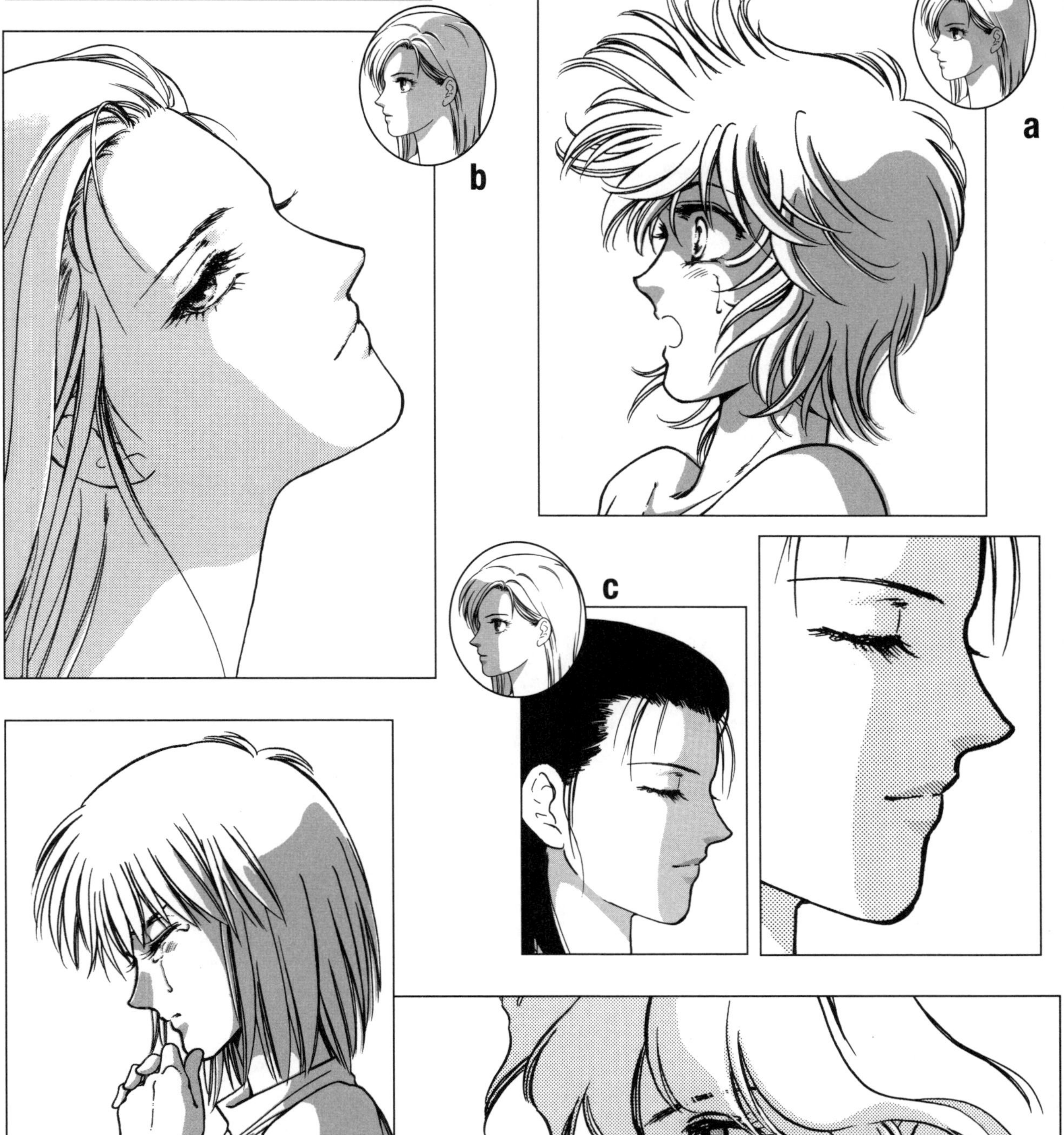

Expanding the negative space in the direction faced by the figure adds to the effectiveness of e-type shadows. This technique is suited toward long panels.

Moderate Low Angle

a

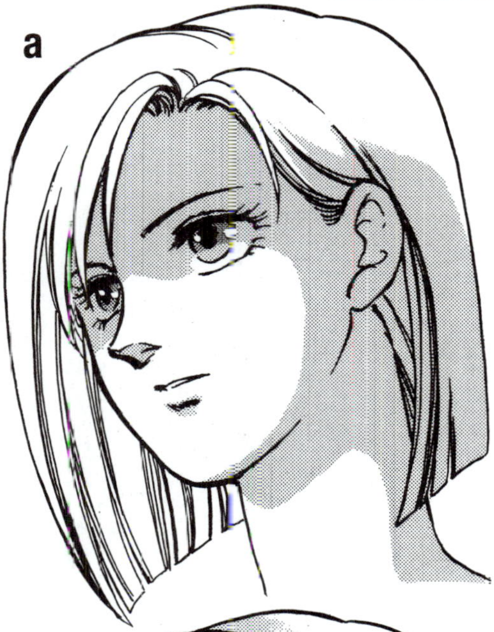

b

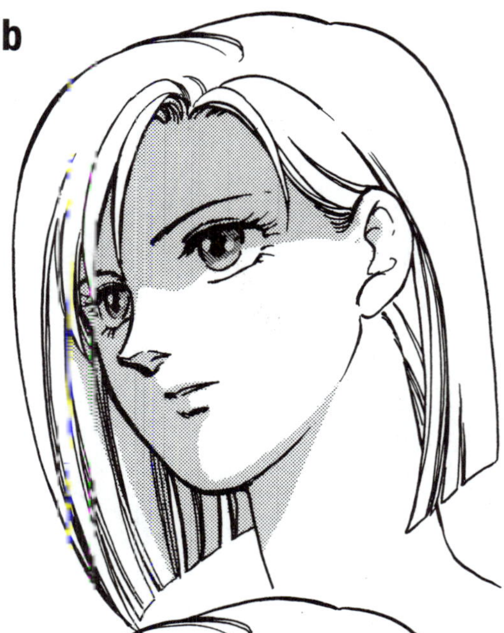

c

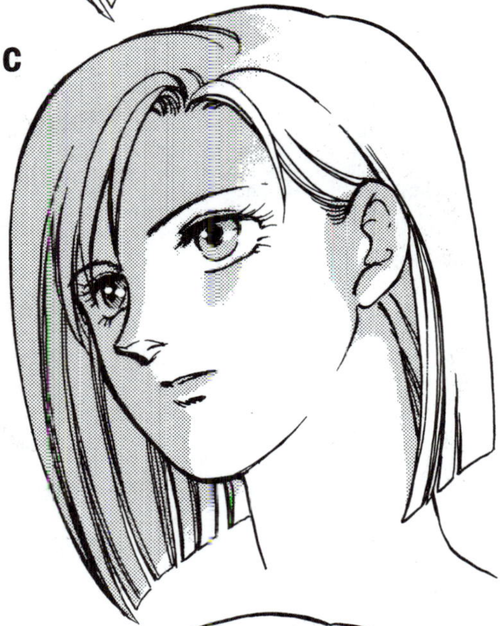

d

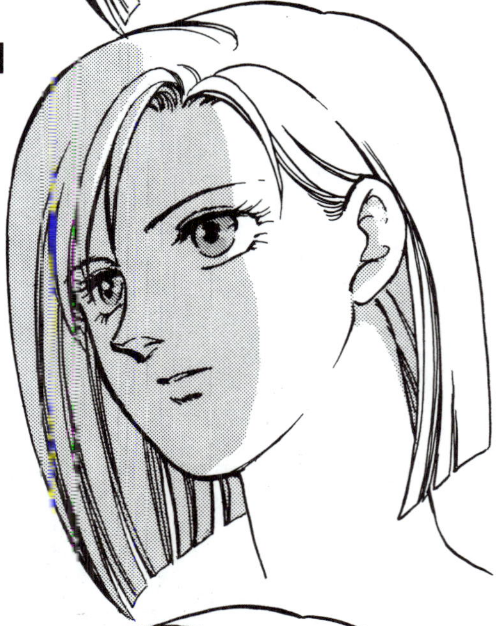

e

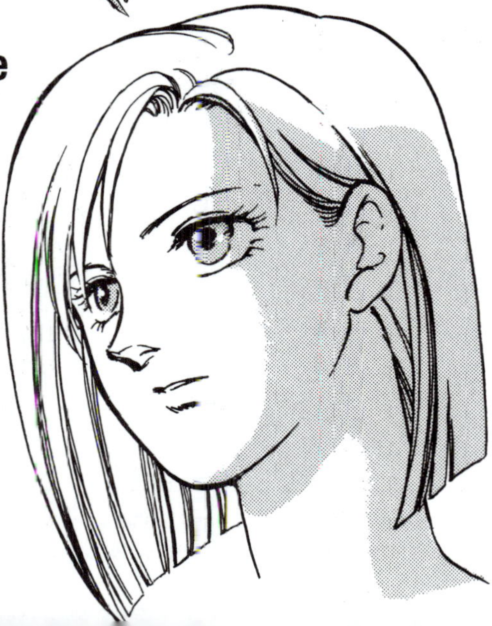

f

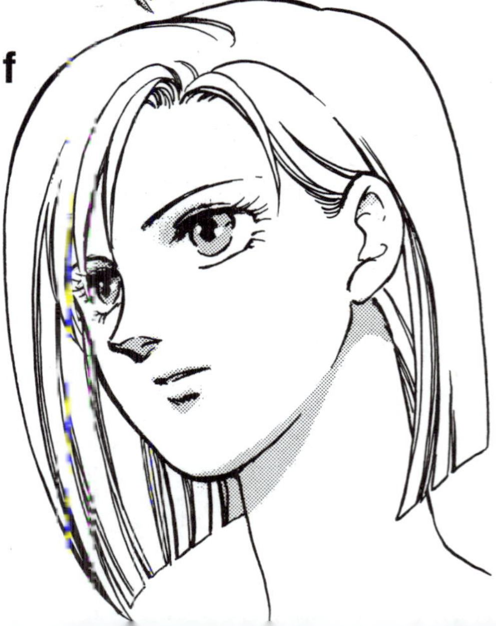

Practical Applications to Panels (Moderate Low Angle)

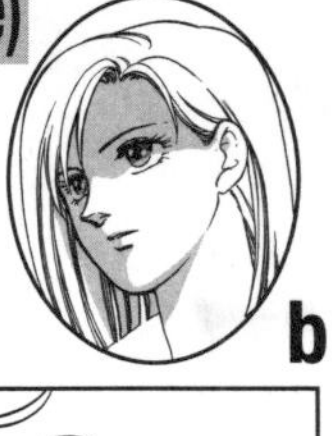
b

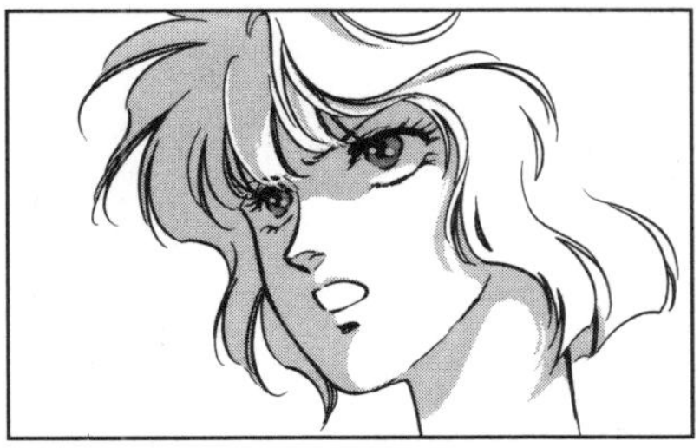

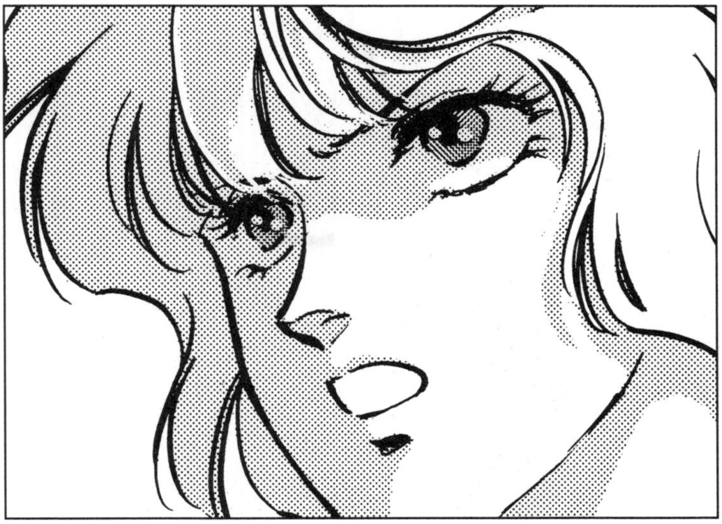

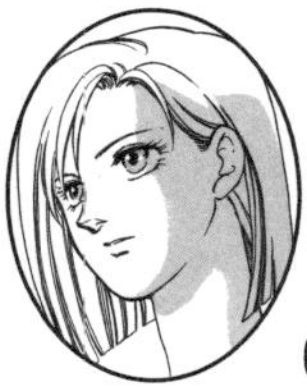
e

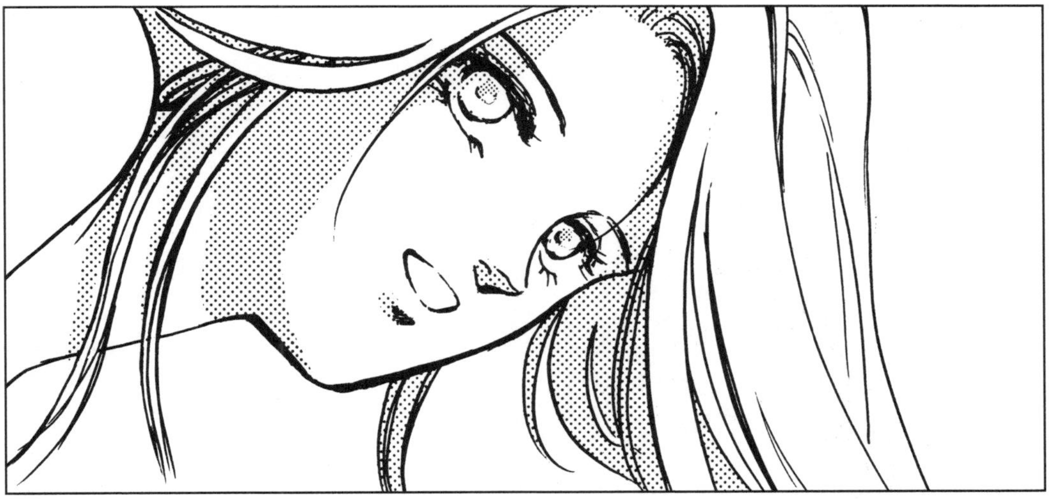

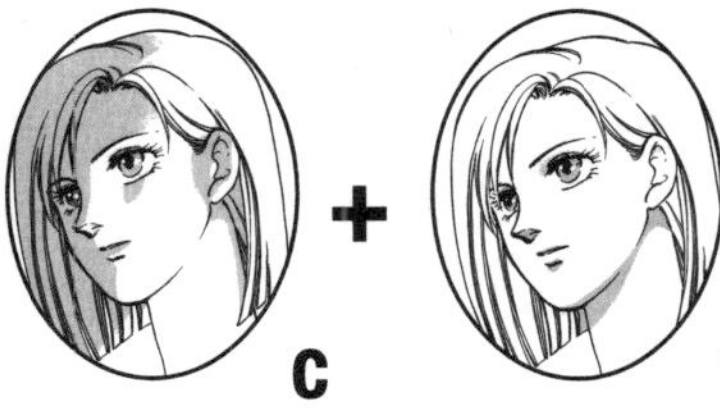
c + f

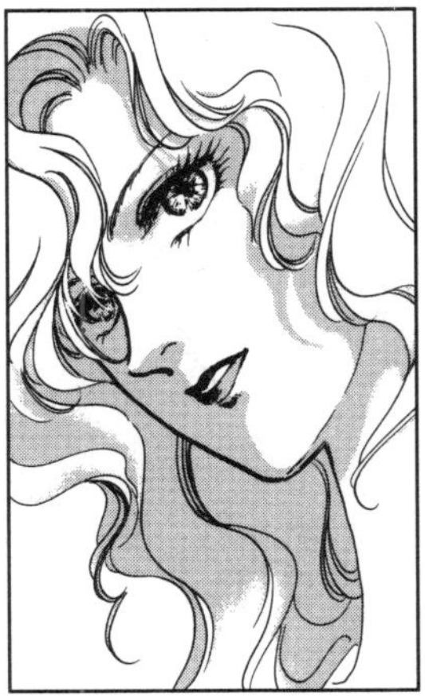

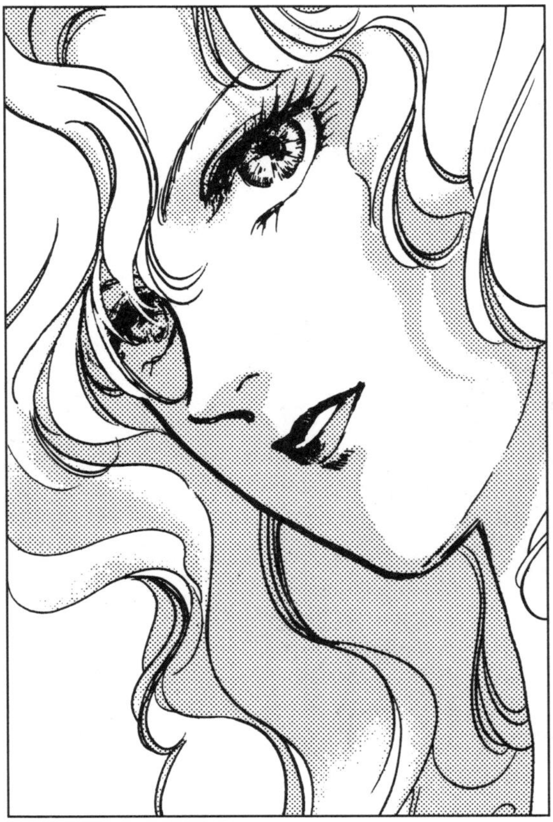

The shapes of the hair shadows are intricate. Contrary to what you might expect, duplicating the exact shape of the hair in the shadows will make the composition unnatural.

Moderate High Angle

a

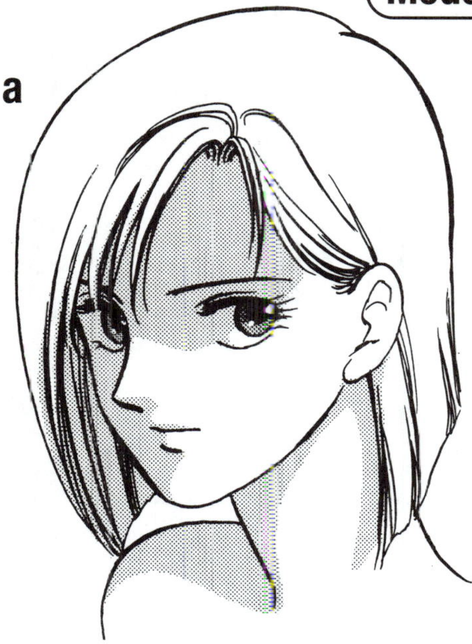

b

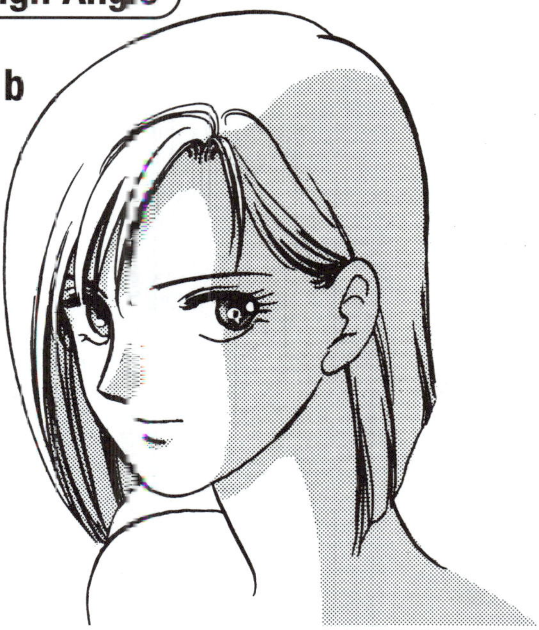

c

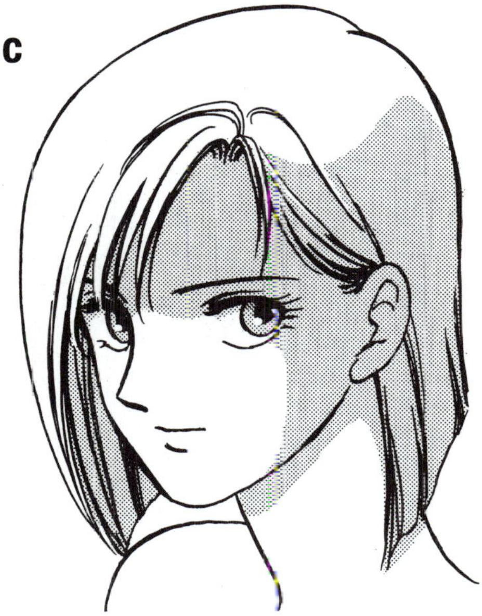

d

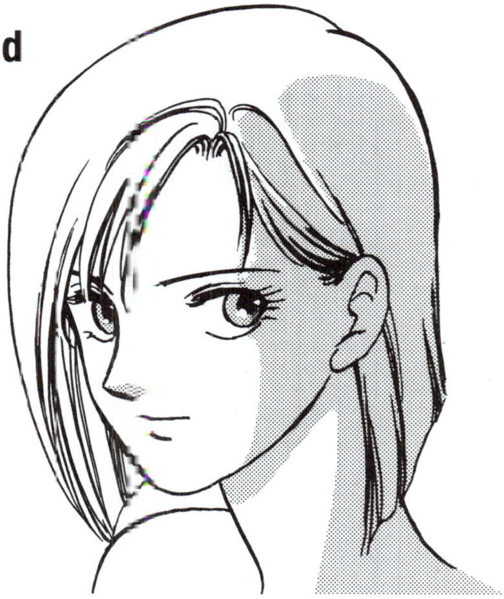

e

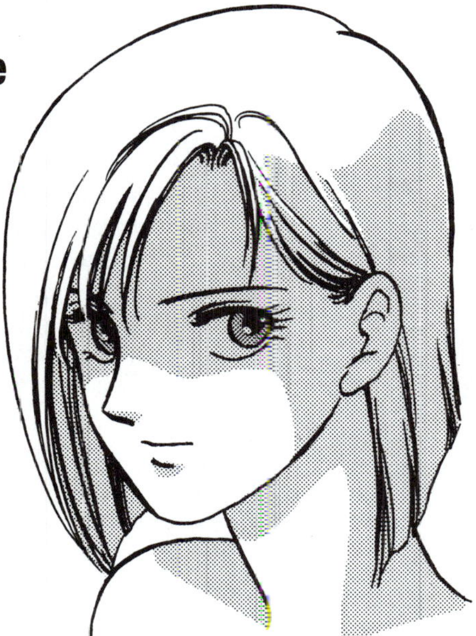

f

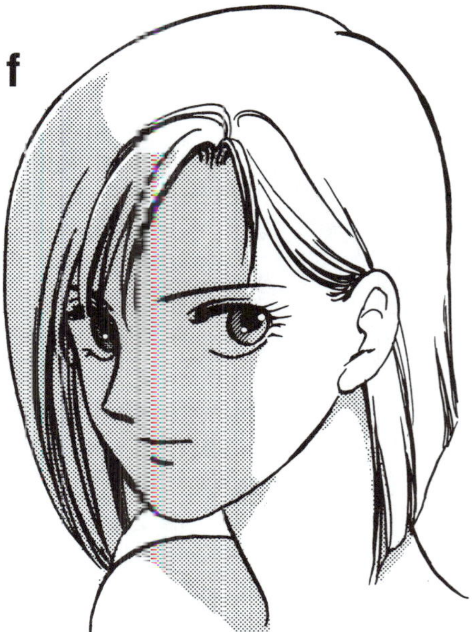

Practical Applications to Panels (Moderate High Angle)

c

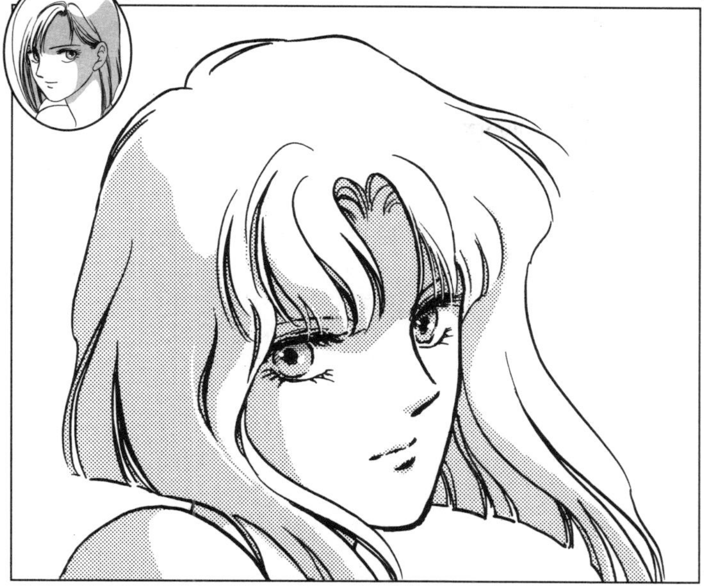

b

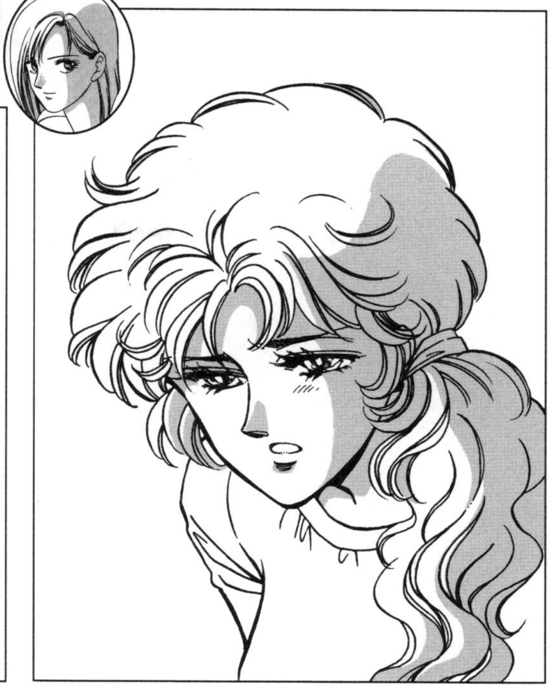

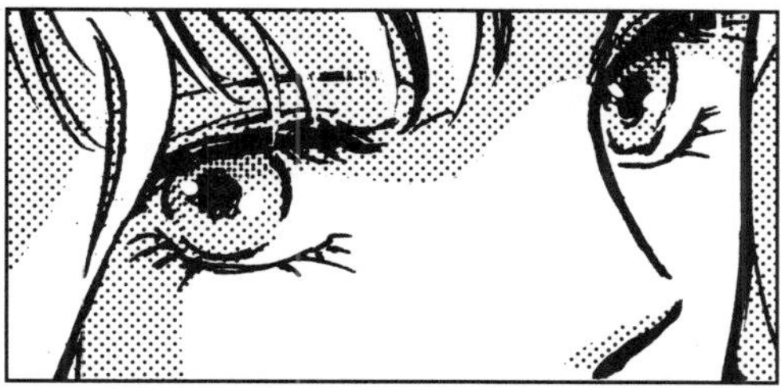

c-type shadows, which fall across the forehead and eyes, are effective in close-ups.

a

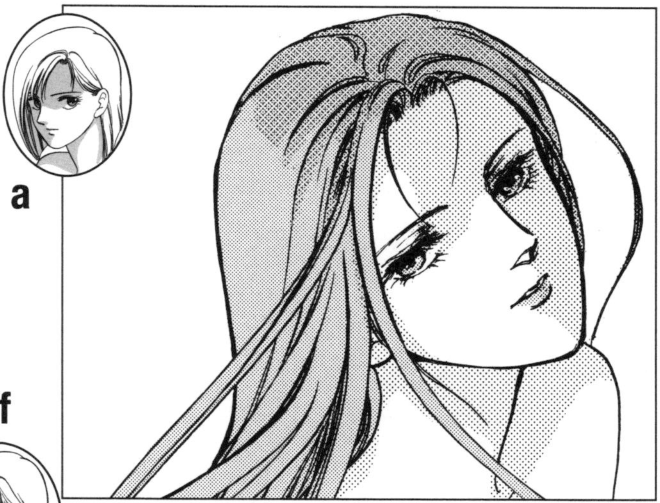

f

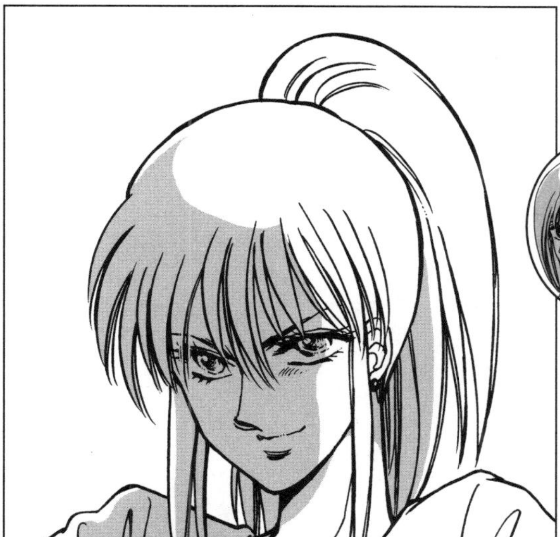

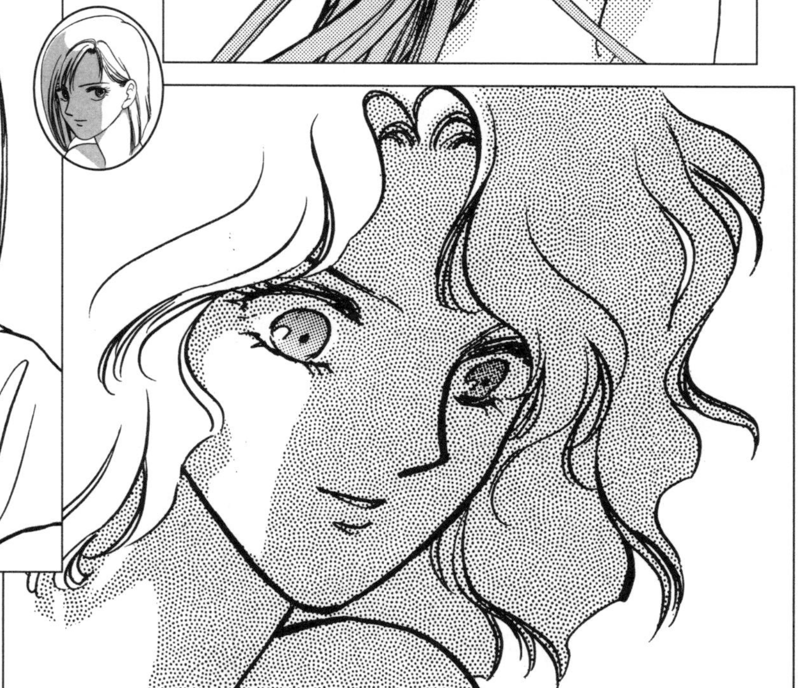

f-type shadows are effective both when showing the entire head and when cropping it and just showing a portion.

Common Body Shadows

Shadows are added to the body primarily to give the figure a sense of volume or to accentuate its forms. Consequently, poses and compositions that draw attention to the figure's contours or musculature tend to be favored.

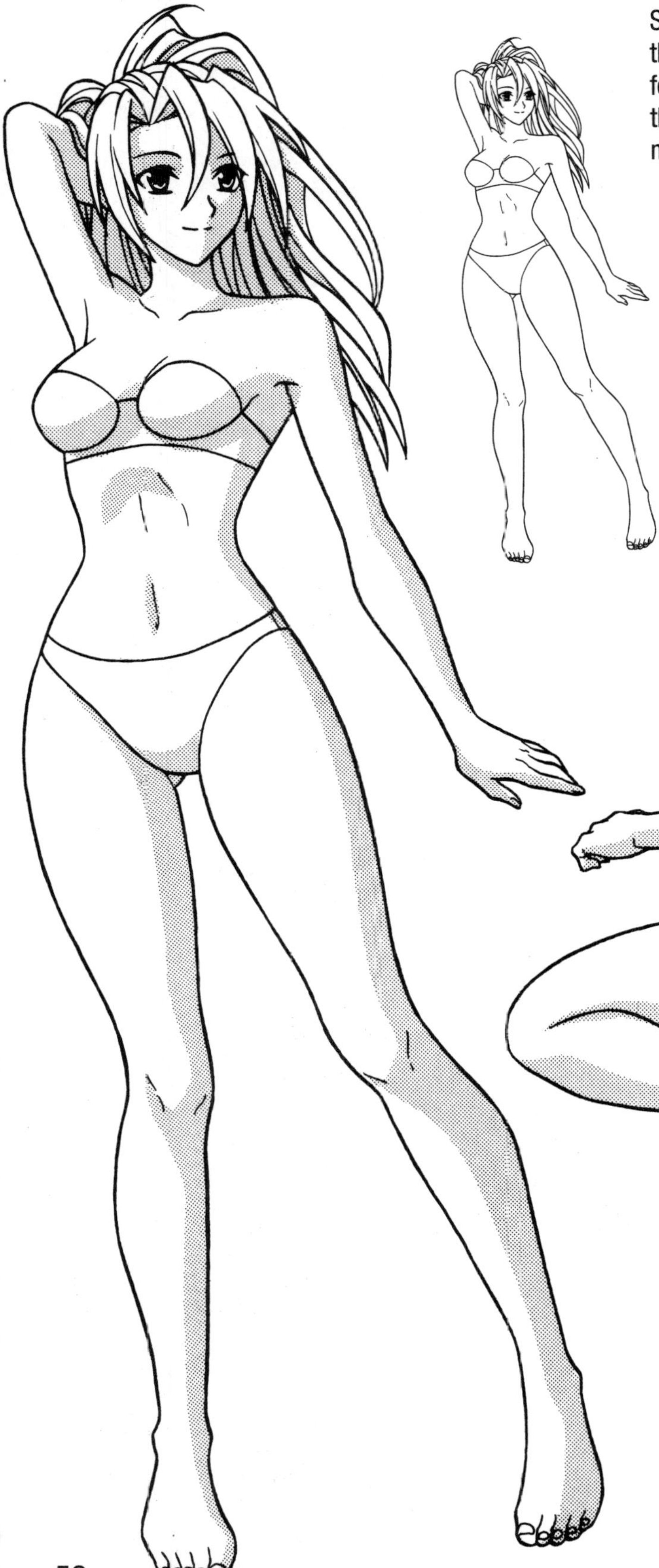

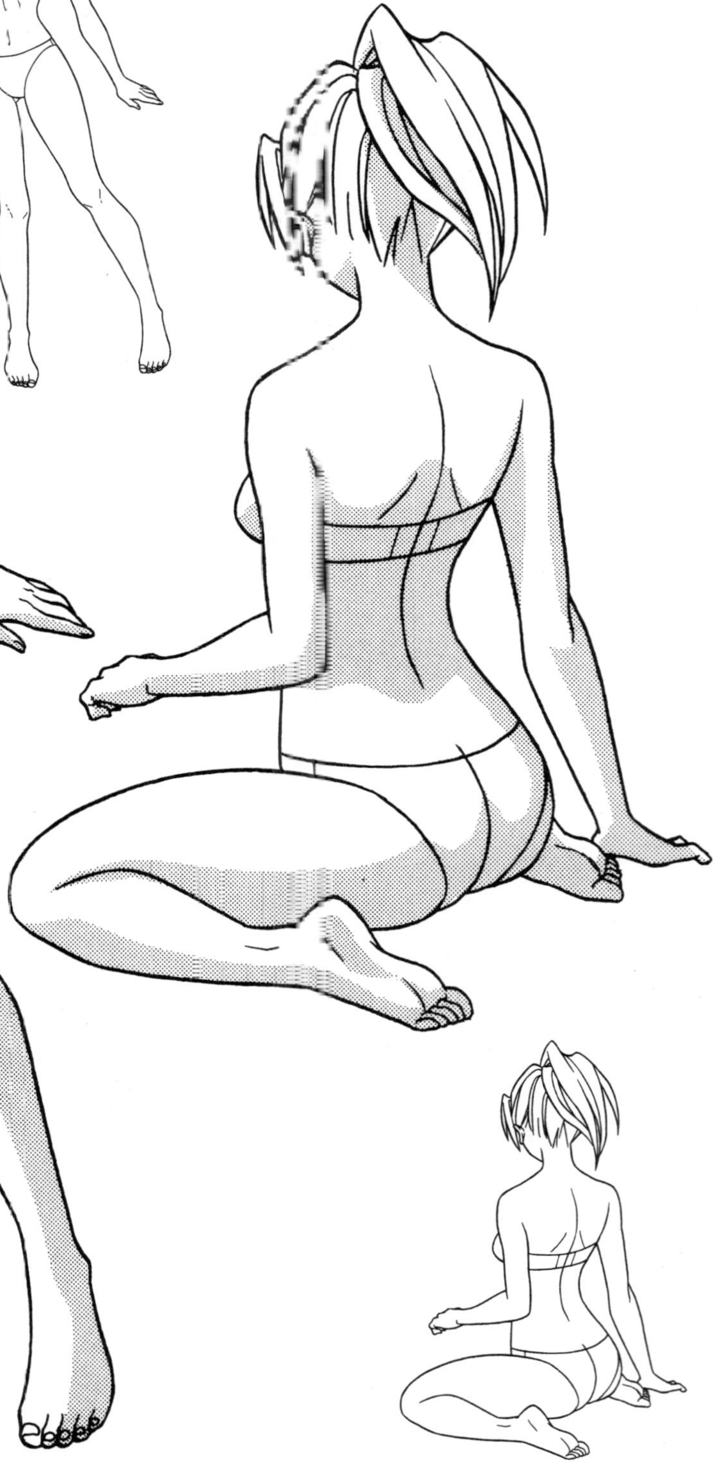

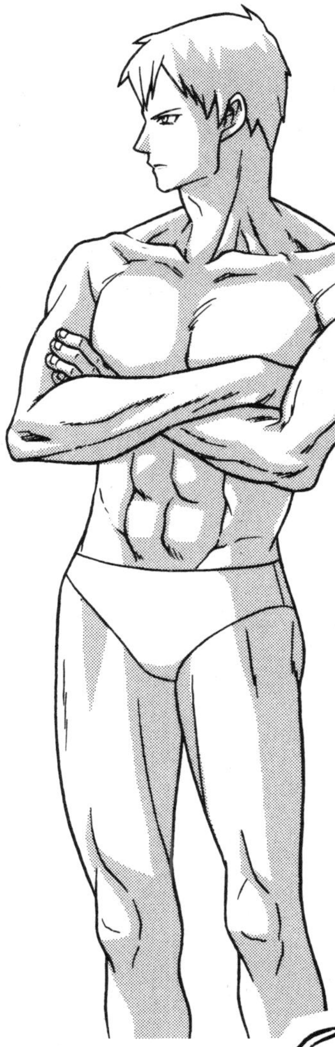

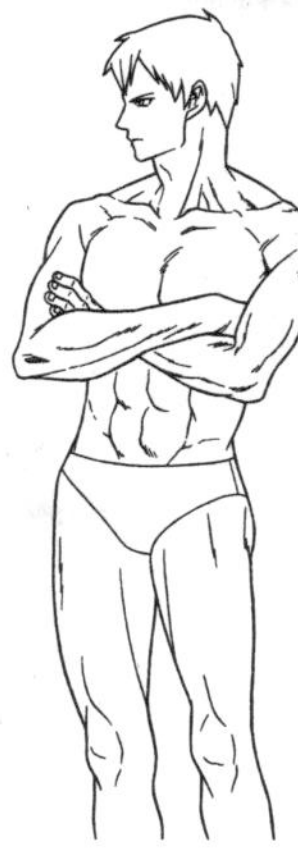

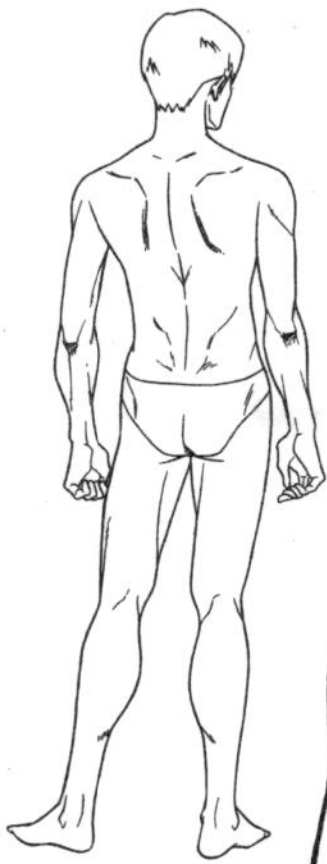

Adding to the girths of the arms and thighs generate a weightier feel.

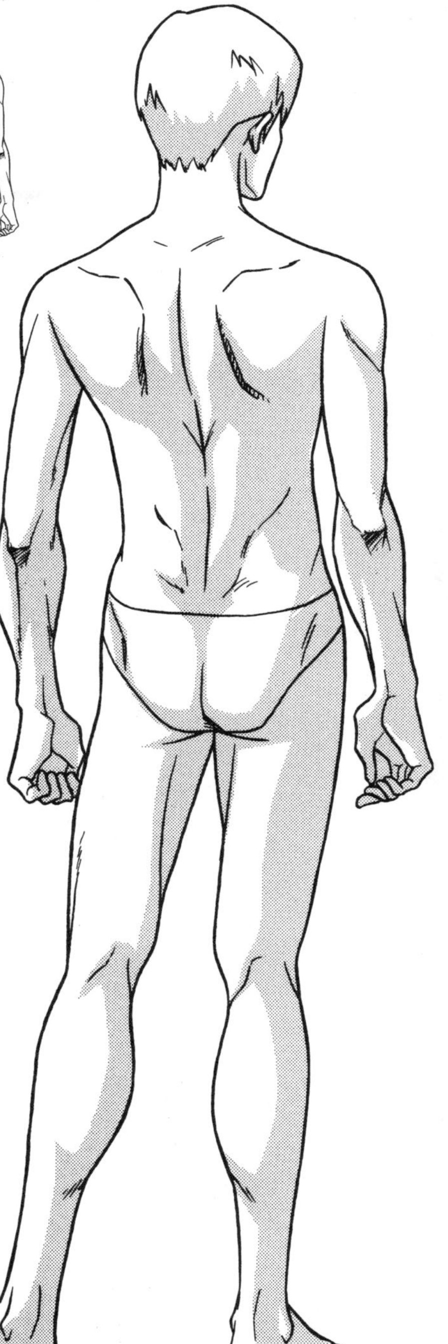

The key to exquisite, lithe muscles is to draw the arms and legs on the lean side and maintain balance.

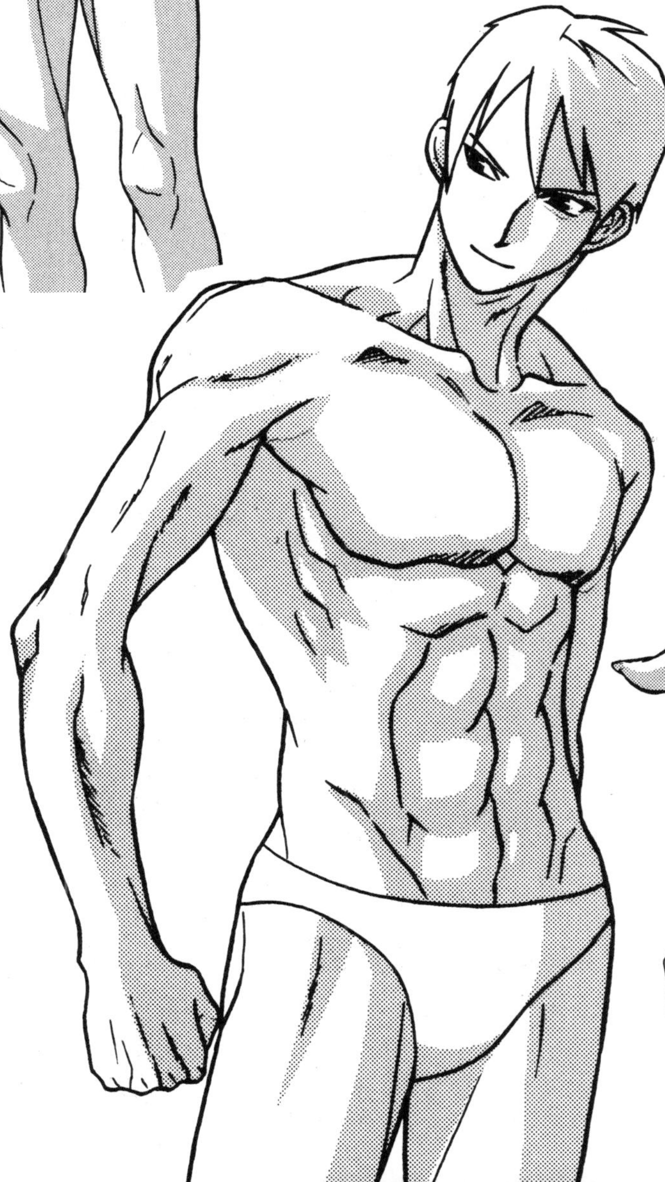

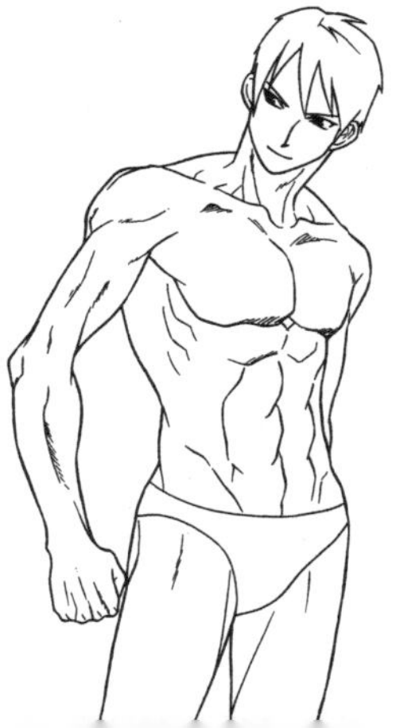

Action scenes, which primarily comprise martial arts scenes, tend to draw attention to male characters' muscles. Have a look at pro-wrestlers and body builders for reference. To draw handsome, lean muscles, look to the bodies of dancers.

Principles in Figure Shading

Limit lighting to a single source
(i.e. add shadows from a uniform direction)

Light source

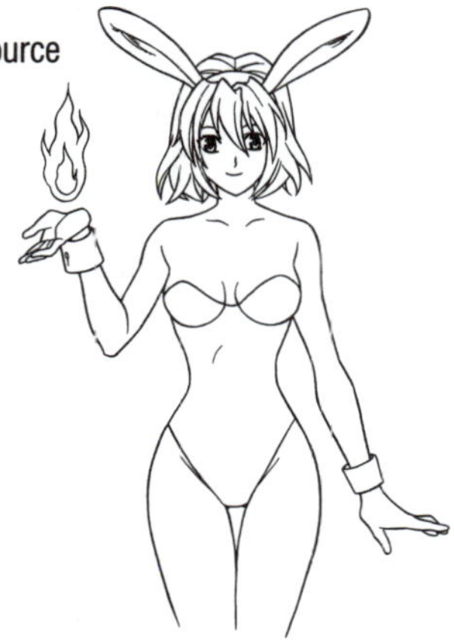

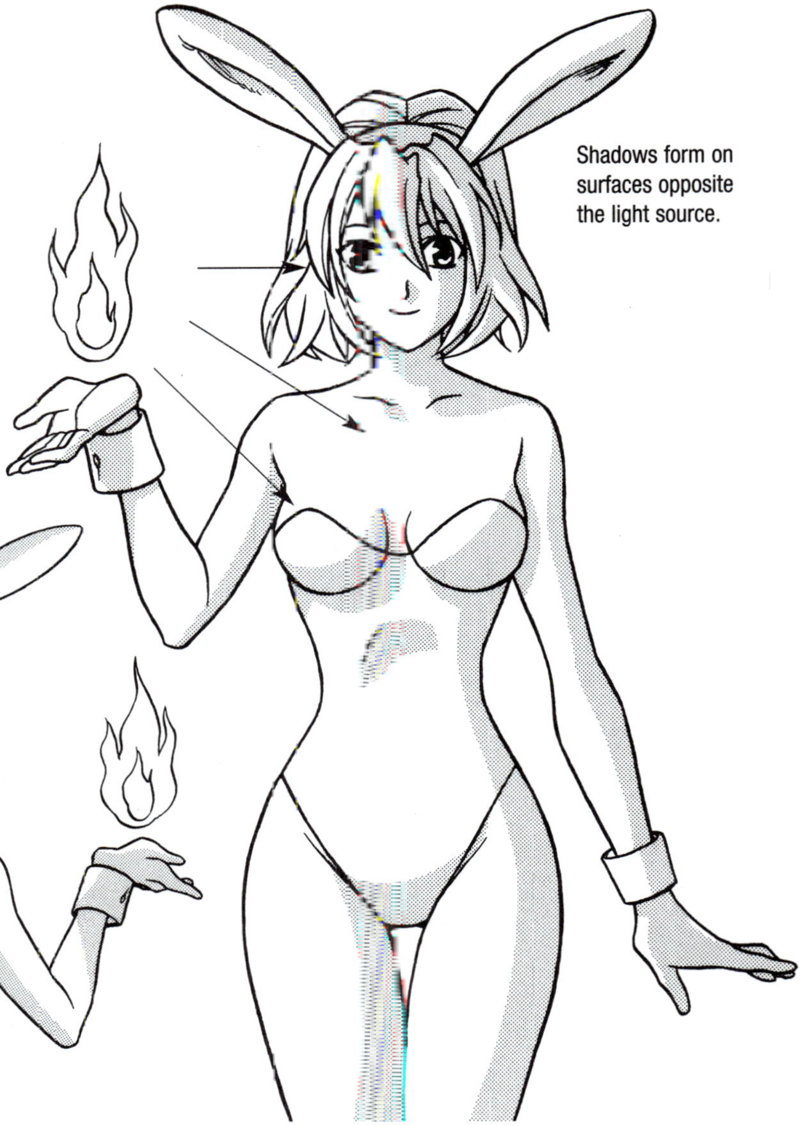

Shadows form on surfaces opposite the light source.

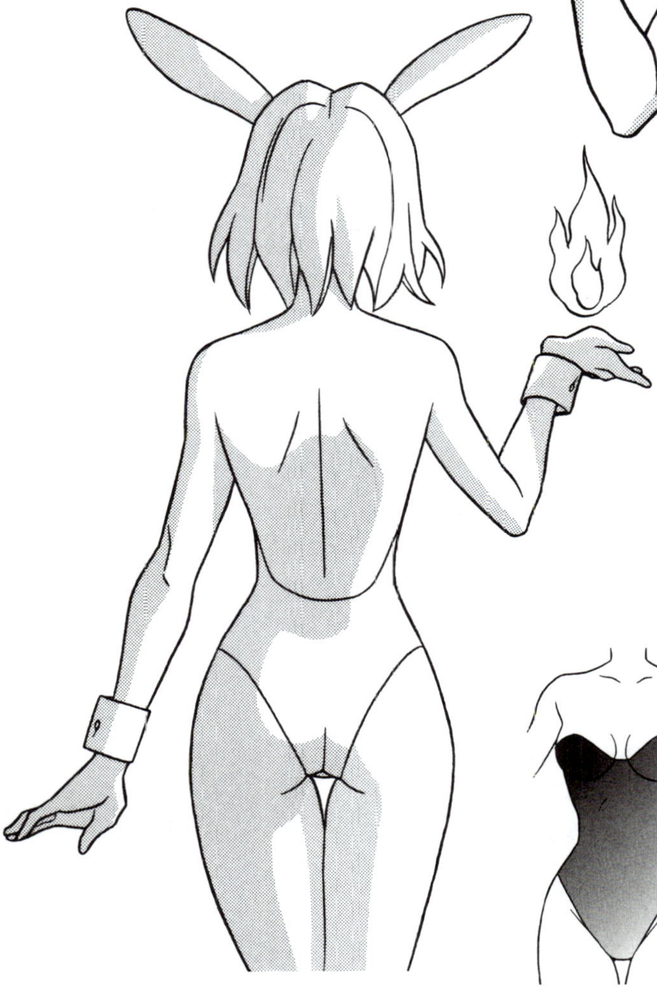

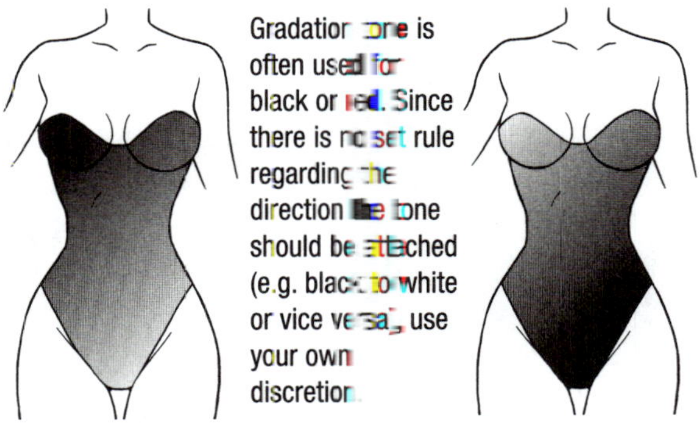

Gradation tone is often used for black or red. Since there is no set rule regarding the direction the tone should be attached (e.g. black to white or vice versa), use your own discretion.

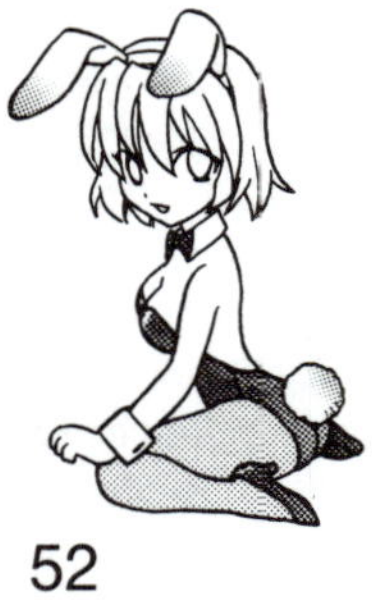

Note: Traditional bunnies have cotton tails.

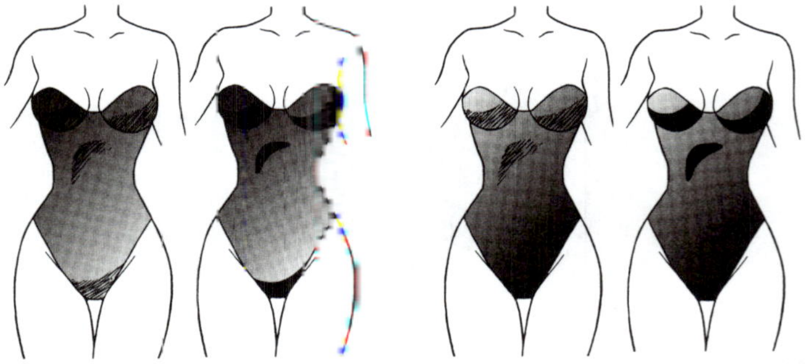

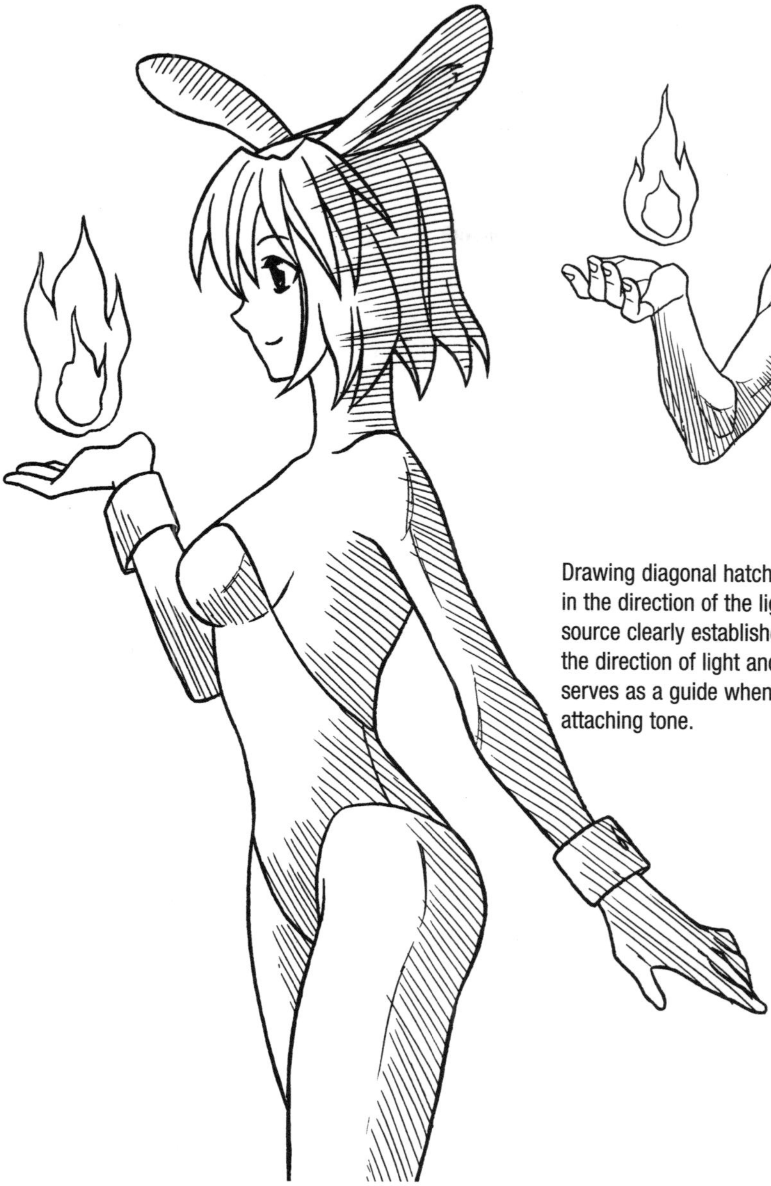

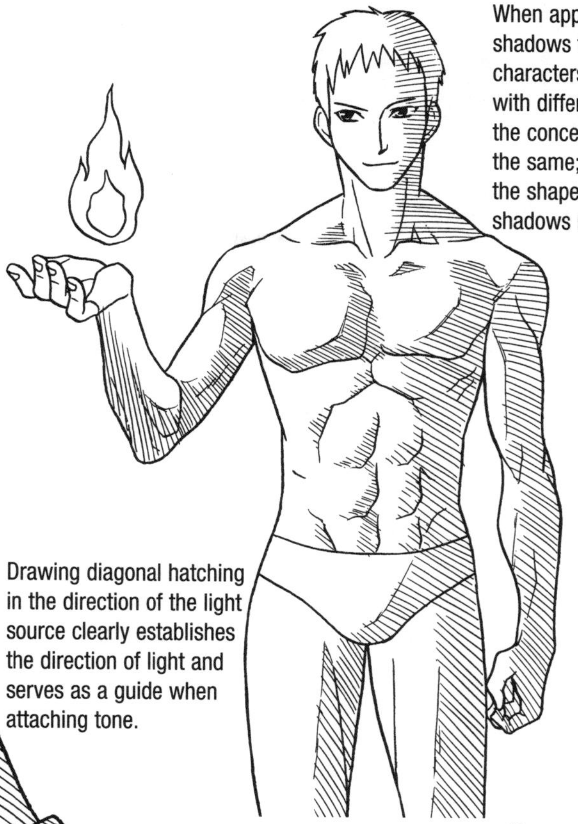

When applying shadows to male characters or figures with different builds, the concept remains the same; although, the shapes of the shadows may change.

Drawing diagonal hatching in the direction of the light source clearly establishes the direction of light and serves as a guide when attaching tone.

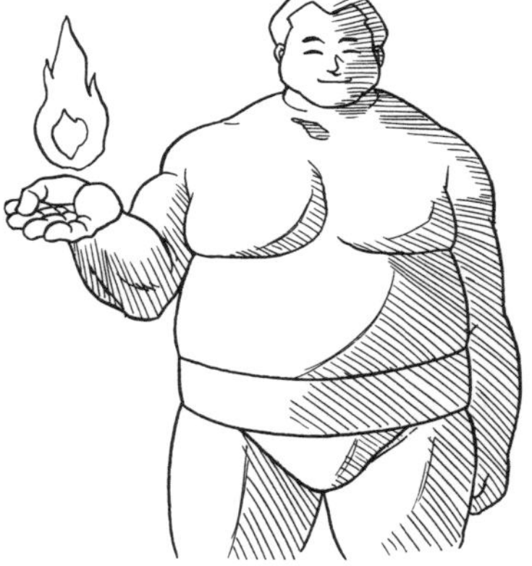

Caution There should usually be a single light source.

Not good

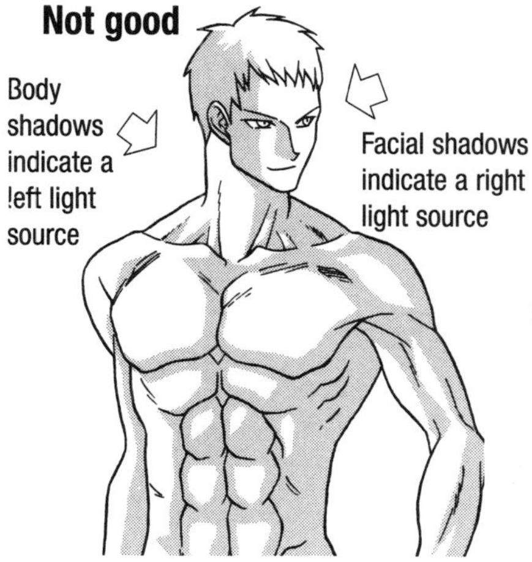

Shading the face and body with shadows indicating different light sources results in an unacceptably awkward composition.

Good

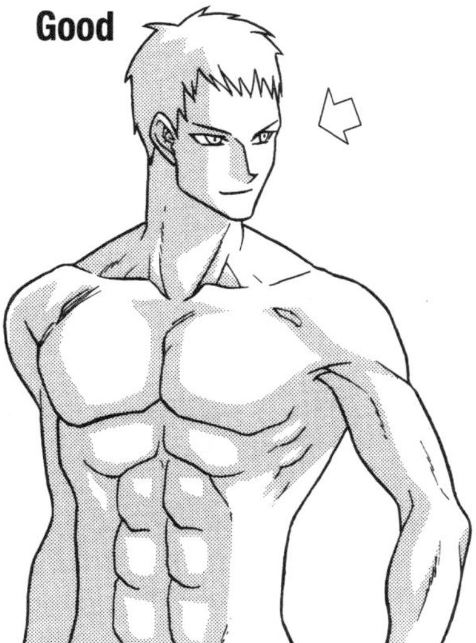

Here, I drew the body's shadows to match those on the original face.

Good

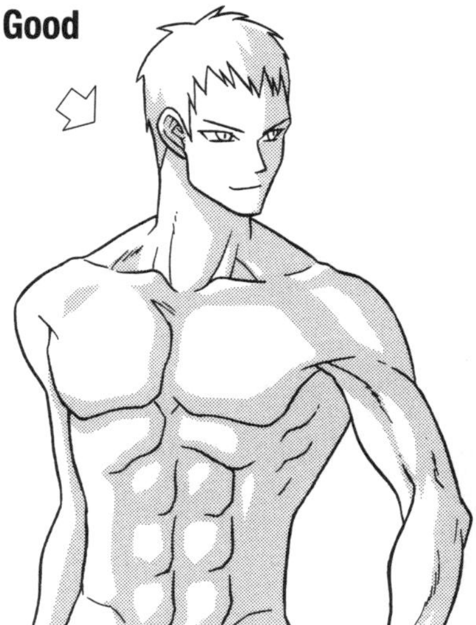

Here, I drew the facial shadows to match those on the original body.

Tricks to Drawing Body Shadows

Male Characters

Even masters at sketching find it difficult to identify with absolute certainty how shadows form depending on the lighting.

Light source

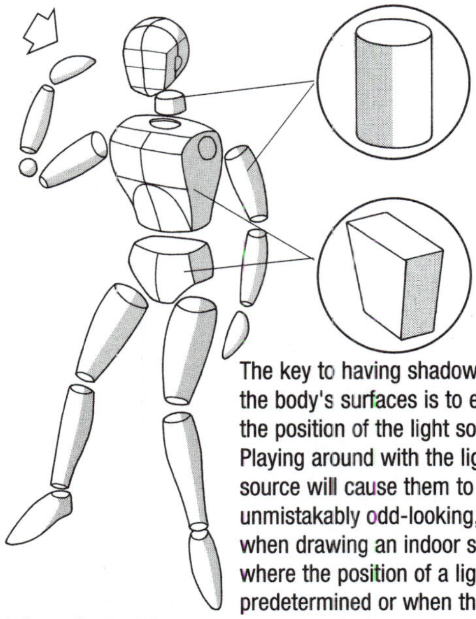

Draw the neck, arms, and legs as cylinders.

Use a block for the torso.

Jot down the body's parts as blocks when laying out shadows.

The key to having shadows form on the body's surfaces is to establish the position of the light source. Playing around with the light source will cause them to become unmistakably odd-looking, such as when drawing an indoor scene where the position of a light is predetermined or when the position in relation to the sun is clearly established. In these cases, shadows must be clearly drawn according to positional relationships. However, you may establish a special light source when drawing shadows specifically to "make the character look good" for the sake of character portrayal.

Not good

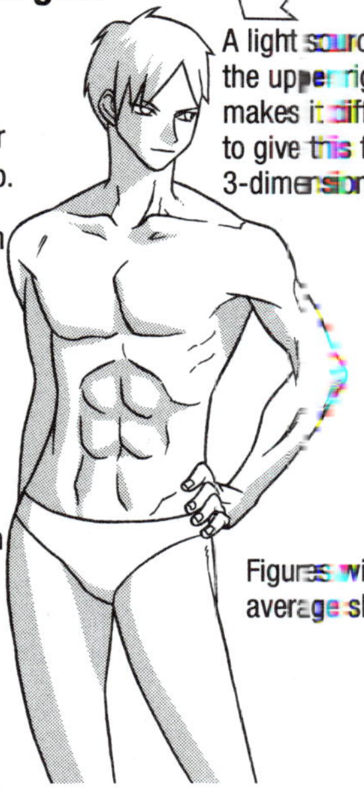

A light source from the upper right makes it difficult to give this figure 3-dimensionality.

Figures with average shading

Good

Figure with upper left light source

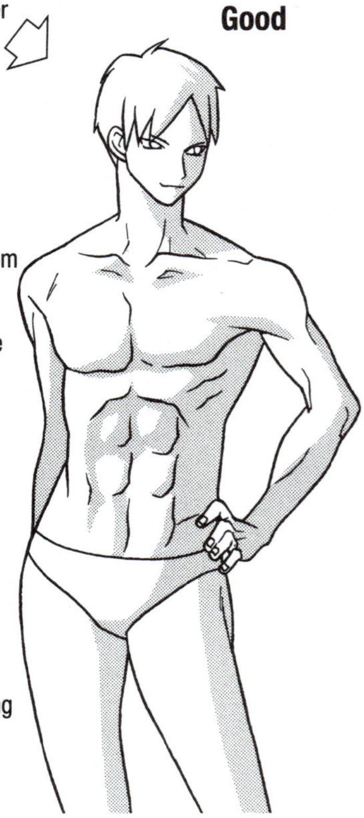

Common Shading Patterns

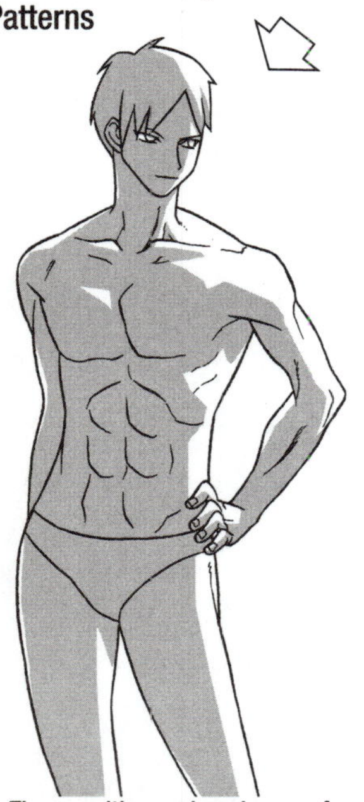

Figure with an abundance of shadow (e.g. Sun to figure's back)

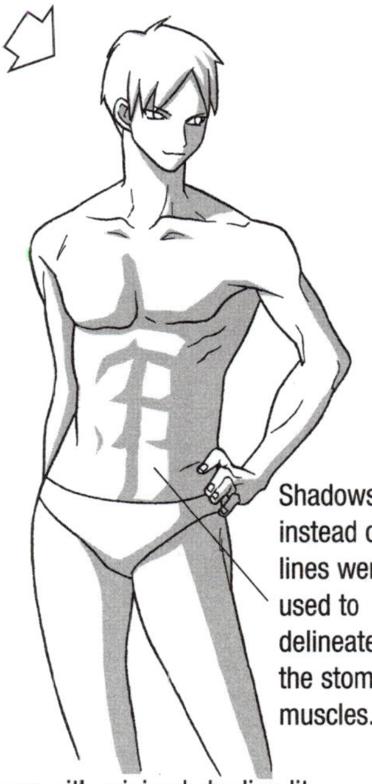

Shadows instead of lines were used to delineate the stomach muscles.

Figure with minimal shading lit from the upper left (Light source at upper left front)

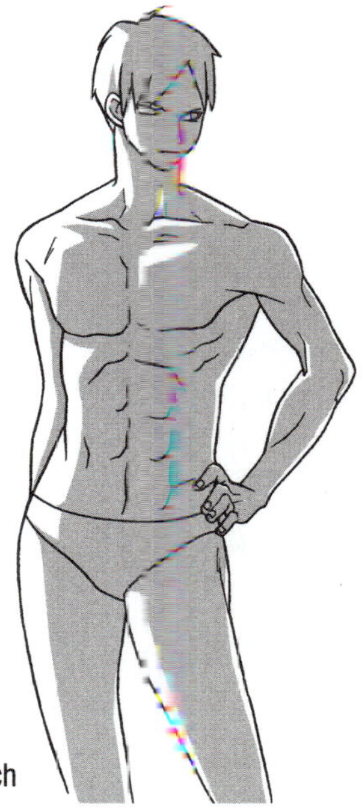

Figure with an abundance of shadow (e.g. Sun to figure's back; light source at upper left back)

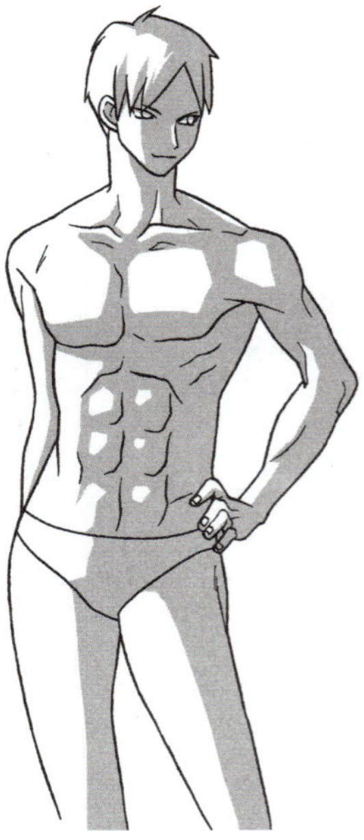

Moderately abundant shadows

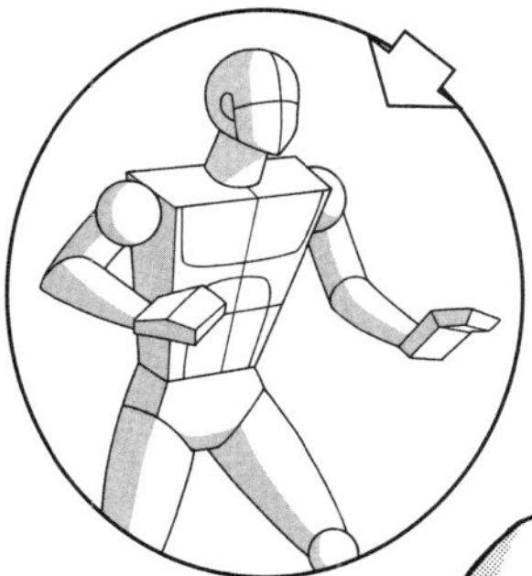

Common Shading Styles

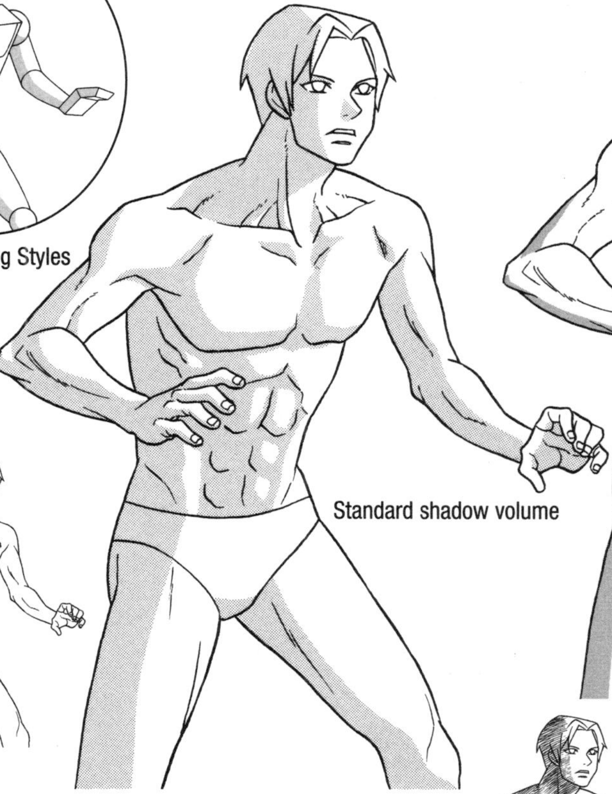

Standard shadow volume

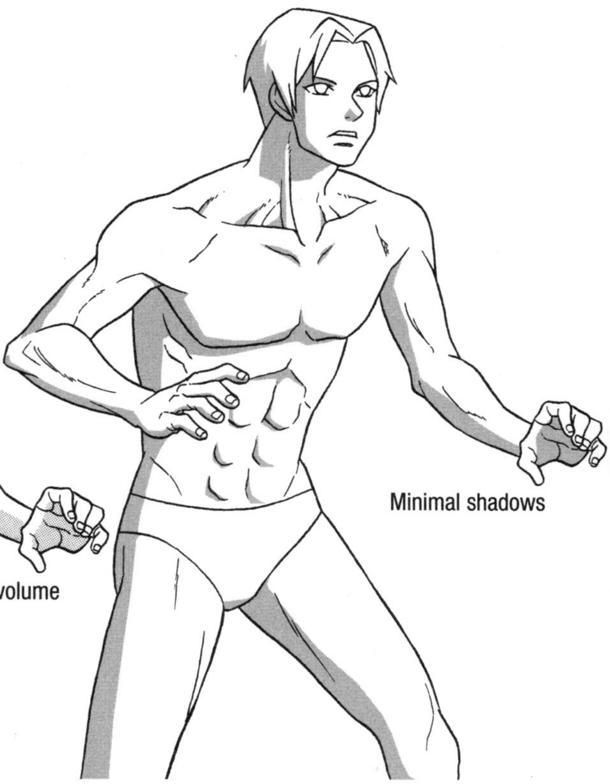

Minimal shadows

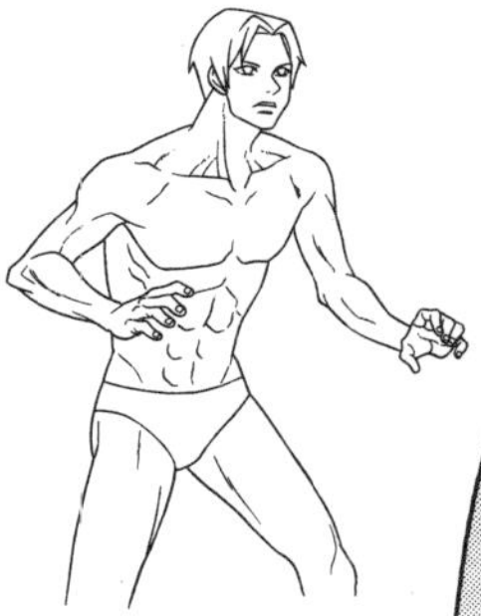

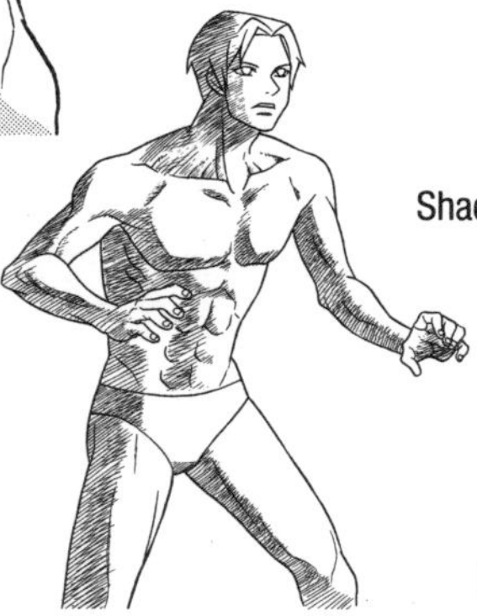

Shadows rendered in hatching

Shadows form on clothed figures approximately the same as they would on a nude.

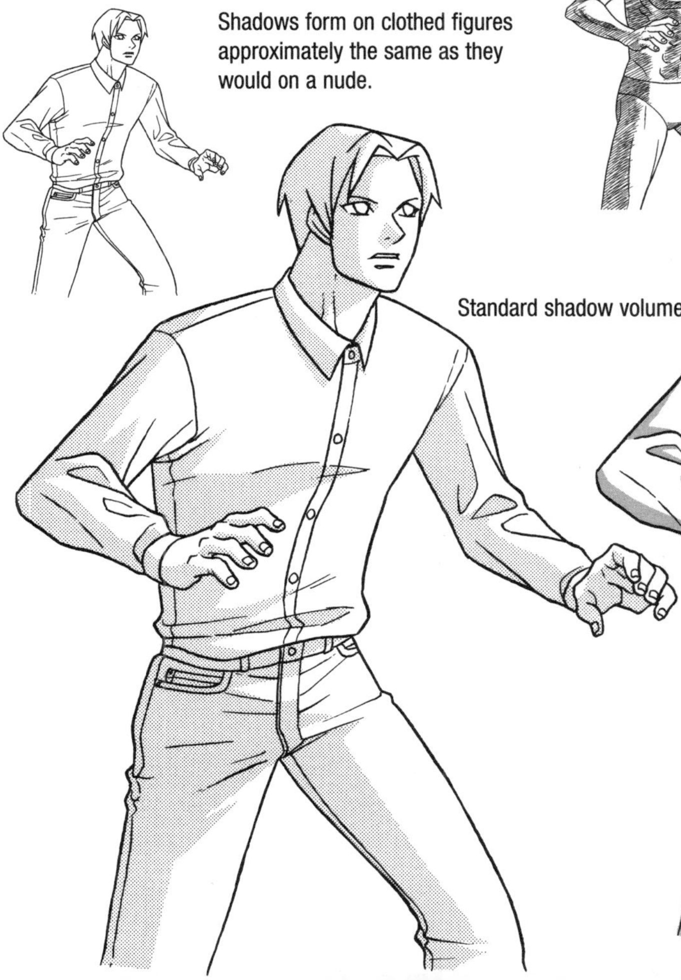

Standard shadow volume

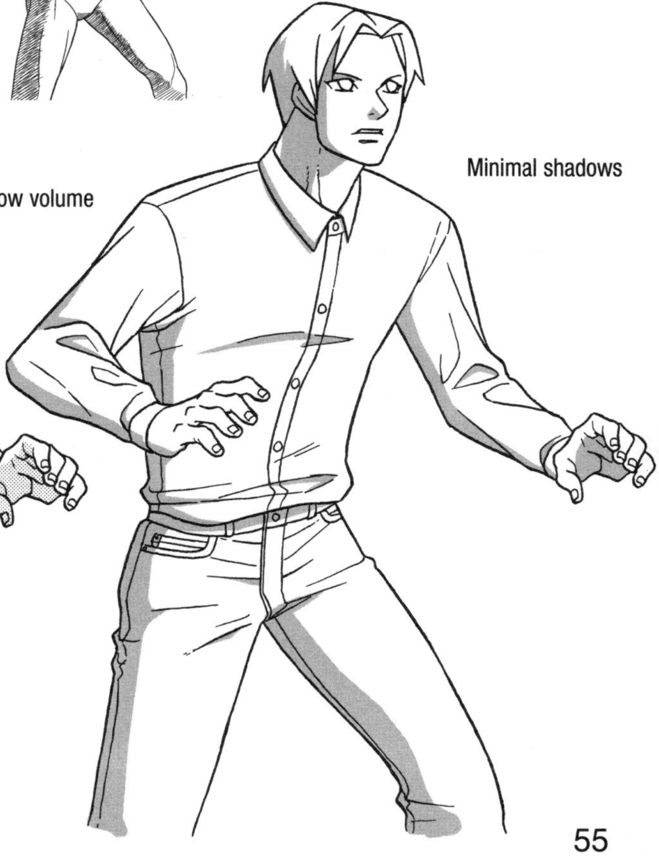

Minimal shadows

Shading the Back

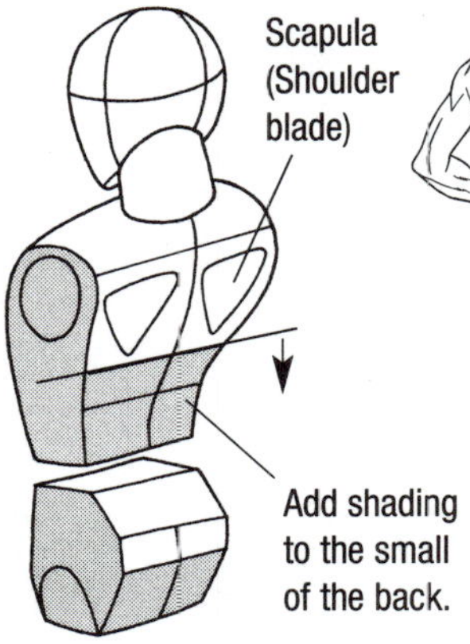

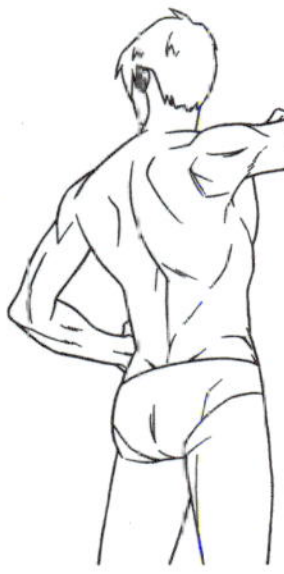

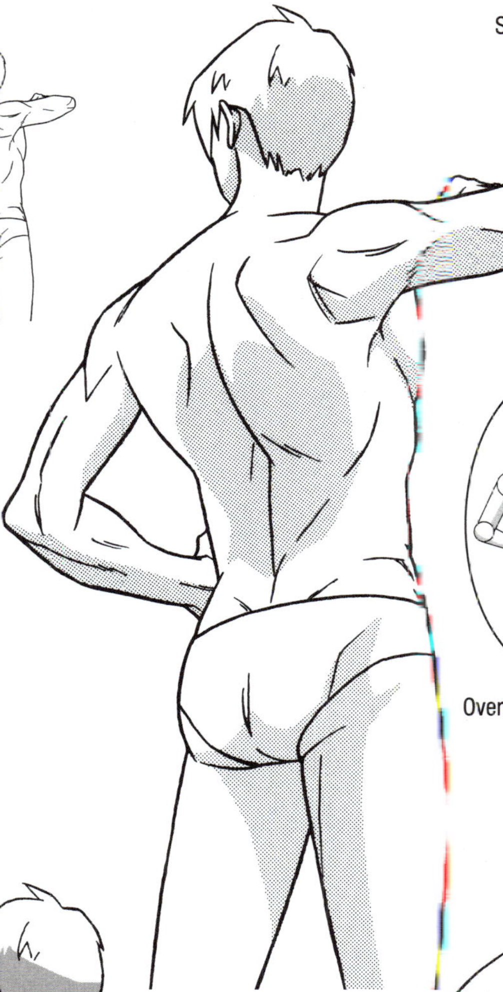

Shadows rendered in hatching

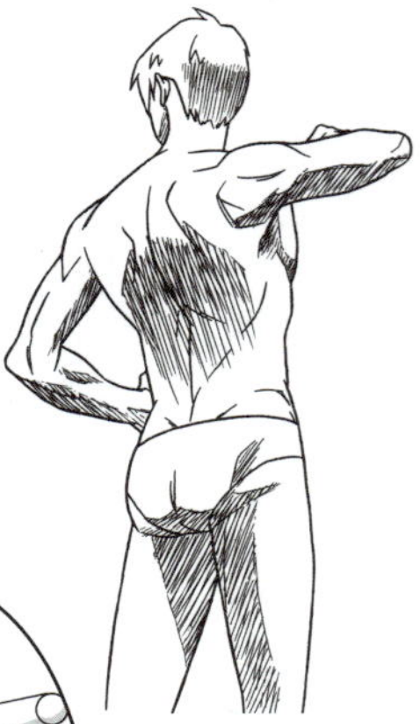

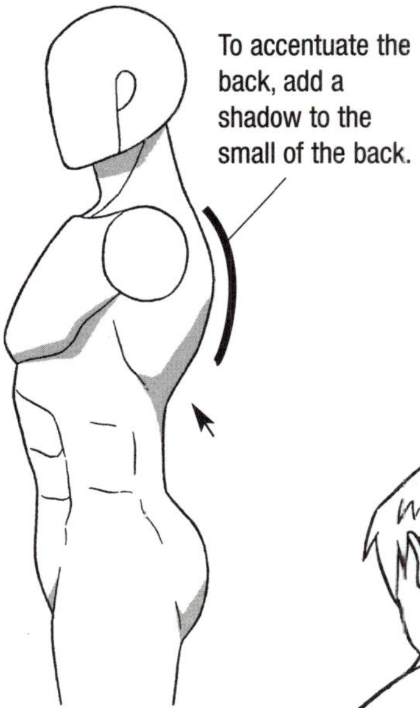

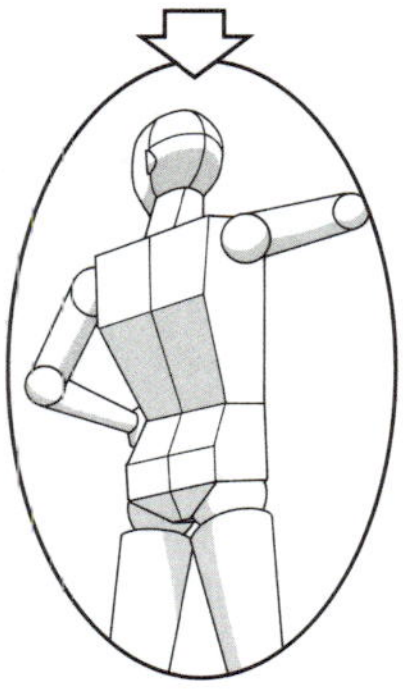

Overhead light source

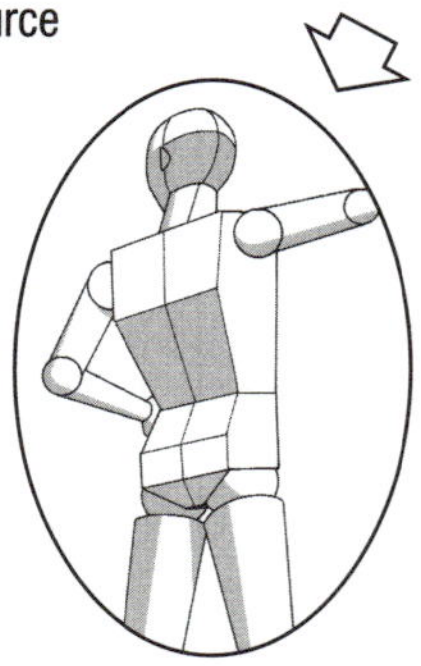

Upper right light source

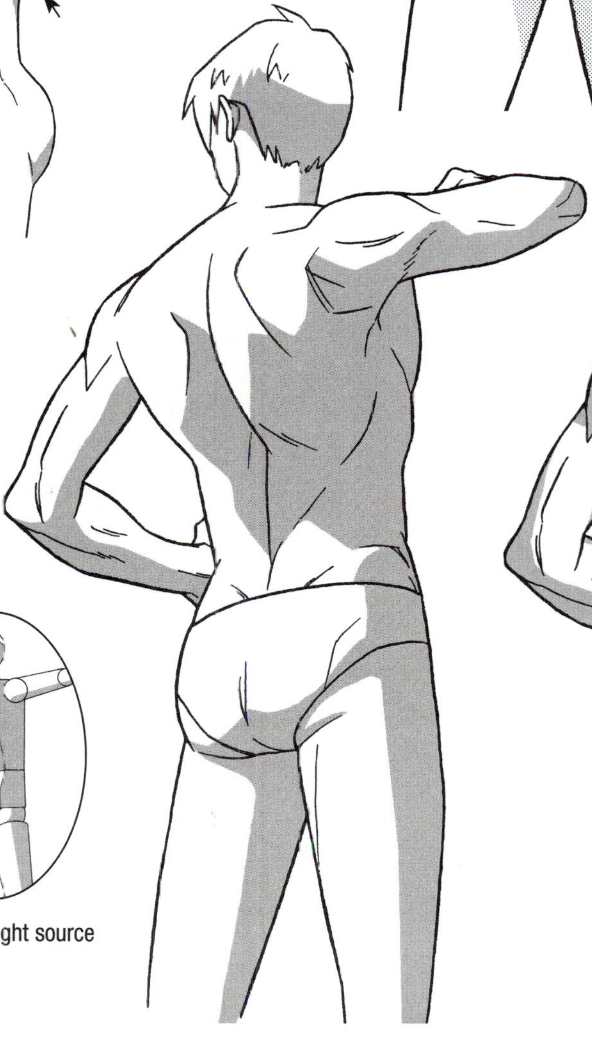

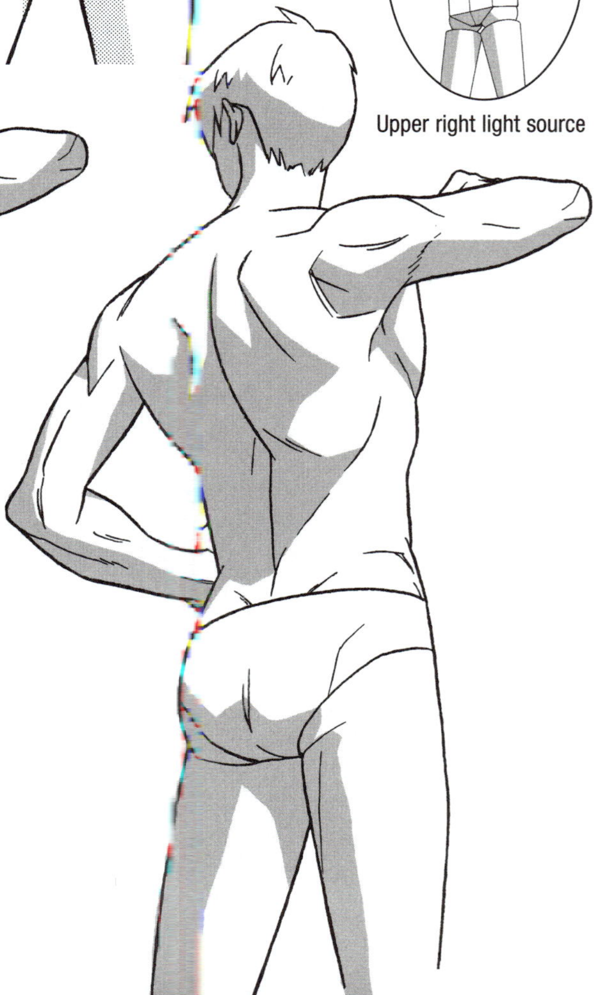

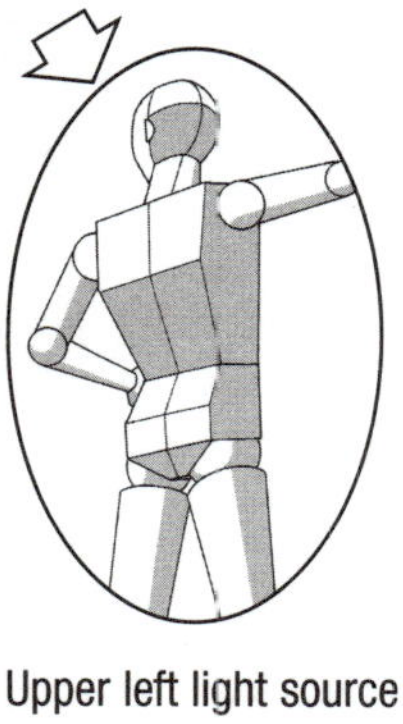

Upper left light source

Shadows on the Back of a Jacket

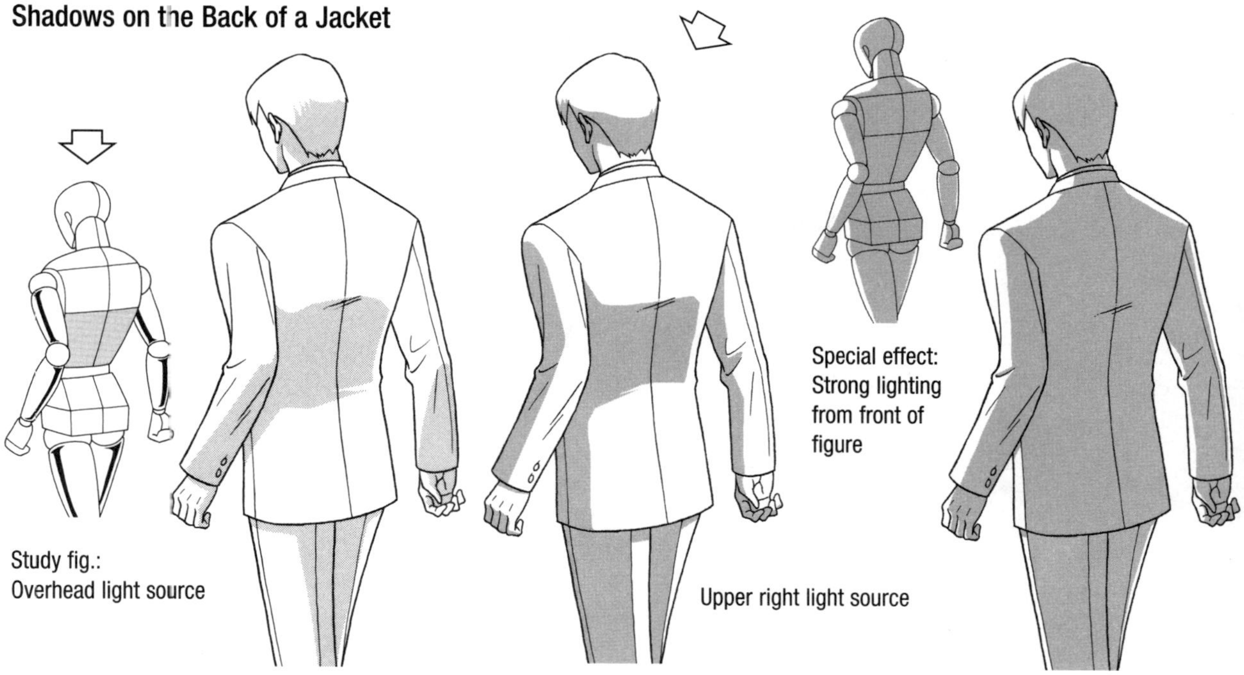

Study fig.:
Overhead light source

Upper right light source

Special effect:
Strong lighting from front of figure

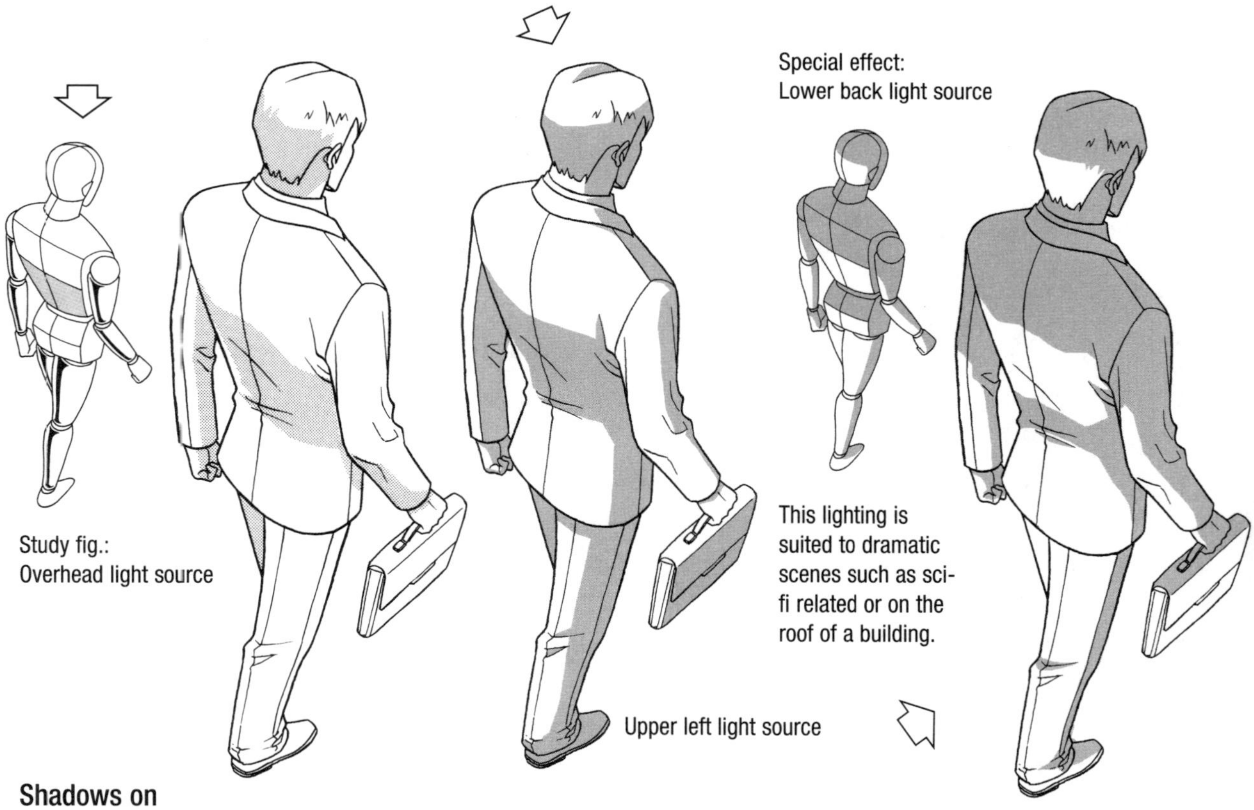

Study fig.:
Overhead light source

Upper left light source

Special effect:
Lower back light source

This lighting is suited to dramatic scenes such as sci-fi related or on the roof of a building.

Shadows on the Posterior

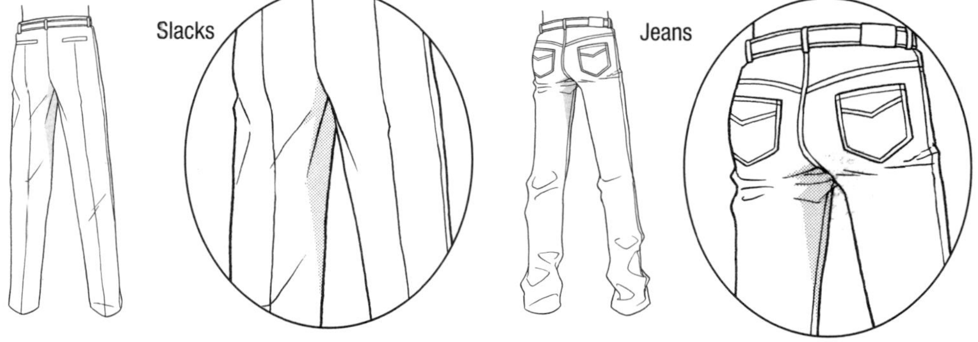

Slacks

Jeans

Close-ups of a male character's derriere are not common, and shadows are not typically added.

Female Characters

The female figure is composed of curves, causing the edges of shadows to curve as well.

Figure Study

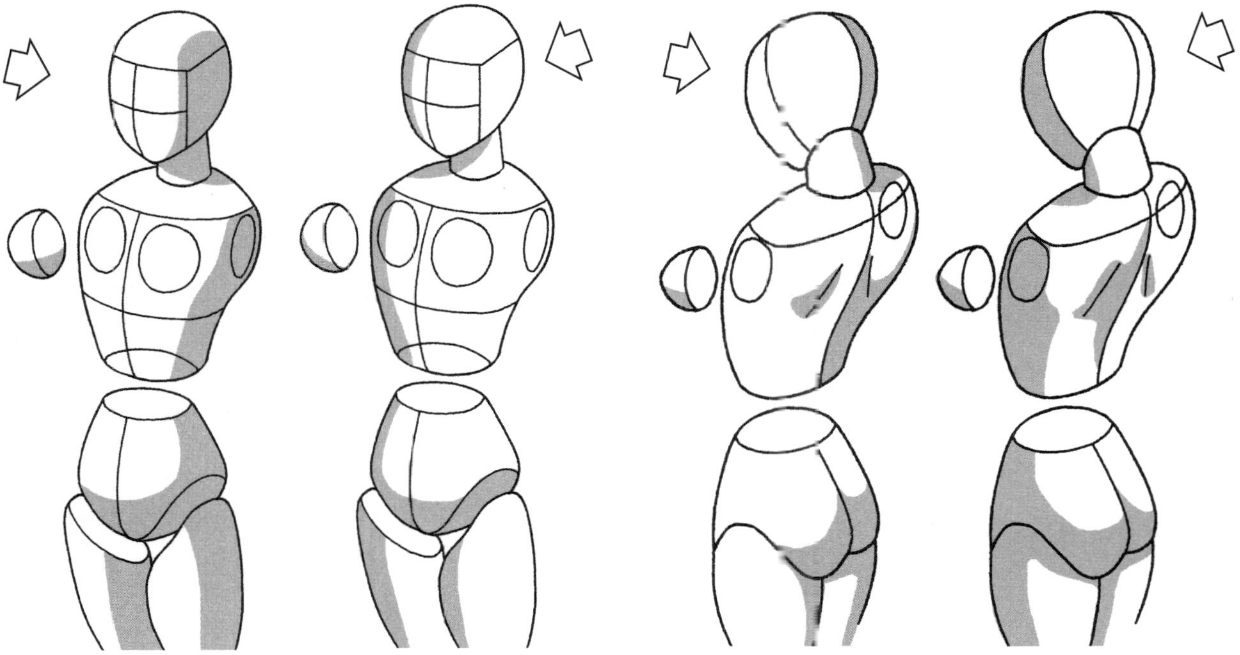

Upper left light source   Upper right light source   Upper left light source   Upper right light source

2 Common Shadow Types Used to Accentuate the Chest and Posterior

Study how shadows form on spherical objects when adding them to the chest and backside. The most common styles are crescent-shaped shadows and bottom shadows.

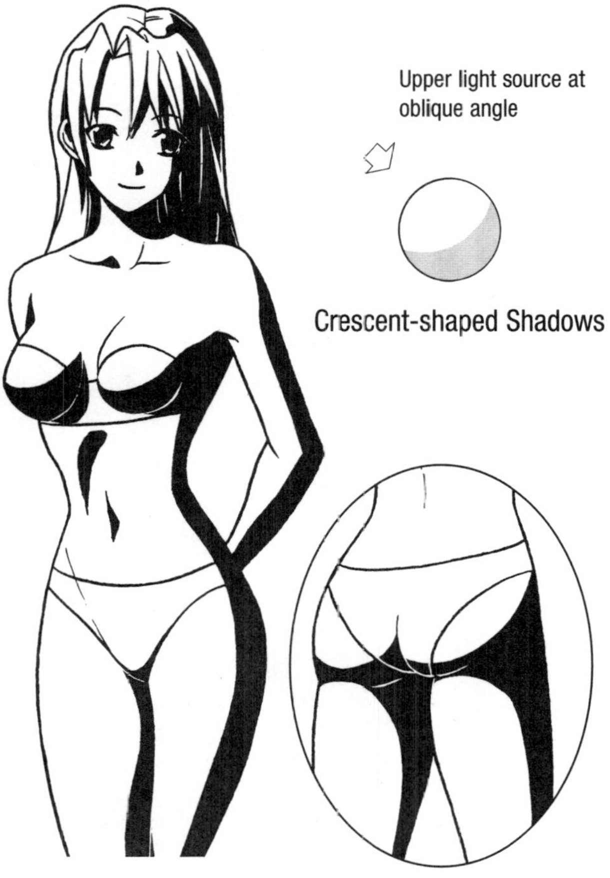

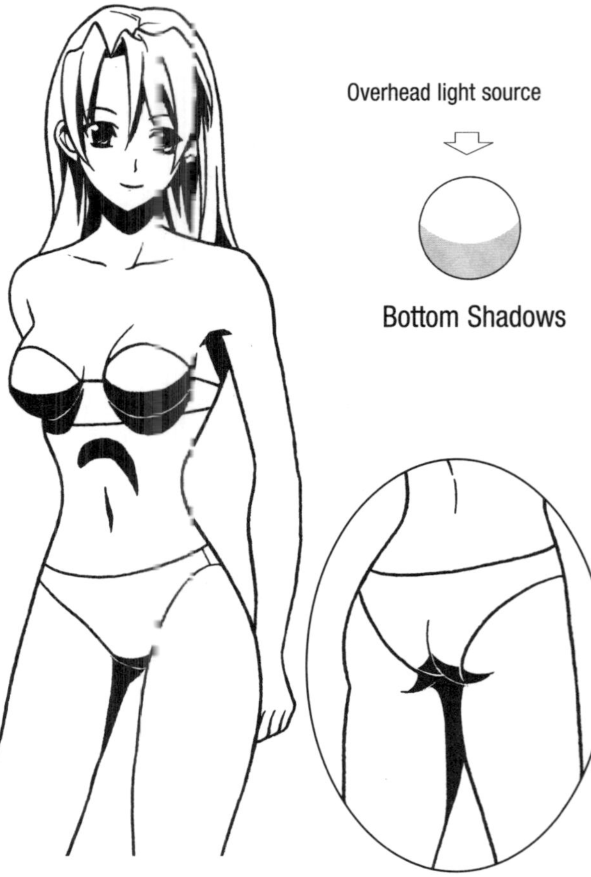

Crescent Shadows

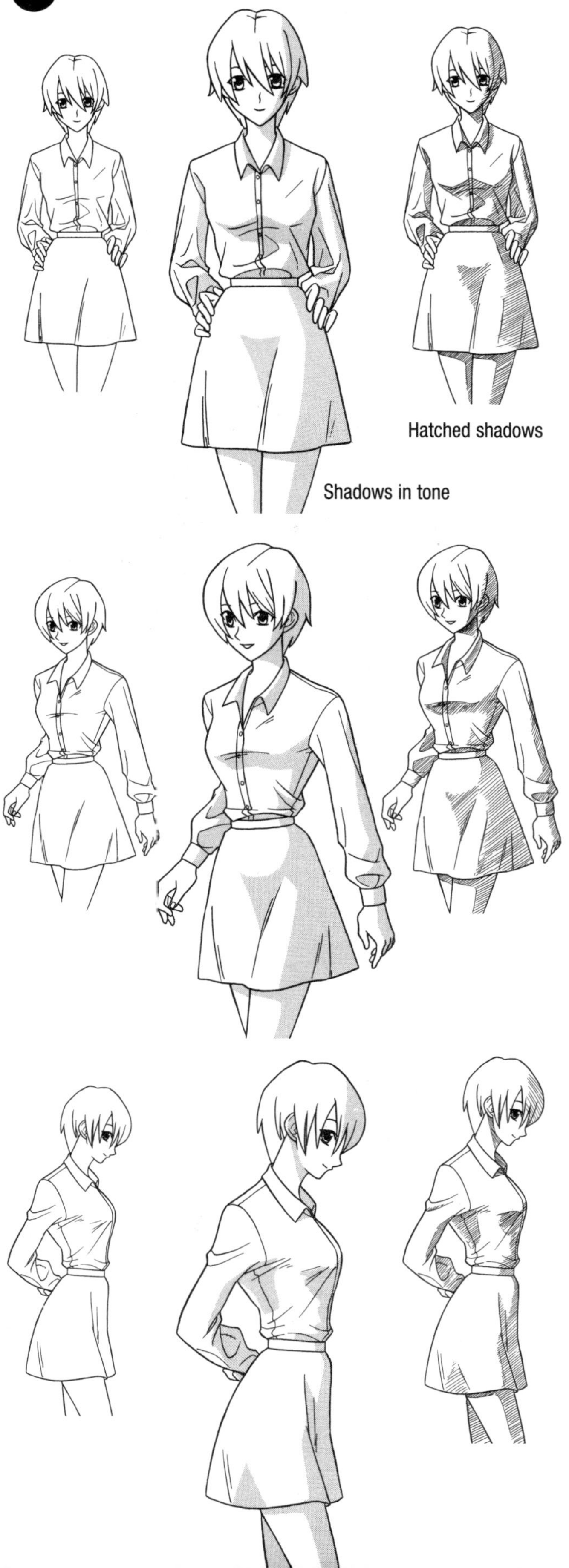

Bottom Shadows

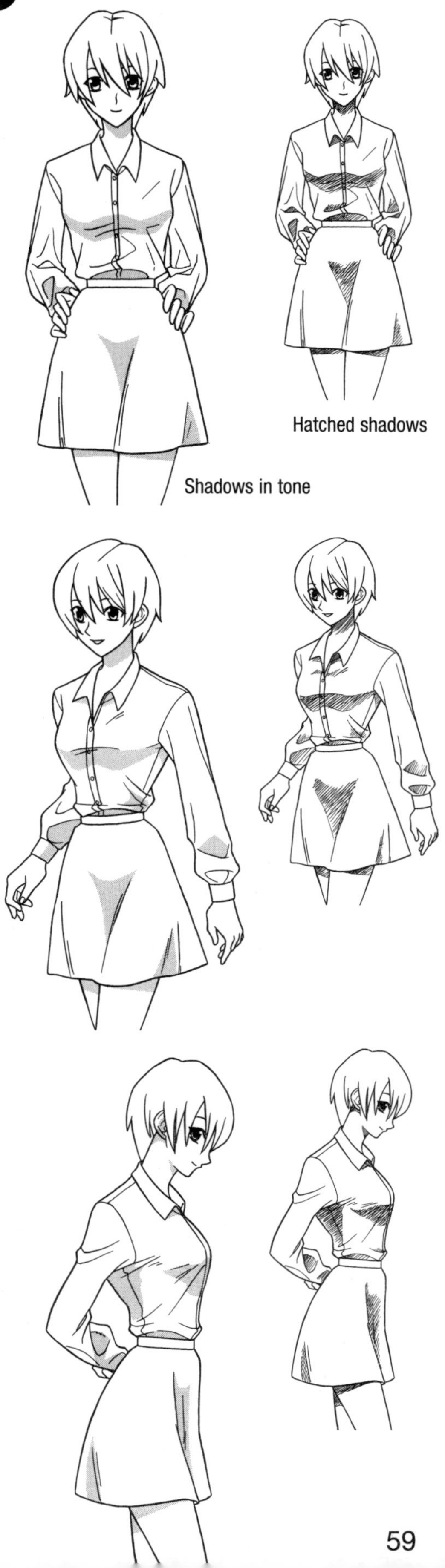

Side Shadows

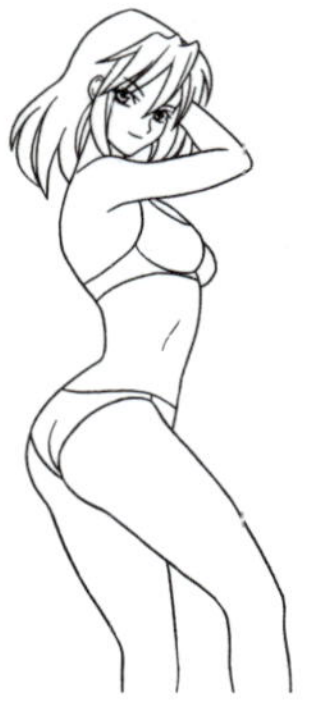

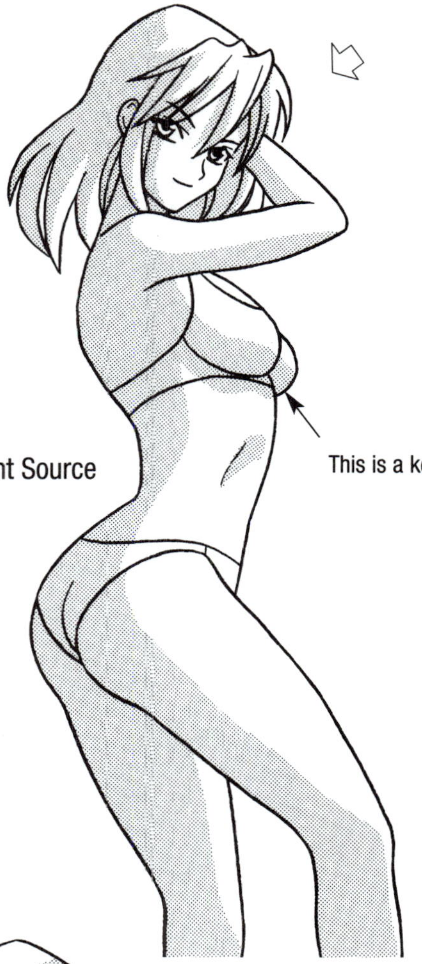

Front Light Source

This is a key shadow.

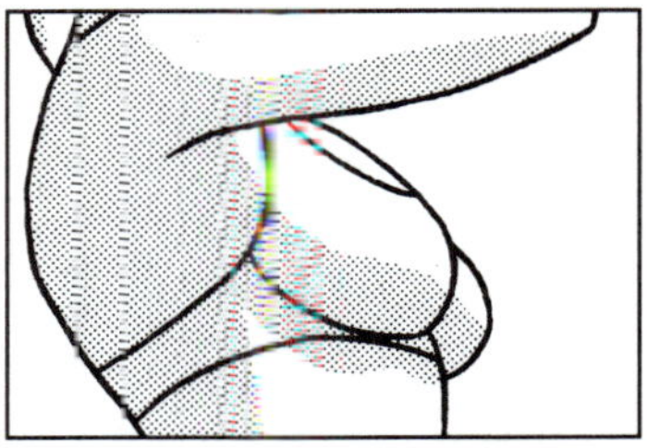

Front light sources are suited to emphasizing the chest.

Combined Lighting

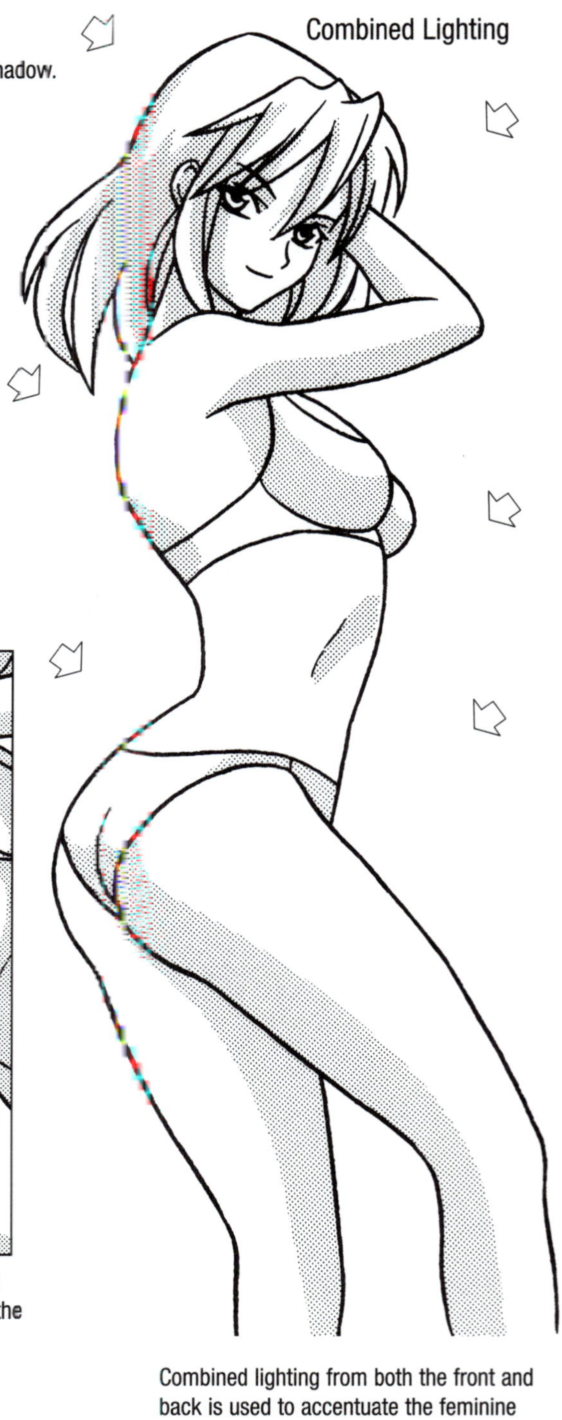

Combined lighting from both the front and back is used to accentuate the feminine charms of a female character.

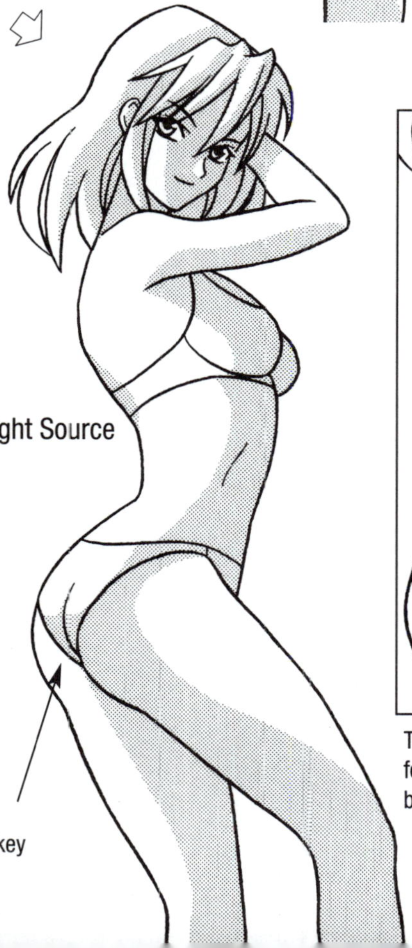

Back Light Source

This is a key shadow.

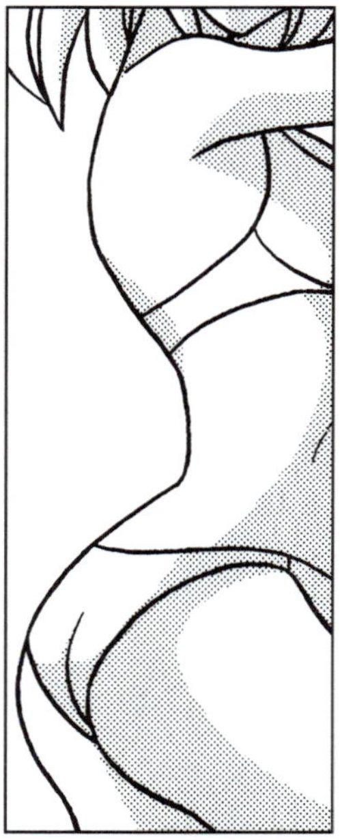

This light source is great for drawing attention to the backside.

Back Shadows

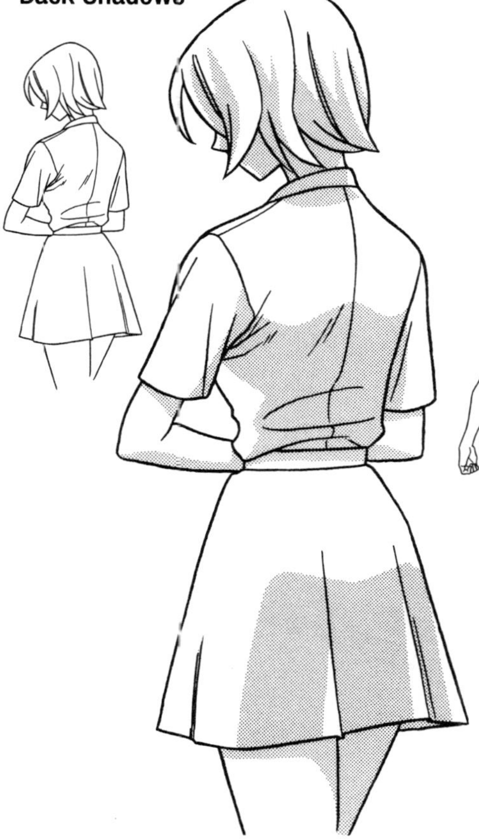

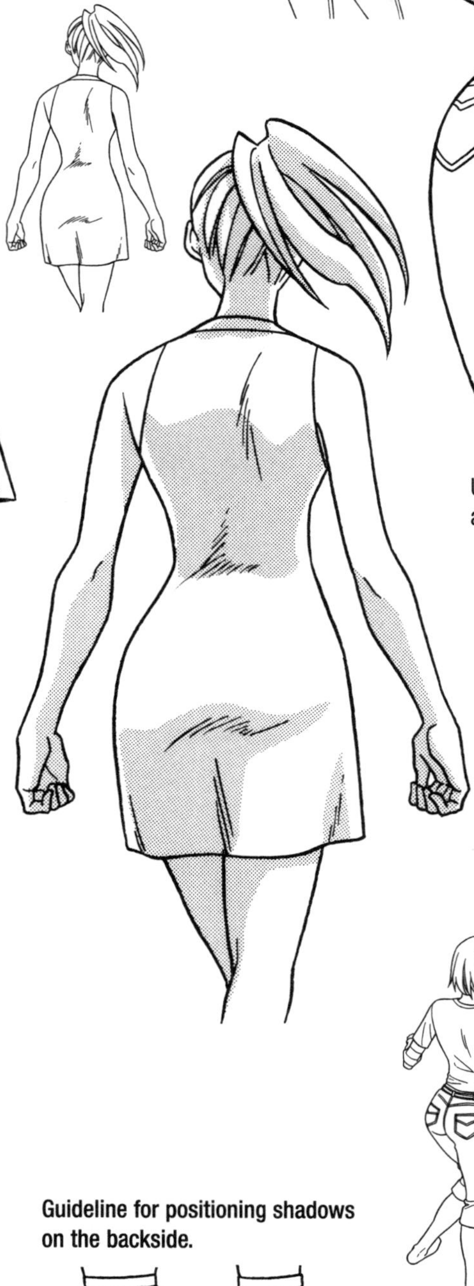

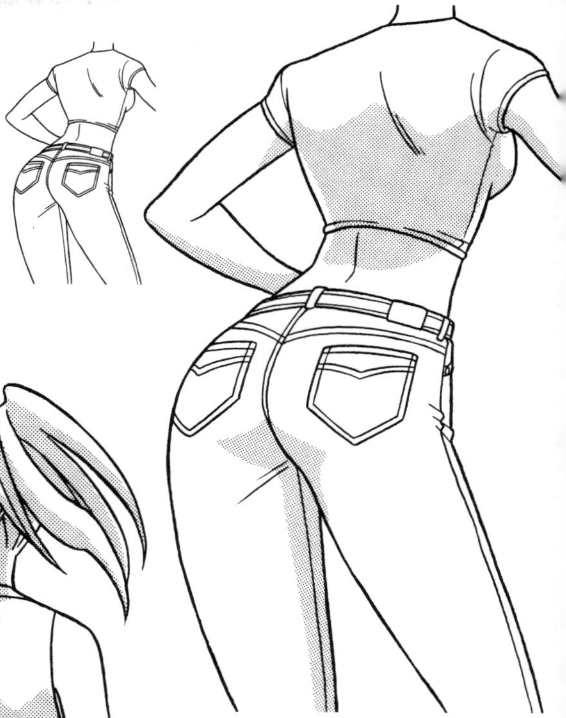

Use these shadows to accentuate a posterior clad in tight jeans.

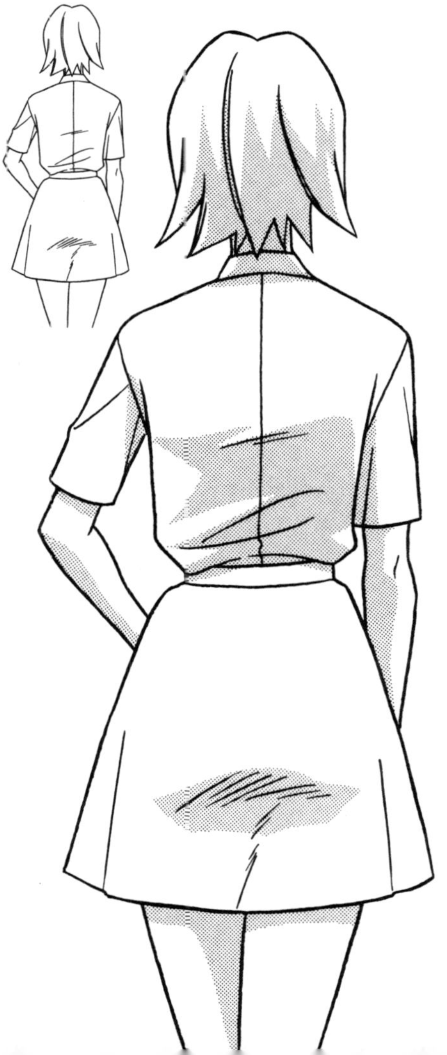

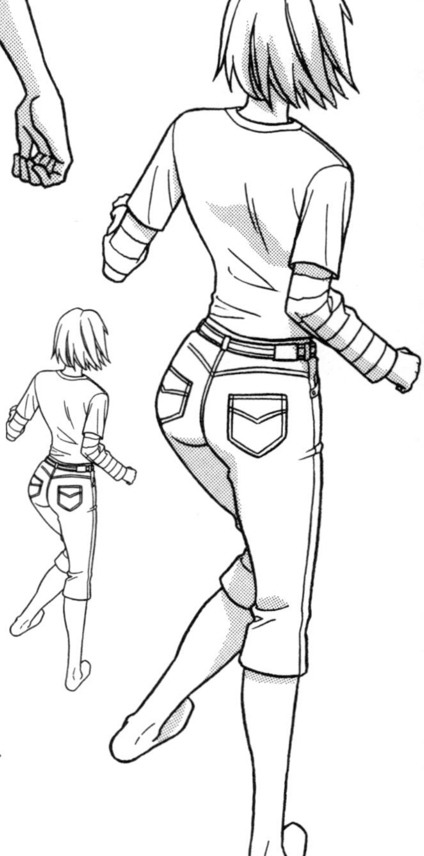

Guideline for positioning shadows on the backside.

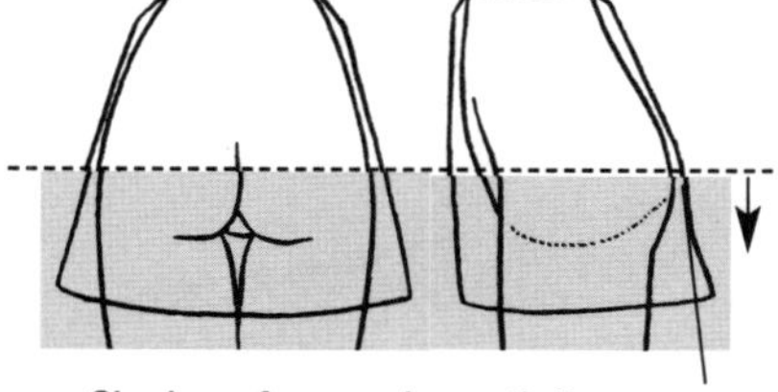

Shadows form underneath the areas that project outward the most.

Shadows at the Feet

These shadows are primarily added to shots of characters ranging from medium full figure to long shots.

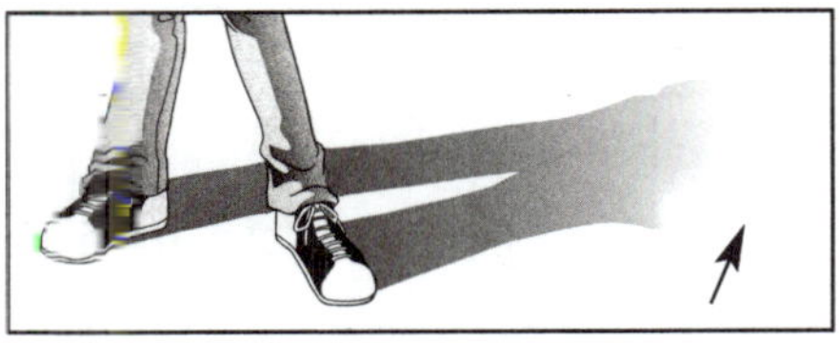

Use gradation tone. Feel free to blur the edge of the "shadow."

Shadows at the Feet (Puddle Shadows)

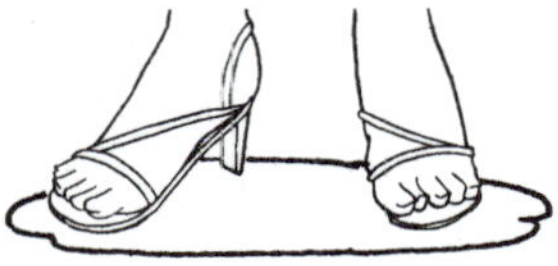

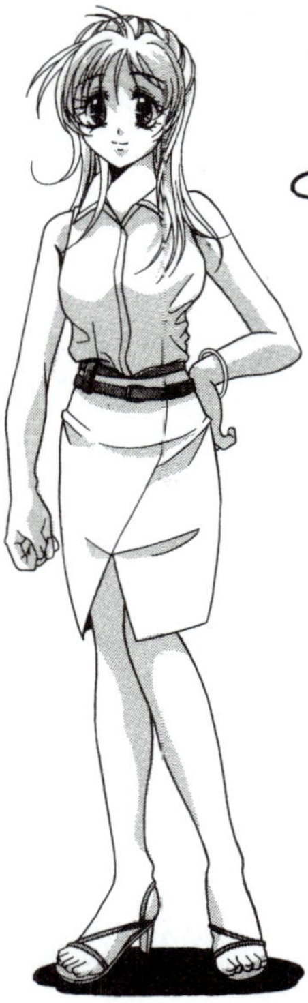

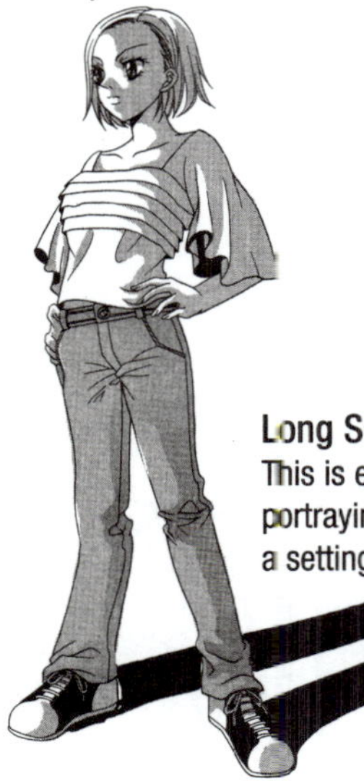

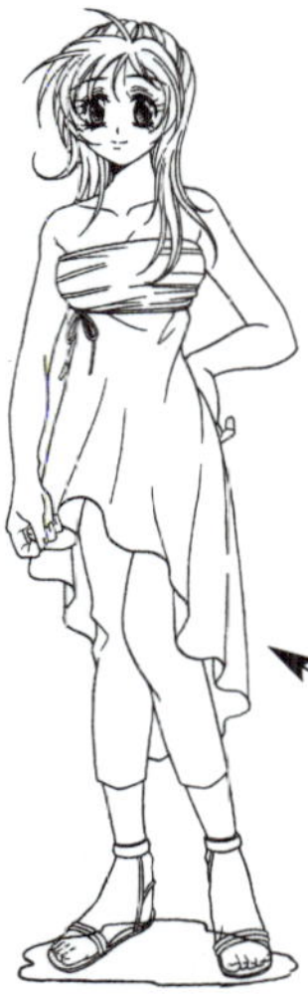

Although the character's skirt is rippled, the shadow at her feet remains simple.

Not good

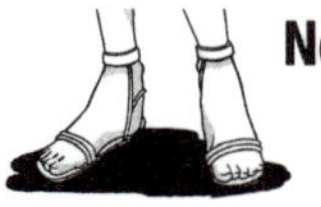

Long Shadows
This is effective for portraying scenes with a setting sun.

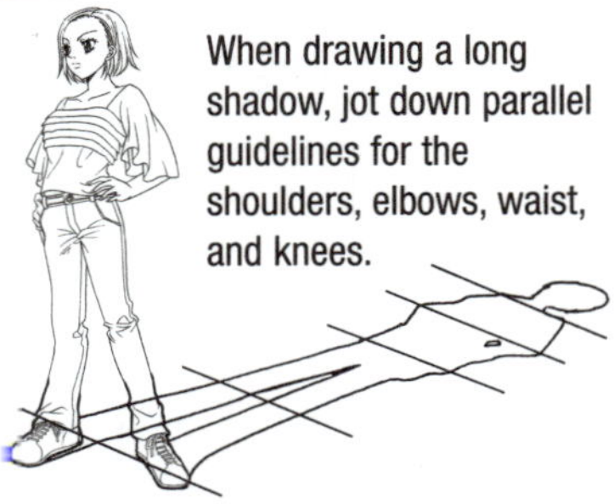

When drawing a long shadow, jot down parallel guidelines for the shoulders, elbows, waist, and knees.

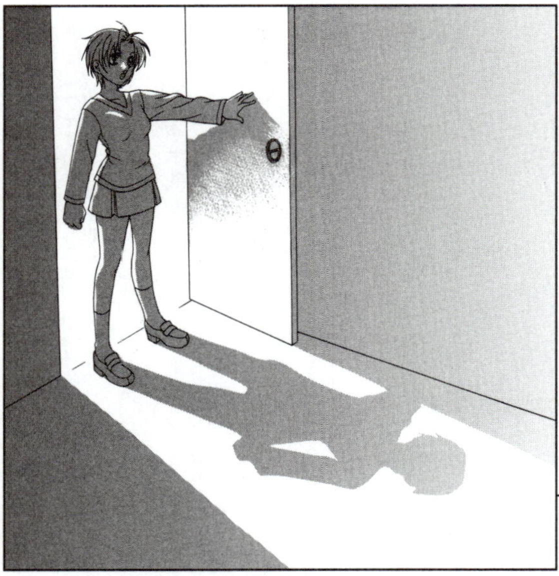

Silhouette Shadows Created by Backlighting
Solid black in lieu of tone makes for a more dramatic portrayal.

Intersecting Shadows
Here we have light shining from multiple directions.

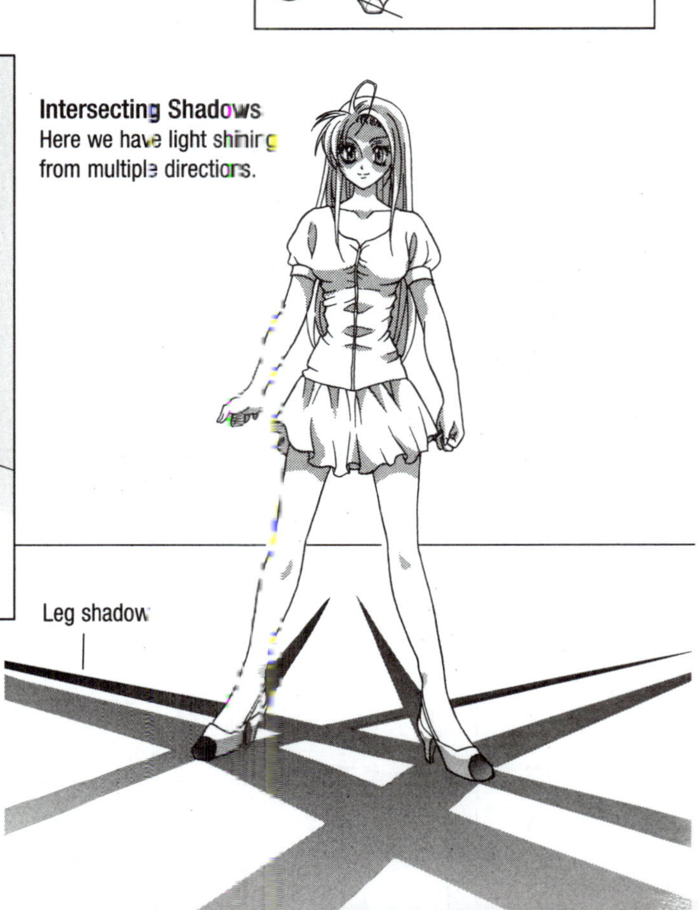

Shadows at the feet are normally omitted from *manga* artwork. However, they are included in long shots or when seeking to create a striking effect.

Assorted Puddle Shadows

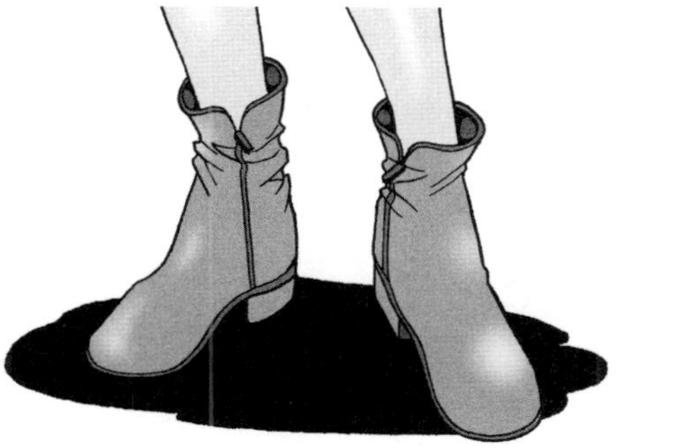

Solid black

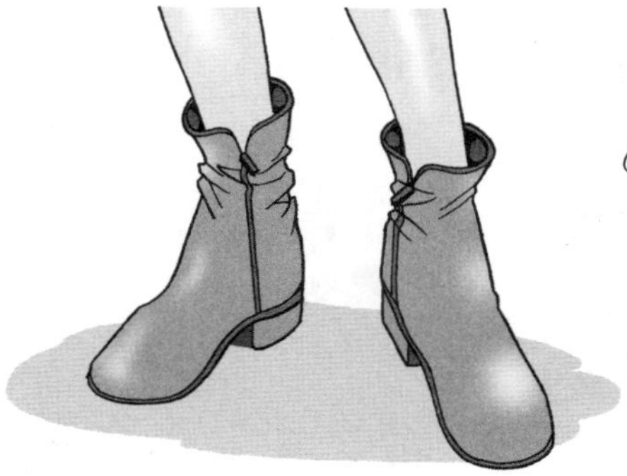

Tone

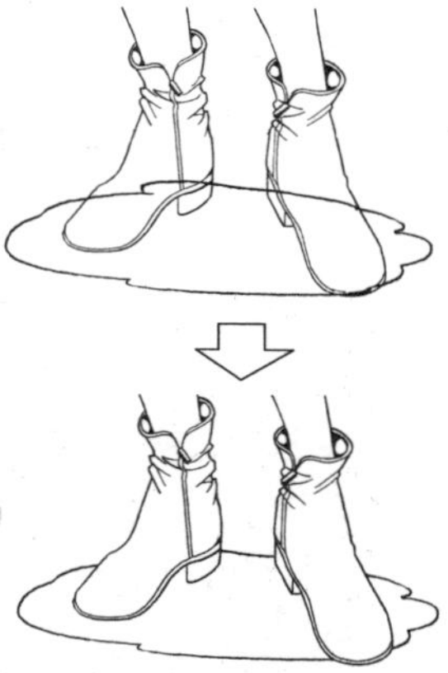

Use an elliptical form for shadows at the feet. Be sure to draw as well portions that will not be visible in the final composition.

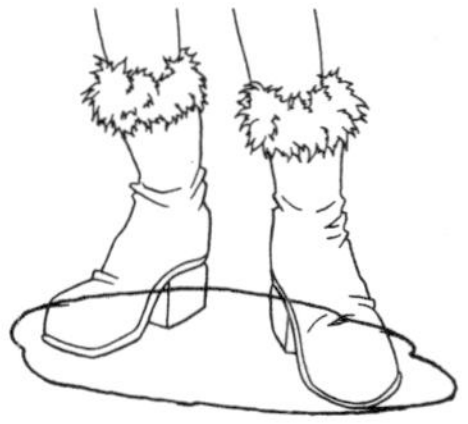

Not good

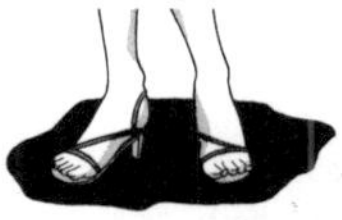

This shadow is too large and should have fewer ripples.

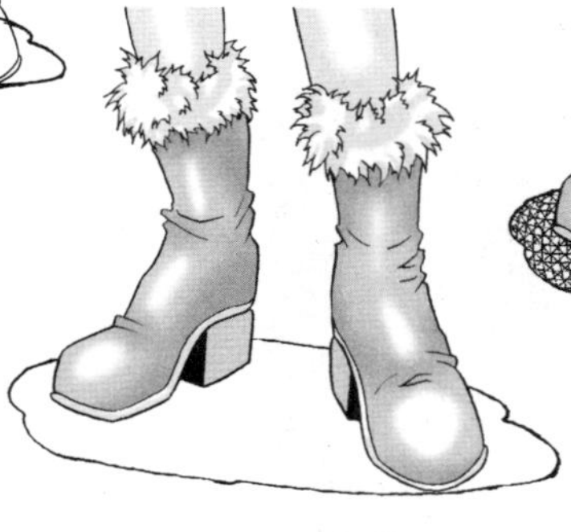

Outline

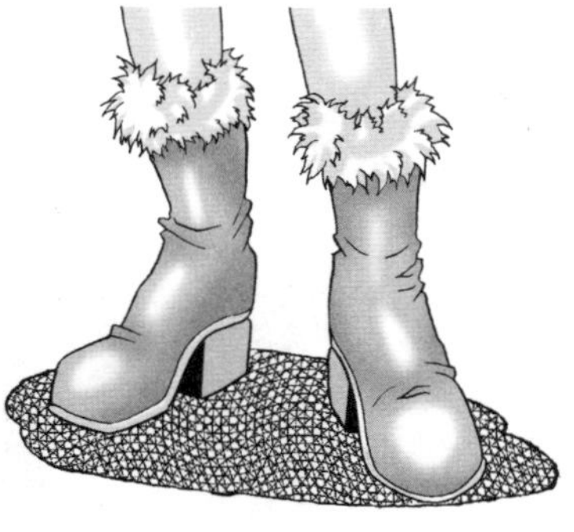

Crosshatched

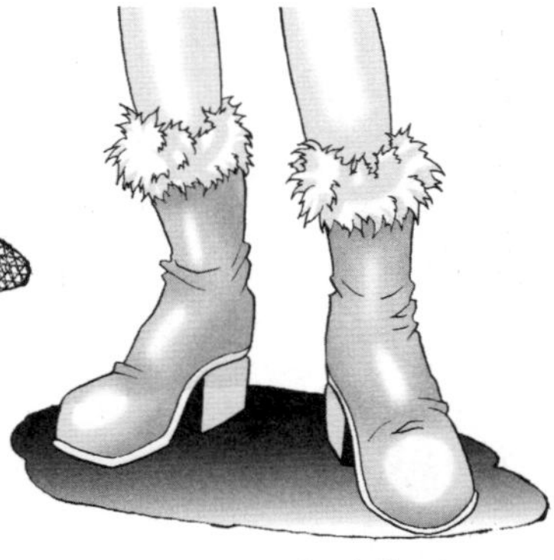

Gradation tone

Reflections

Use shadow-style executions to portray the luster of a floor.

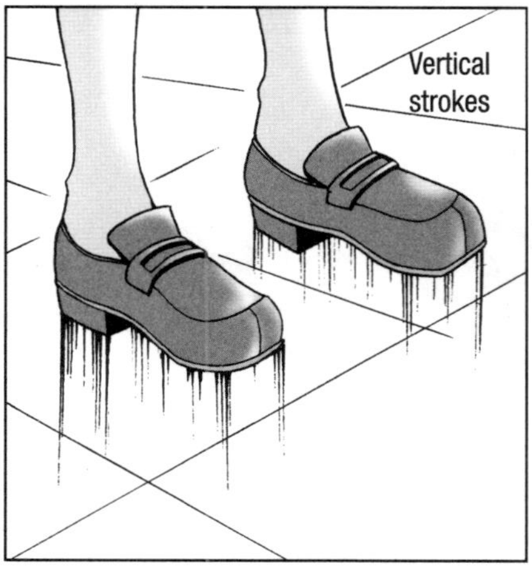

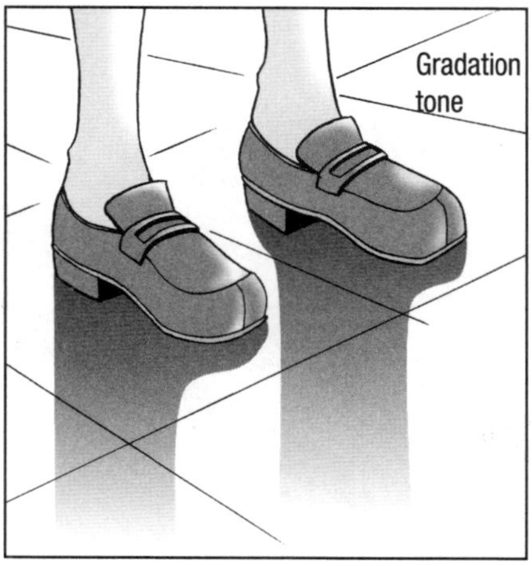

Diagonal hatching

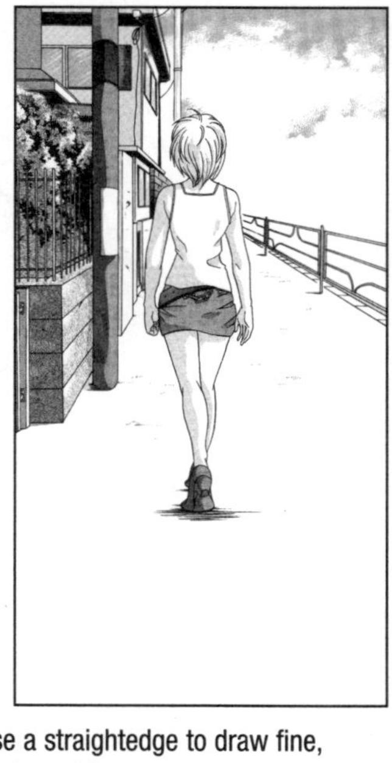

Special Effects

Here, speed lines are used to portray shadows.

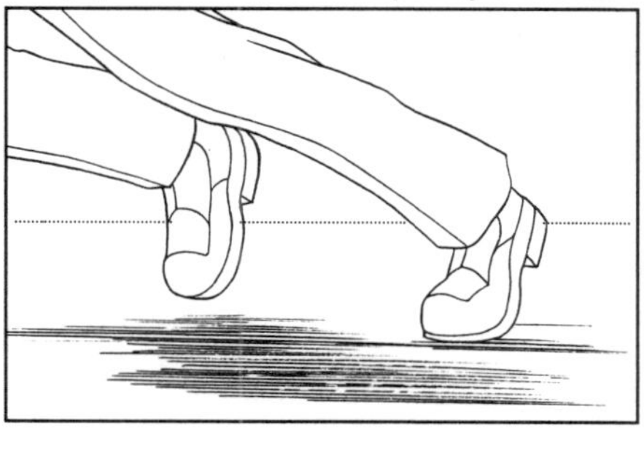

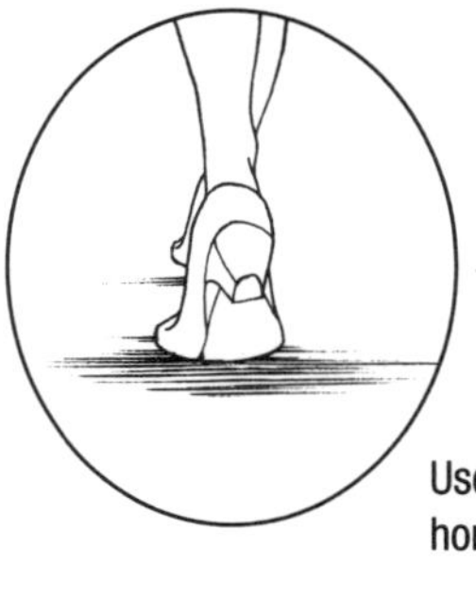

Use a straightedge to draw fine, horizontal lines.

Creating a Composition without Using Tone: Sample Compositions in Pen

Tone used to portray colors and shading by contrasting dark and light shades originate from diagonal hatching created using pen.

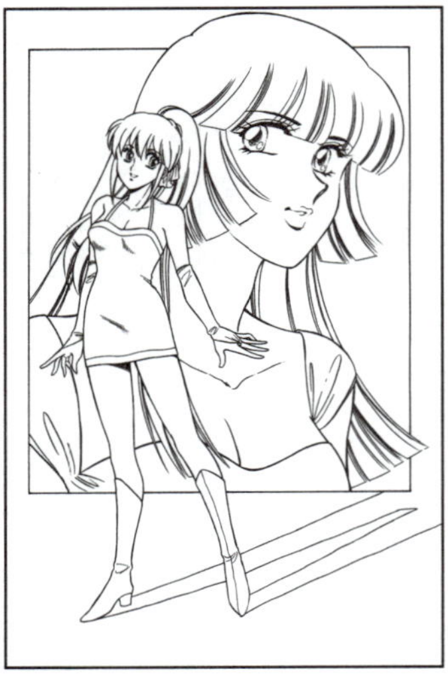

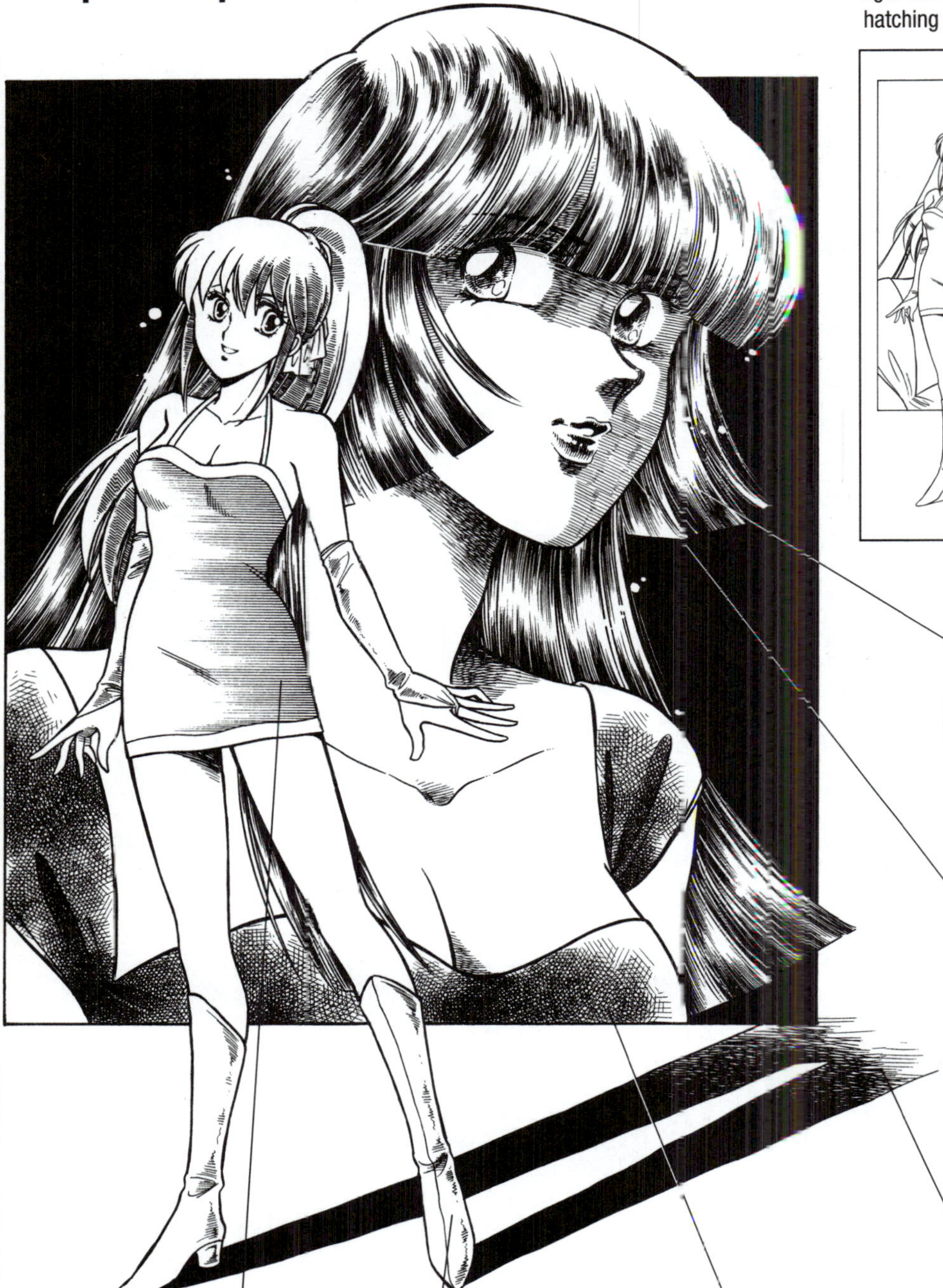

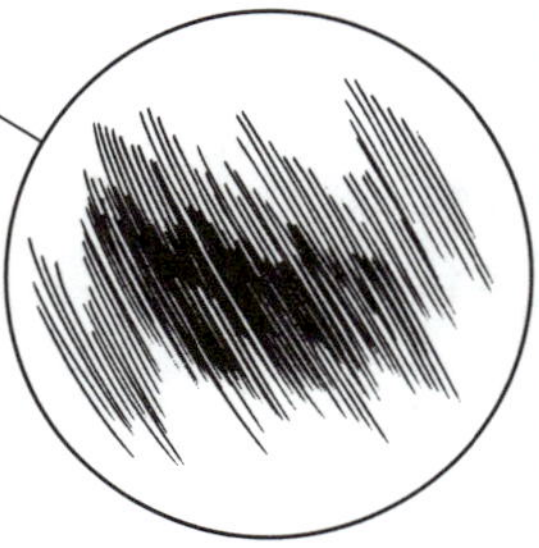

Hair

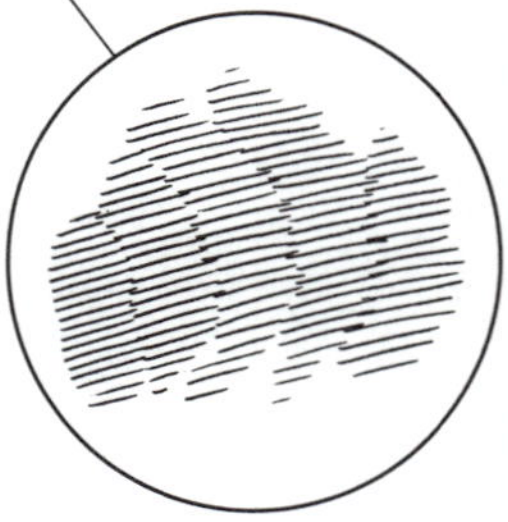

Facial shadows

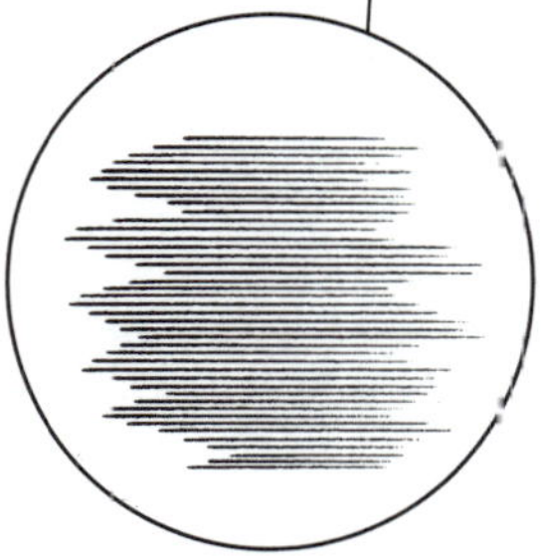

Tapered lines drawn using a straightedge

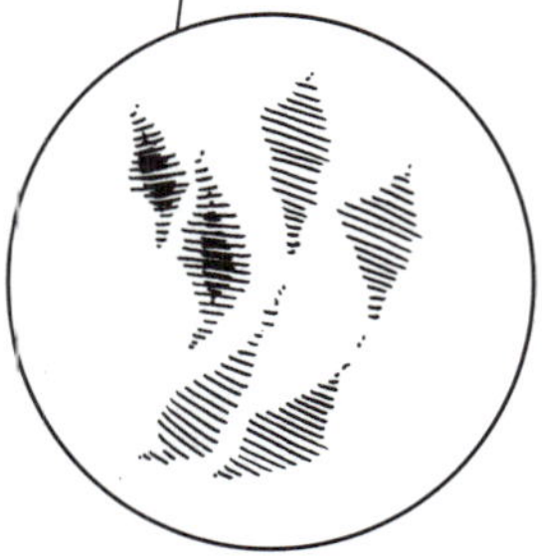

Hatching portraying the color and texture of hair or boots

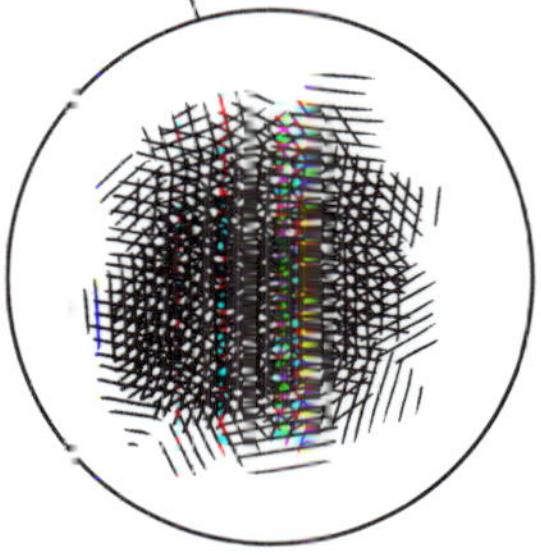

Crosshatching is often used to portray the texture of clothing or blackness. Here it is used for clothing.

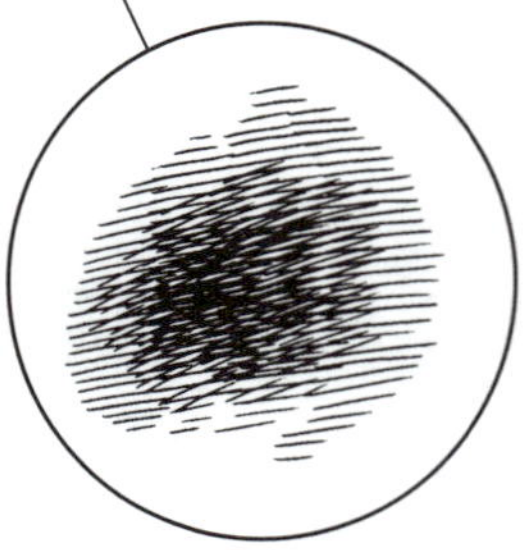

This hatching used under the chin and on the floor creates a gradation effect.

Chapter 3

Movement with a Sense of Presence

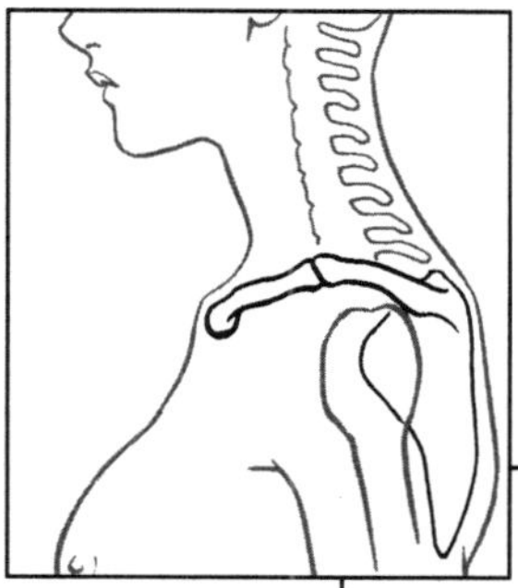

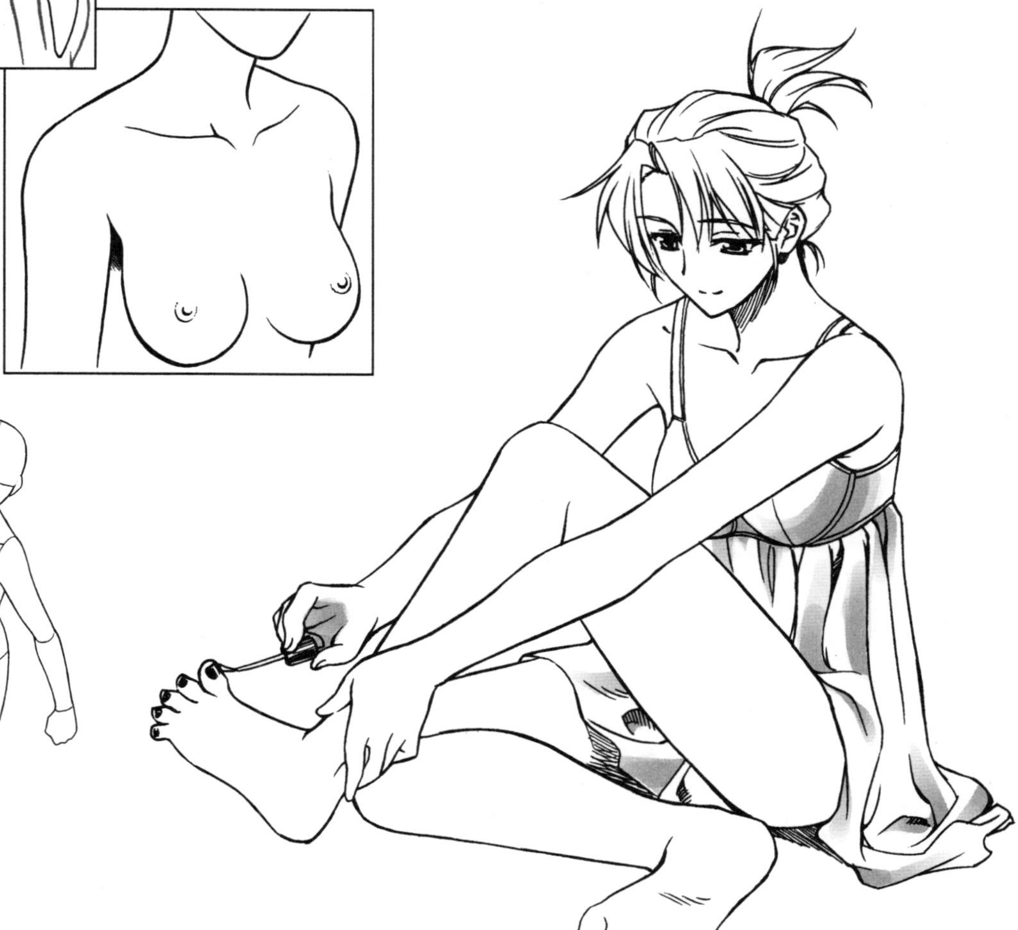

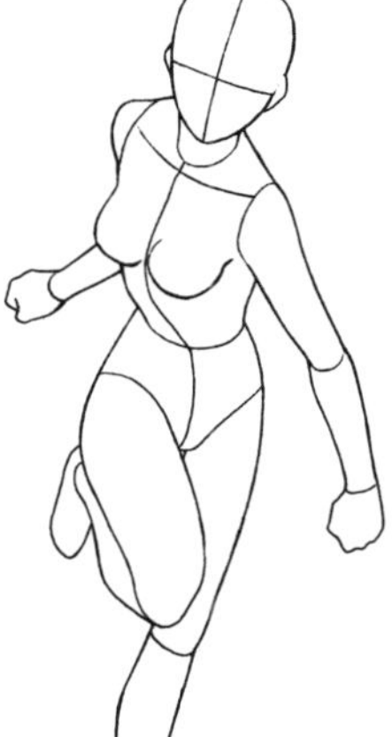

The Key Points to Portraying Natural Movement Lie in the Shoulders

Shoulder Basics

Normally, when a figure is portrayed standing straight, a line connecting the right and left shoulders (shoulder line) is horizontal.

Good

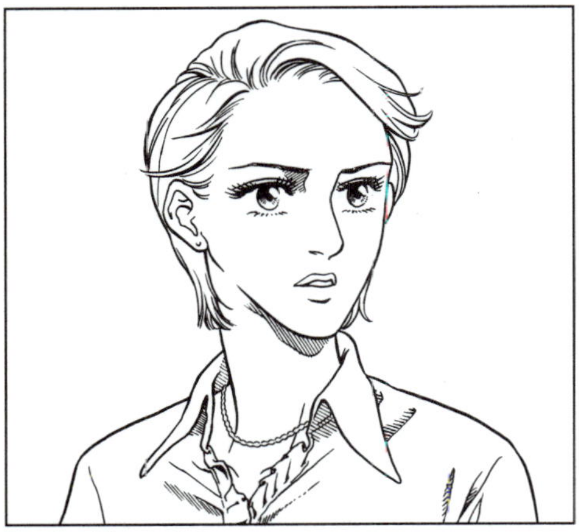

A natural bust shot

Not good

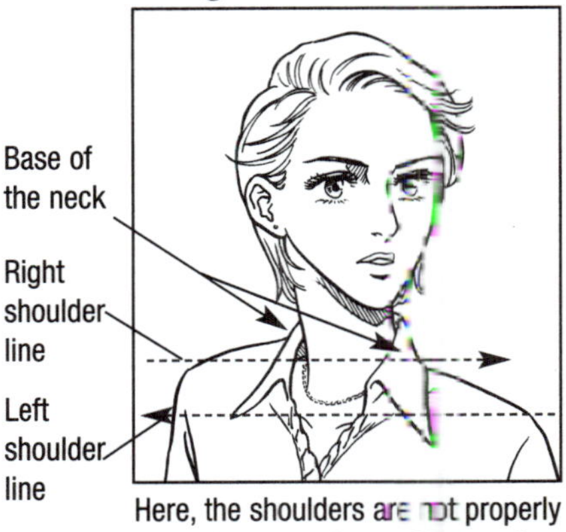

Here, the shoulders are not properly aligned, and the base of the neck (marking the top of the shoulder line) is also tilted.

Not good

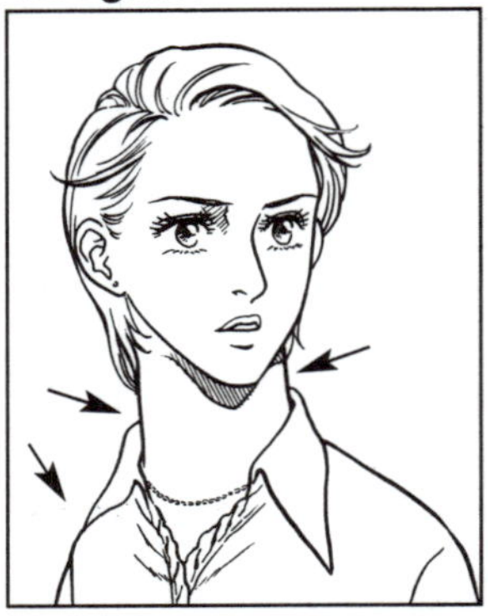

Here, the neck broadens at the base, and the right shoulder is missing.

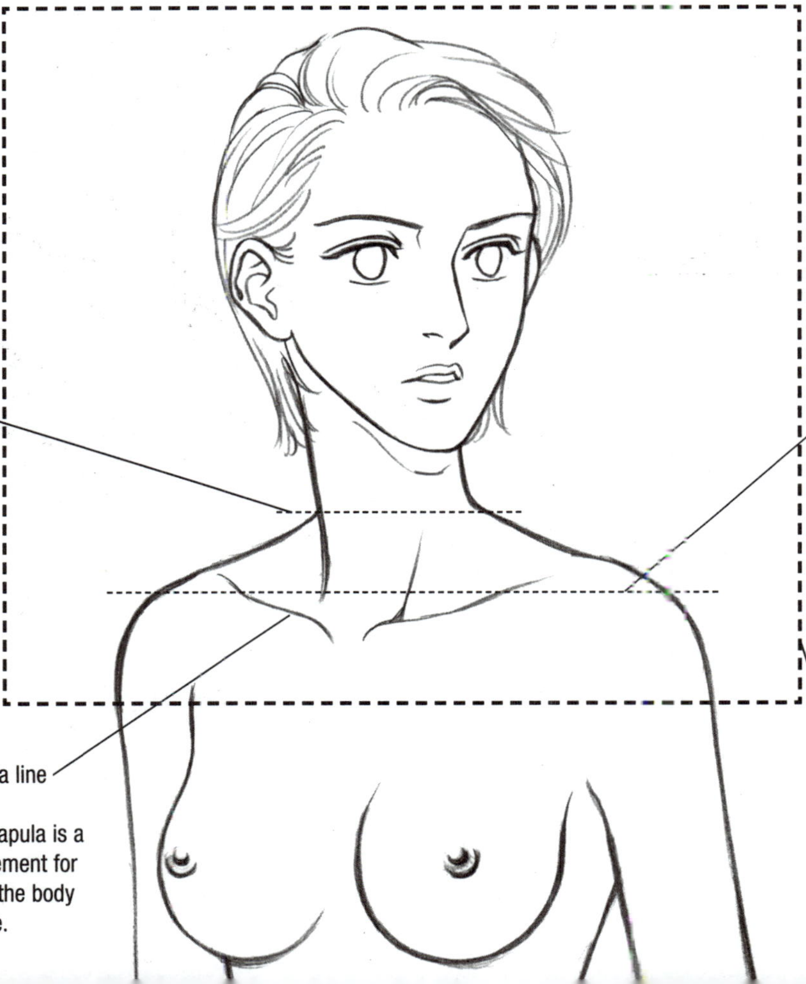

Line connecting the right and left sides of the base of the neck

Horizontal shoulder line

Scapula line

The scapula is a key element for giving the body volume.

Here we see guide framing for a bust shot. A bust refers to a portrait from chest up; however, in Japanese *manga*, a bust shot usually means a portrait that starts somewhere above the chest. The shoulders should be visible.

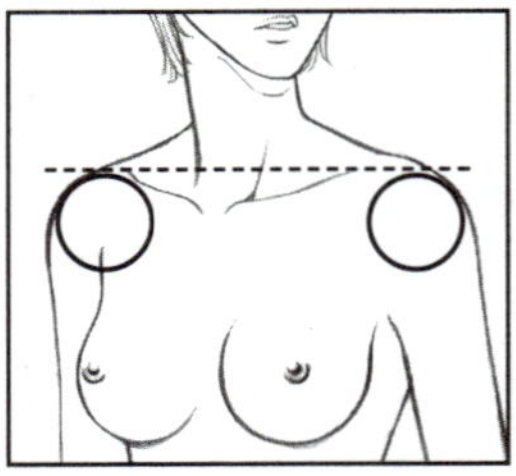

The shoulder line is a line drawn from the top of each shoulder, connecting the two.

Moving the arms up and down causes the shoulder line and the chest line to shift.

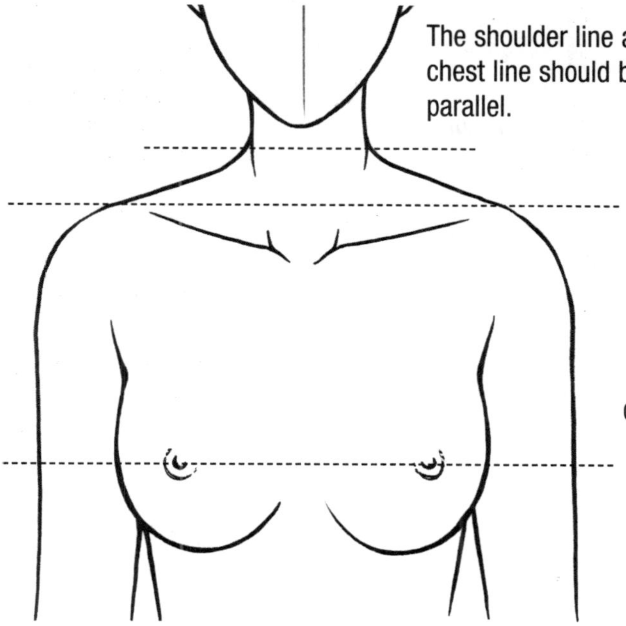

The shoulder line and chest line should be parallel.

Shoulder line

Chest line

Not good

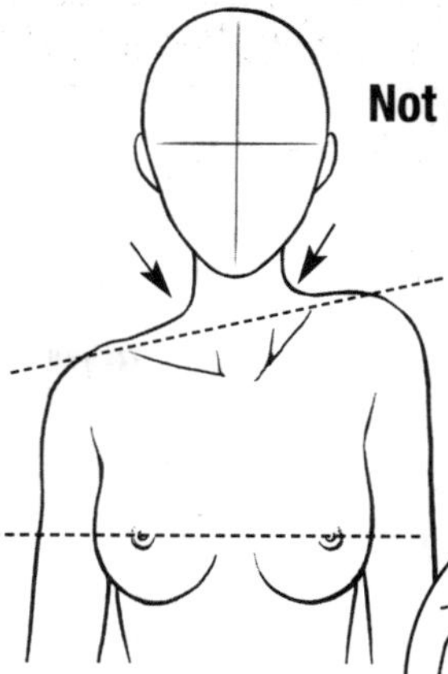

Good

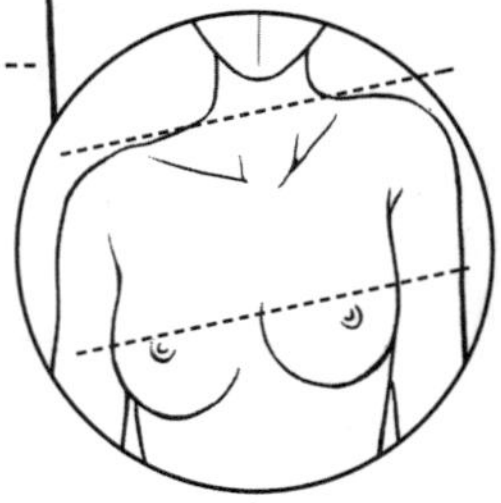

While the shoulders may be skewed in this manner, the chest line should be similarly angled.

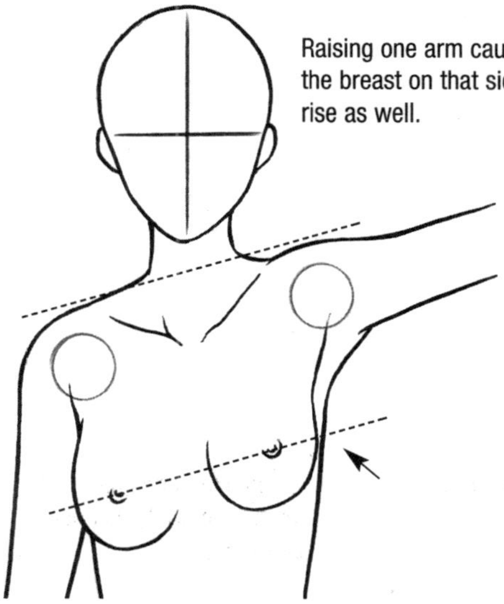

Raising one arm causes the breast on that side to rise as well.

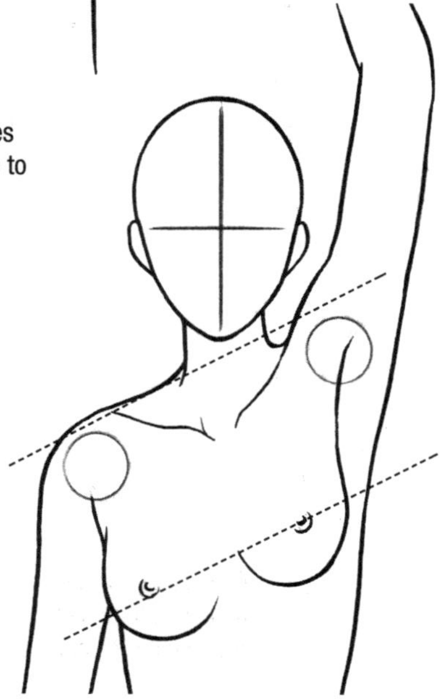

Not good

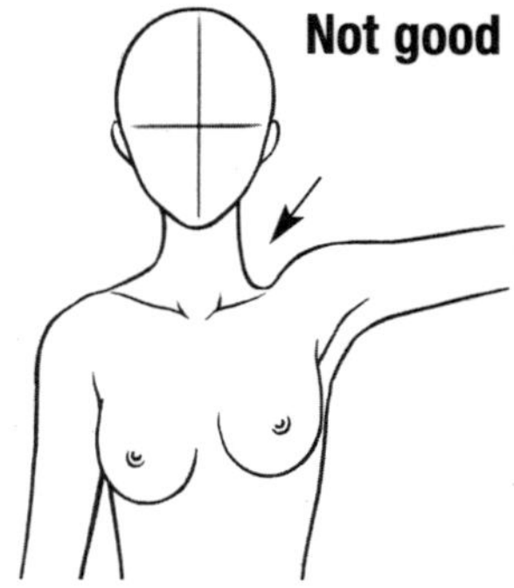

Here, the angle of the chest line is natural for when an arm is raised, but the shoulder line is not.

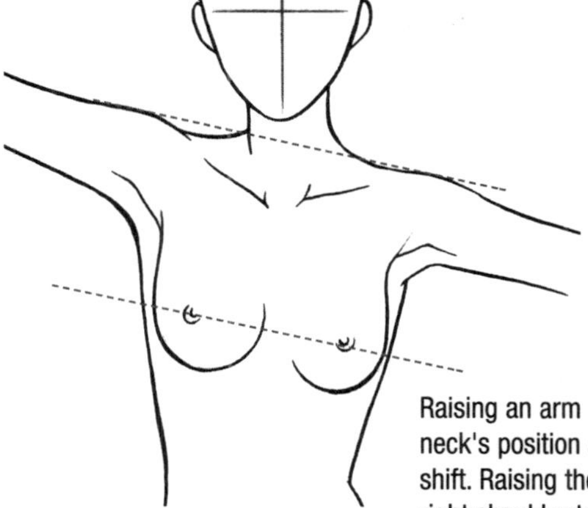

Not good

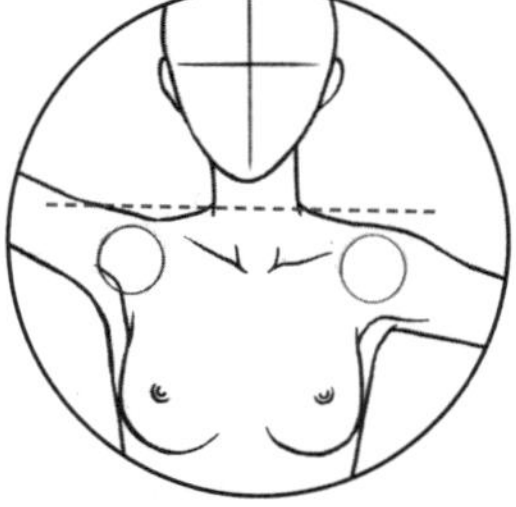

Bad example:
Here, the two shoulders are even.

Raising an arm causes the base of the neck's position and the shoulder line to shift. Raising the right arm causes the right shoulder to rise. The shoulder of the lowered arm is likewise low.

The neck on the side of the raised arm becomes compacted.

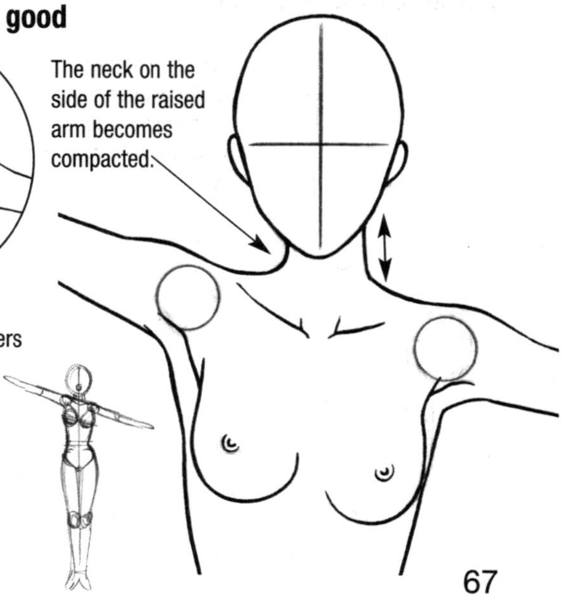

Juncture of the Shoulders and Neck (Shoulder Levels)

This figure was drawn at a moderately high angle. From a 3/4 view, the shoulders appear askew.

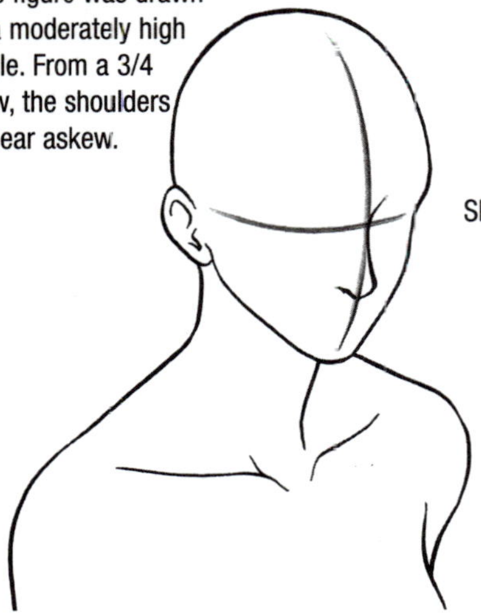

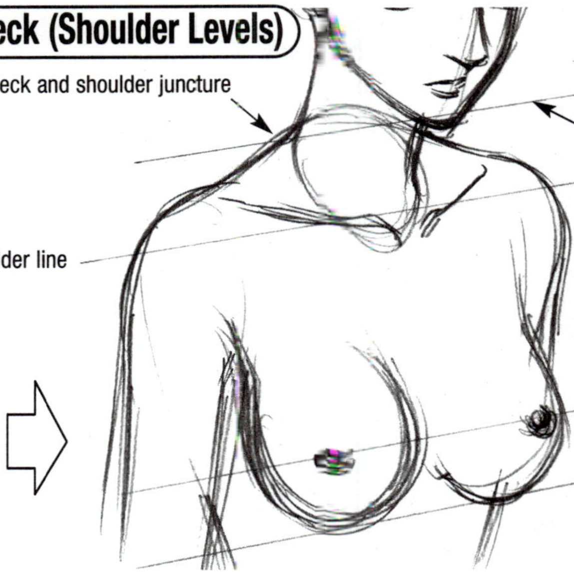

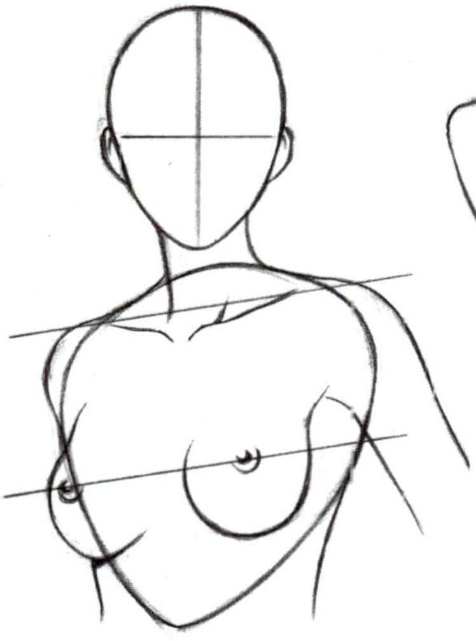

Here we see a leaning pose. The shoulder and chest lines are parallel.

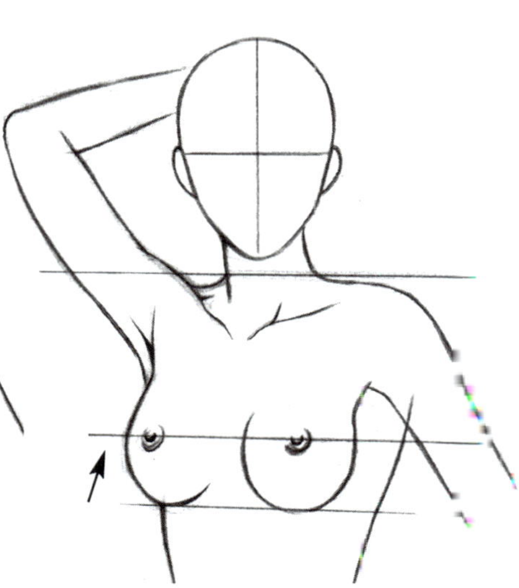

Raising an arm causes the chest on that side to also rise, eliminating the angled feel.

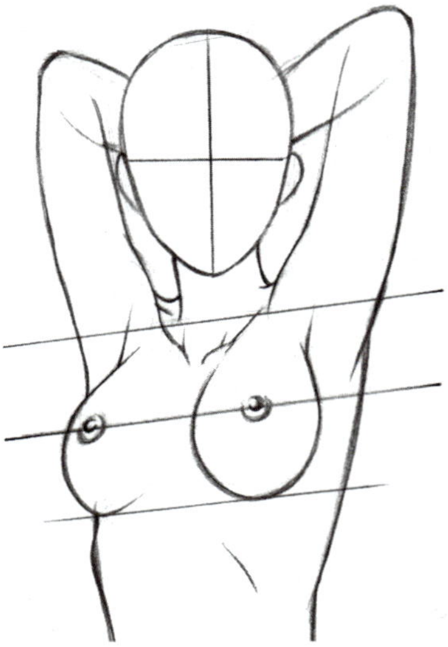

Raising both arms causes the figure to return to its original angled pose.

Successful Drawing Tips

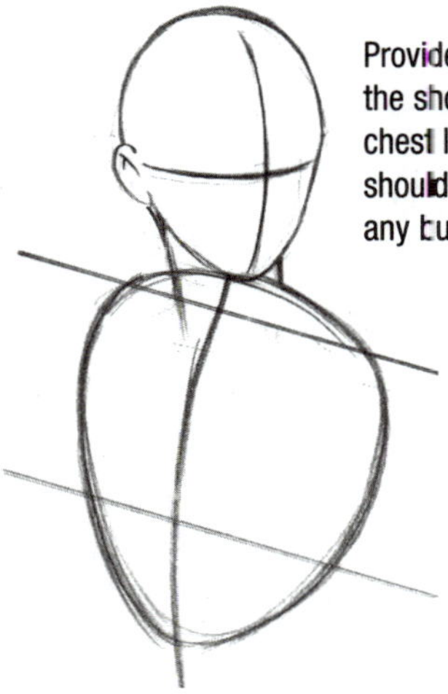

Provided that you keep the shoulder line and chest line parallel, you should be able to draw any bust shot.

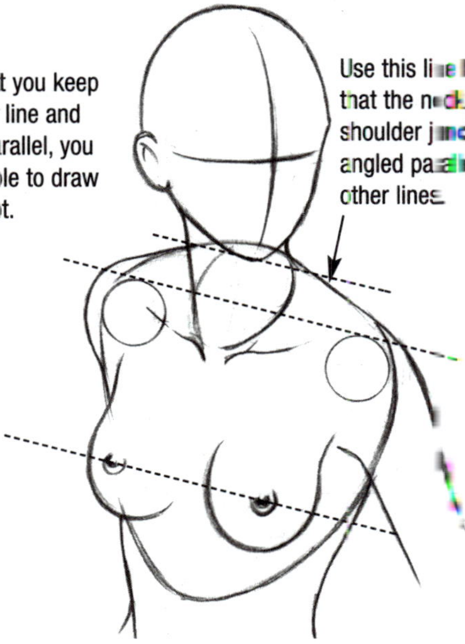

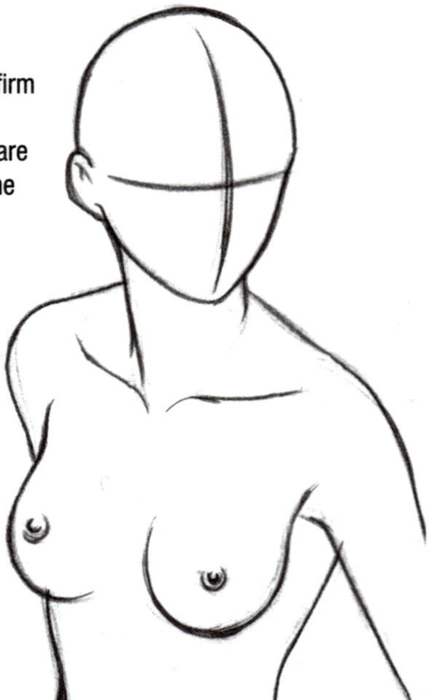

Correcting Mistakes

Here, the right shoulder and breast seem to be in profile.

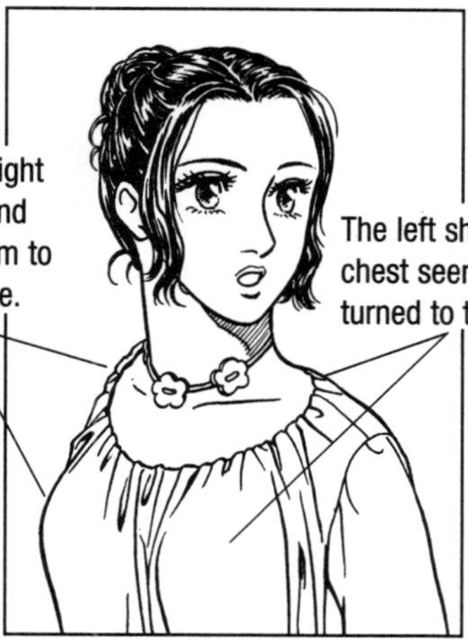

The left shoulder and chest seem to be turned to the right.

- The neck is too thick
- The right shoulder is ambiguous
- The torso seems to part in profile and part in 3/4 view.

Bring the neck contour in from the ear, closer to the face.

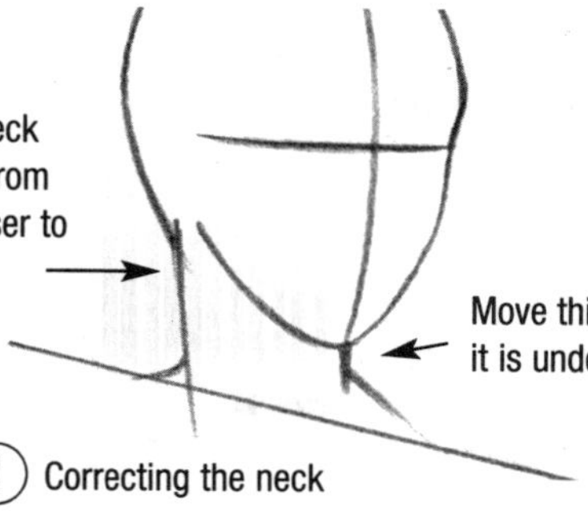

Move this contour so that it is underneath the chin.

Draw the shoulder line

① Correcting the neck

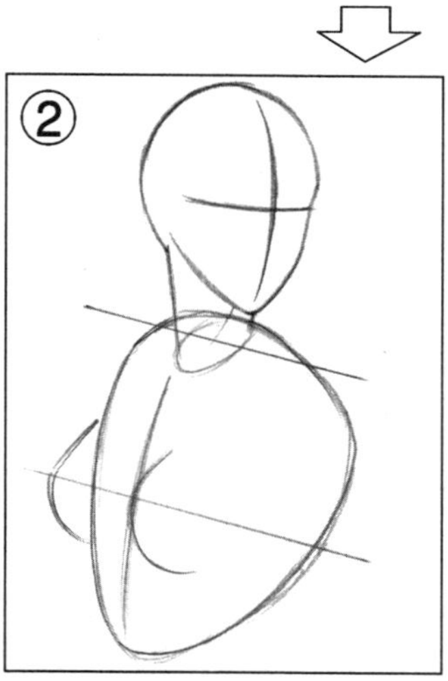

Torso in profile

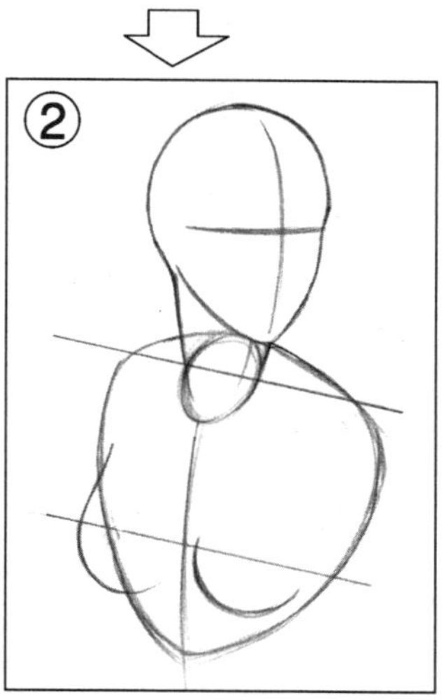

Torso in 3/4 view, facing to the right

When the torso is in 3/4 view, the shoulder should be partially visible.

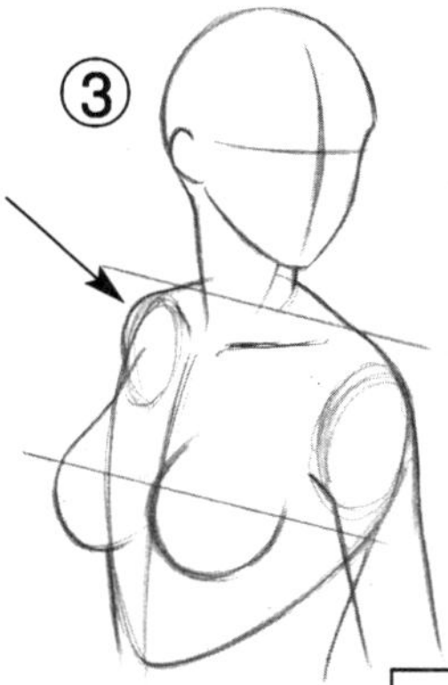

The shoulder is in clear view when the torso faces the right.

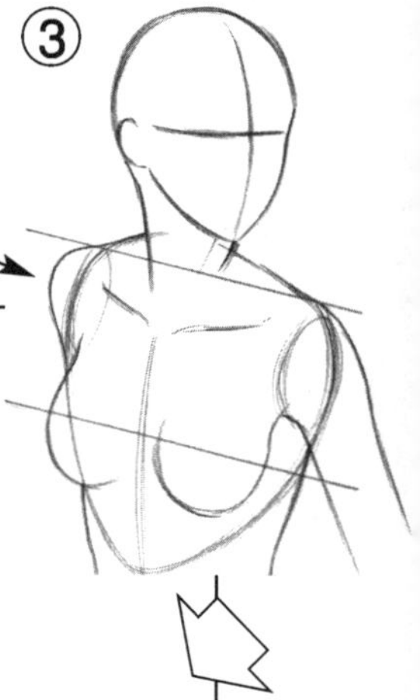

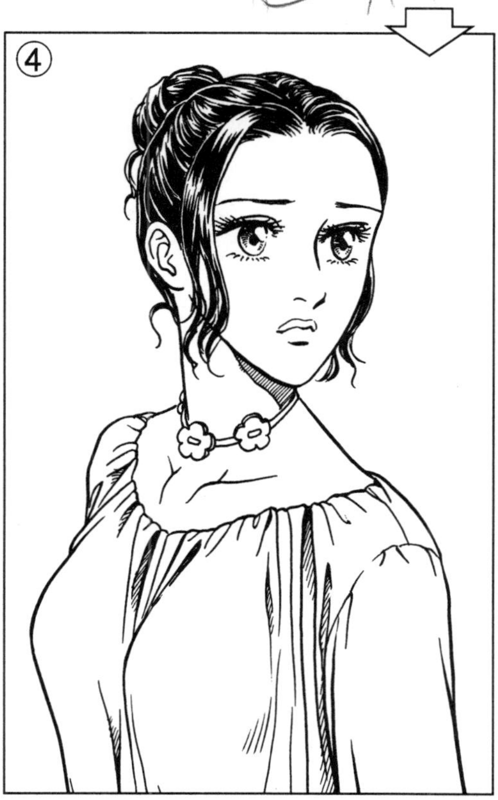

Final Drawing

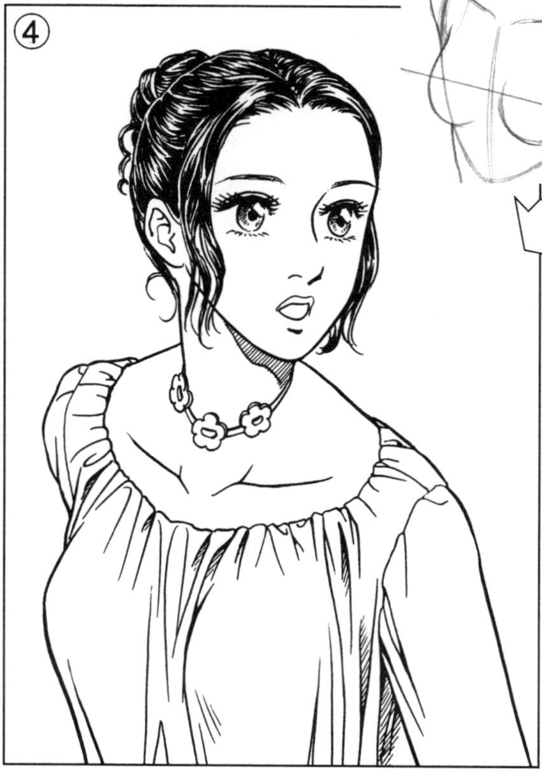

Final Drawing

The Bust Shot Drawing Process

Detailed Example of Using Knowledge of the Body's Structure to Draw

①

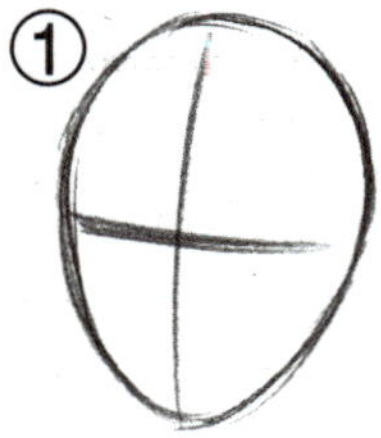

Draw the face
(Crossed lines indicate the direction the head faces).

②

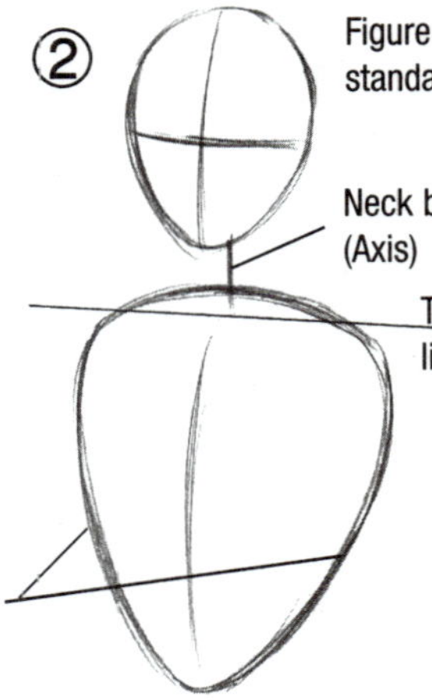

Sketch in the shoulder line and a layout of the torso.

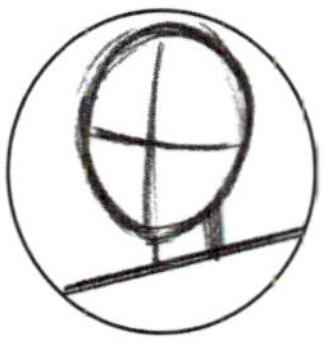

Raising the left arm causes the shoulder line to tilt.

③

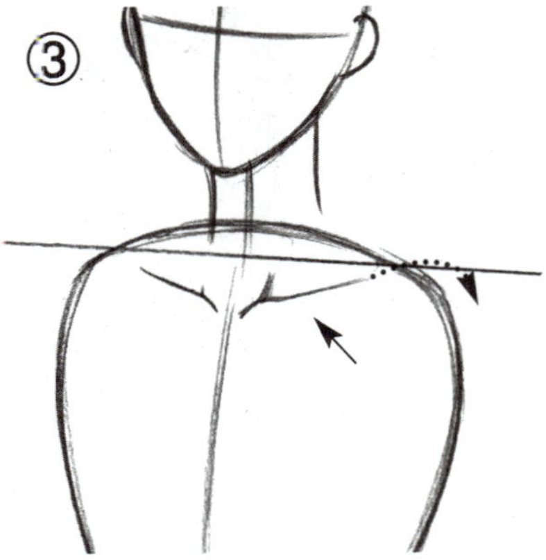

Identify how the clavicle flows into the shoulder and how they connect.

④

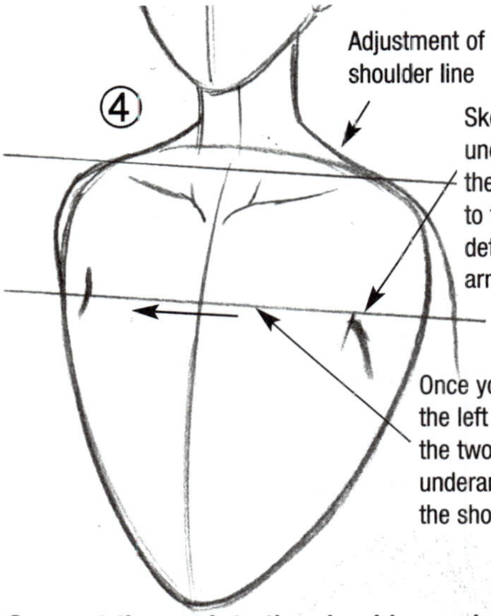

Connect the neck to the shoulders using smooth contours and position the underarms.

⑤ **Draw the chest and the arms.**

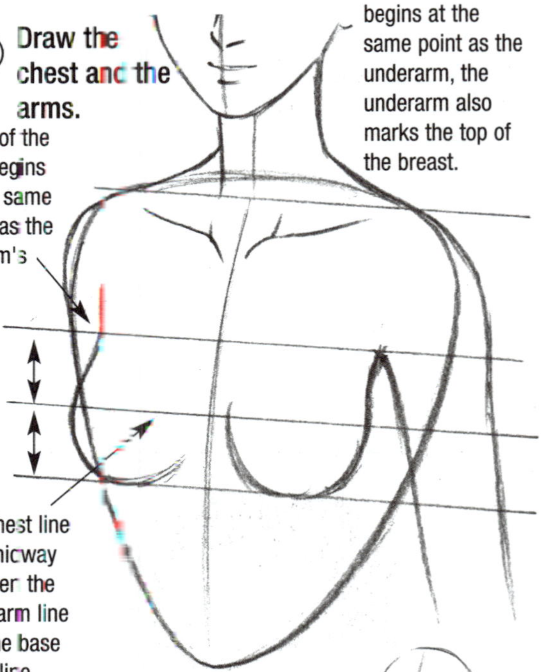

⑥ **Clean up the torso's contours using the chest as a guideline.**

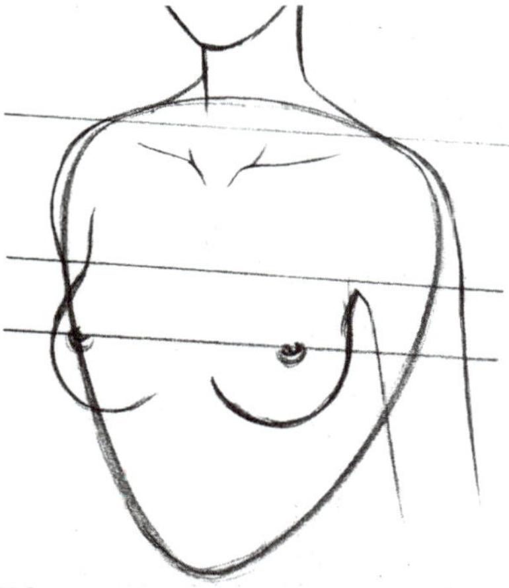

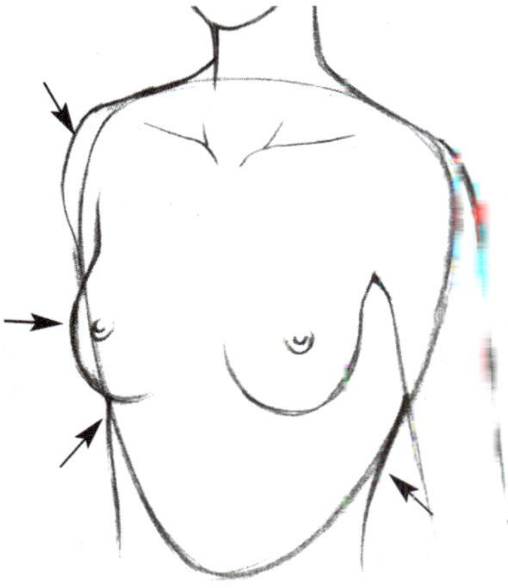

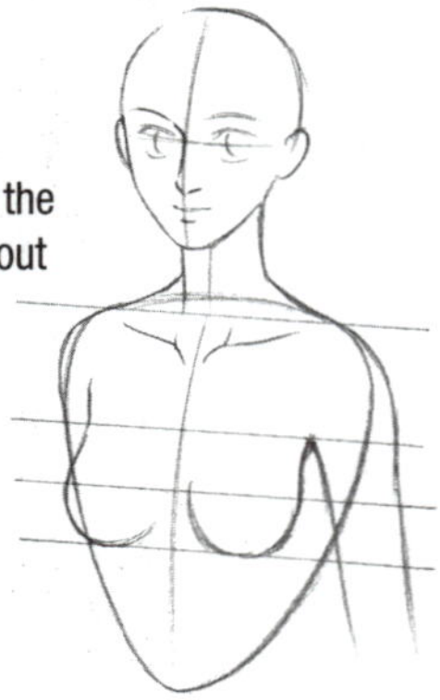

Adjust the shapes of the lower areas of the chest, the shoulders, and the breasts. Clean up the back's contours. Use layout guidelines to arrive at a line drawing of the torso.

⑦ Fill in the details.

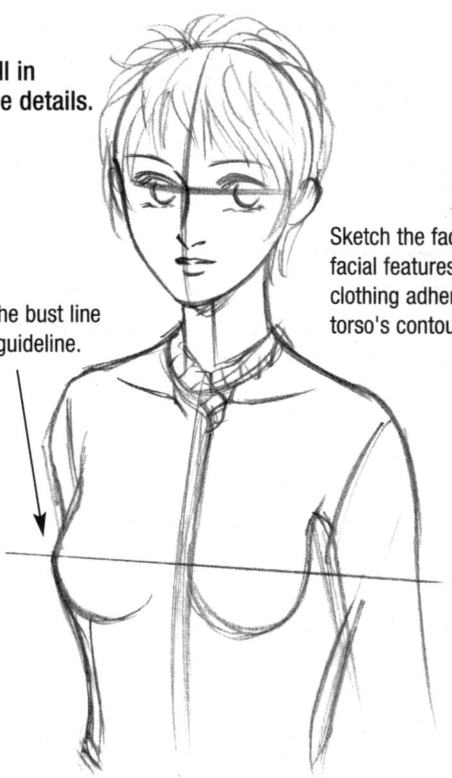

Use the bust line as a guideline.

Sketch the face, filling in the facial features and hair. Add clothing adhering to the torso's contour lines.

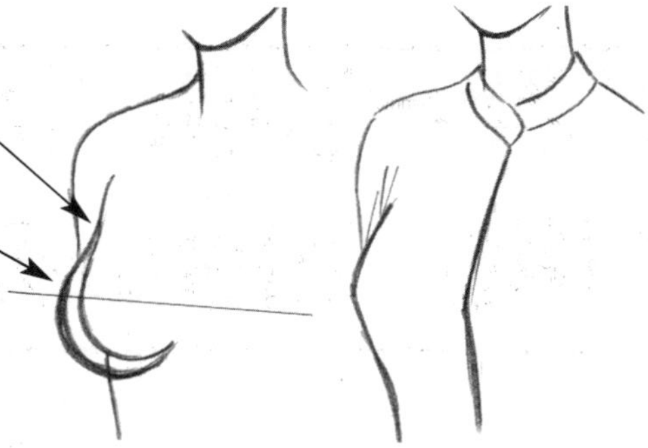

To accentuate the chest, leave the top of the chest at the same position, but shift the breast's peak upward.

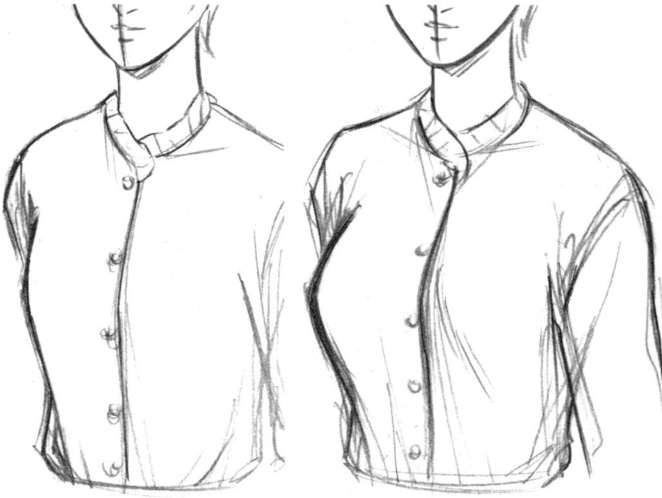

Modest build Voluptuous build

⑧ Final Drawing

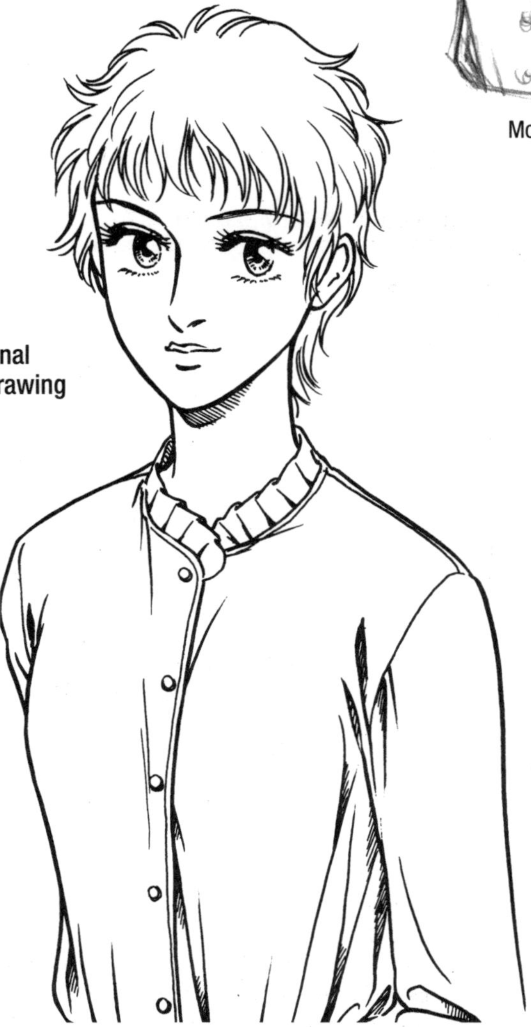

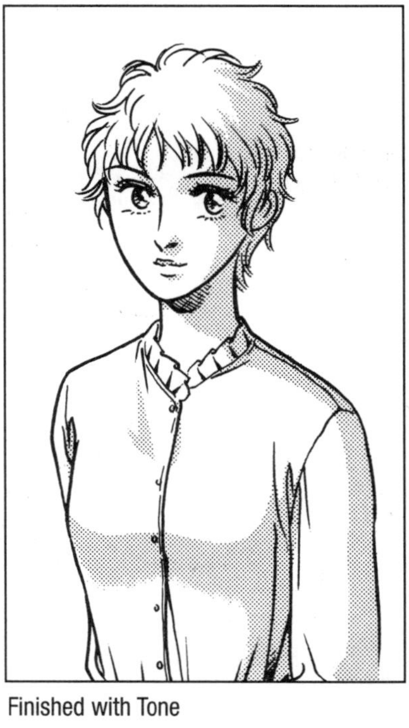

Finished with Tone

The Side Centerline Gives the Torso Volume

The side of a torso is long and narrow and is not visible from the front or back. Yet, the side constitutes a vital point when drawing most poses. The side also contains a "seam" connecting the front and the back. This seam is called the "Side centerline."

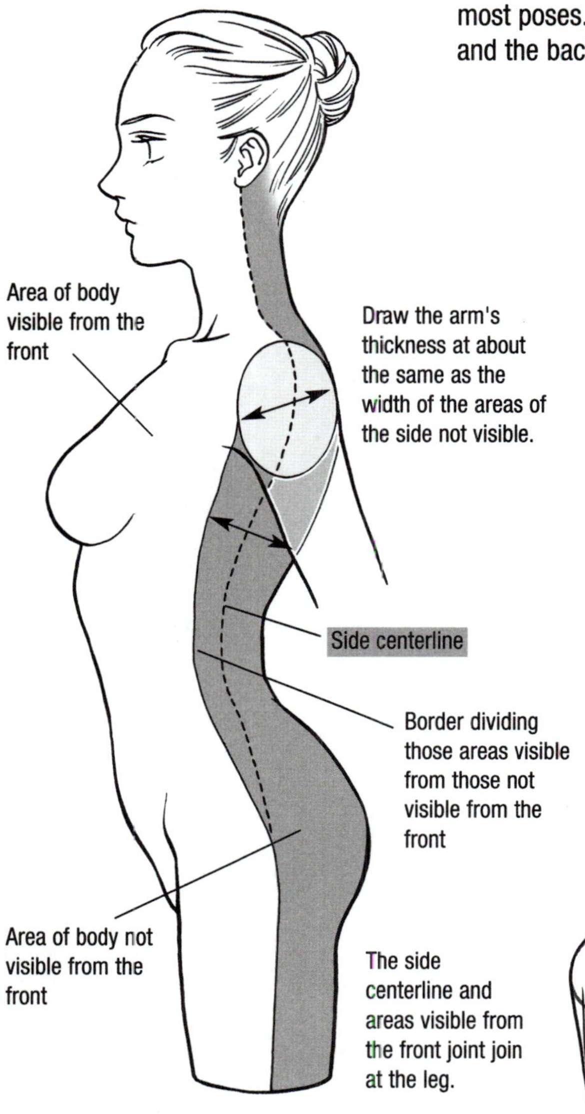

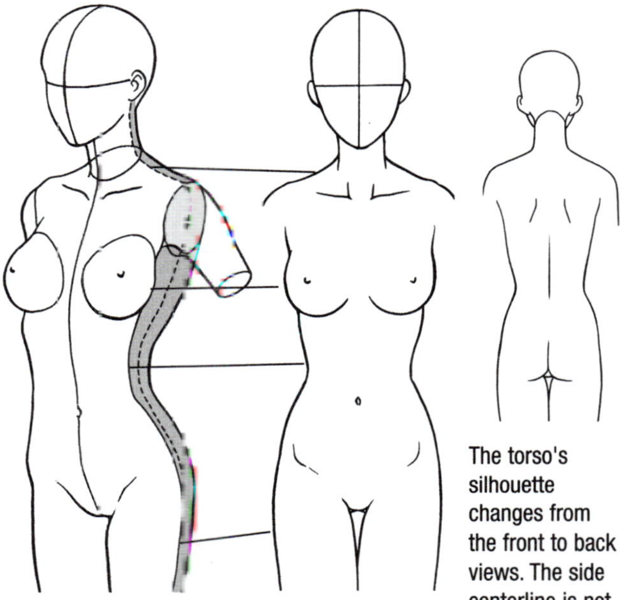

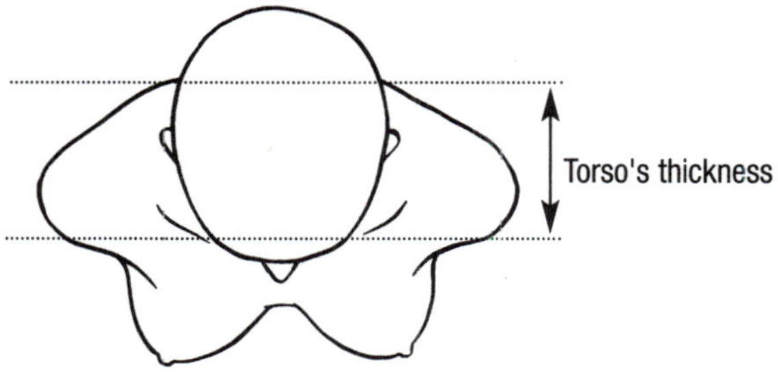

The side centerline appears as a "seam" in the majority of clothing

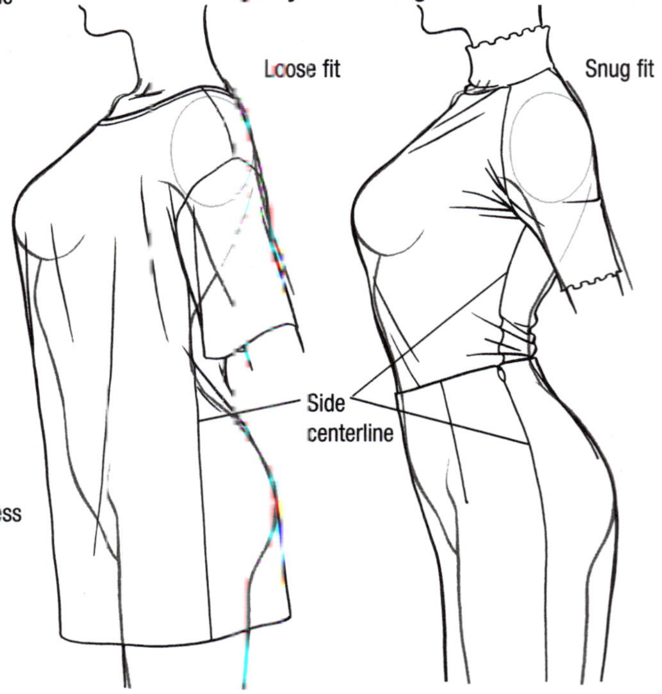

While in actuality, clothes do add a bit more girth to the torso all around, in *manga*, it is perfectly acceptable to use the same layout for the character's figure nude as for it clothed.

Slim Build

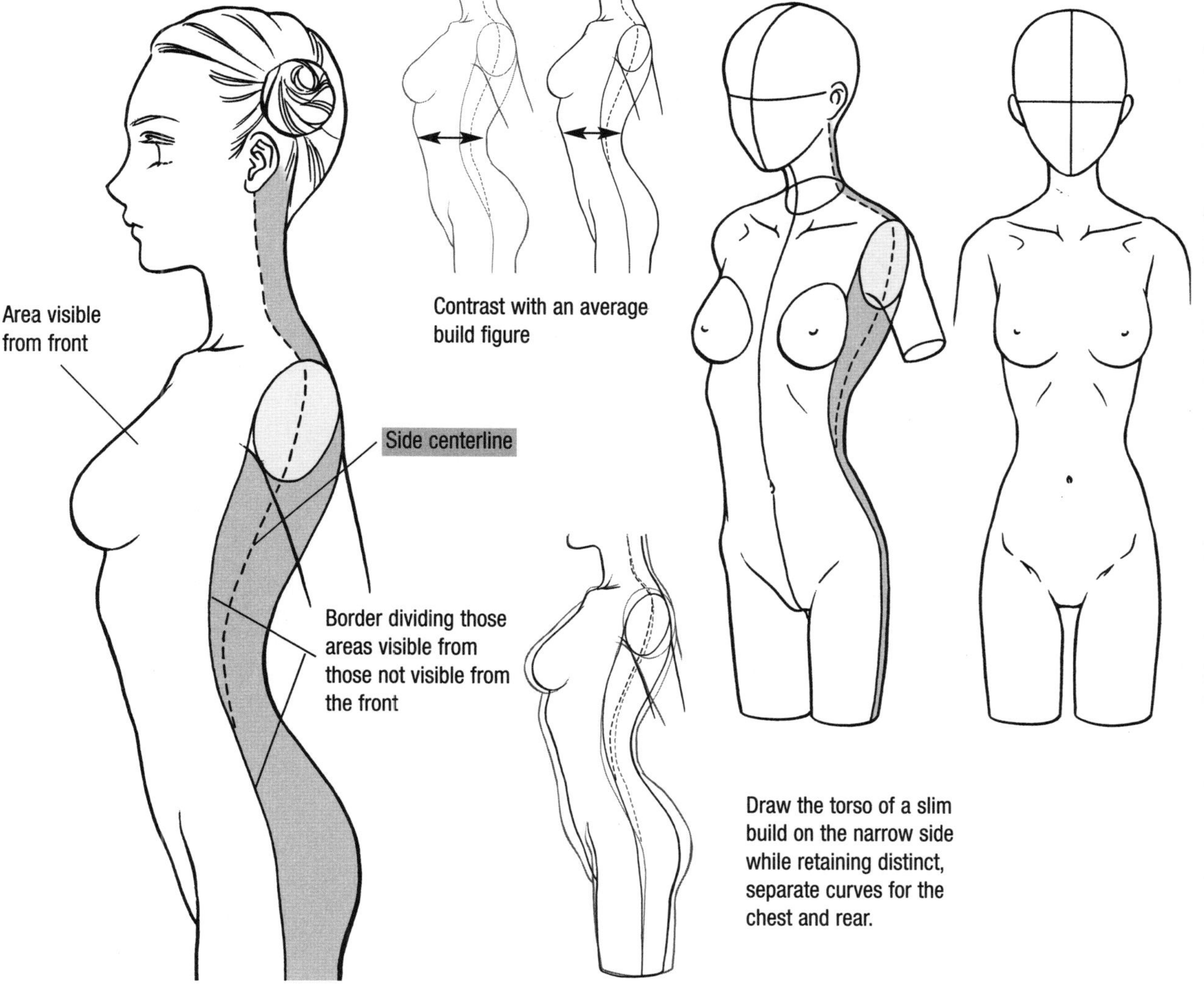

Male Characters

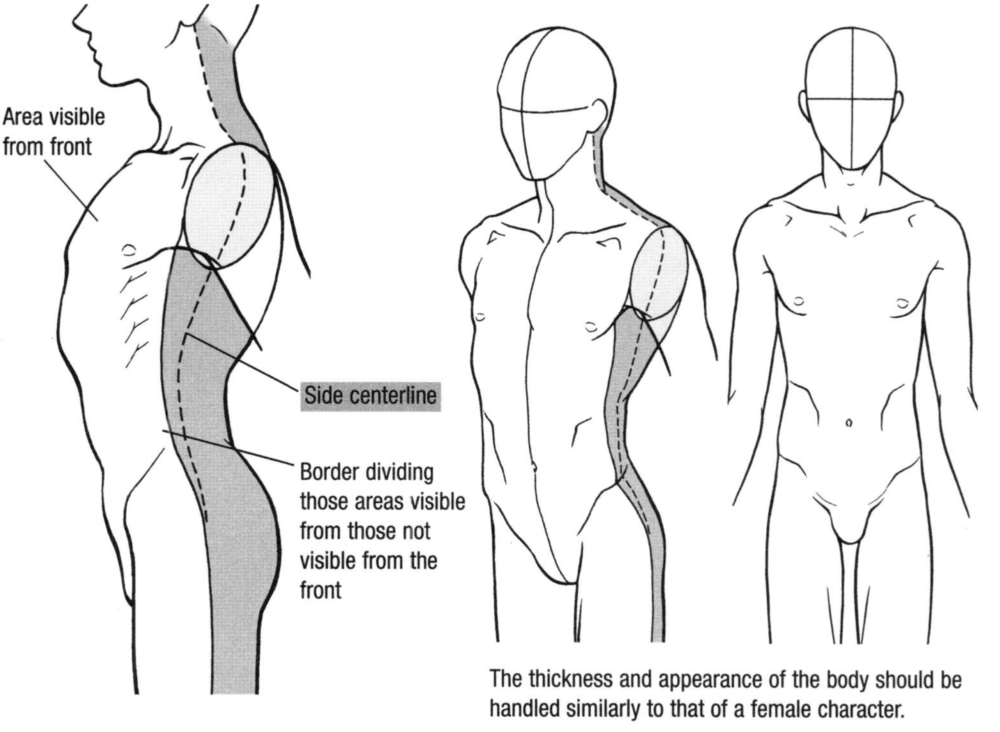

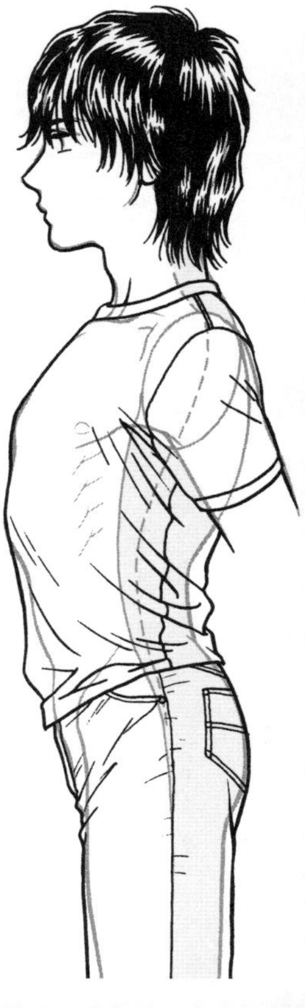

6 Lines Vital to Successful Drawing

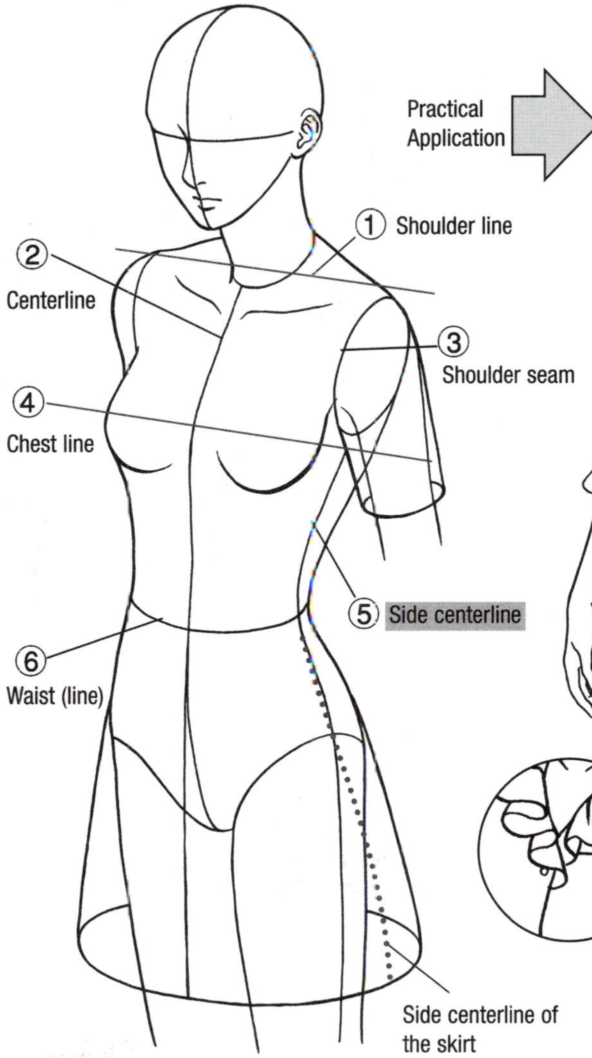

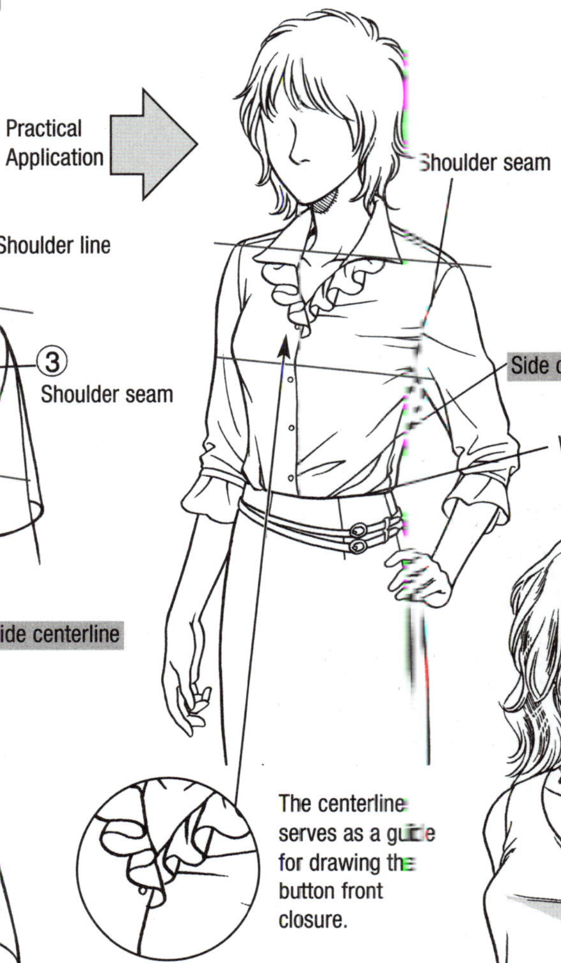

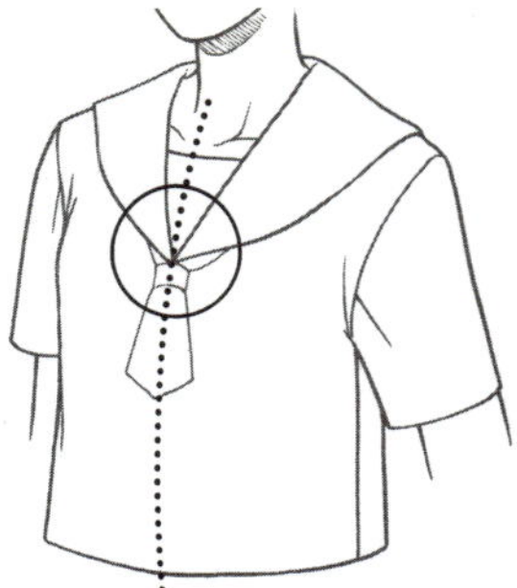

Front closure of a sailor suit

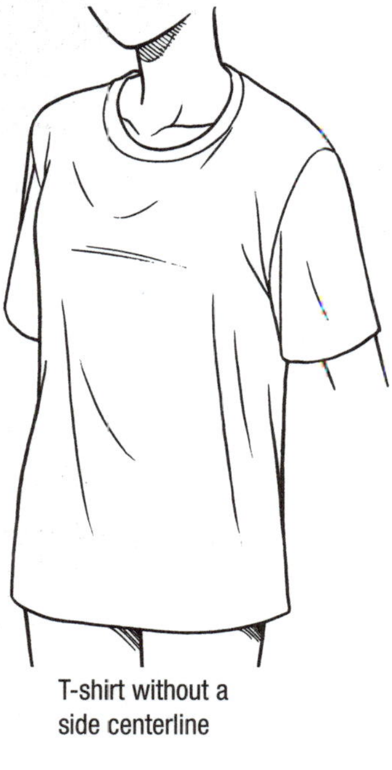

T-shirt without a side centerline

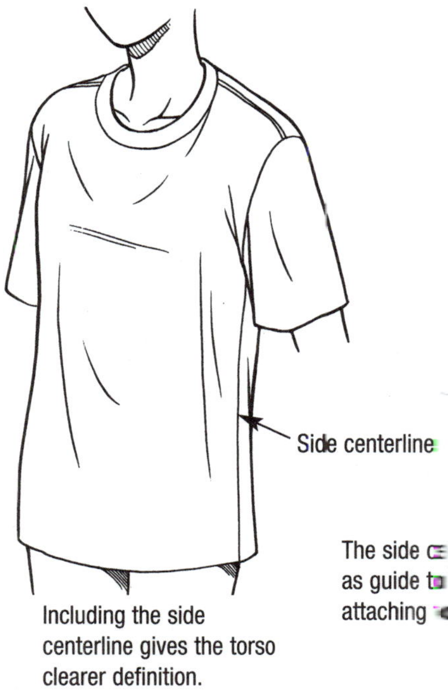

Including the side centerline gives the torso clearer definition.

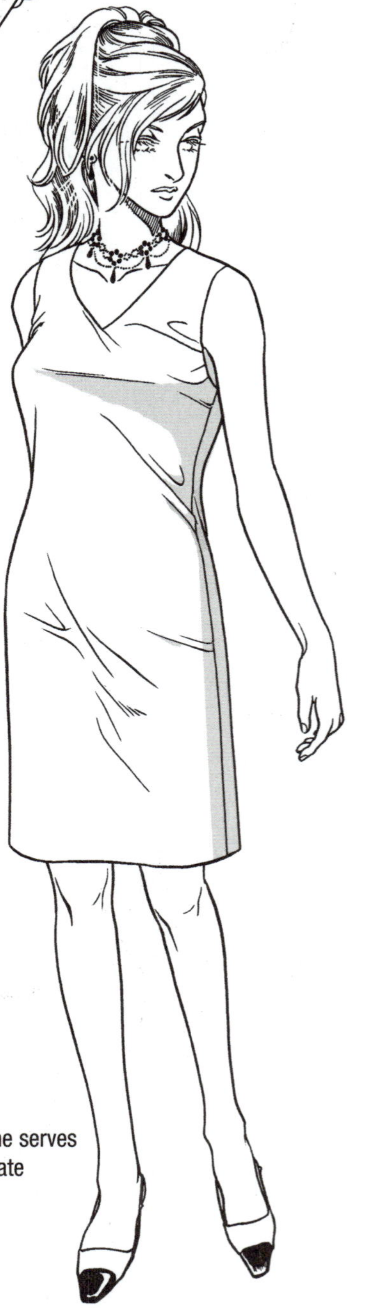

The side centerline serves as guide to facilitate attaching tone.

Note: Some T-shirts lack the side seams from the underarm down.

Back View

The side centerline along with the torso's thickness gives the torso clear definition.

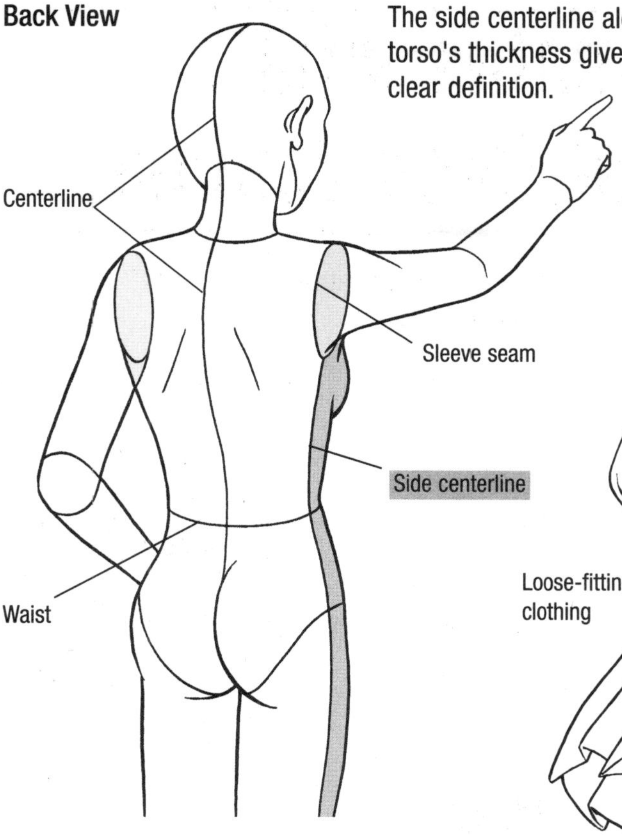

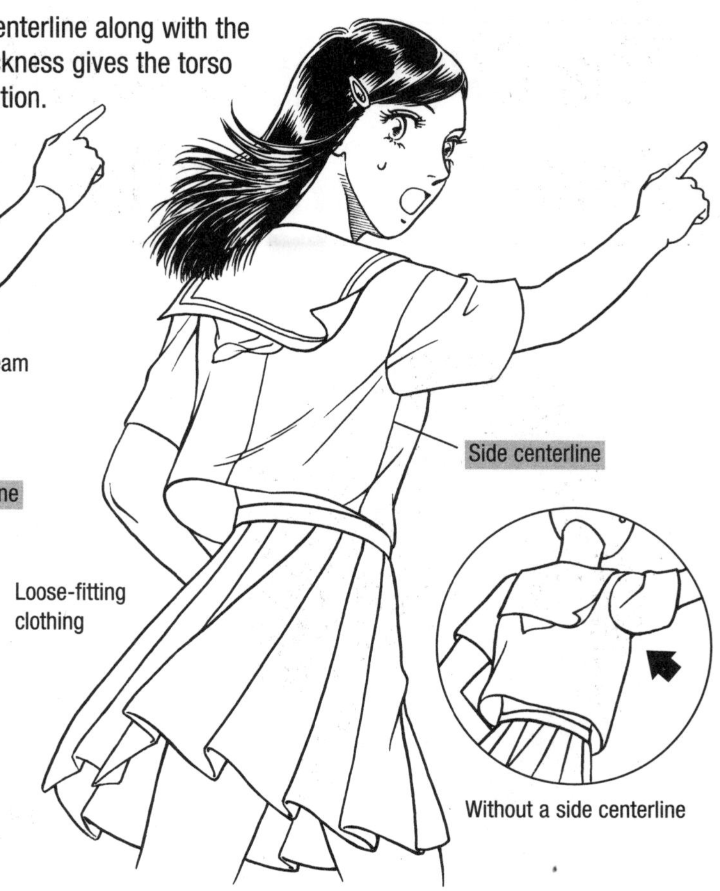

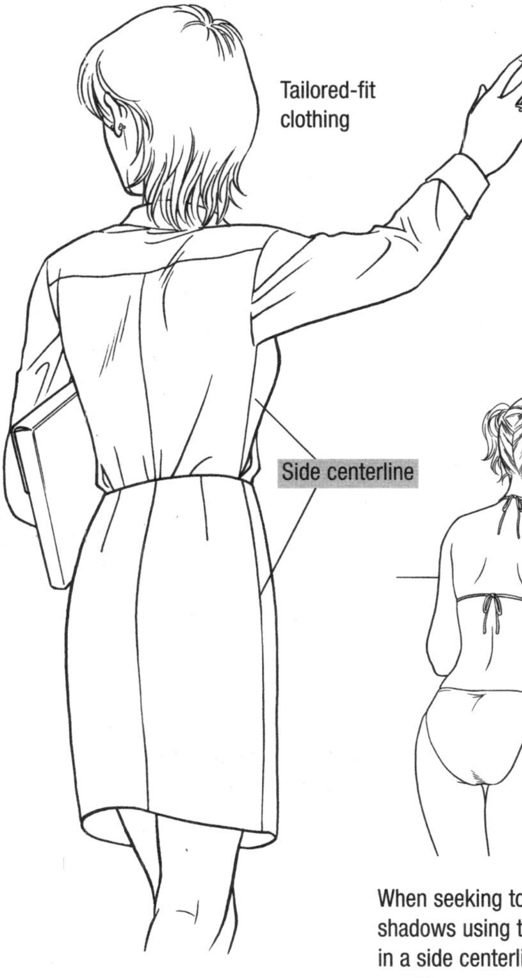

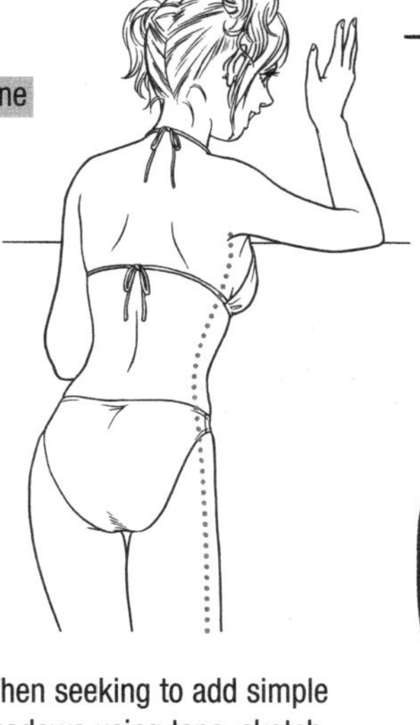

When seeking to add simple shadows using tone, sketch in a side centerline to use as a guide.

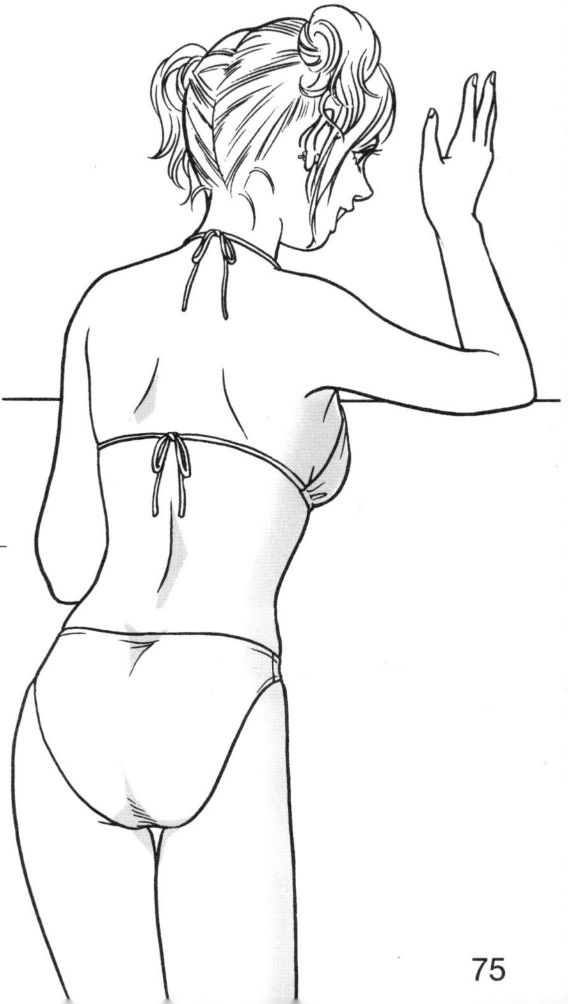

The Clavicle Is Another Vital Point to Giving the Torso Volume

The clavicle is key to constructing the upper front of the torso.

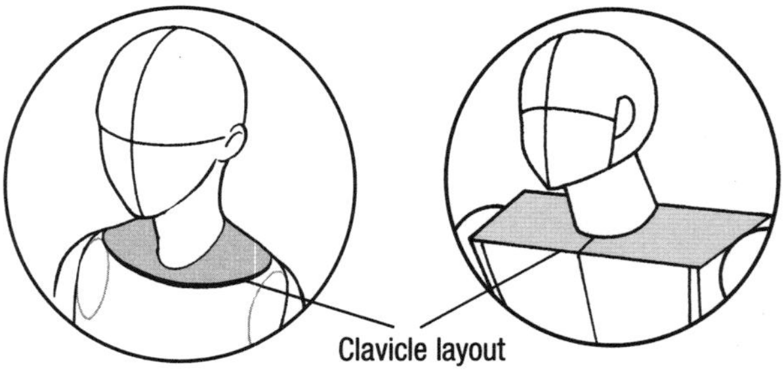

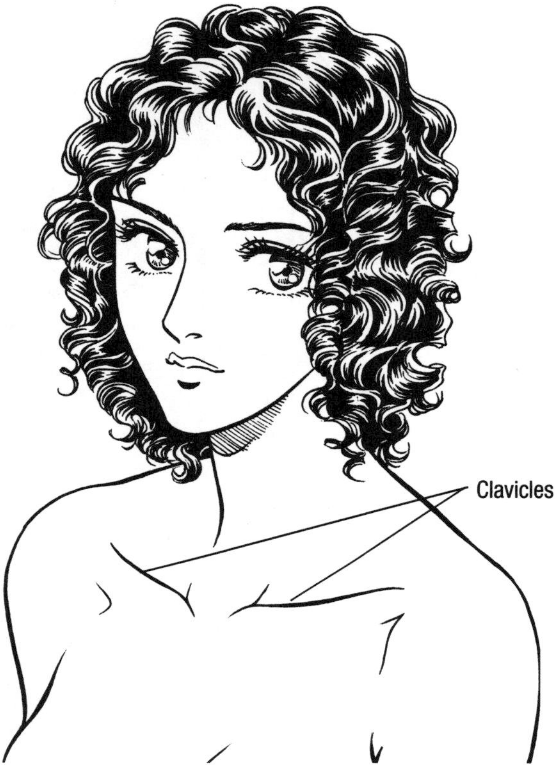

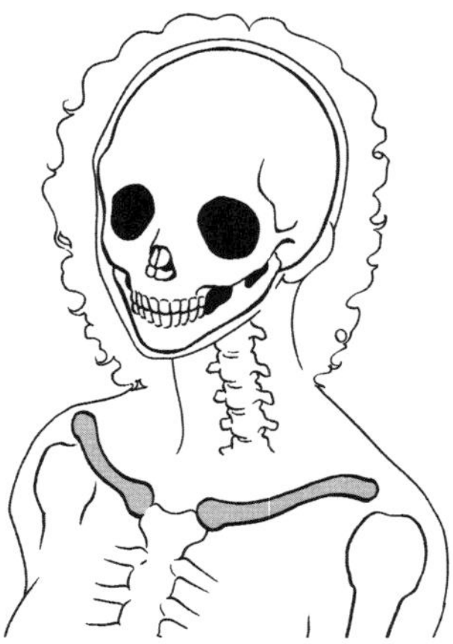

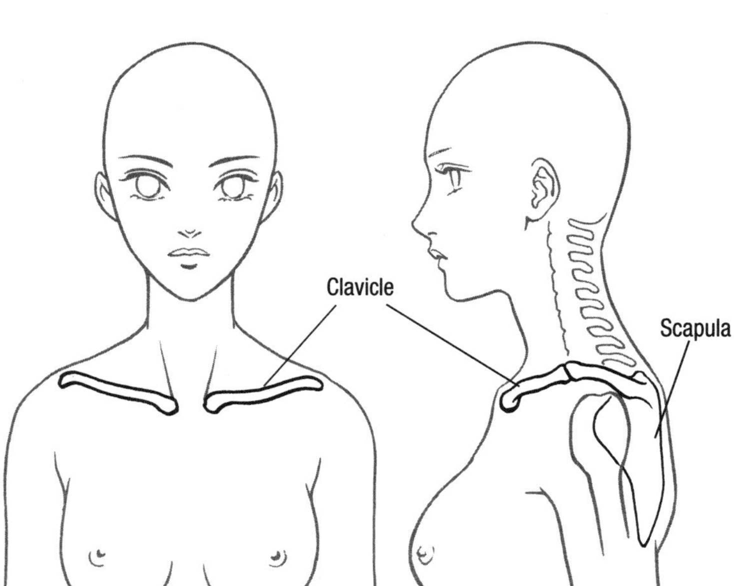

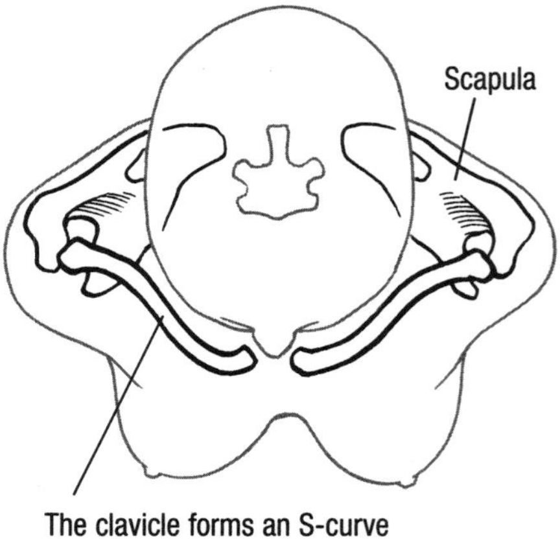

Depicting the Shoulders and Movement of the Clavicles

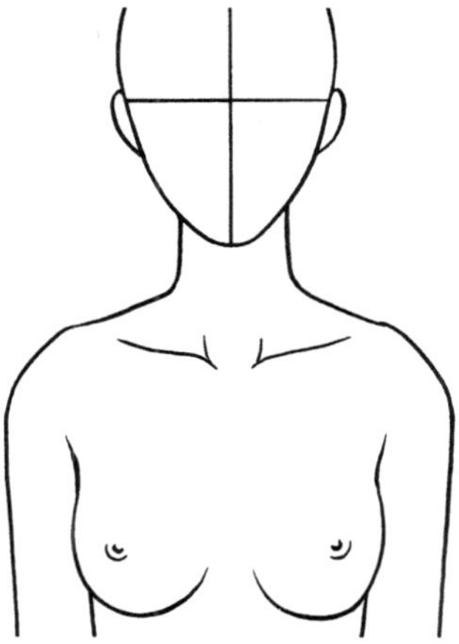

Front

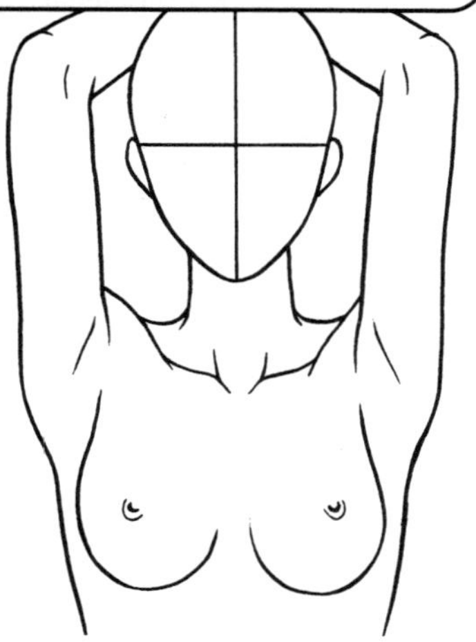

Raising both arms

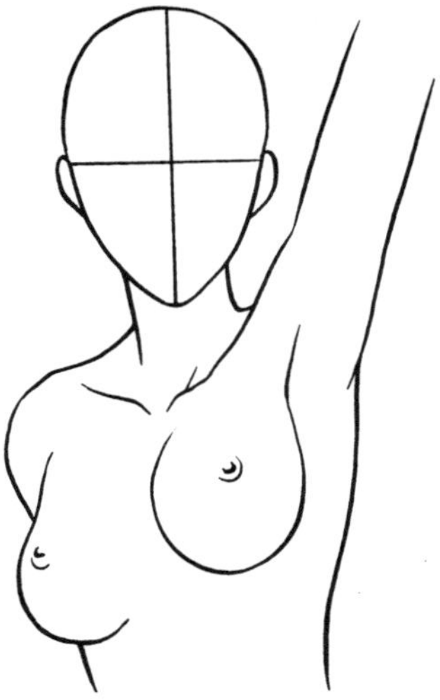

From a normal stance, the clavicles do not really change in appearance even when an arm is raised.

Motions That Make the Clavicles Stand Out

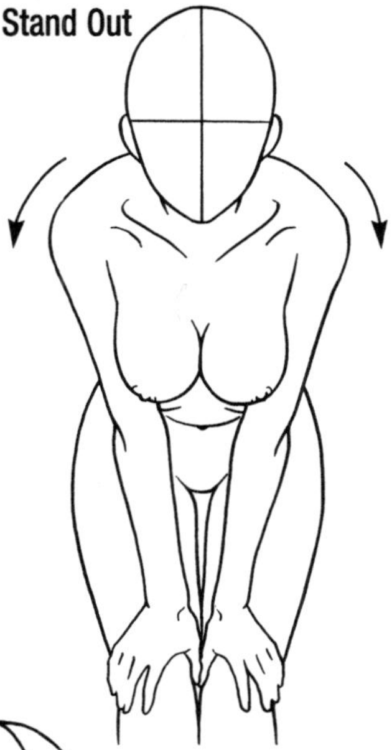

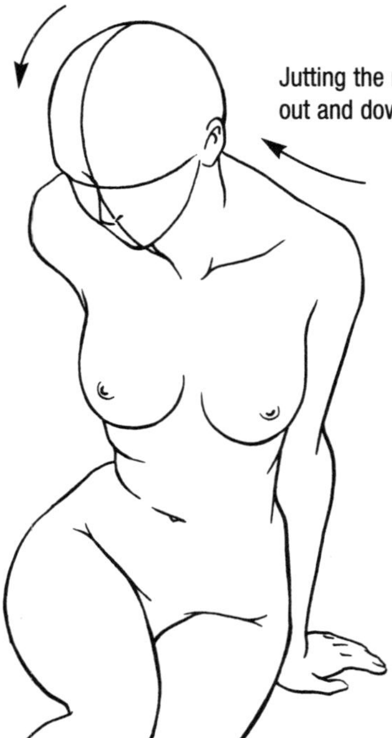

Jutting the neck out and down

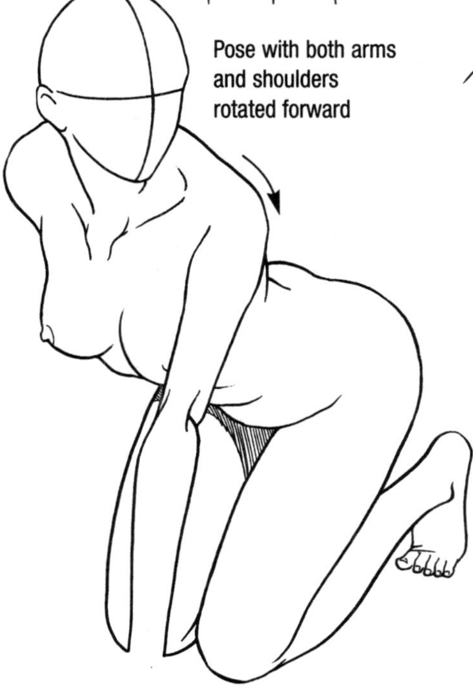

Pose with both arms and shoulders rotated forward

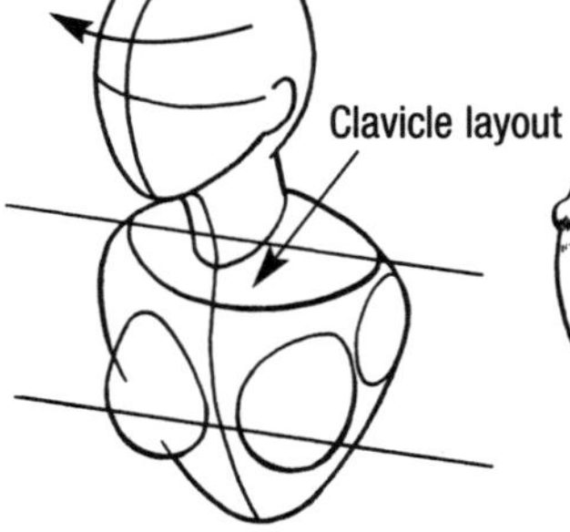

The more the neck is rotated to the side from the front, the more the clavicles and the neck muscles (tendons) protrude.

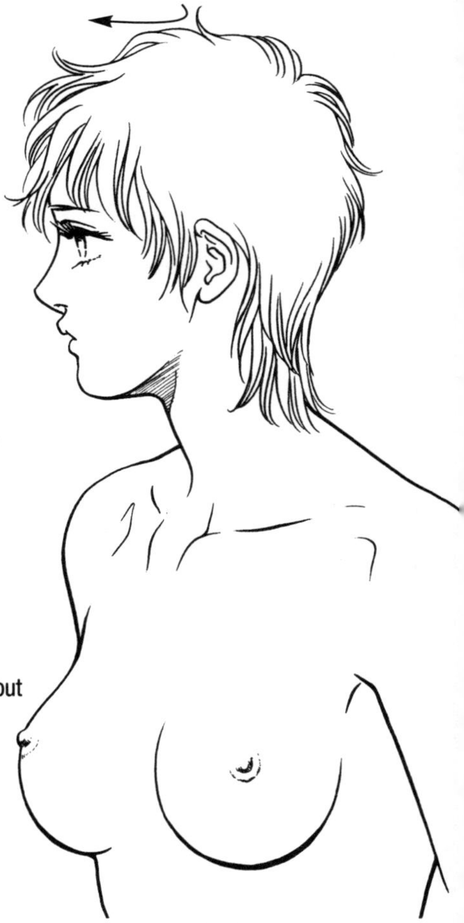

Clavicles often become prominent accompanying neck movement, or when both shoulders are rotated forward or when the shoulders are tensed.

Sample Clavicles

The clavicles are prominent on thin builds and relatively hidden on fleshy figures.

Female Characters

Clavicles rendered in detail

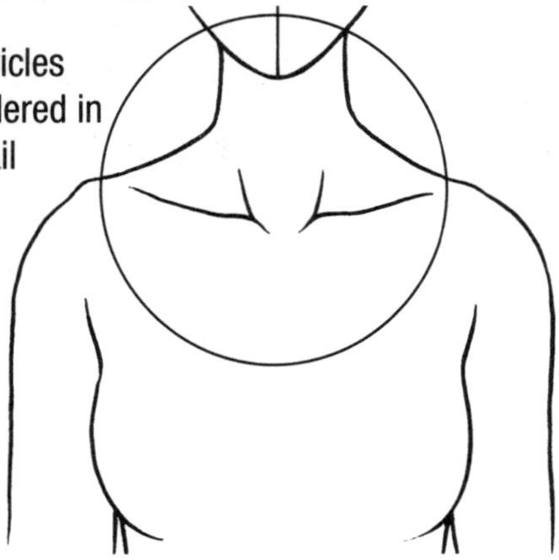

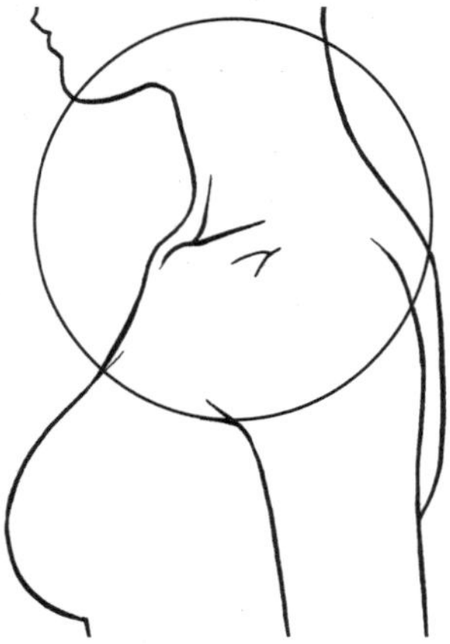

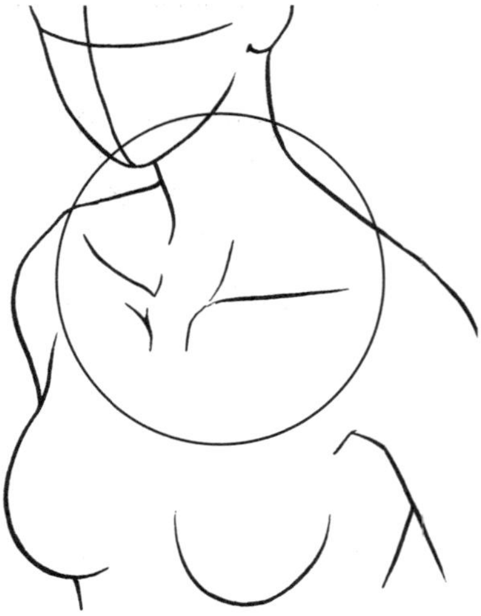

Abbreviated clavicles

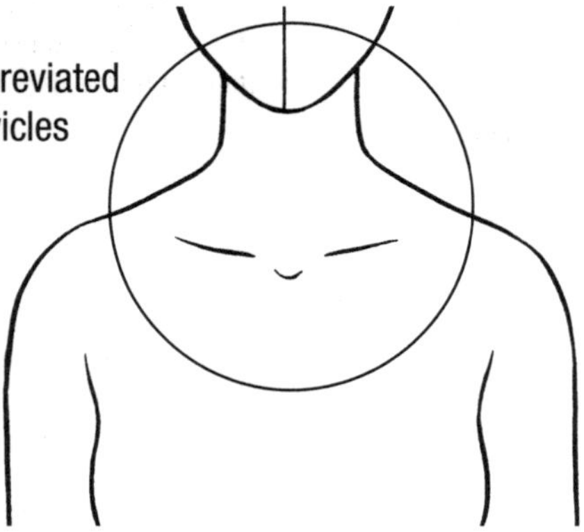

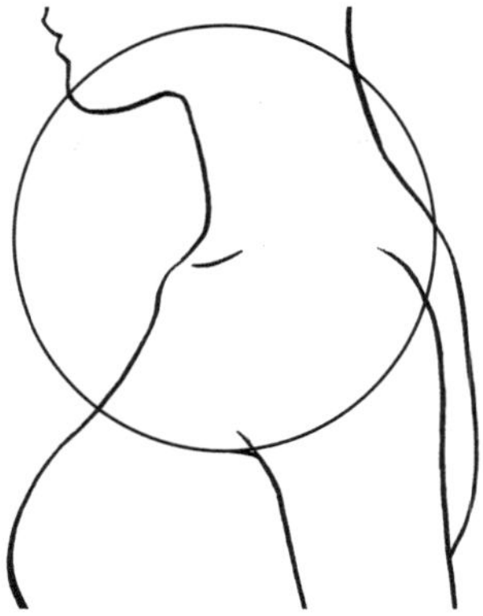

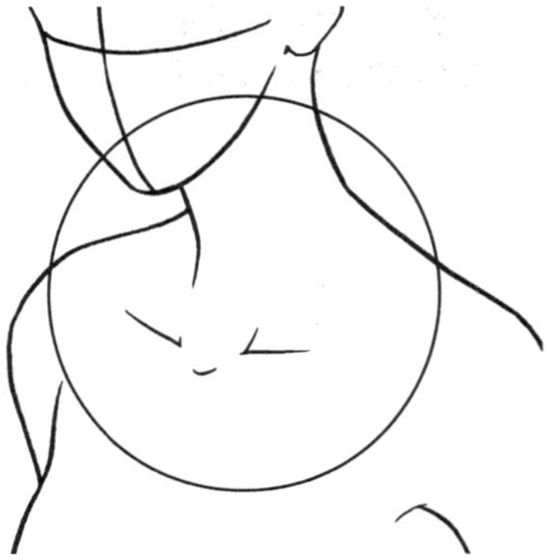

Because the clavicles allow you to portray the maleness, femininity, or adultness in a character, they are often included when the artist intends to draw out these traits.

Children

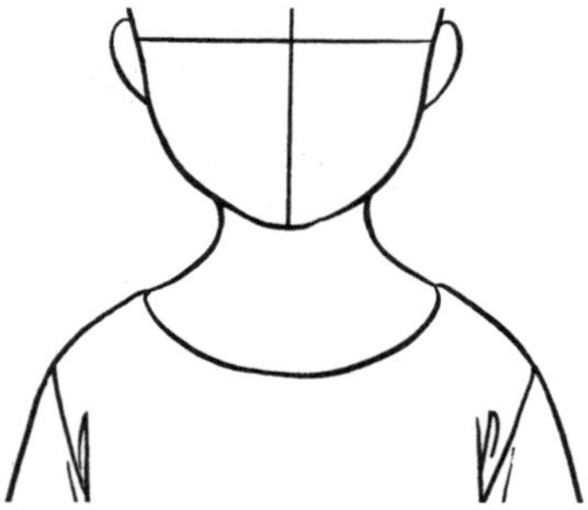

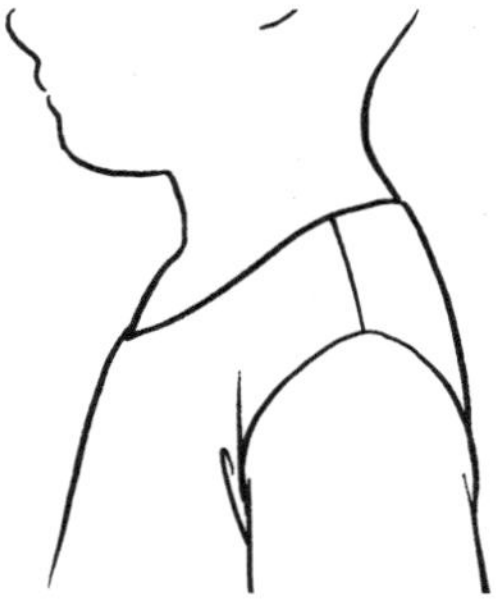

Leave out the clavicle when drawing children (this will make them more "childlike").

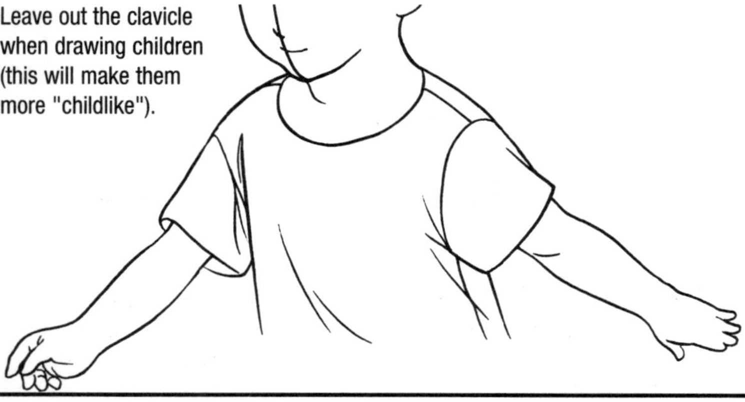

Incorrect Clavicles

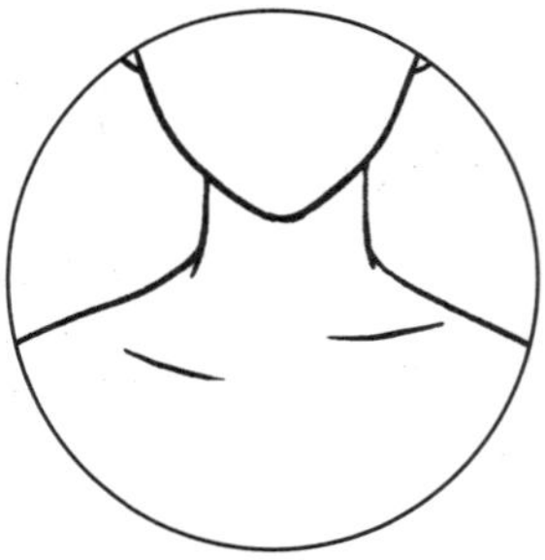

The levels and positions of the two do not correspond.

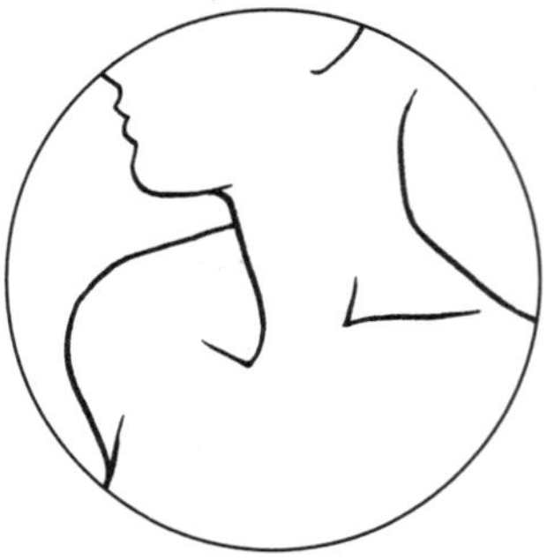

Here, the length and position do not match.

Male Characters

Average Build

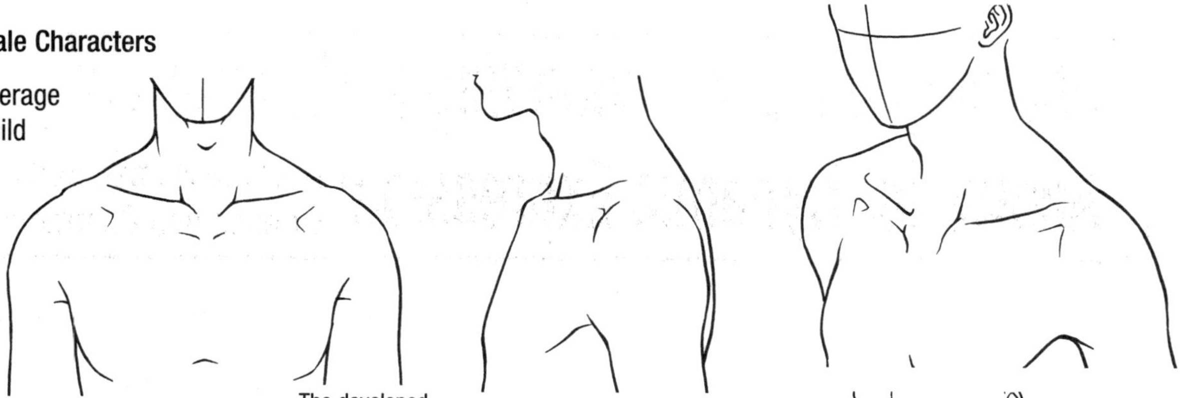

Muscular Build

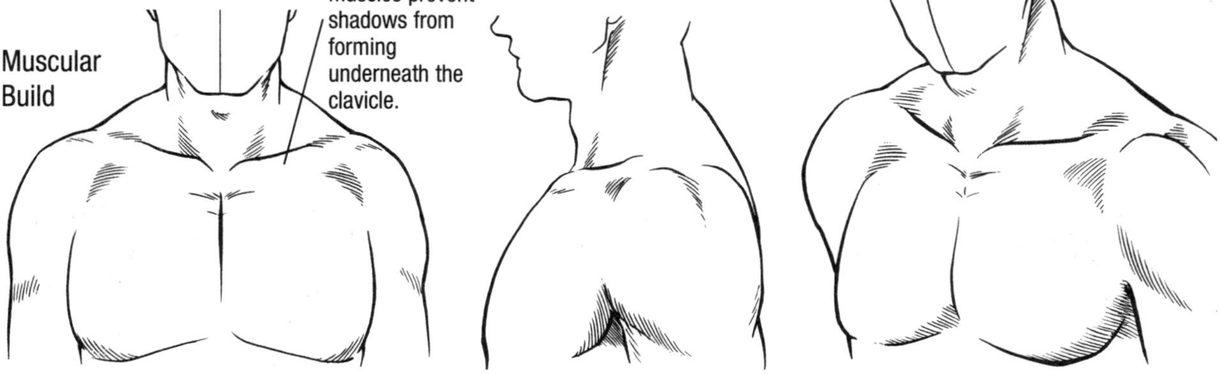

Use hatching and shadows to beef up a muscular character's bone structure.

Distinguishing Male and Female Characters

Draw the clavicles so that the reader can distinguish the character's gender at a single glance, even when wearing a T-shirt and only a portion of the figure is visible.

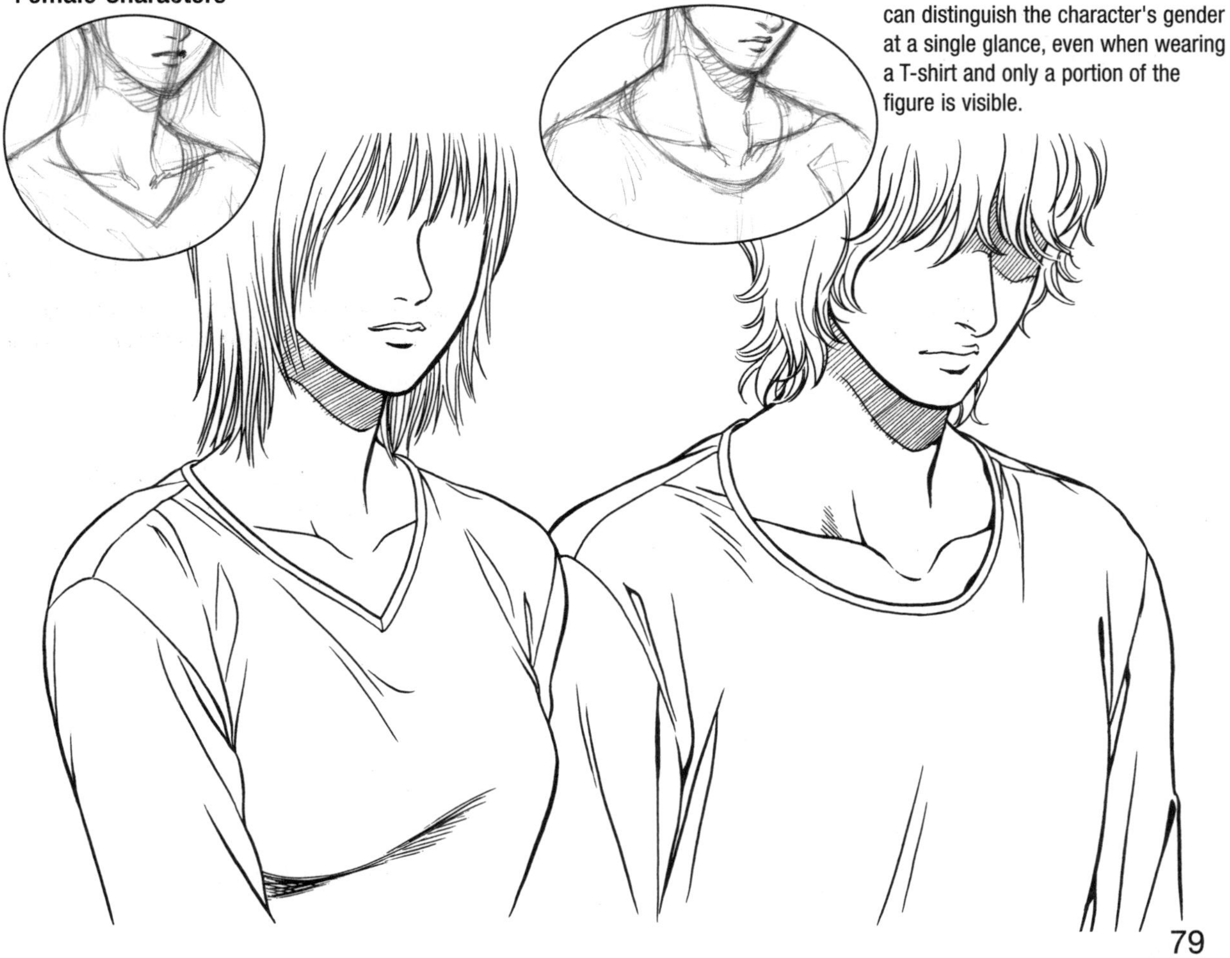

Showing a Figure Extending and Contracting Allows for Dynamic Expression: How the Human Body Extends and Contracts

Our hands, legs, and torso extend and contract. Being aware of how far a limb bends forward or back will allow you to draw your characters' movements convincingly.

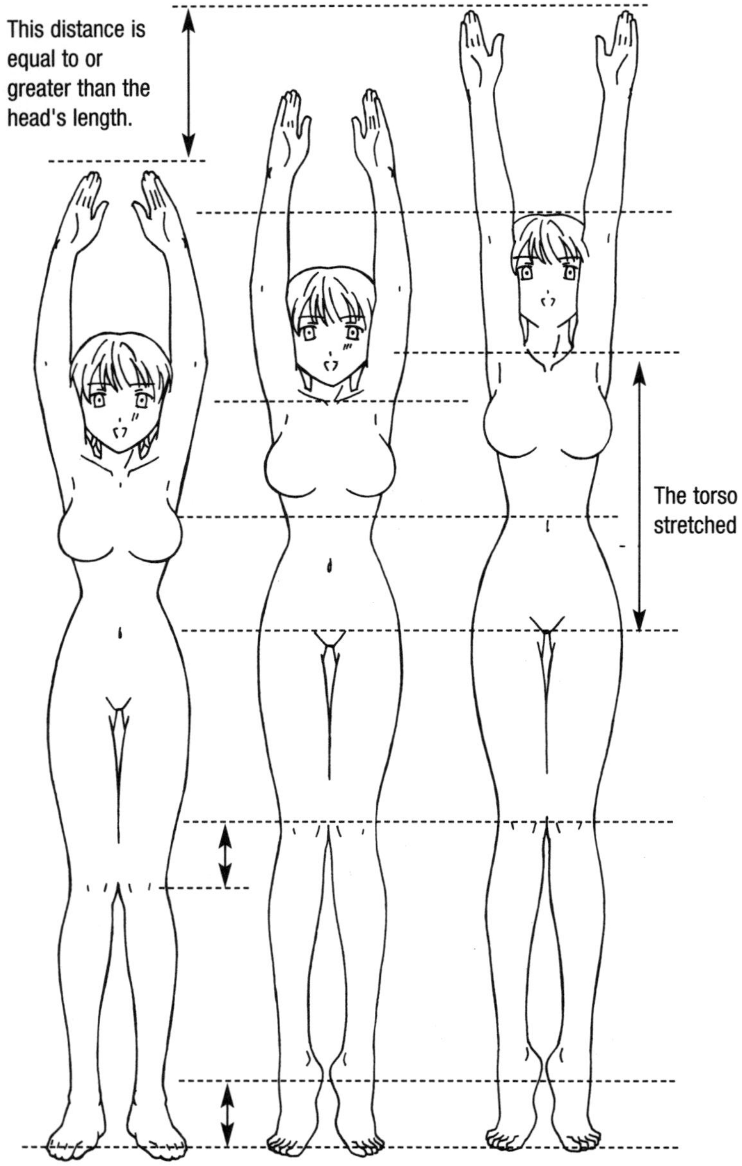

The figures height expands by the length of the feet when standing on toe tips.

Stretching the body to the extent possible lengthens even further the torso and upper body and the arms.

The arms also stretch.

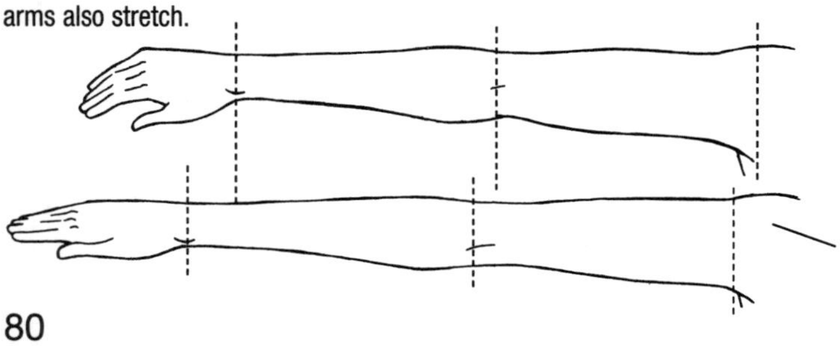

Stretching occurs at the shoulder (joint).

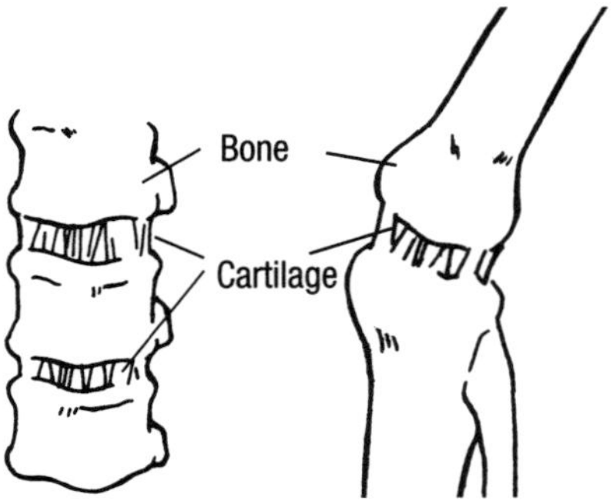

Ref. Fig.: Spine

Ref. Fig. Knee

The Principles behind Stretching

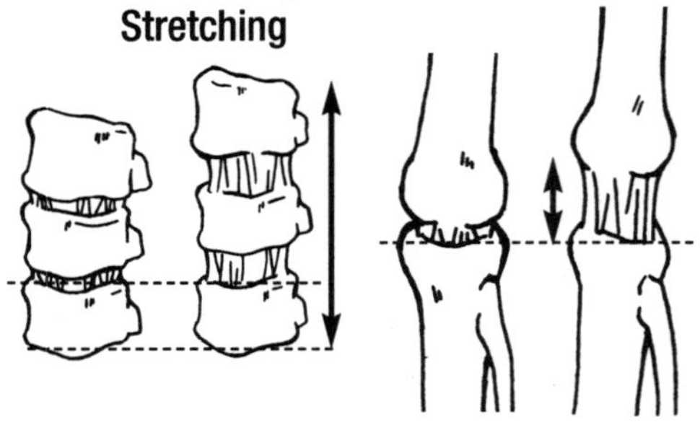

Hard bones are connected to each other by soft cartilage. Cartilage has elasticity that can be likened to rubber.

Stretching and Contracting Caused by Bending

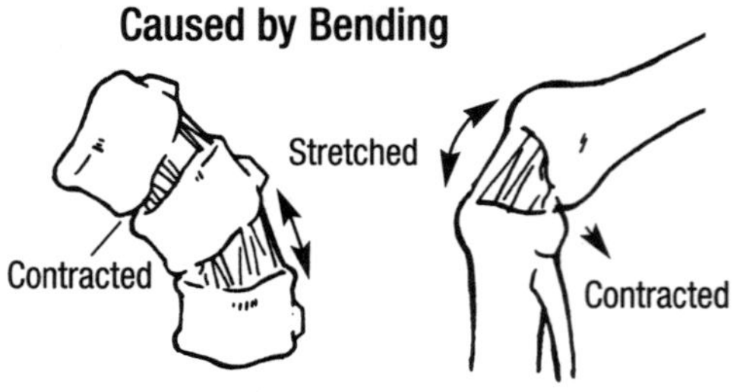

Stretching and contracting both occur during the act of "bending."

Figure in Clothing

Clothing is designed with movement (the body extending) in mind. While some clothing is made of fabrics capable of stretching and contracting (stretch fibers), typically, clothing is pulled with the body, altering its silhouette.

Typical Blouse

Cropped Top

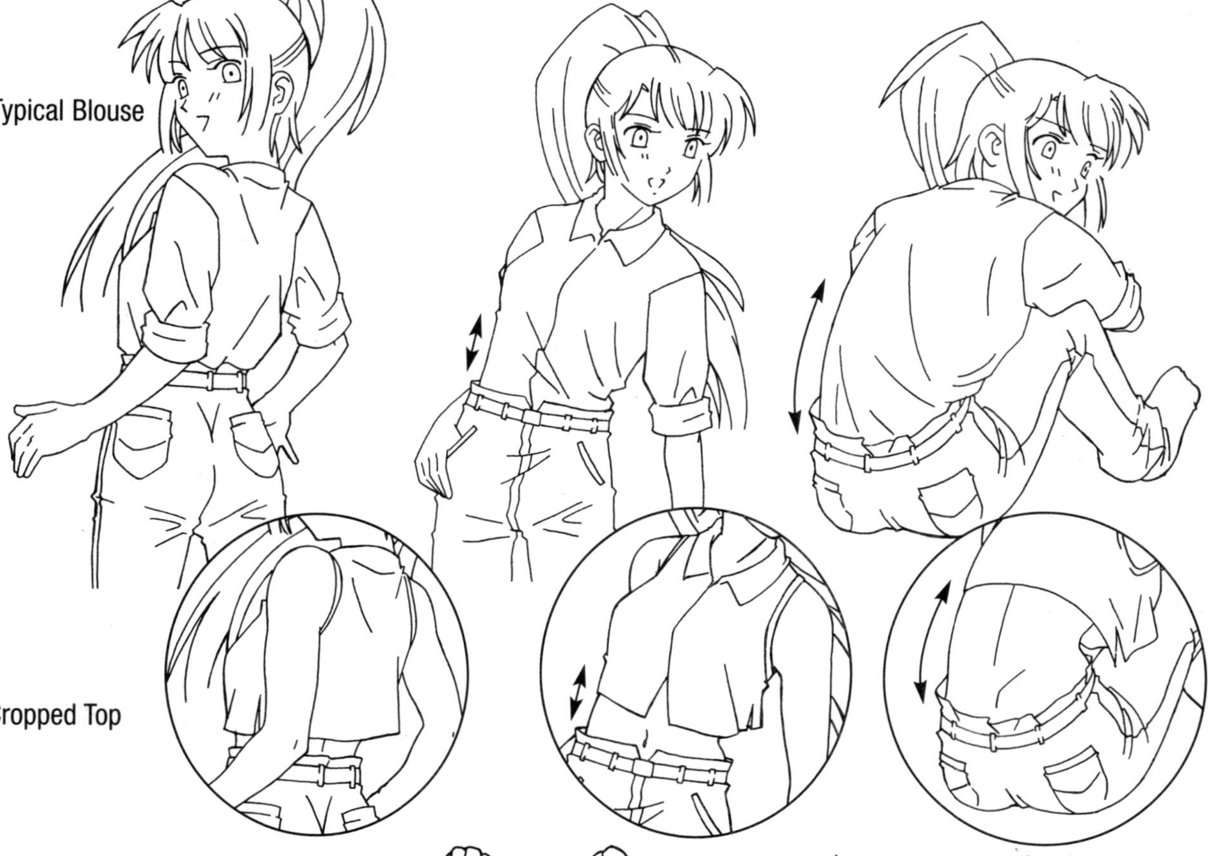

Loosely Fitted Clothing

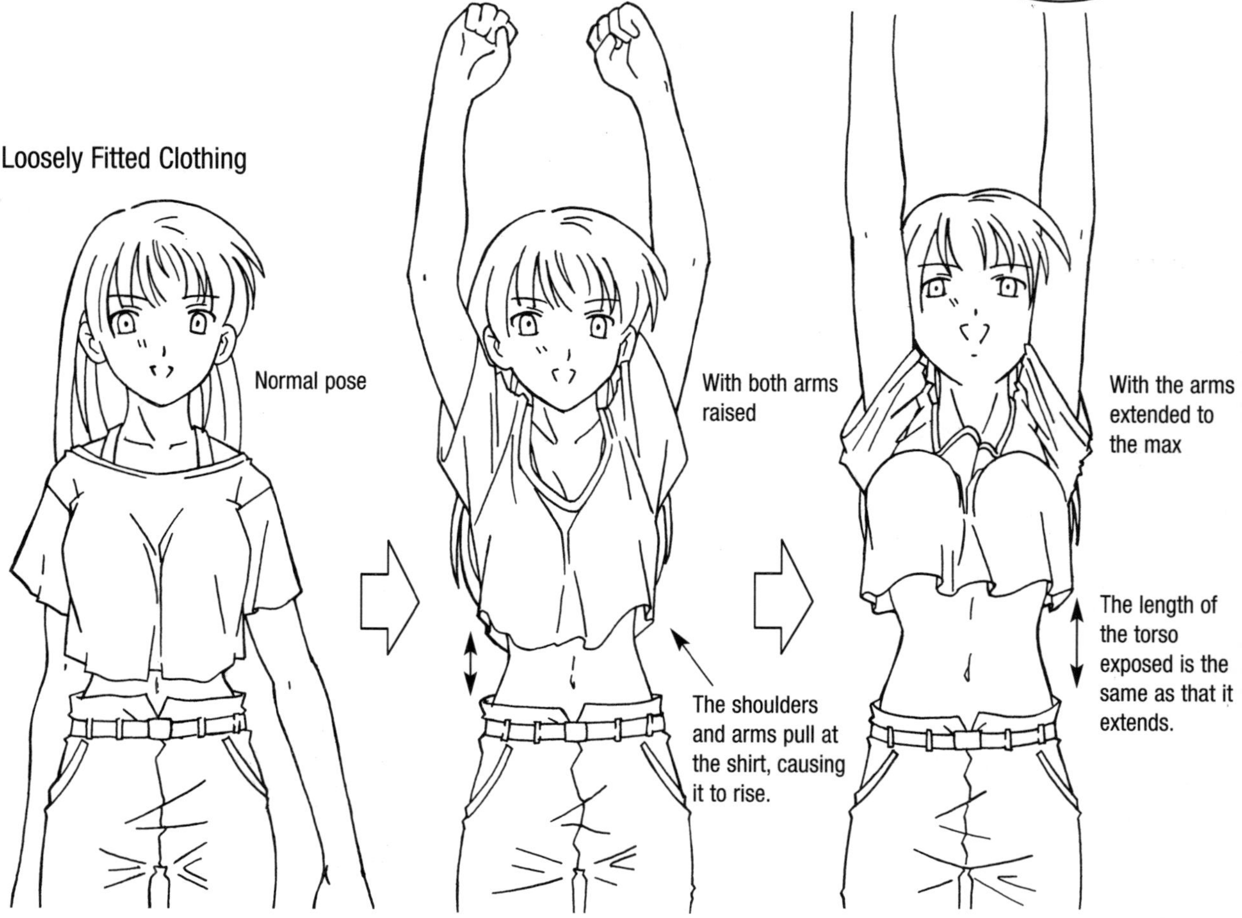

Bending the Neck

Stretching and contracting of the neck is a frequently used, key motion.

Common Stretching and Contracting of the Neck

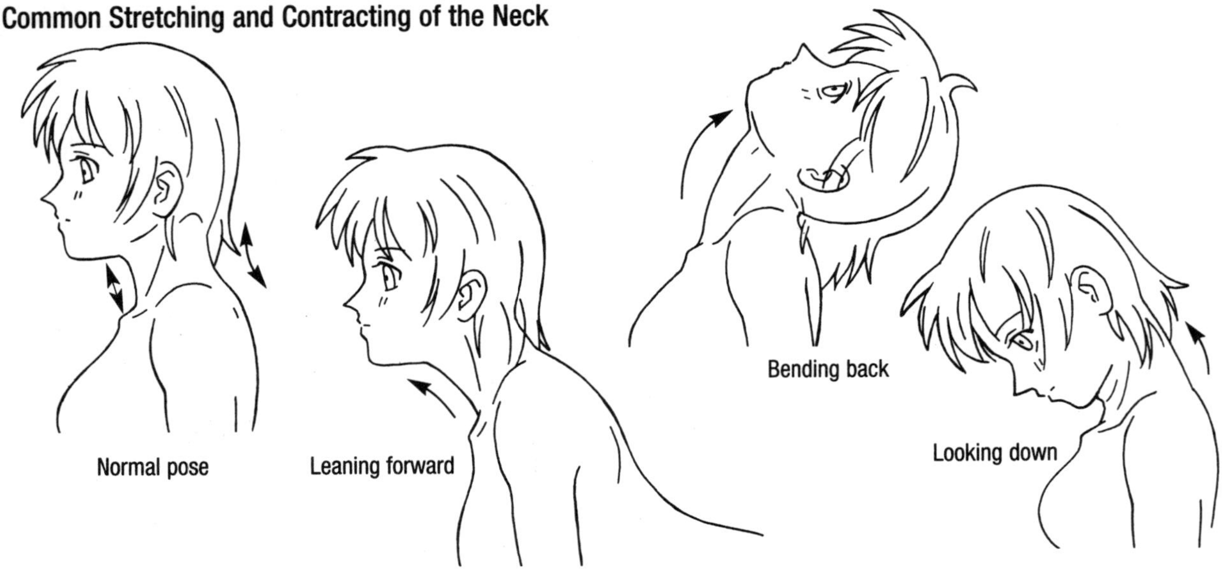

Stretching and Contracting to the Side

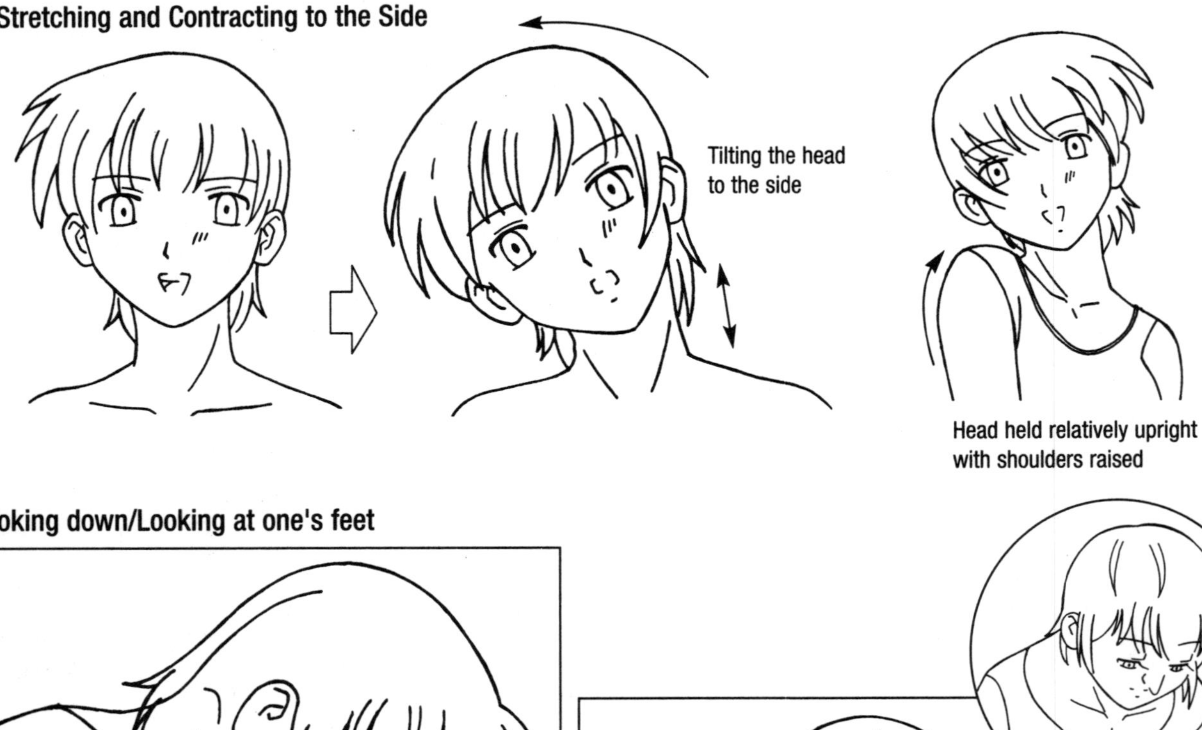

Looking down/Looking at one's feet

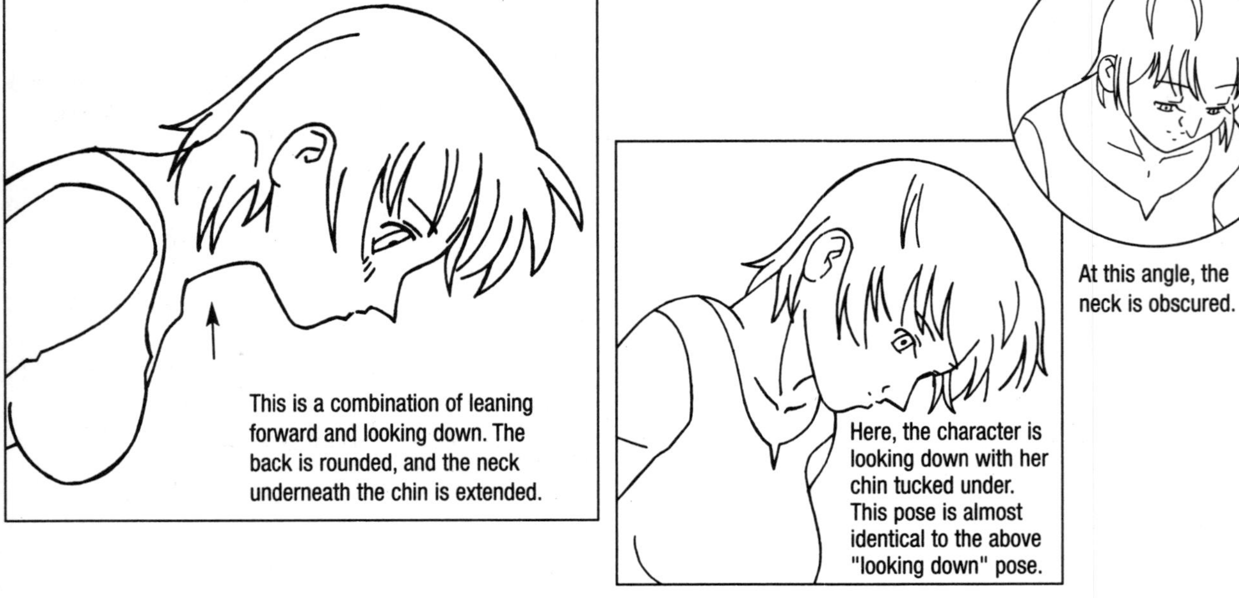

Twisting the Head up

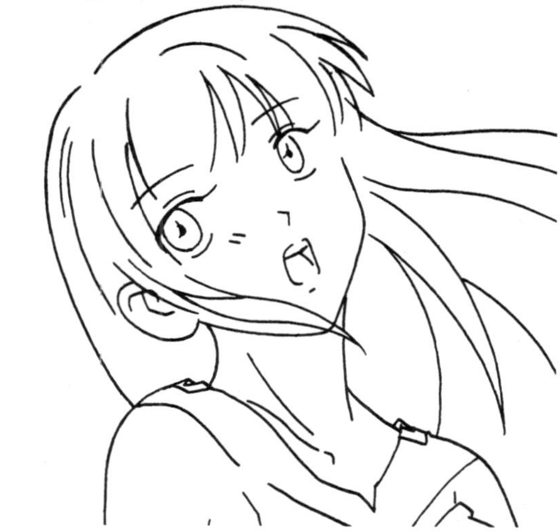

Bad example.

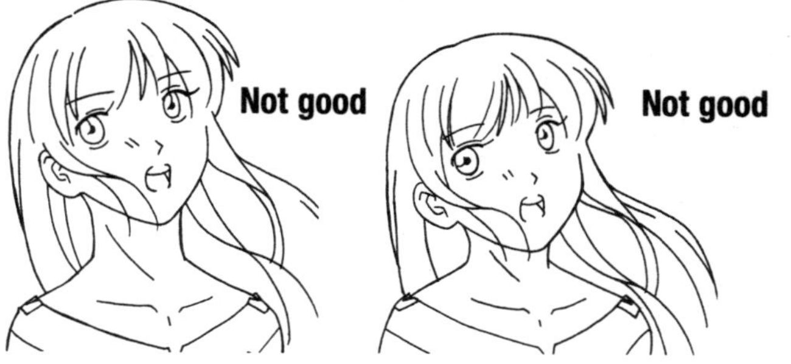

The head should be tilted more.

The neck should be longer.

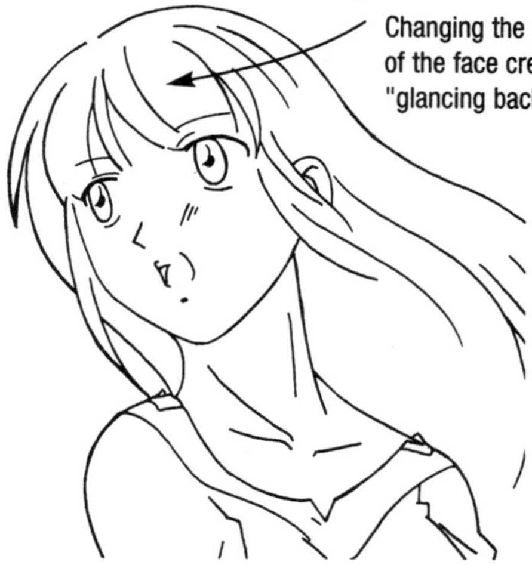

Changing the direction of the face creates a "glancing back" pose.

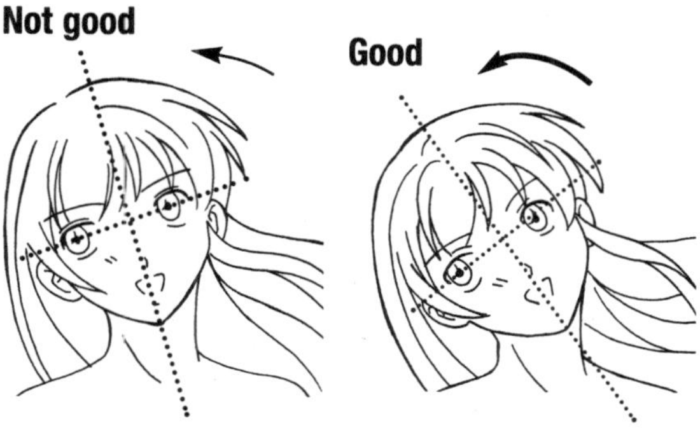

The trick is to give the neck a dramatic angle.

Leaning Forward with the Body

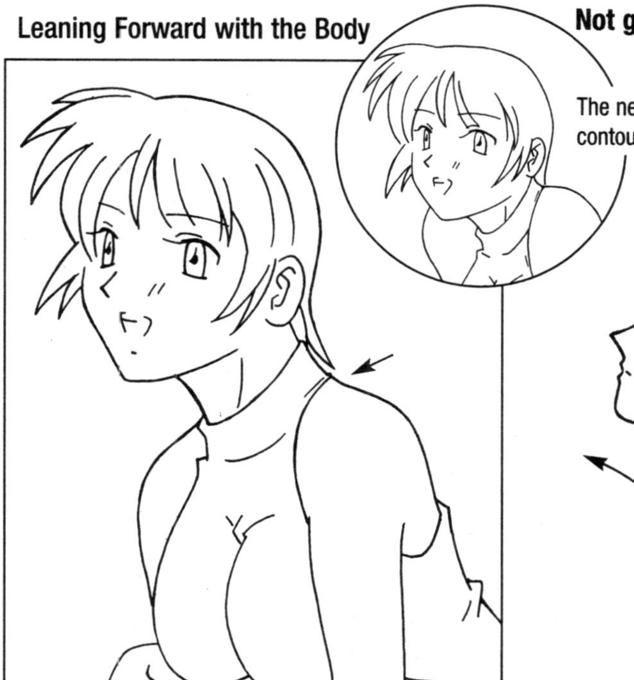

Not good

The neck-to-shoulder contour is too short.

The contour from the neck to the shoulder is critical.

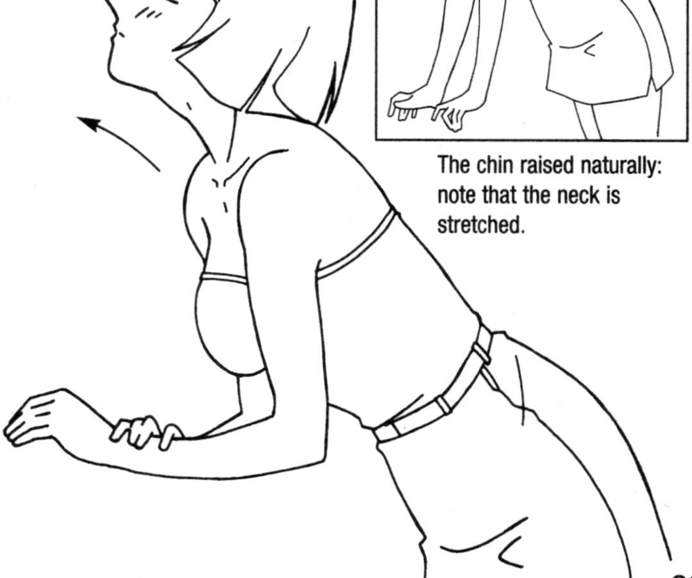

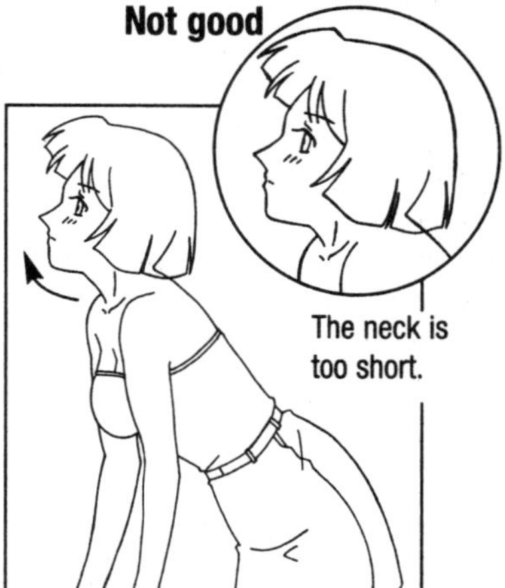

Not good

The neck is too short.

The chin raised naturally: note that the neck is stretched.

The Arms

Scenes in *manga* of a character toting a heavy load require that you take extra care with drawing the arms in an extended position.

Carrying a Load of Normal Weight

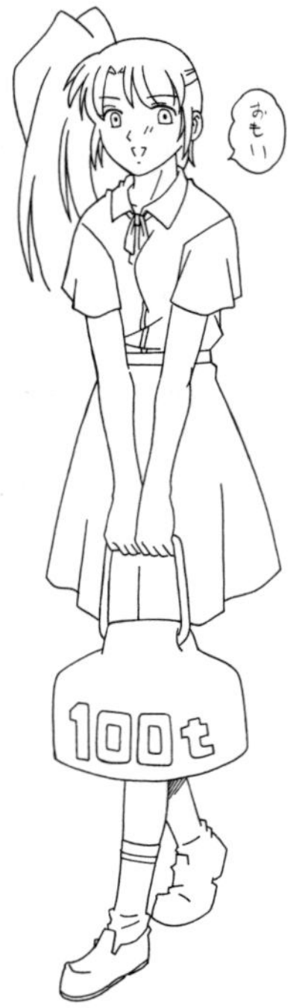

Lifting a Moderately Heavy Load

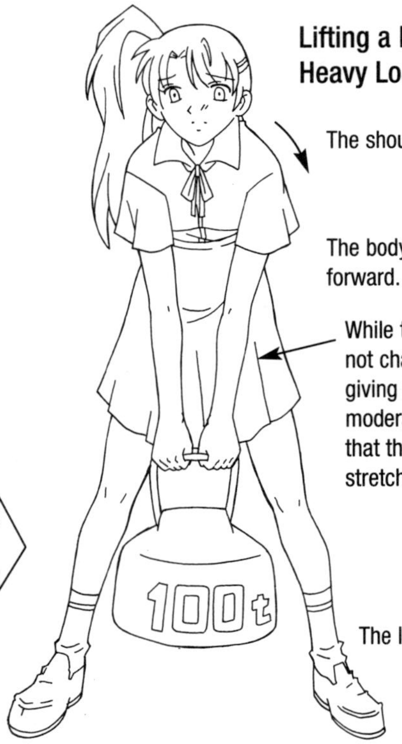

The shoulders drop.

The body hunches forward.

While the arms' length do not change dramatically, giving the muscles a moderate bulge shows that the arms are being stretched.

The legs are spread.

Lifting an Ultra-Heavy Load

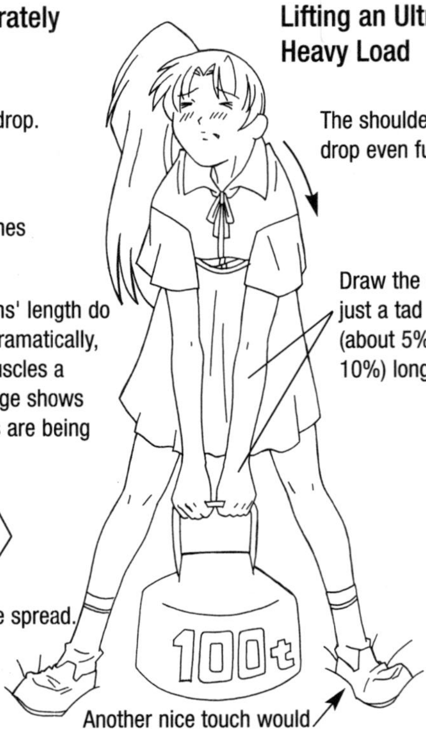

The shoulders drop even further.

Draw the arms just a tad (about 5% to 10%) longer.

Another nice touch would be to show the feet sinking into the ground.

Not good

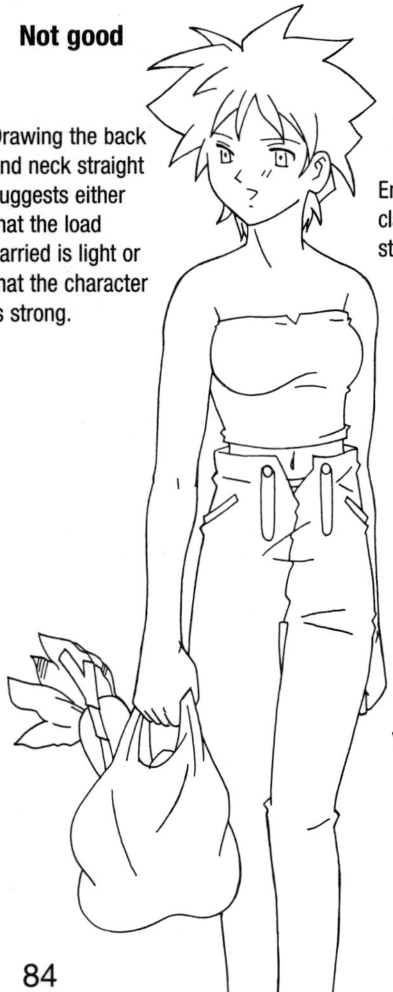

Drawing the back and neck straight suggests either that the load carried is light or that the character is strong.

Good

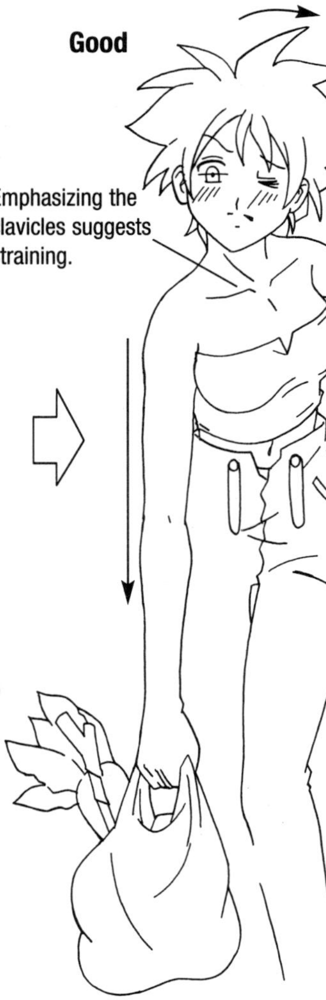

Emphasizing the clavicles suggests straining.

The body is pulled to the right by the bag, causing the character to want to lean toward the left, and the head to tilt to the left.

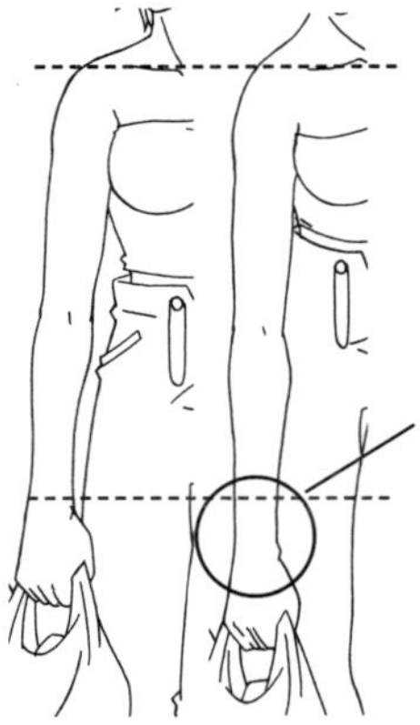

Contrast of arm lengths: Draw the forearm and wrist narrower.

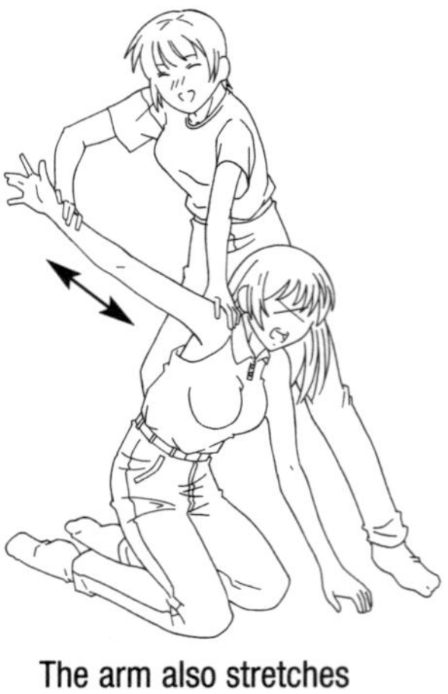

The arm also stretches when grabbed and pulled back.

The Elbow and Wrist

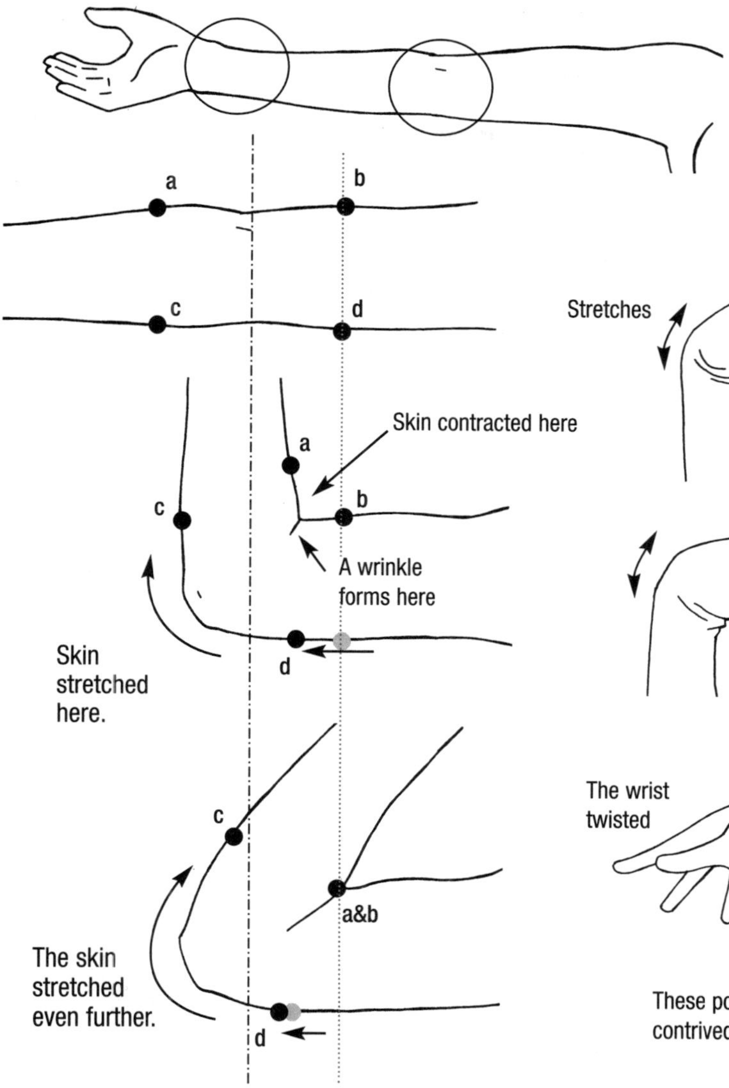

Wrist

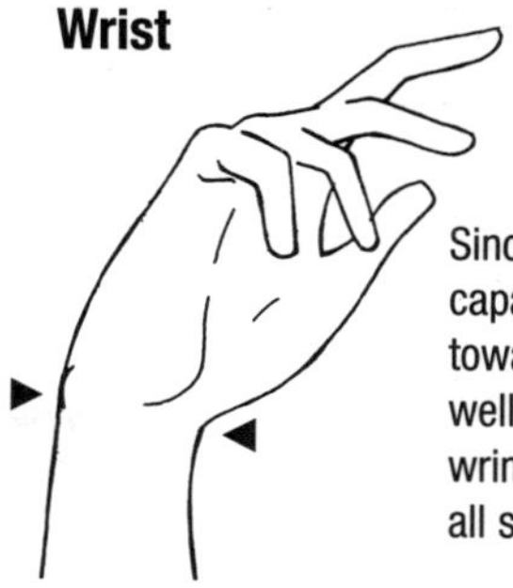

Since the wrist is capable of bending toward the front as well as the back, wrinkles form around all sides.

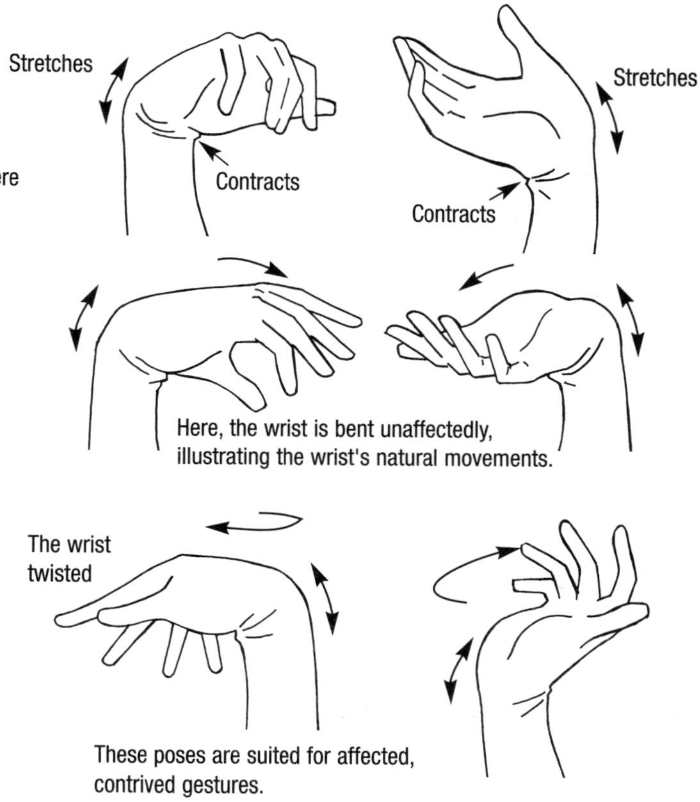

Resting on the Elbows

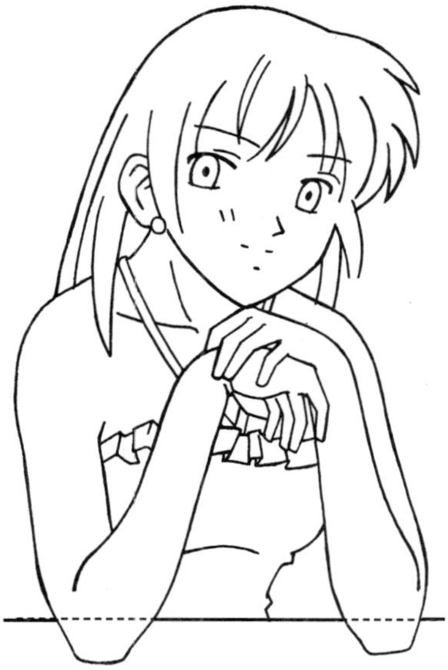

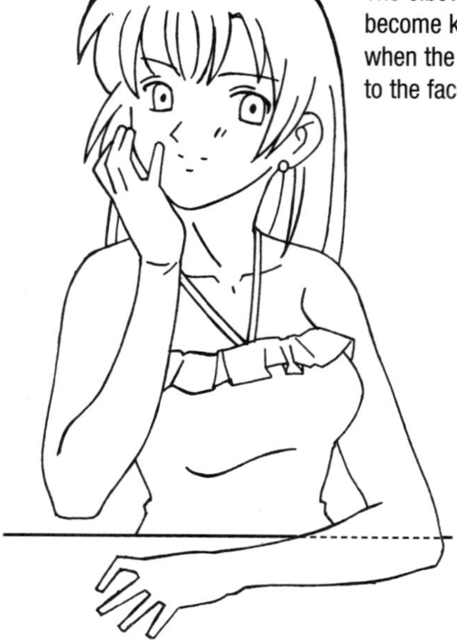

The elbows and wrists become key elements when the hand is brought to the face.

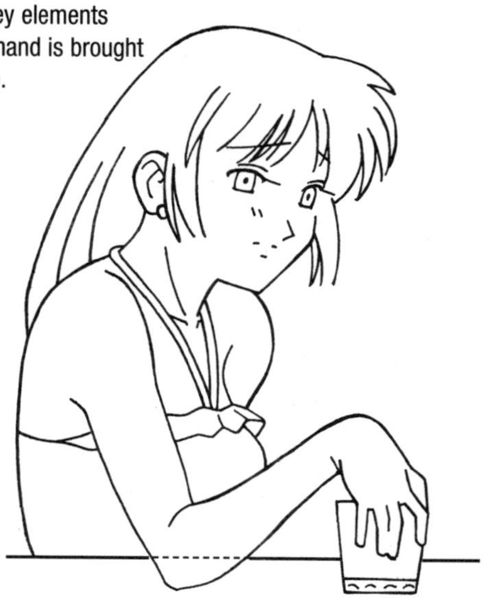

The Hands and Fingers

The stretching and contracting of the hands and fingers is tied into the opening and gripping of the hand.

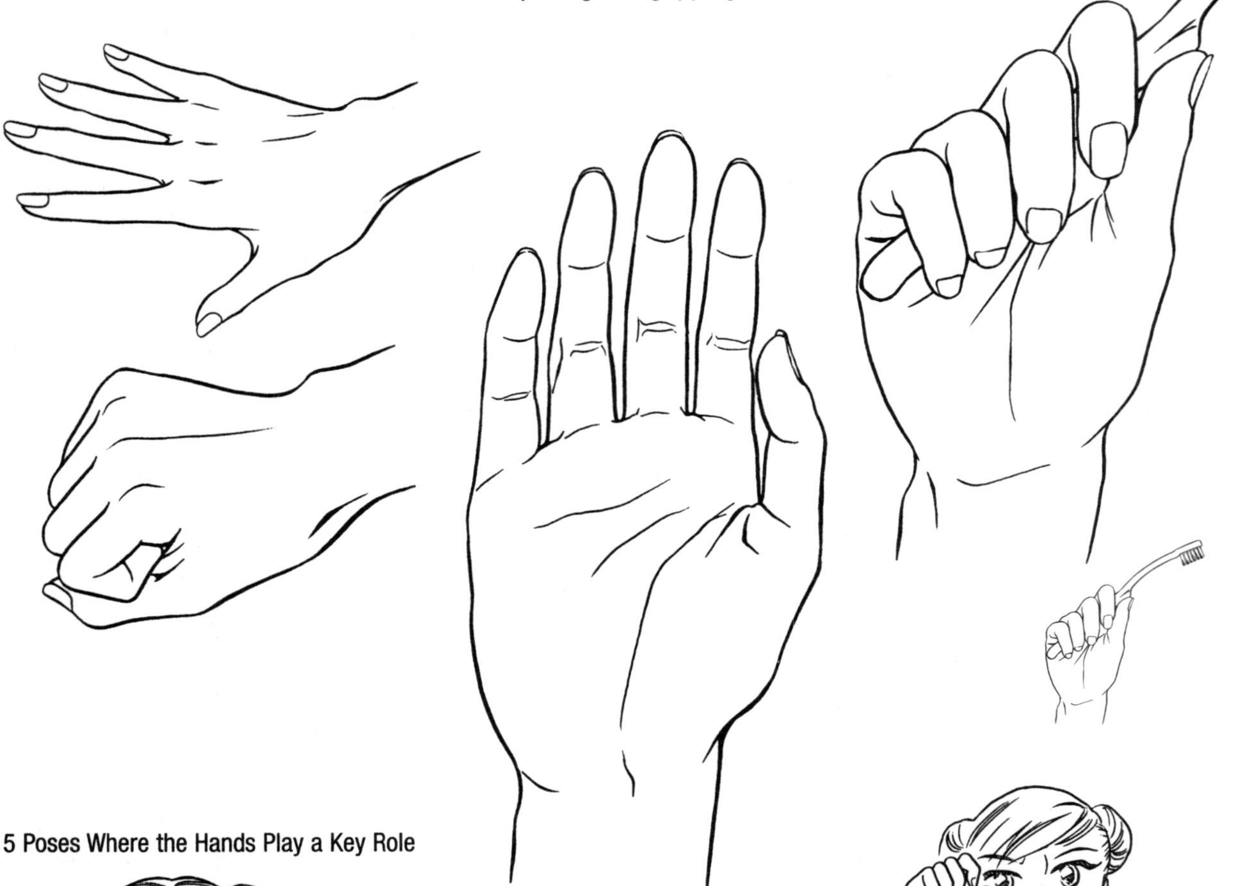

5 Poses Where the Hands Play a Key Role

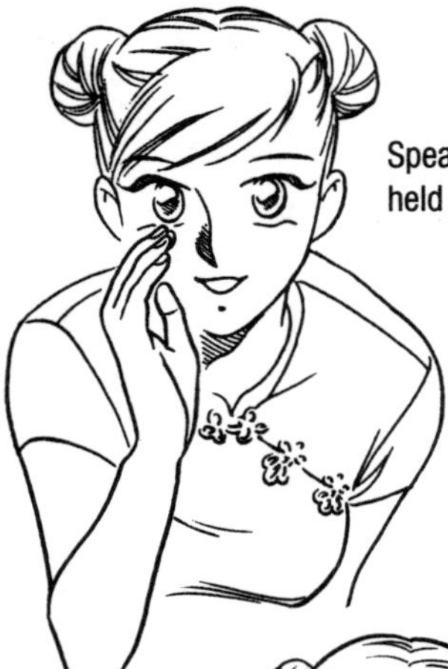

Speaking (with the hand held to the face)

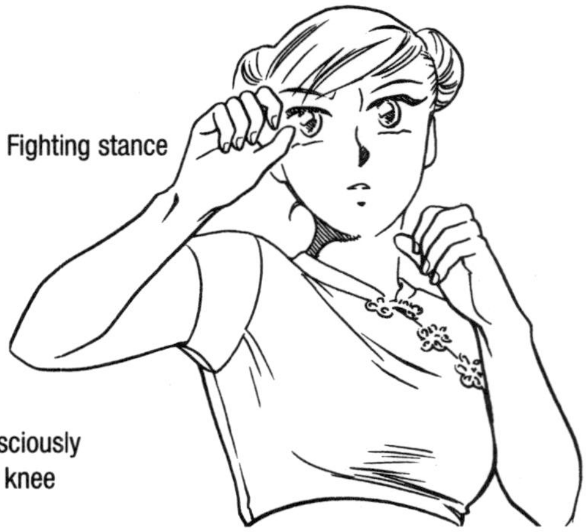

Fighting stance

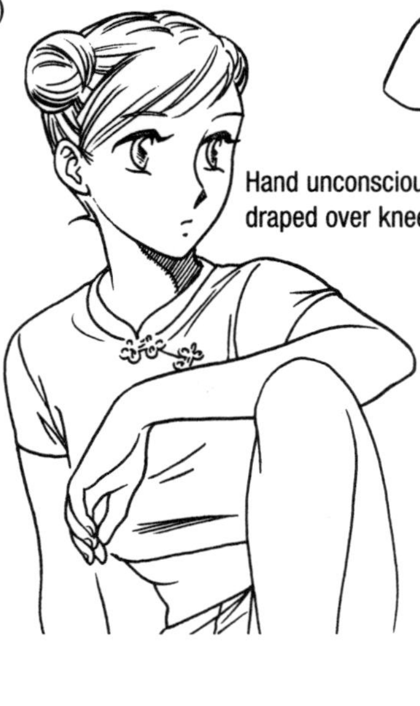

Hand unconsciously draped over knee

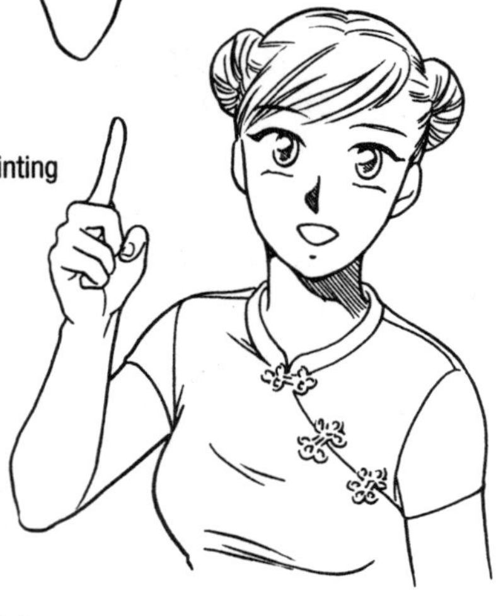

Pointing

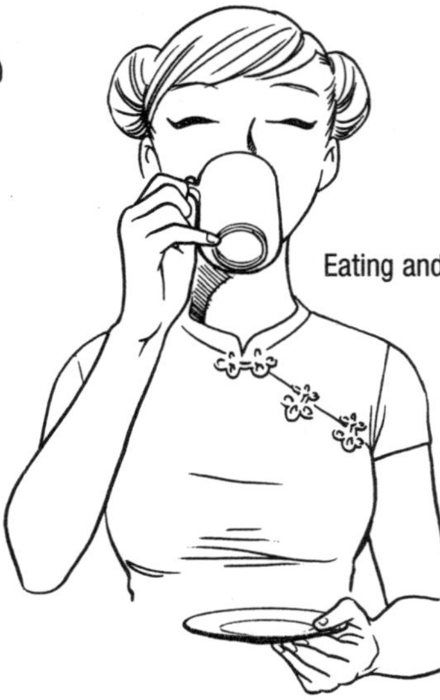

Eating and drinking

Key Points in Drawing the Hands and Fingers:
Matching up Thicknesses and Lengths

Artists tend to concern themselves with the shape of the hands. Still, you should be able to produce a satisfying hand even if you do botch up the shape somewhat, provided that the fingers' thicknesses, lengths, and nail shapes match.

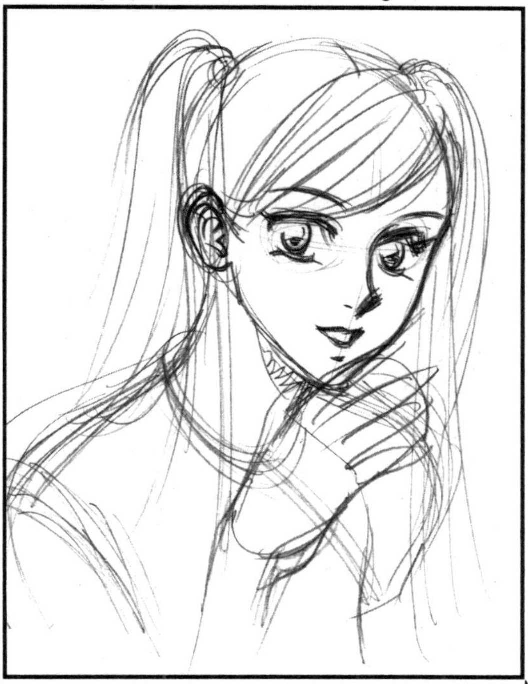

When producing a rough drawing, sketch the approximate positions, shapes, and sizes of the hands. You should establish the image in general terms.

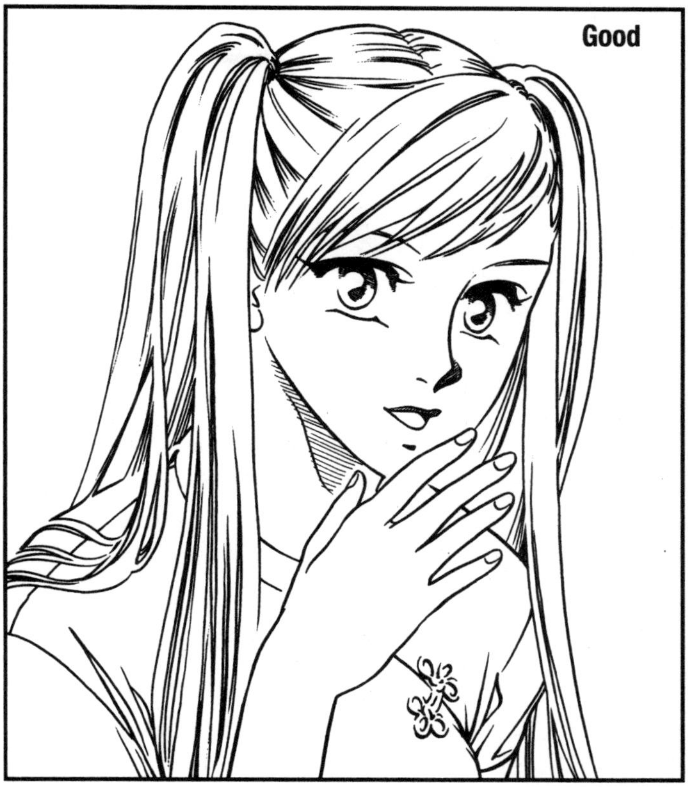

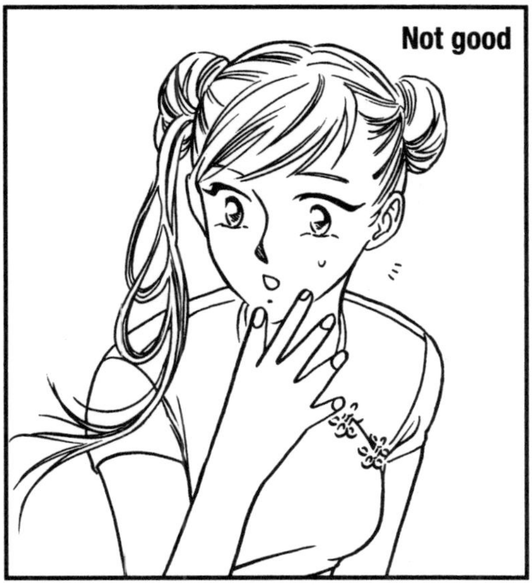

Major mistakes have been made in the figure above.

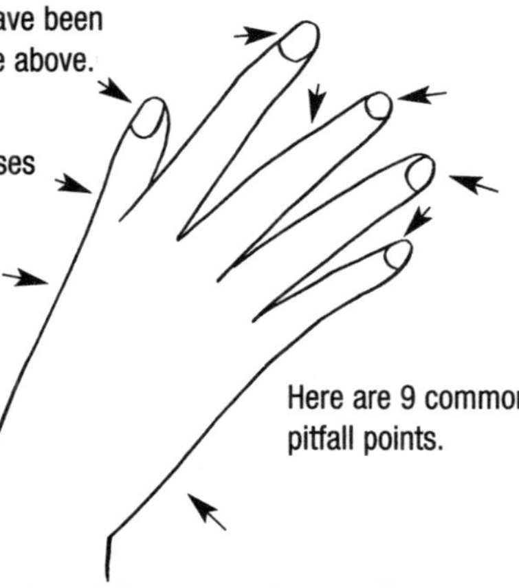

The fingers are different thicknesses and the nails are different sizes.

Here are 9 common pitfall points.

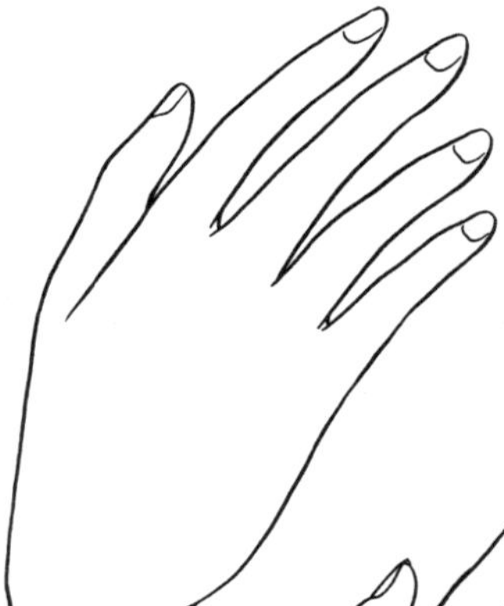

Simple Rendition
Here we see a clean line drawing.

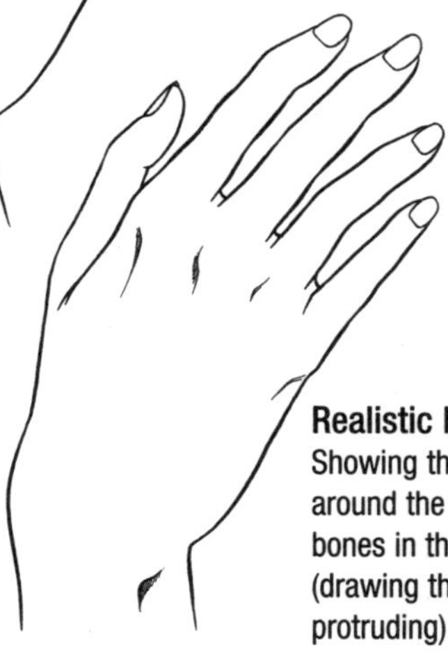

Realistic Rendition
Showing the muscles around the fingers and bones in the hand (drawing the tendons protruding) gives the hand a realistic flavor.

The Hand Held Unaffectedly

Use these gestures when drawing a figure held naturally or when standing normally.

The hands add to expression of the character's emotional state. It is important to distinguish gestures. To portray a normal or casual atmosphere, show the hands in a relaxed state. To portray tension, show the hands clenched in fists. Take care when drawing the hands, as both natural and contrived or awkward compositions show up clearly to the viewer.

Standing Normally

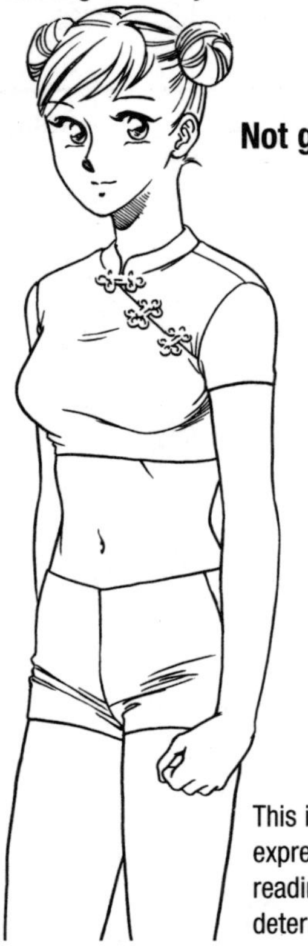

Not good

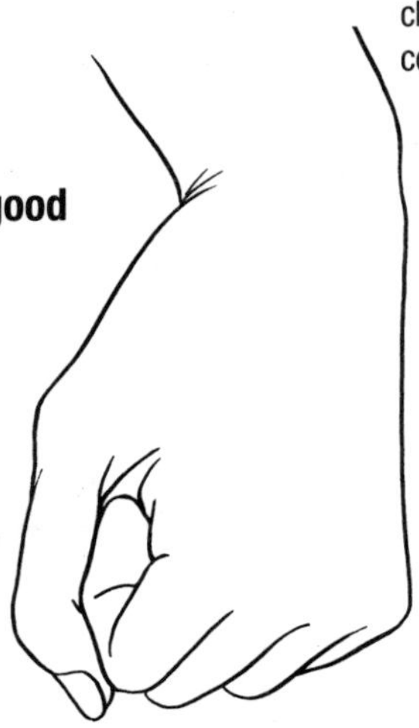

This strongly clenched fist suggests that the character is either about to engage in battle or is feeling oddly tense.

This is a better facial expression for suggesting readiness to fight or determination.

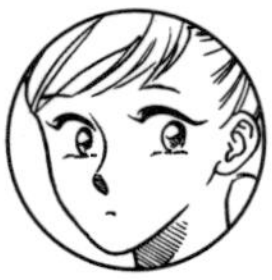

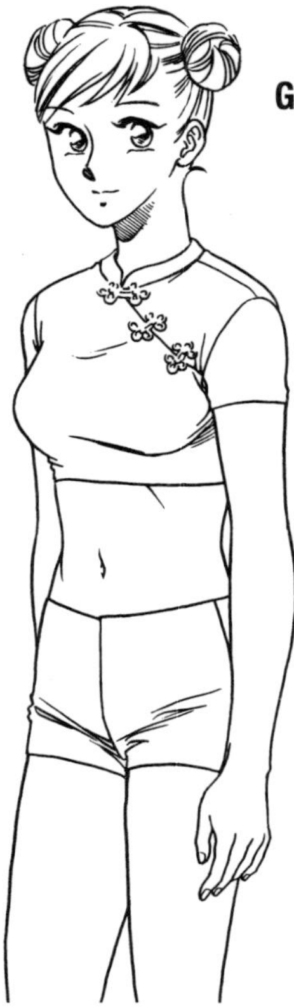

Good

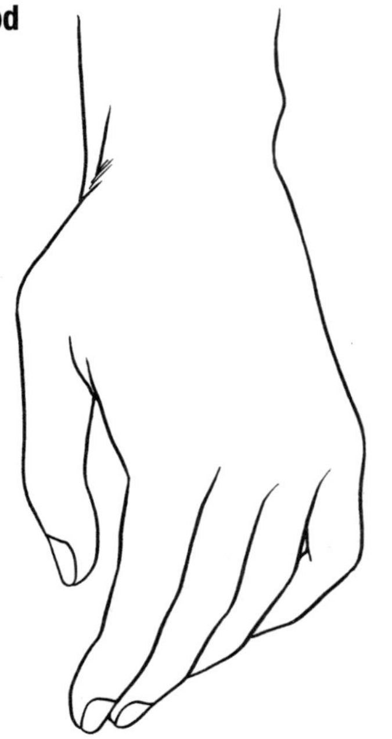

Character in relaxed state

Lightly Clenched Fist

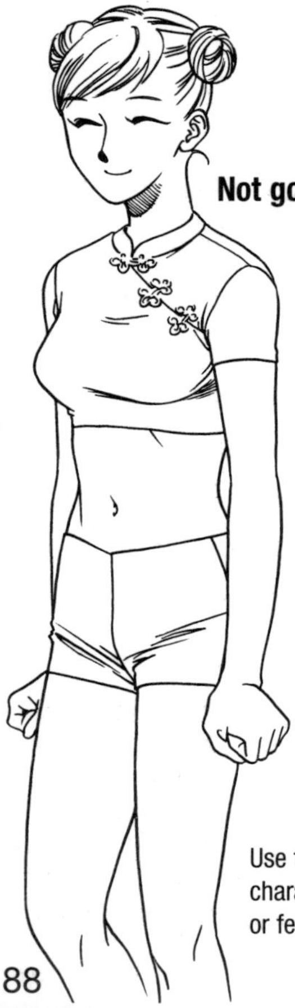

Not good

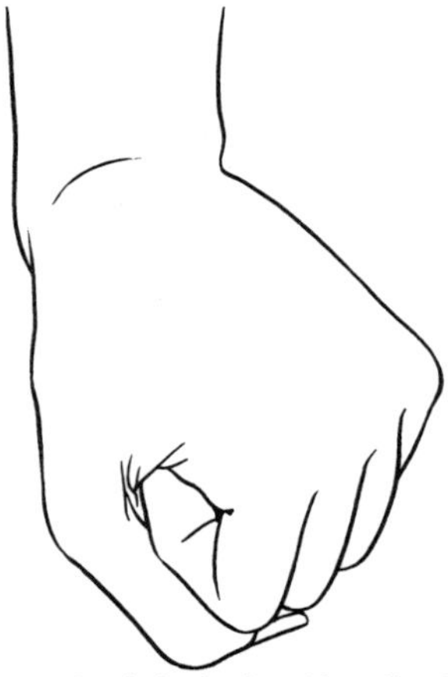

Here, not only is the hand in a fist, but the wrist is bent back. This generates an even more awkward image. Hands drawn like this should only be used in special circumstances or with an odd, eccentric character. It could also be used in combat scenes.

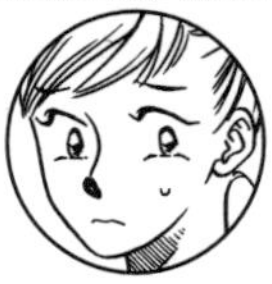

Use this face to show that a character is alerted to something or feeling tense.

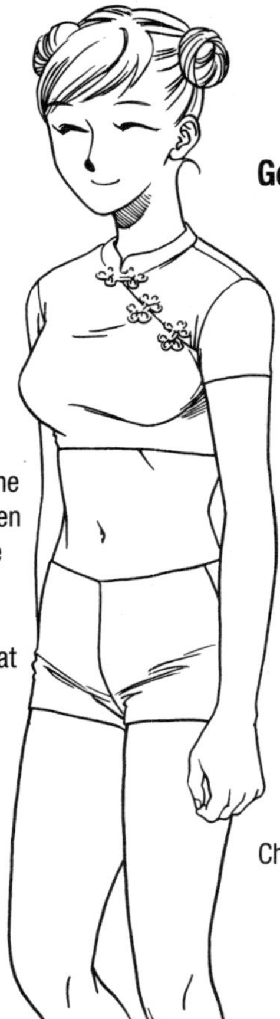

Good

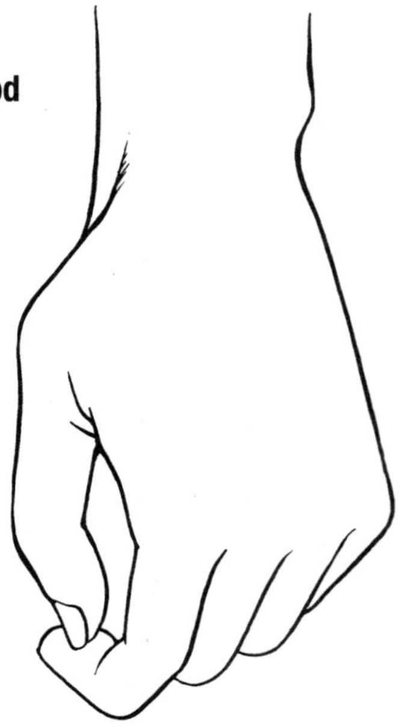

Character in normal state

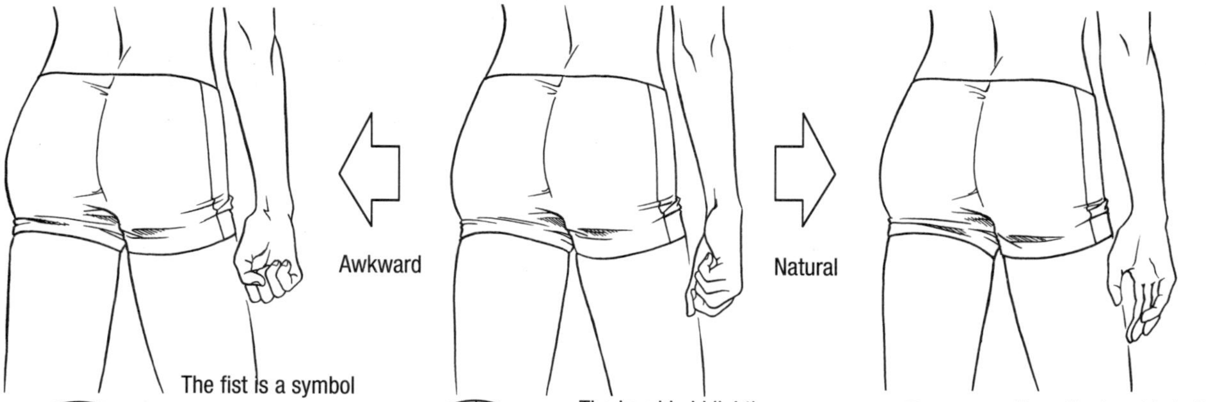

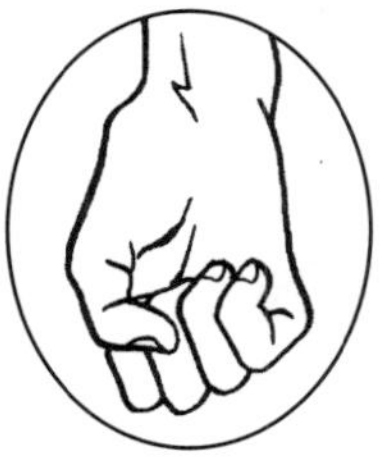

The fist is a symbol of the intent or feeling of tension in the owner. The unconscious clenching of the hand acts as evidence that the character is tense.

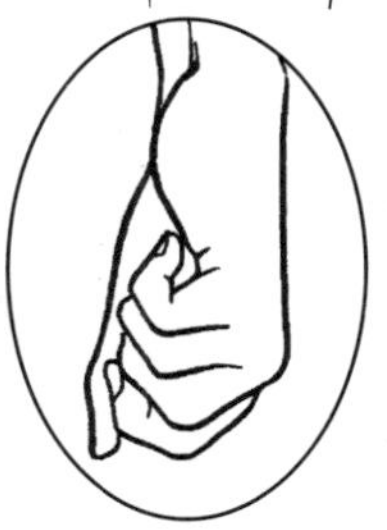

The hand held lightly clenched when the character feels slightly tense or when deep in thought. The character is unconsciously tensing her hand. However, since the hand is not balled into tight fist, the thumb is slack.

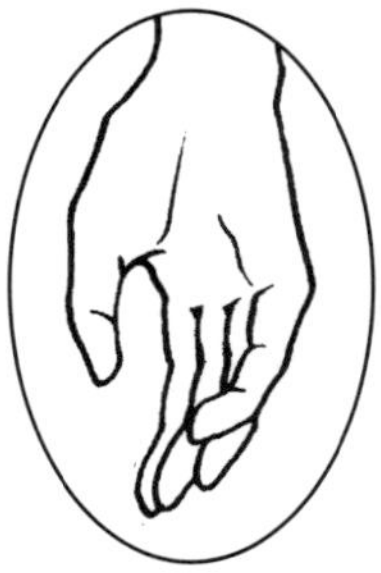

Here, the hand is held open in a normal state. The hand is unconsciously relaxed. The fingers are bent into gentle curves.

Use the hands to show a character's emotional state when glancing back

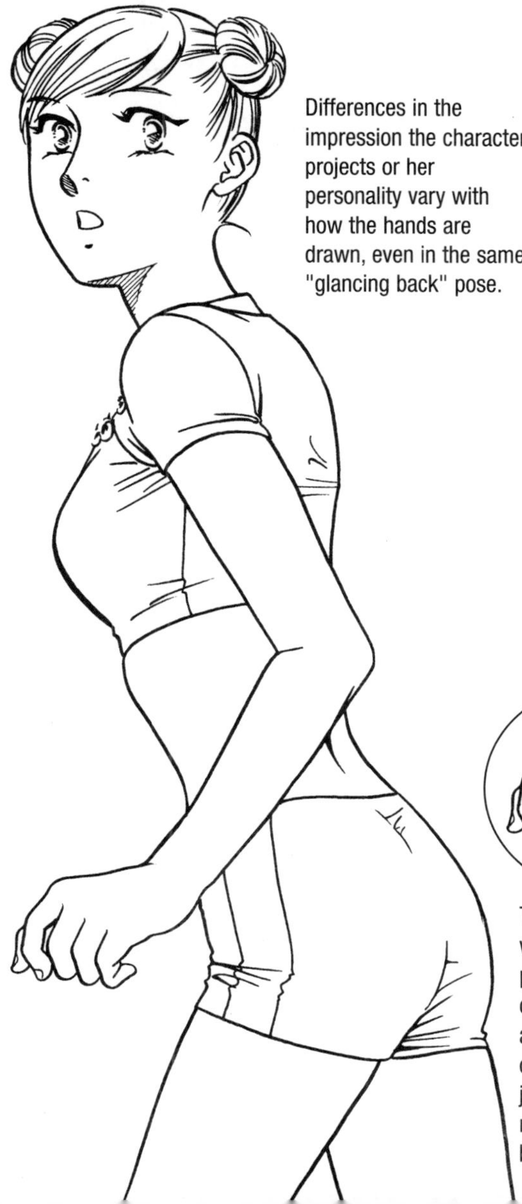

Differences in the impression the character projects or her personality vary with how the hands are drawn, even in the same "glancing back" pose.

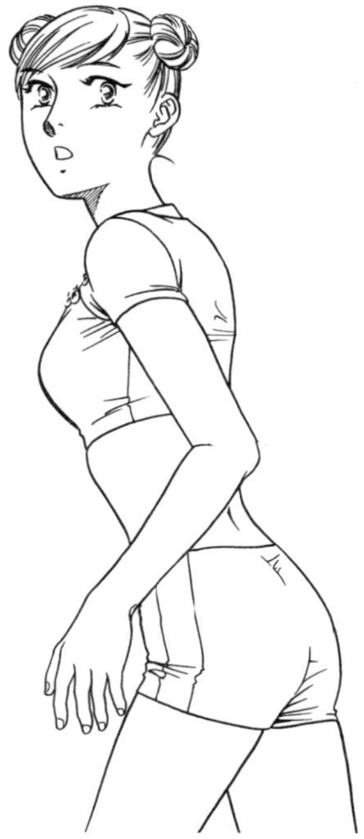

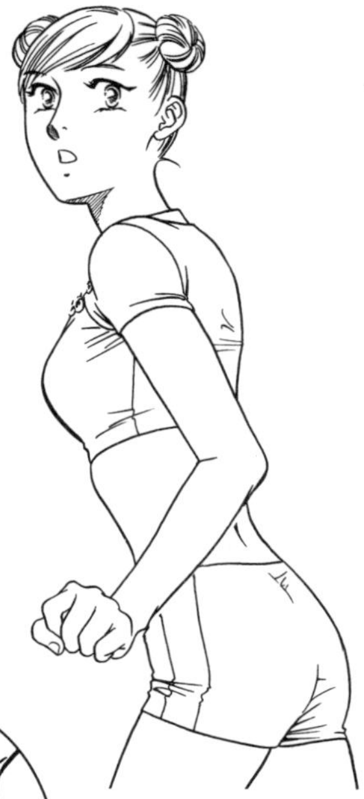

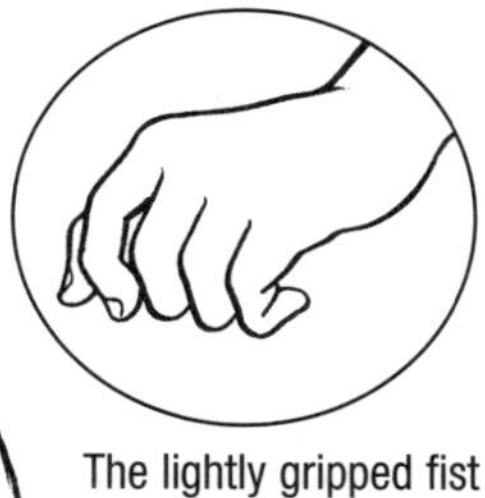

The lightly gripped fist is works well when portraying the moment a character glances back and is slightly surprised or experiences a little jolt. This is the hand most suited to looking back unaffectedly.

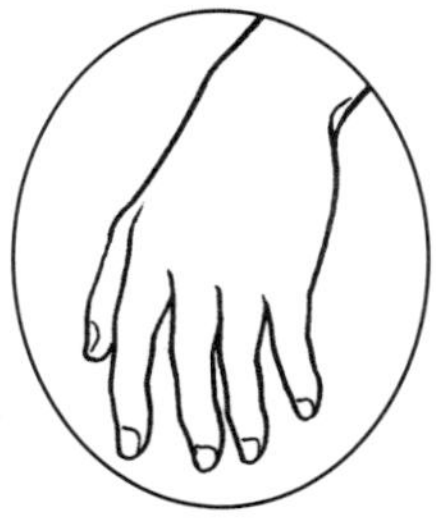

The open hand suggests that a limply held hand. This hand is suited to suggesting disappointment.

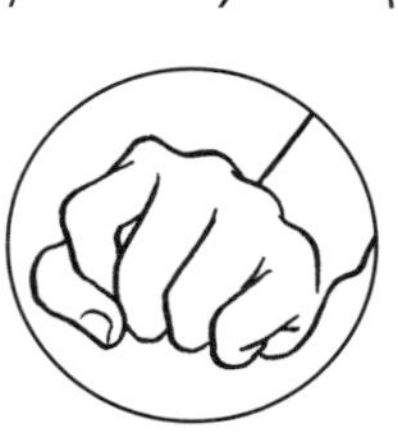

The clenched fist works well when showing the character in mid-sprint or to suggest a determined state ("You can't make me!" etc.)

The Legs

Extension and contraction of the legs are primarily allocated to kick scenes. The prevailing trend is to indicate that the leg is extended using special effects lines or other means to blur the foot.

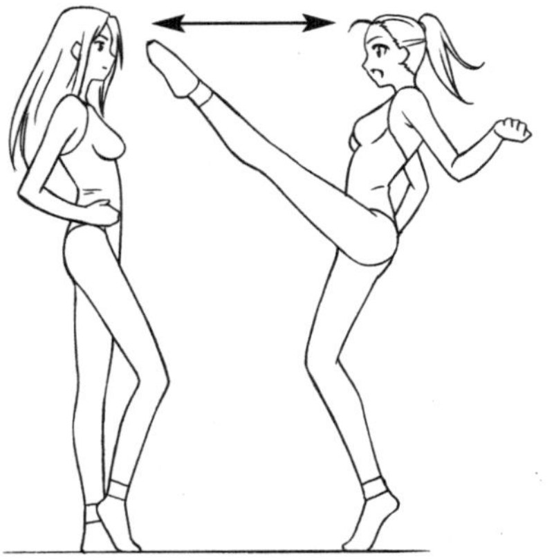

There is no way the kick can be delivered from this distance.

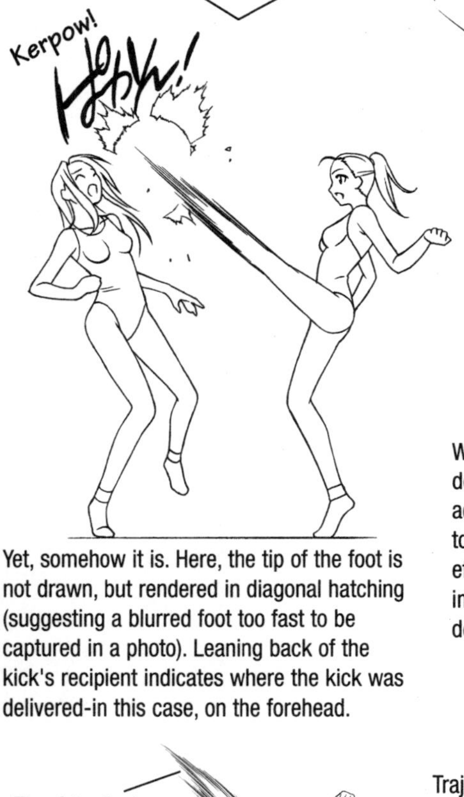

Yet, somehow it is. Here, the tip of the foot is not drawn, but rendered in diagonal hatching (suggesting a blurred foot too fast to be captured in a photo). Leaning back of the kick's recipient indicates where the kick was delivered-in this case, on the forehead.

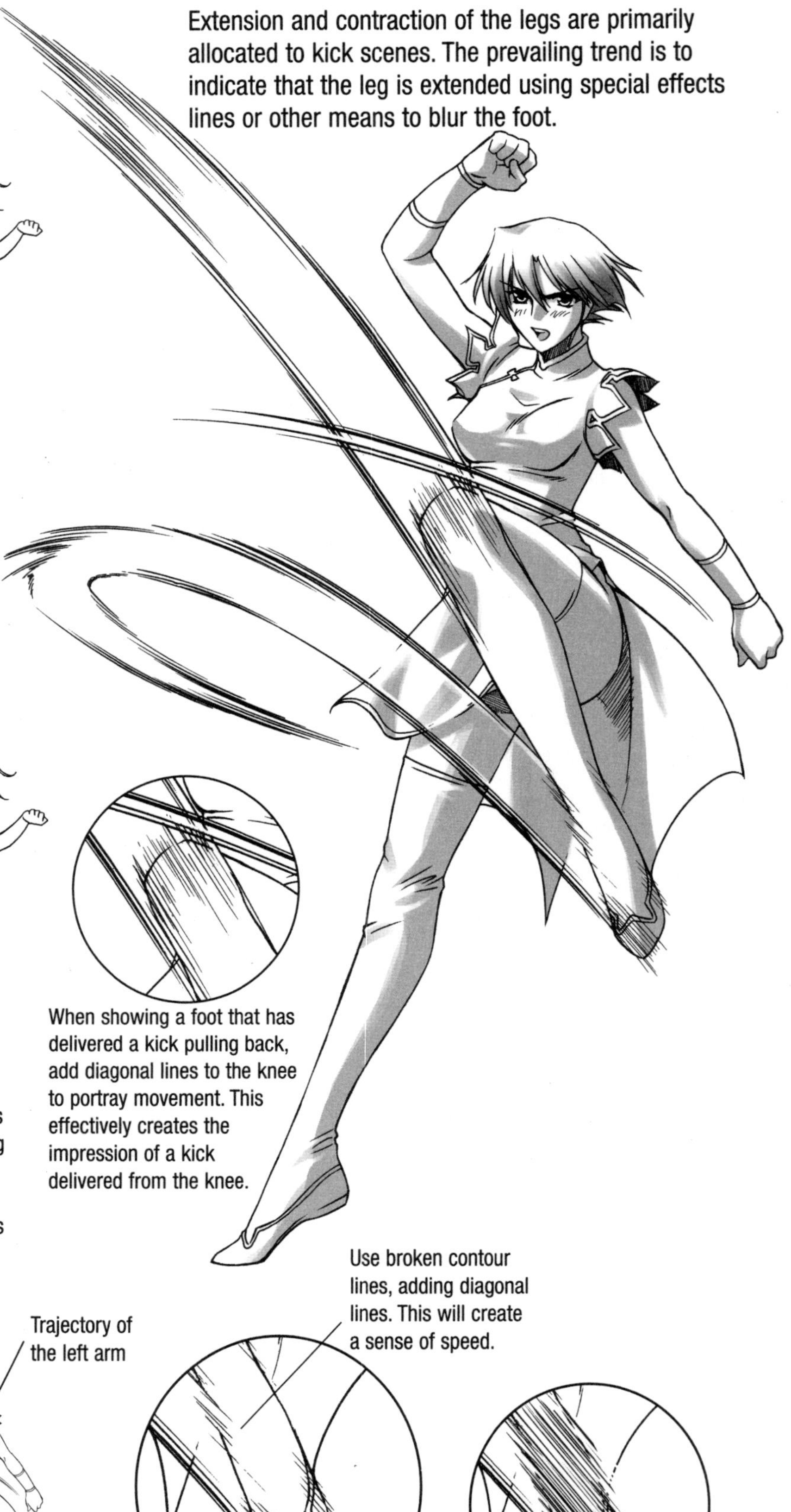

When showing a foot that has delivered a kick pulling back, add diagonal lines to the knee to portray movement. This effectively creates the impression of a kick delivered from the knee.

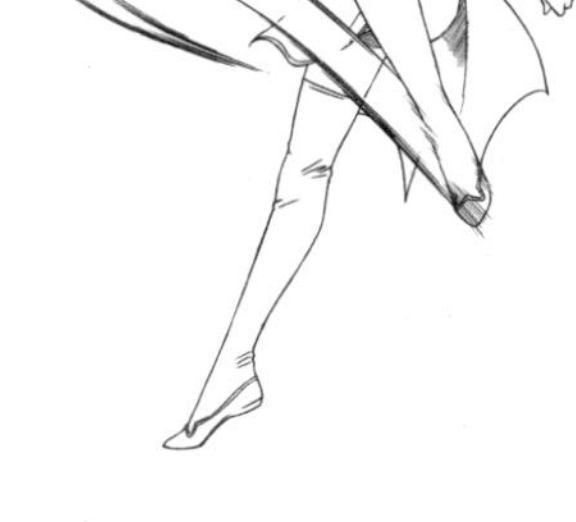

Use broken contour lines, adding diagonal lines. This will create a sense of speed.

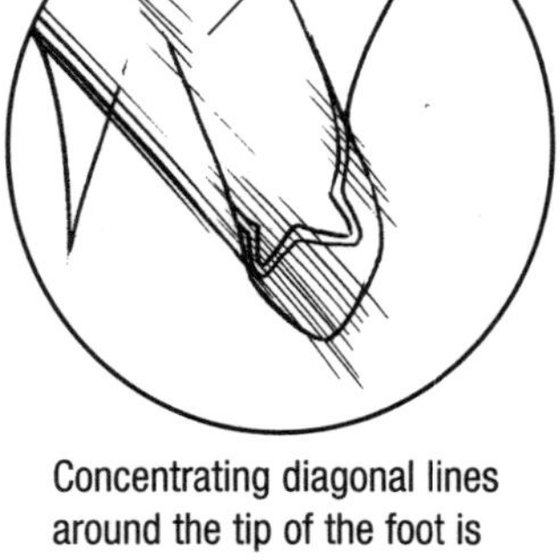

Concentrating diagonal lines around the tip of the foot is a standard technique for suggesting speed.

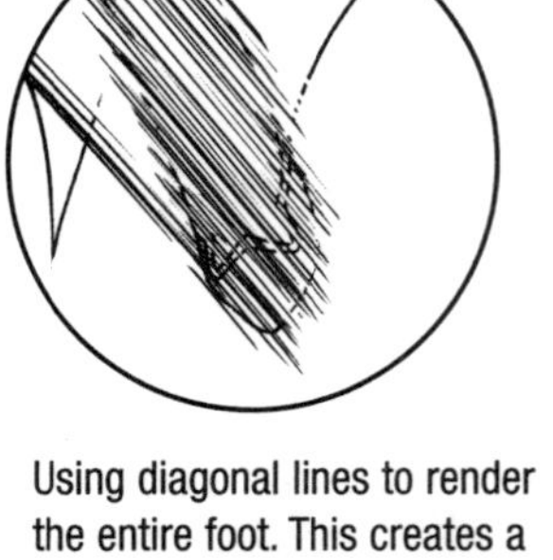

Using diagonal lines to render the entire foot. This creates a "shadow," suggesting extreme blurring.

The Feet

This page shows key points in the bending (extending and contracting) of the ankle and tip of the foot. There is not a wide range for portraying the toes themselves bending and stretching.

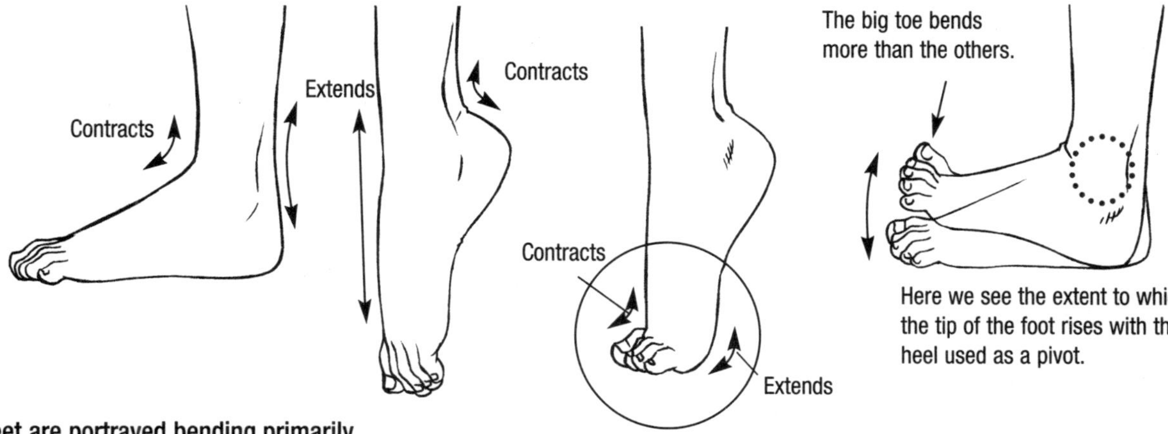

Feet are portrayed bending primarily in walking scenes.

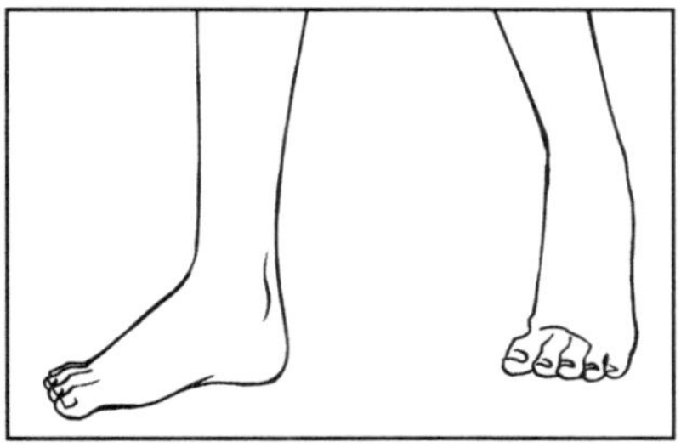

Barefoot

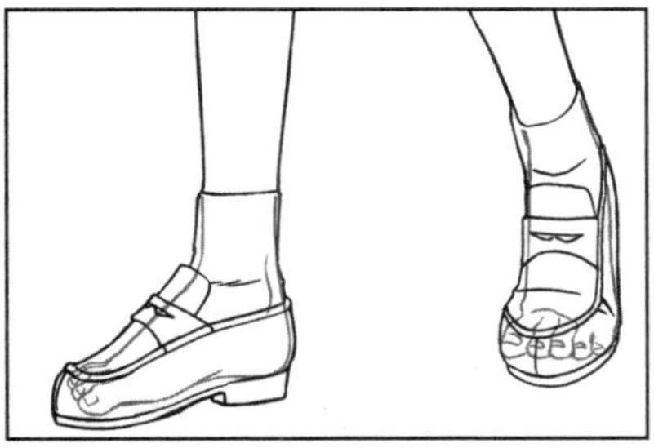

When drawing the feet in shoes, the feet may be drawn the same size as when barefoot or made bigger all around.

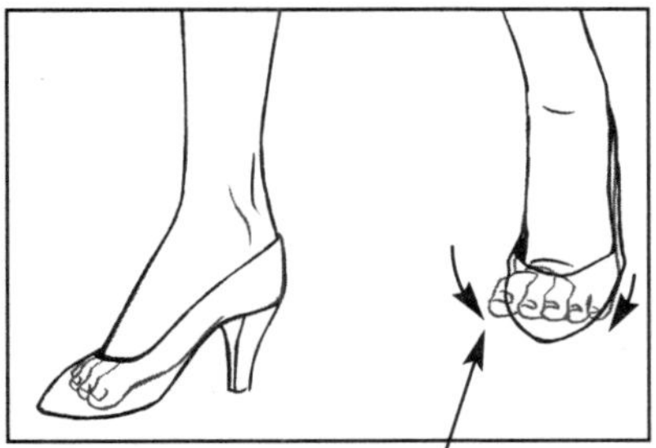

Note that the foot takes on a different shape when clad in high heels.

The toes are actually crammed tightly together in the shoe.

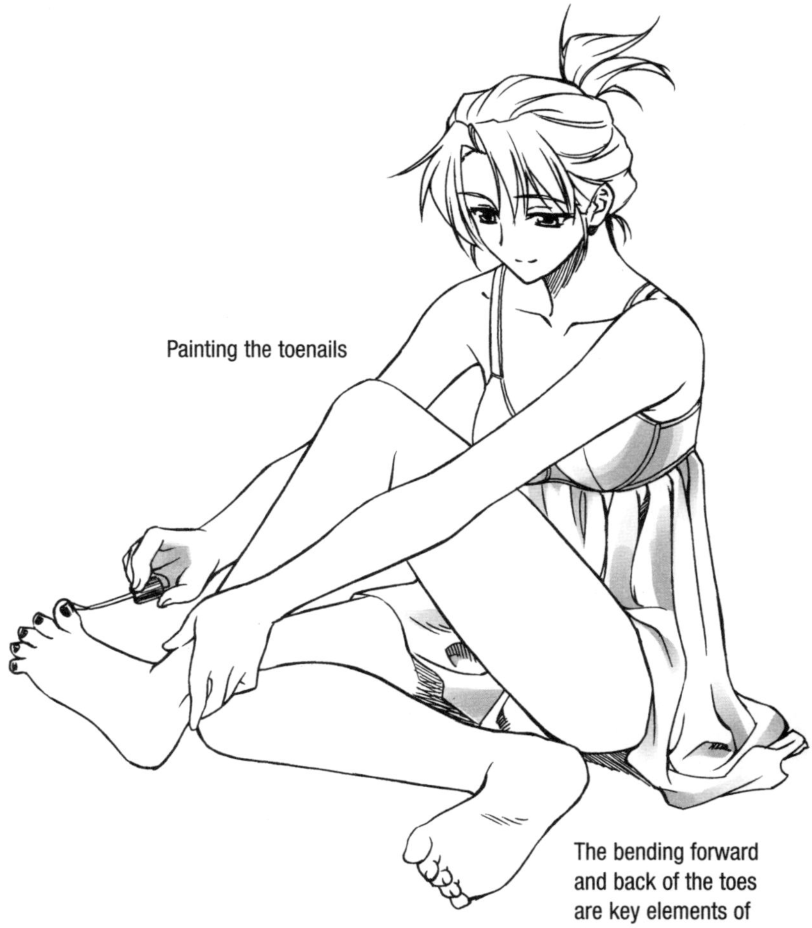

Painting the toenails

The bending forward and back of the toes are key elements of this pose.

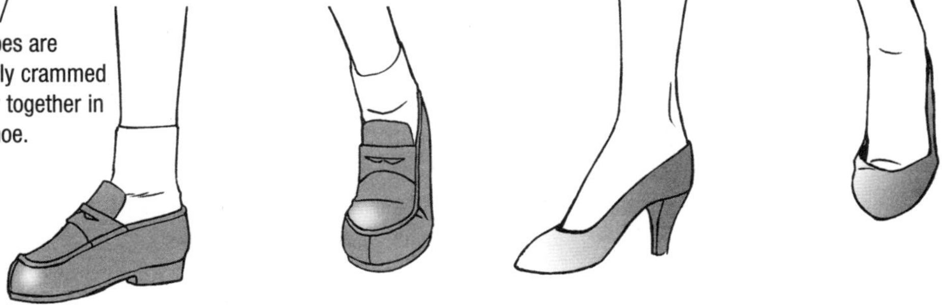

The Waist and Back

Bending over causes skin folds to form in the abdomen.

Bending Over and Hunkering Down

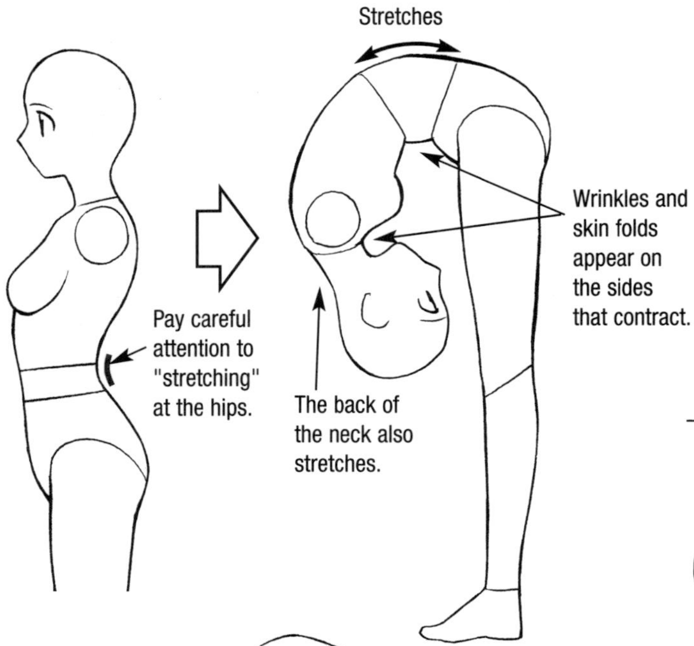

Common Poses with the Back Rounded

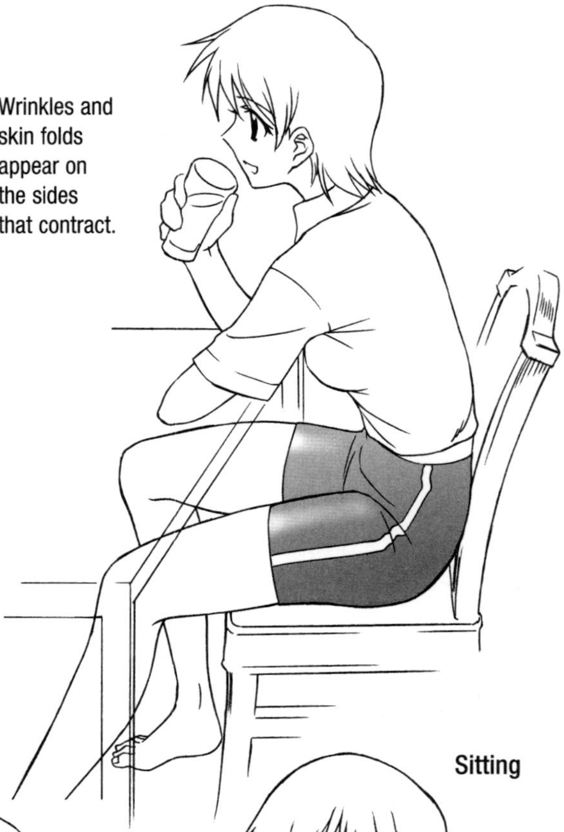

Sitting

Bowing

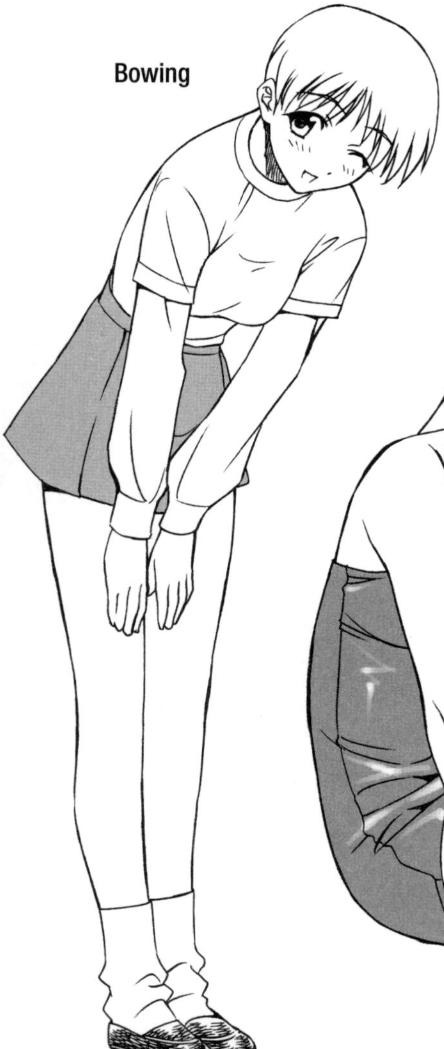

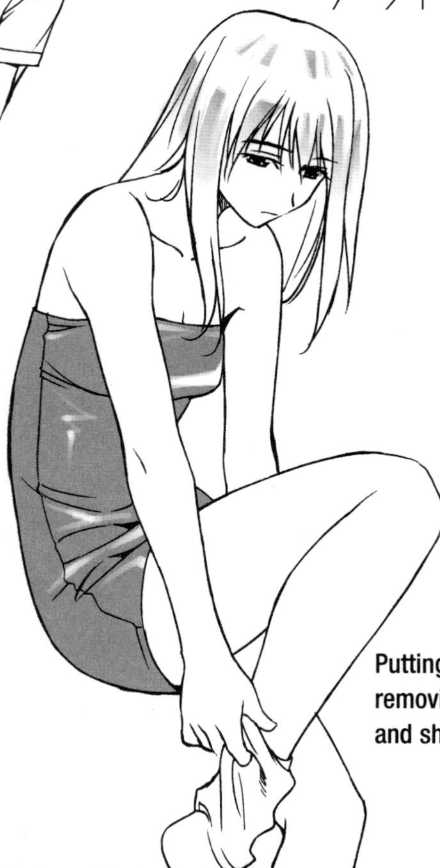

Putting on or removing socks and shoes

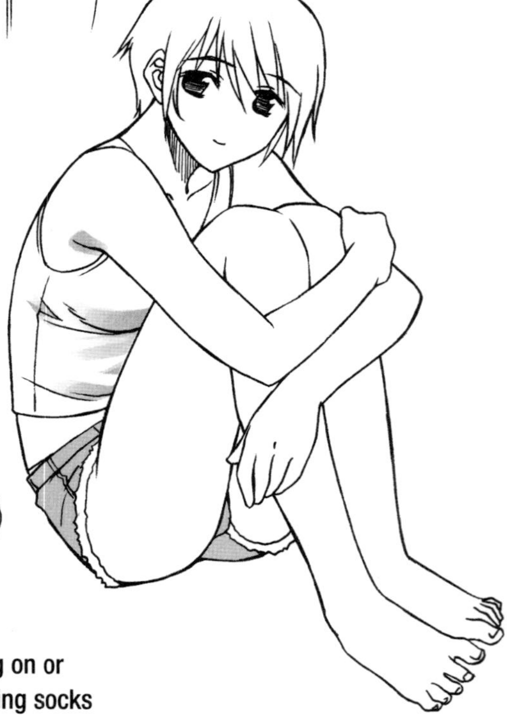

When the back is rounded, the shoulders roll forward

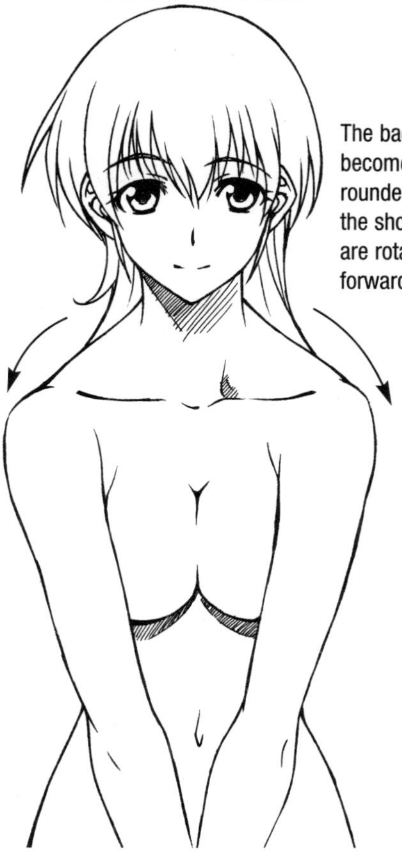

Pay careful attention to how the shoulders rotate forward and back.

The back becomes rounded when the shoulders are rotate forward.

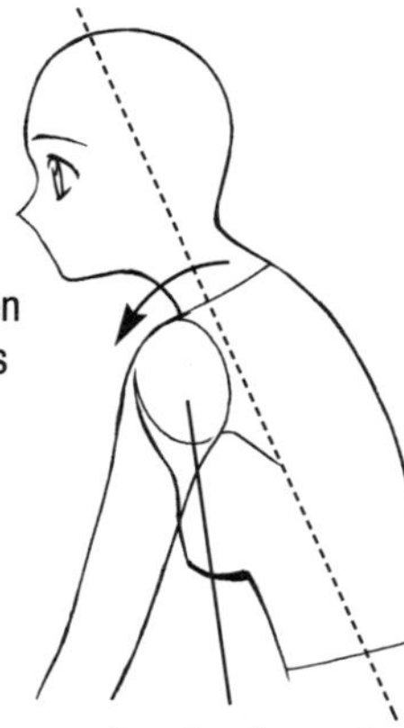

Leaning forward

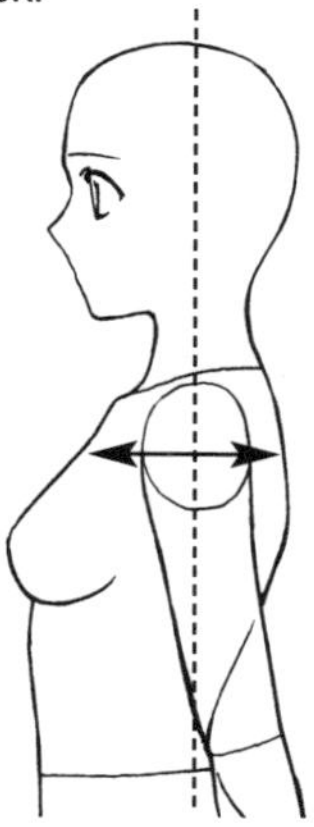

In a normal stance, the shoulders are fairly much centered.

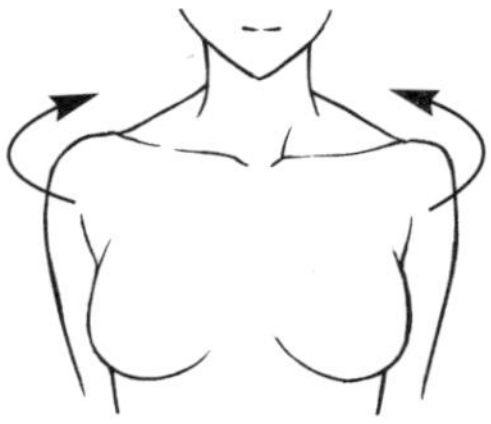

Drawing the shoulders back causes the chest to thrust outward and the back to arc rearward.

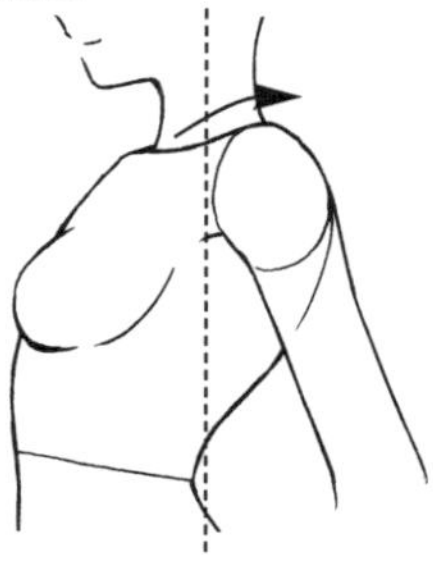

Bow in Greeting

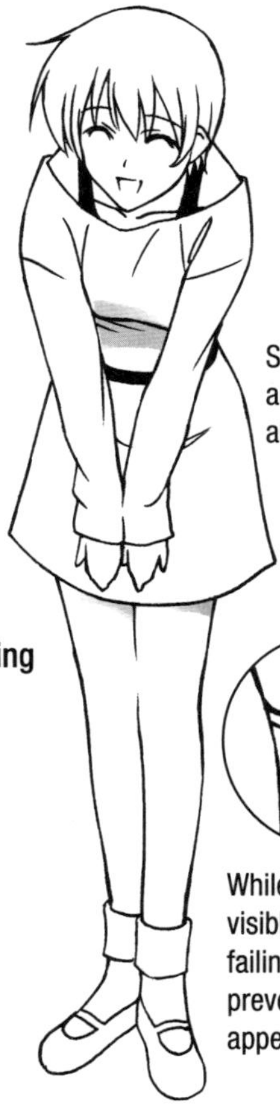

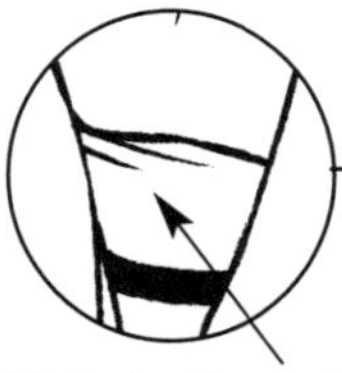

While hardly any folds are visible from the front, failing to draw them will prevent the figure from appearing to be bowing.

Deep Bow

The small of the back stretches.

The muscles along the spine follow a natural curve.

Skin folds appear in the abdomen.

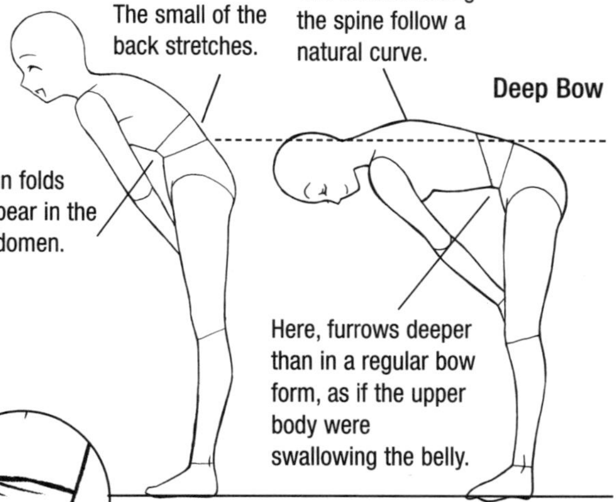

Here, furrows deeper than in a regular bow form, as if the upper body were swallowing the belly.

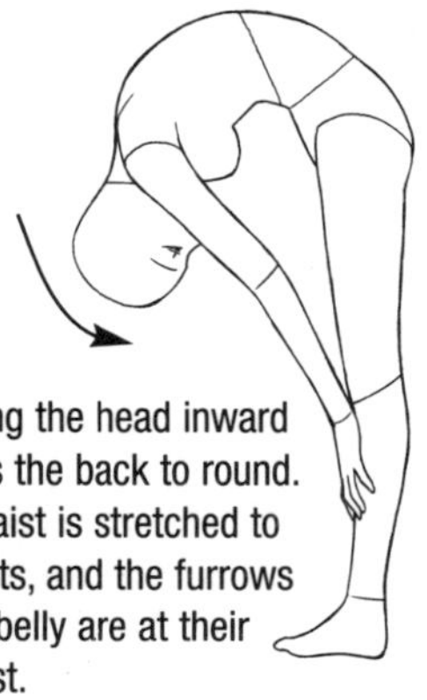

Drawing the head inward causes the back to round. The waist is stretched to its limits, and the furrows in the belly are at their deepest.

Disappointed

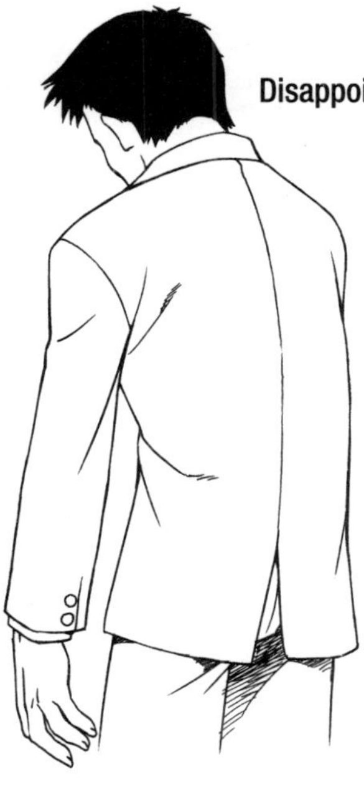

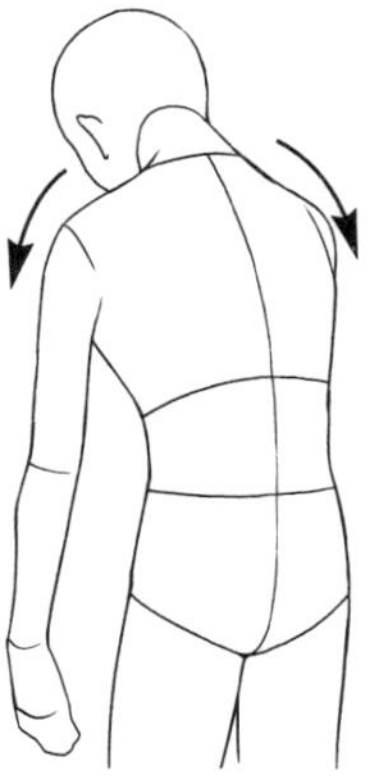

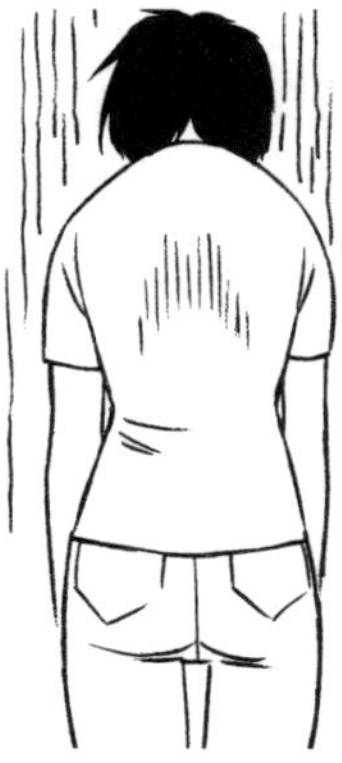

In disappointed and tired backs, the shoulders are rotated forward, and the back is rounded. Exaggerate the look of the sloping shoulders when drawing.

Sitting

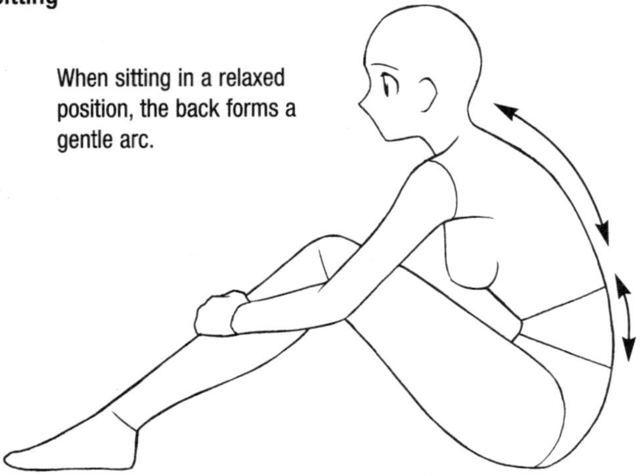

When sitting in a relaxed position, the back forms a gentle arc.

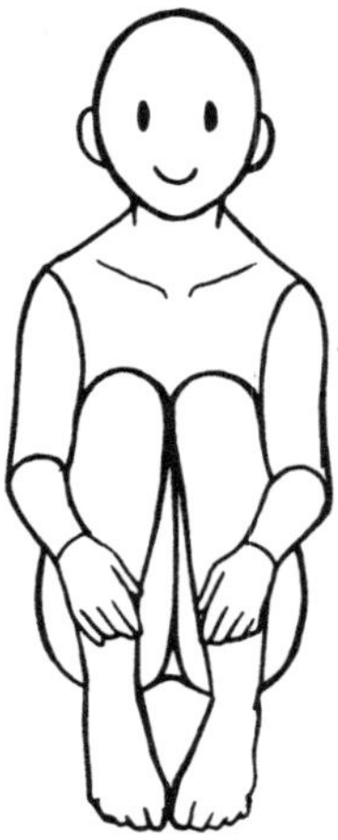

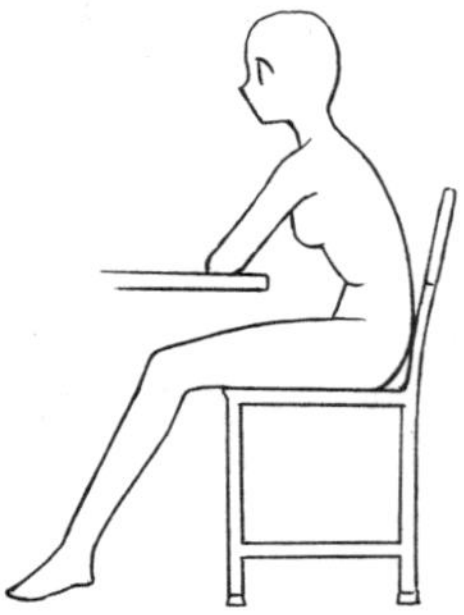

The same holds true for sitting in a chair.

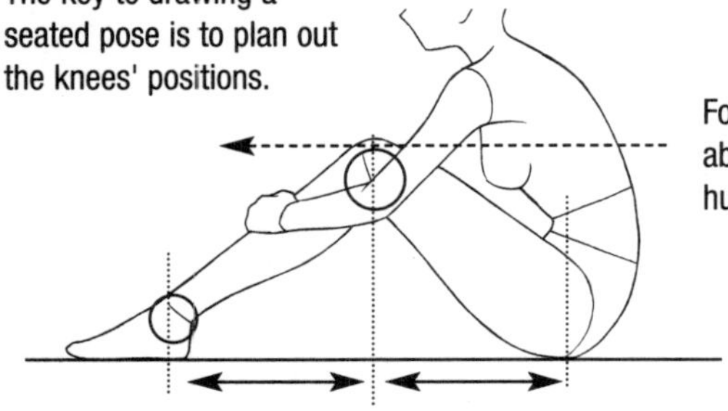

The key to drawing a seated pose is to plan out the knees' positions.

Folds form in the abdomen when slightly hunched forward.

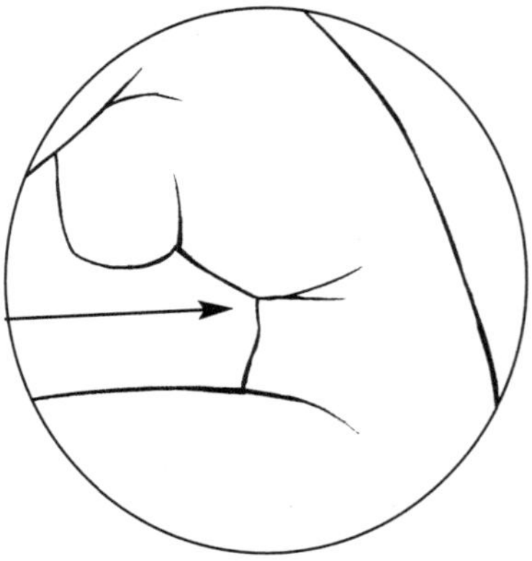

When dressed, creases at the abdomen vary according to the clothing worn.

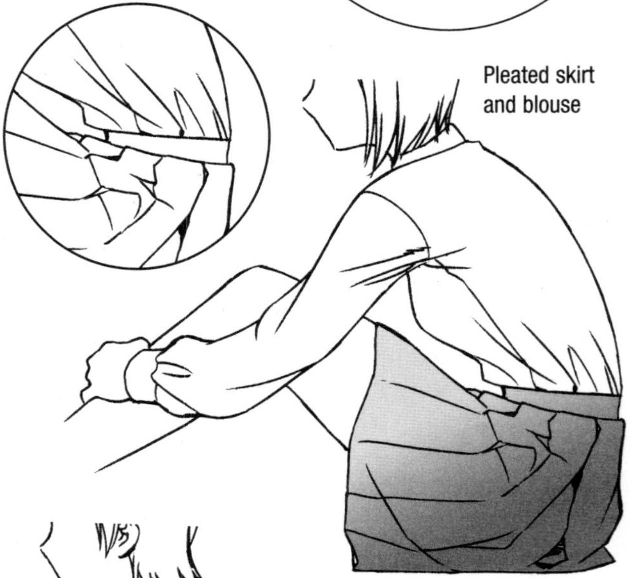

Pleated skirt and blouse

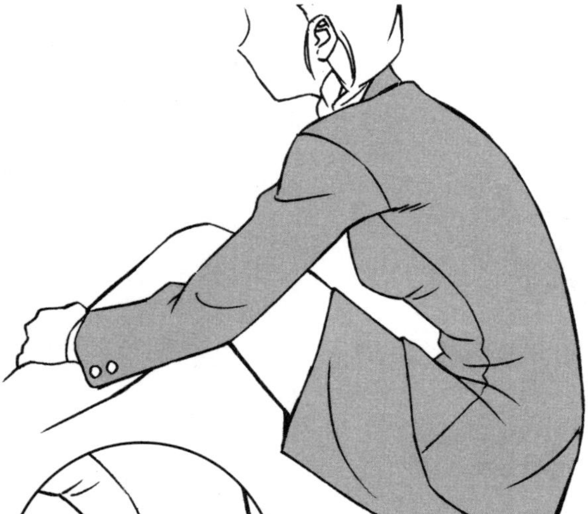

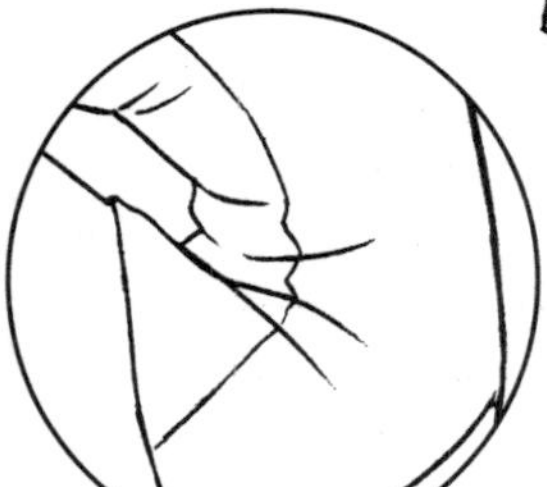

Suit skirt and jacket

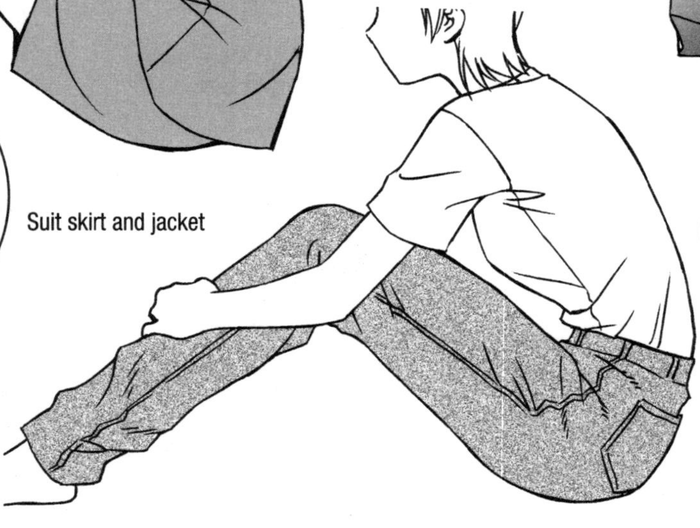

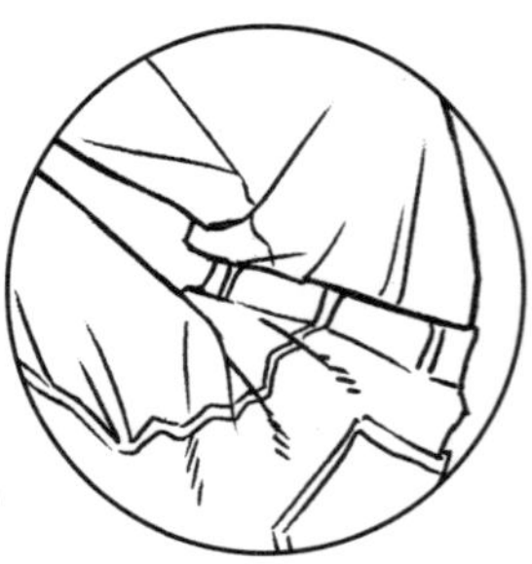

T-shirt and jeans

Sitting Regularly, But Slightly Hunched Forward

In both the back study diagram and the high, oblique angled study diagram, the roundness of the back looks best when not overemphasized. Use a gentle curve for the slope of the back.

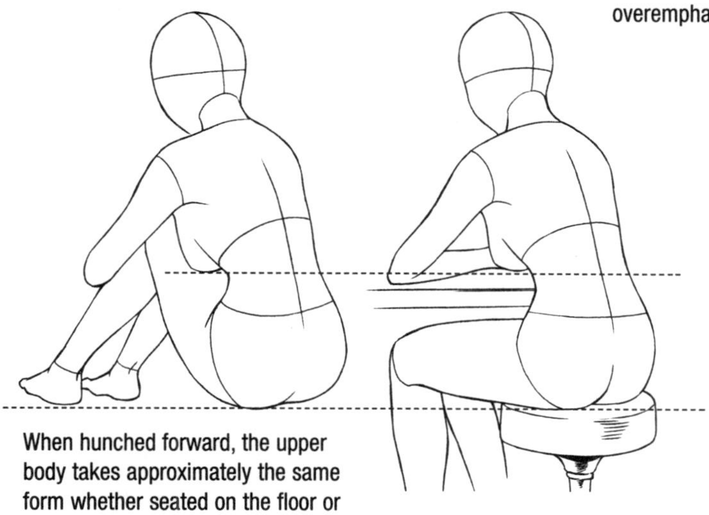

When hunched forward, the upper body takes approximately the same form whether seated on the floor or in a chair.

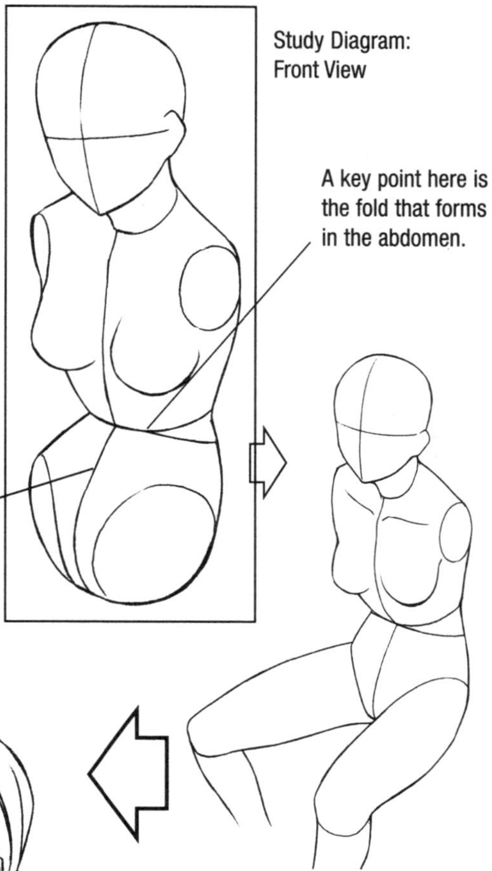

Study Diagram: Front View

A key point here is the fold that forms in the abdomen.

A key point when drawing the figure facing the picture plane is to draw the centerline of the hips facing forward.

Study Diagram for Practical Application

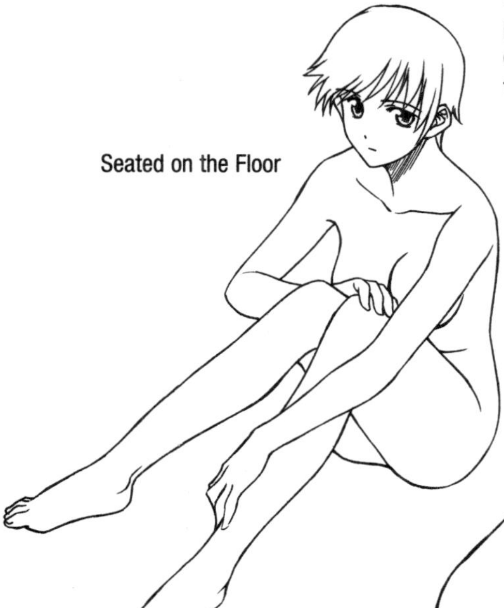

Seated on the Floor

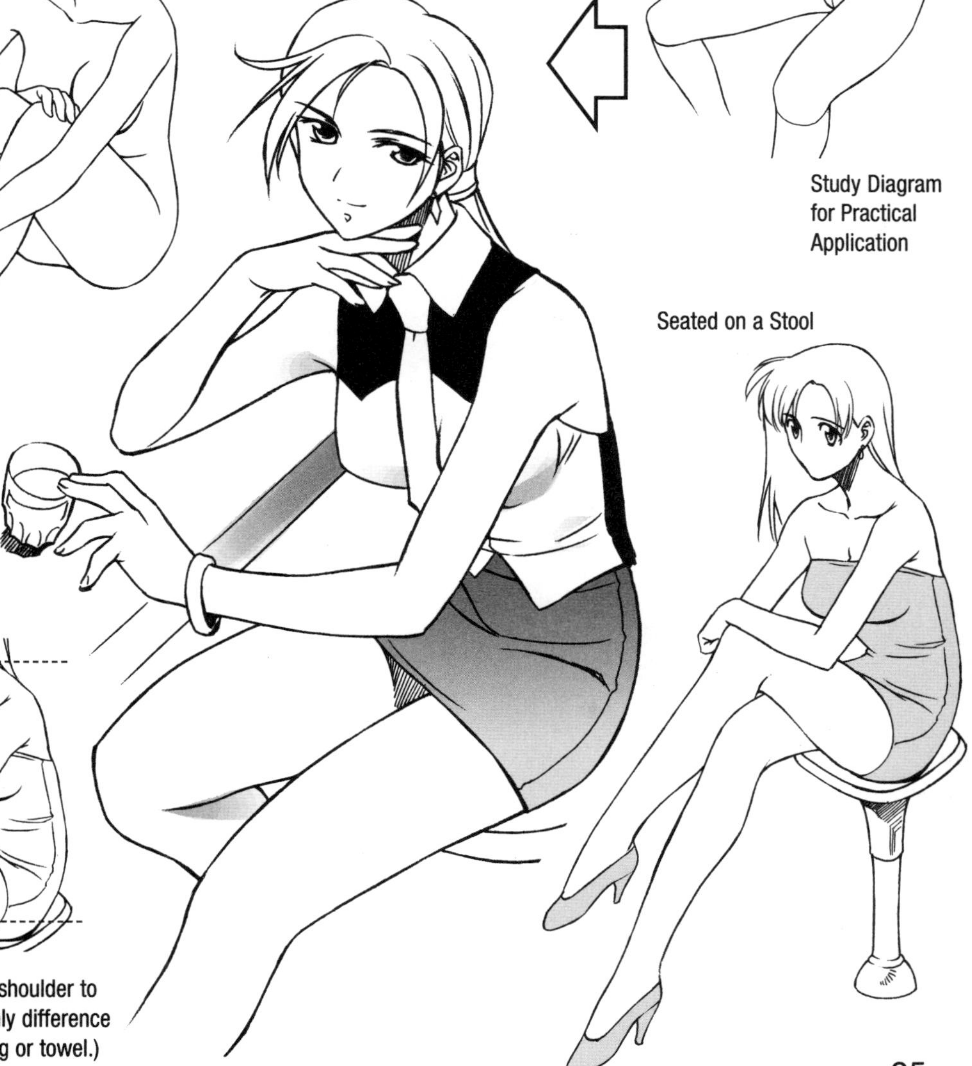

Seated on a Stool

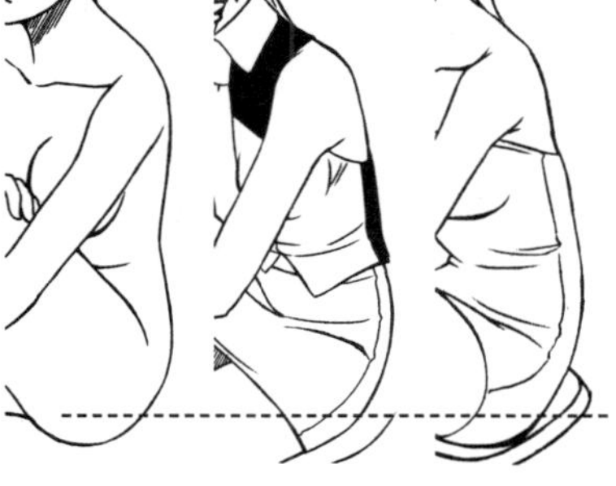

In all 3, the contour from the shoulder to the back is the same. (The only difference is the thickness of the clothing or towel.)

Sitting While Hugging a Knee

①

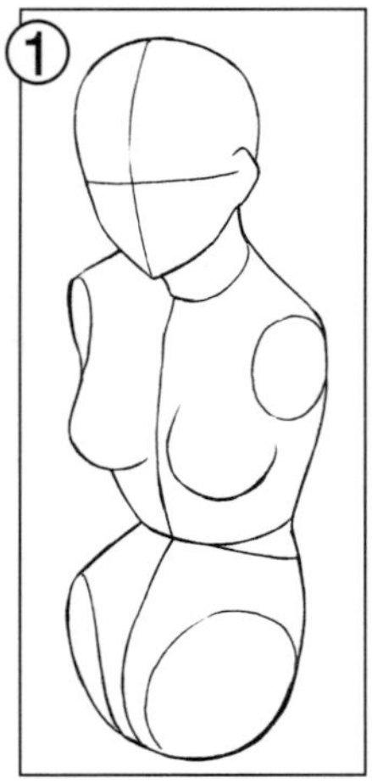

Study Diagram

②

Rough sketch (under drawing)

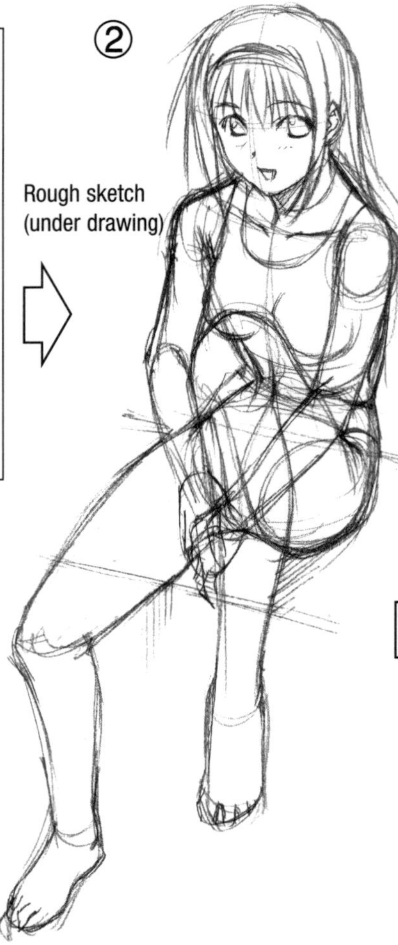

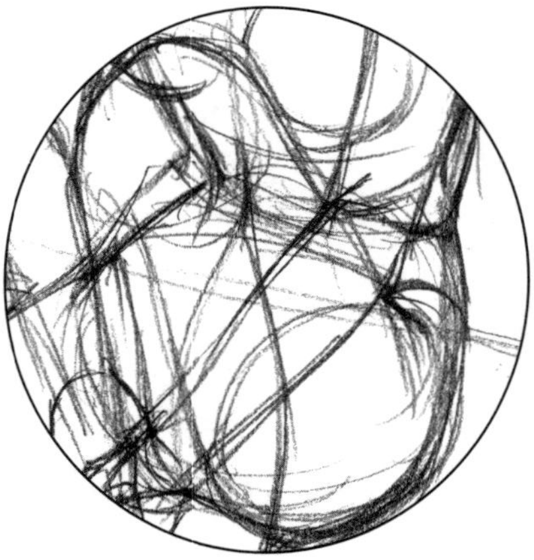

Establish the shapes of the waist and abdomen, even though the arms and leg will obscure them in the final drawing. Identifying the body's entire structure will help you balance the legs.

③

Line drawing

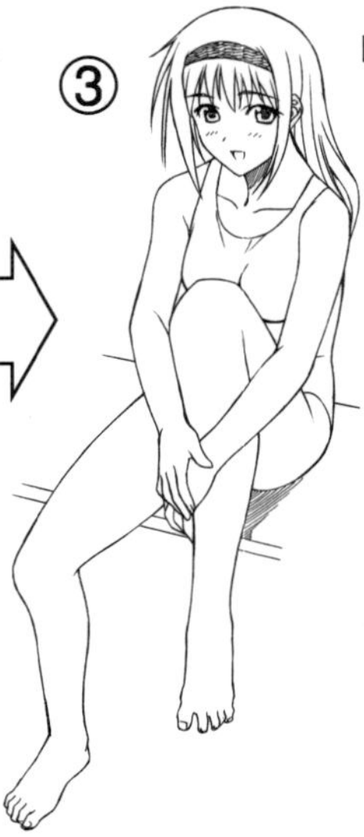

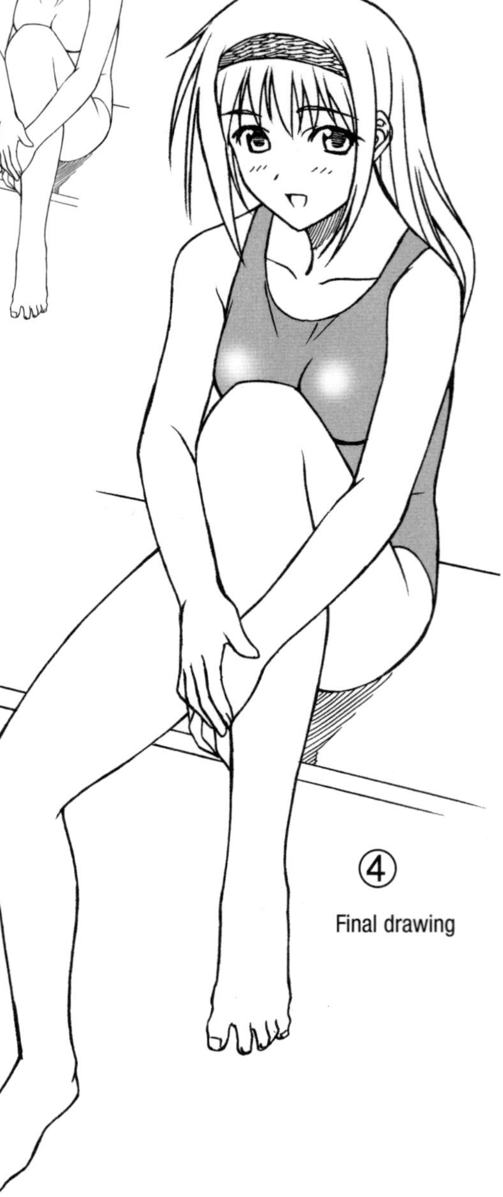

④

Final drawing

Back View

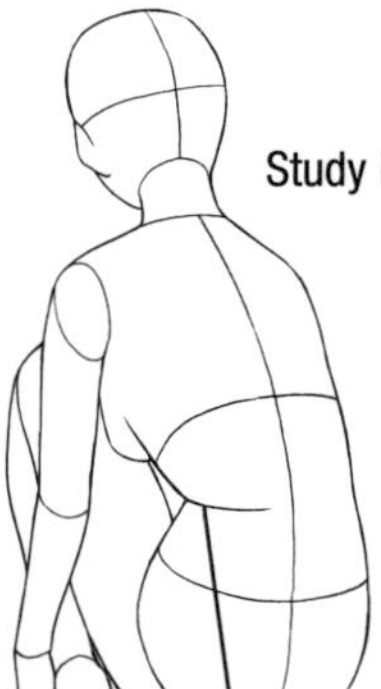

Study Diagram

This skin fold in the back is a key point.

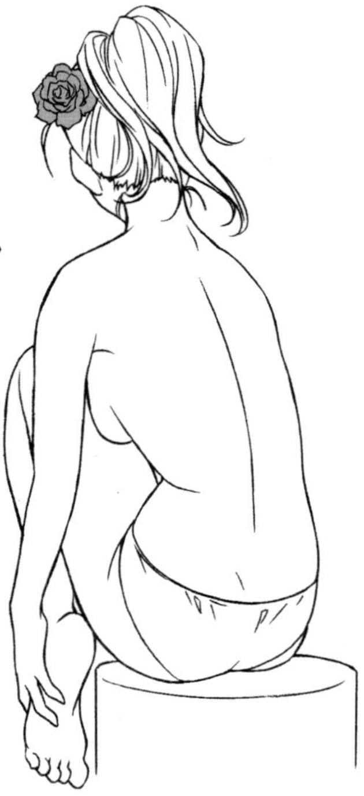

Not good

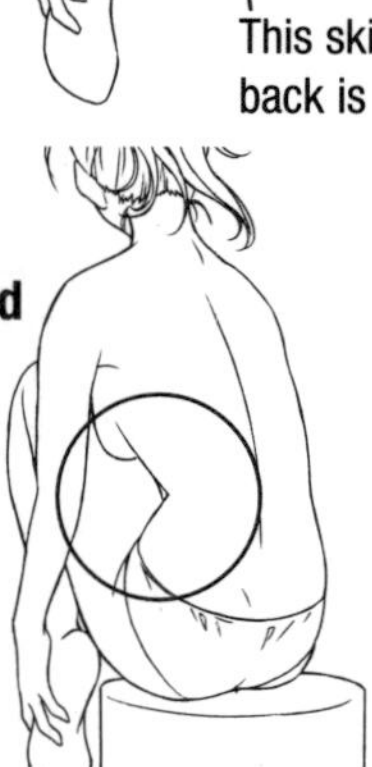

Failing to include a skin fold in the back will make the character appear contrived, causing her to lose her sense of presence.

2 Postures for Sitting on the Floor with the Knees Bent

Hunched over

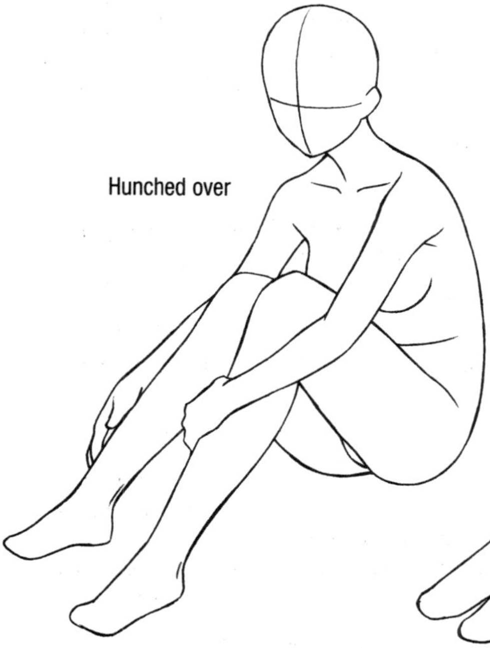

Straight back

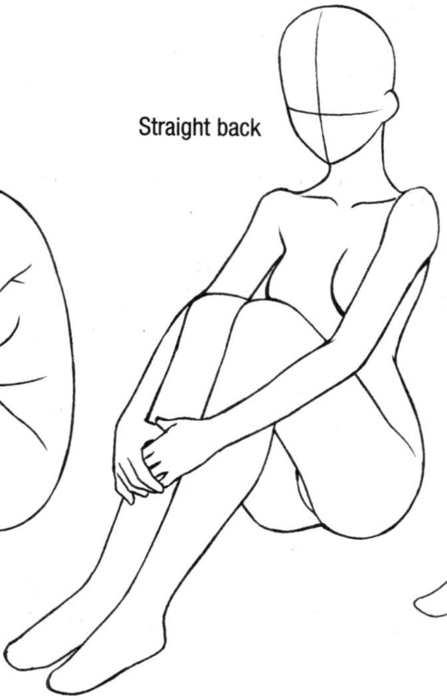

The 2 postures overlapped

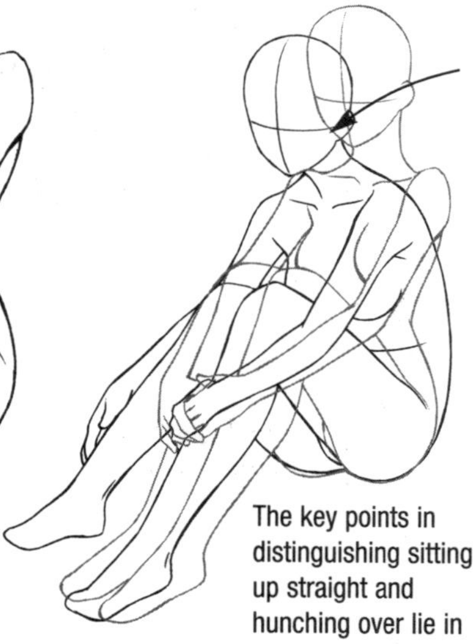

The key points in distinguishing sitting up straight and hunching over lie in the shoulder line and waist.

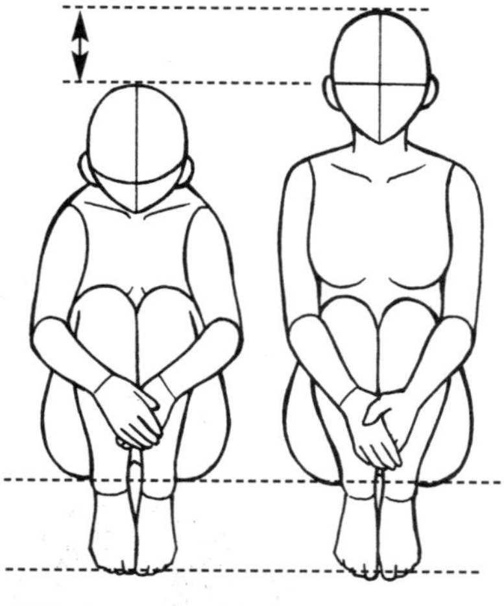

With characters of identical height, the 2 postures result in a half-head difference in height.

Differences in the back contours

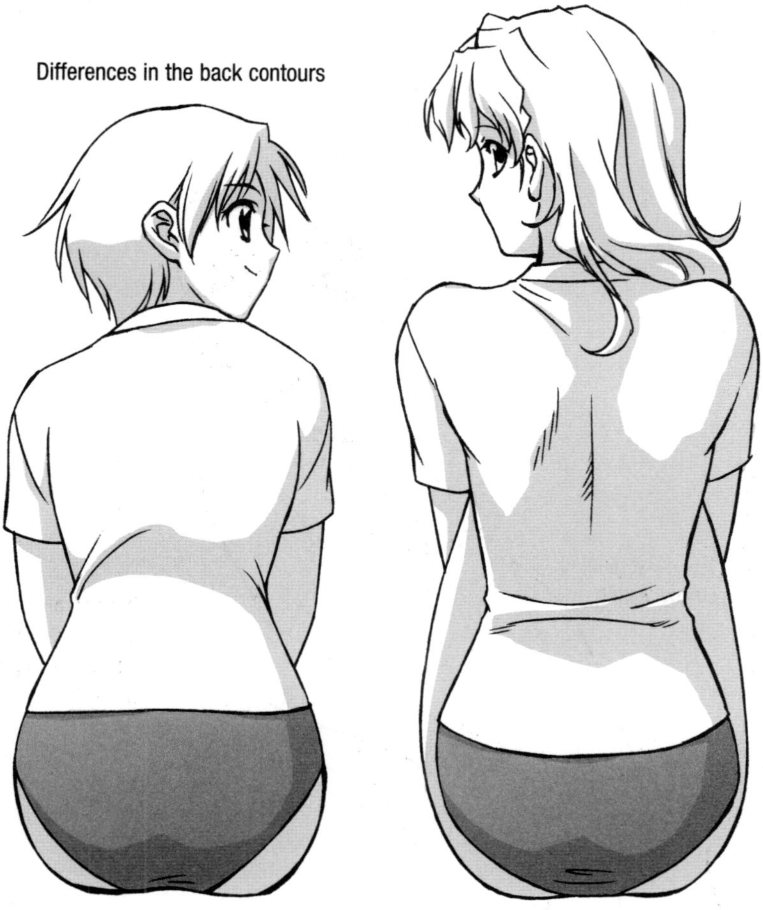

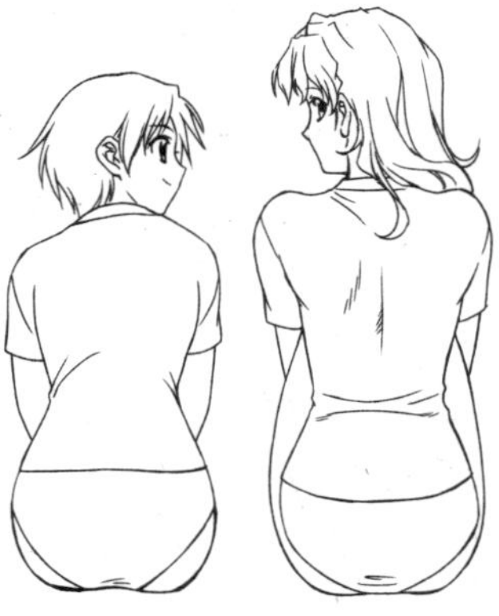

Key Points in Distinguishing the 2 Postures

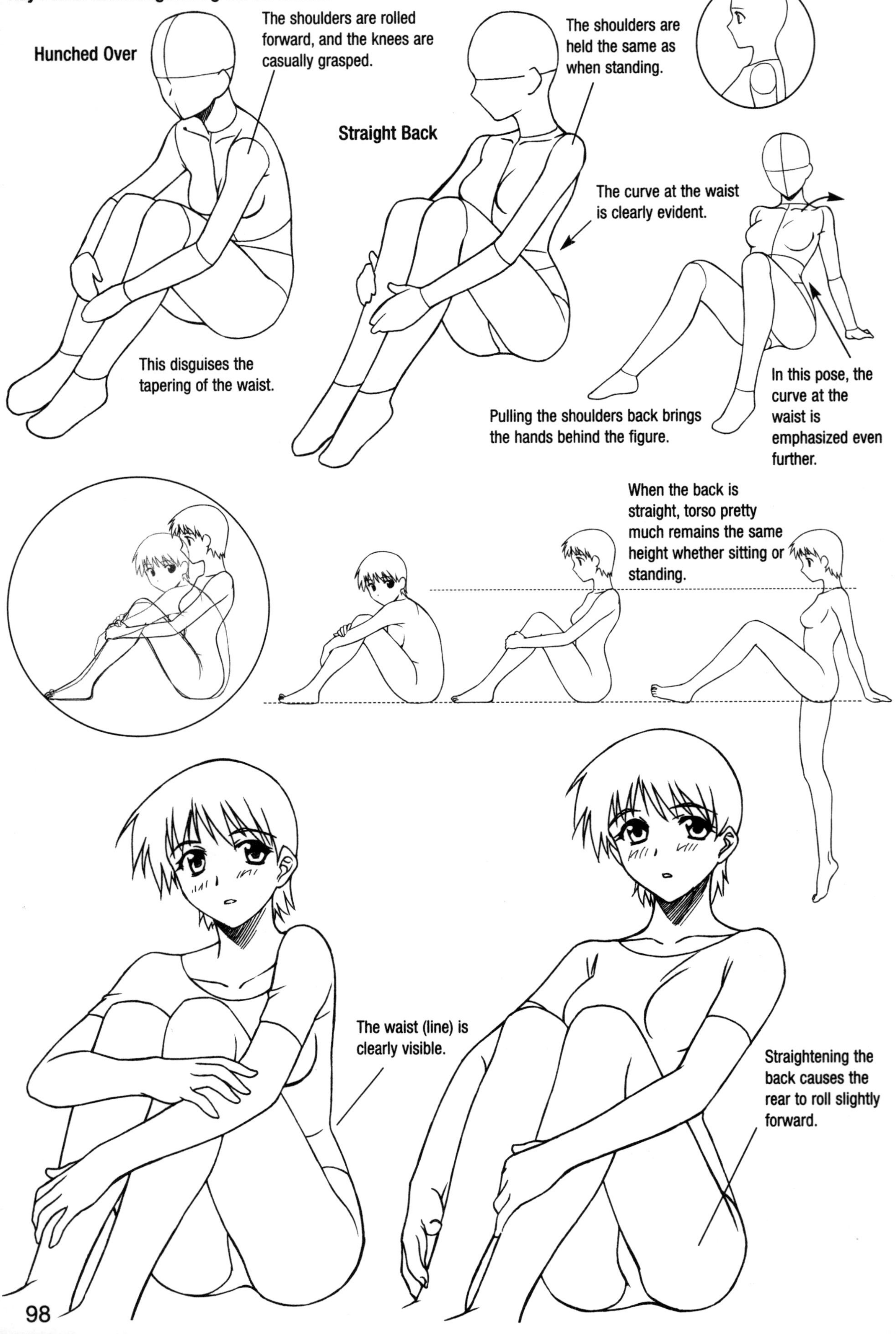

Hugging the Knees

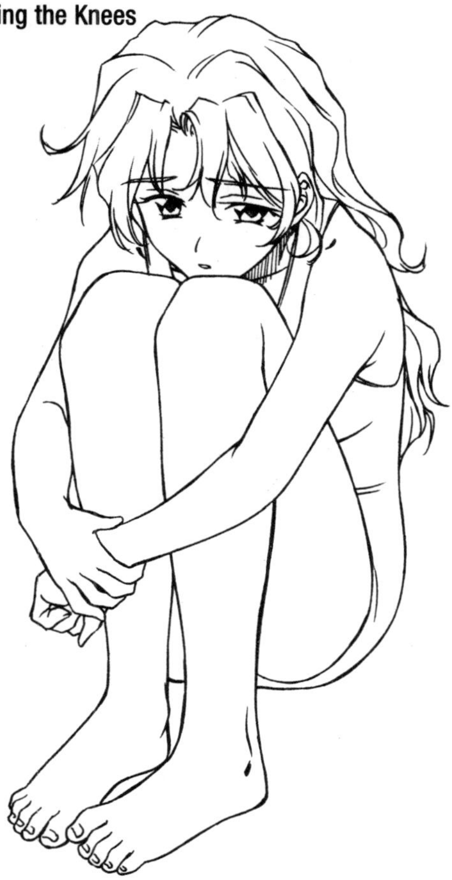

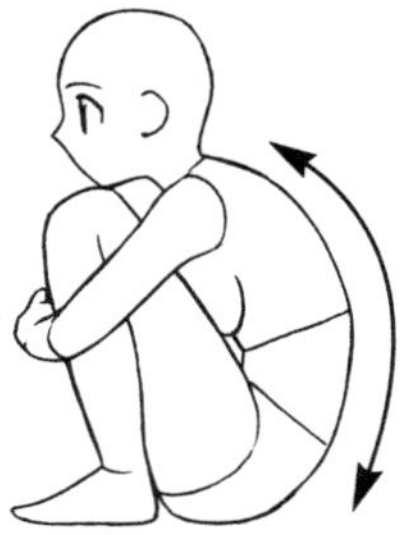

Balling up to the extent that the chin rests on the knees molds the back into a semicircle.

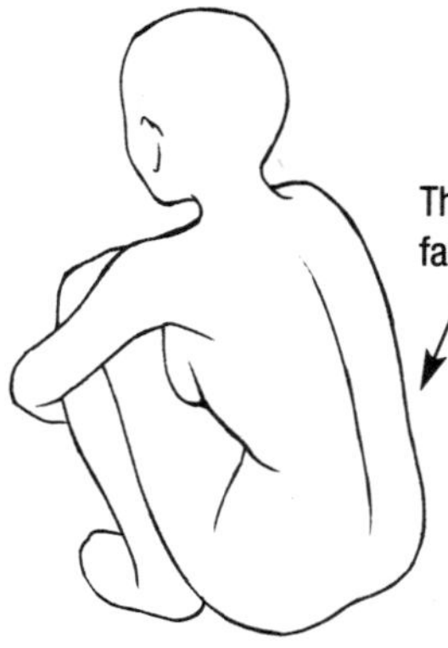

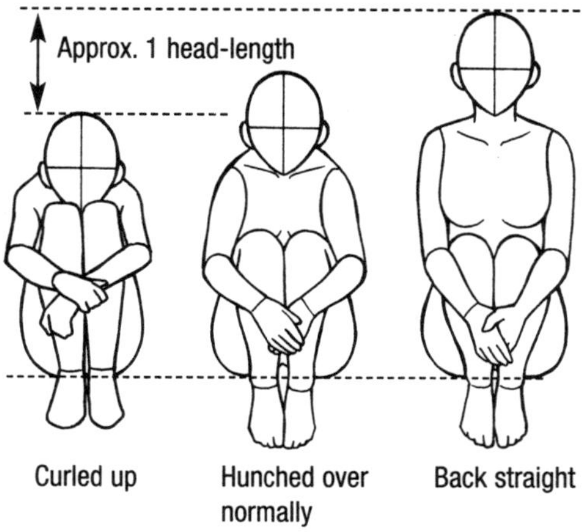

Variations on Sitting on the Floor with the Knees Bent

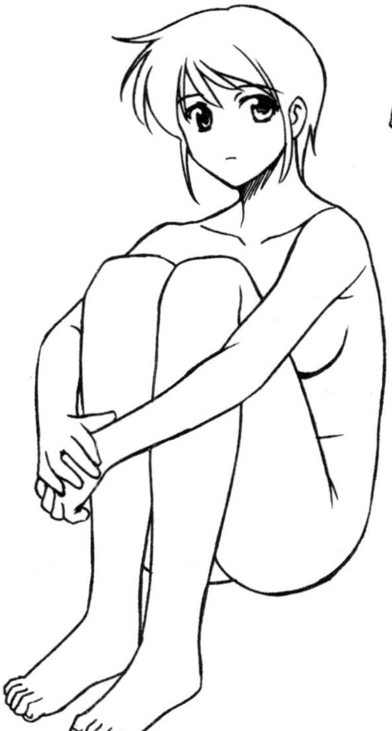

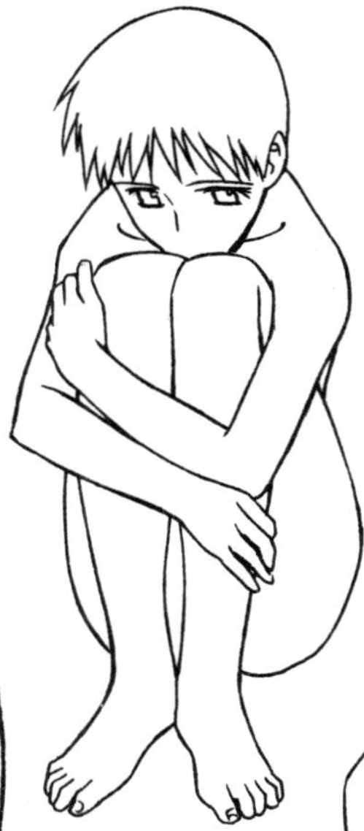

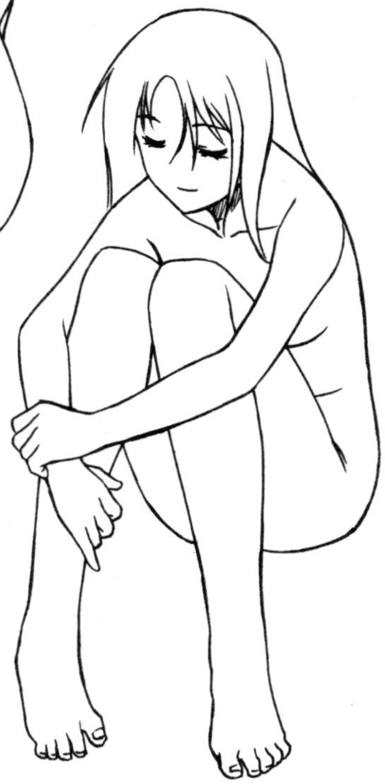

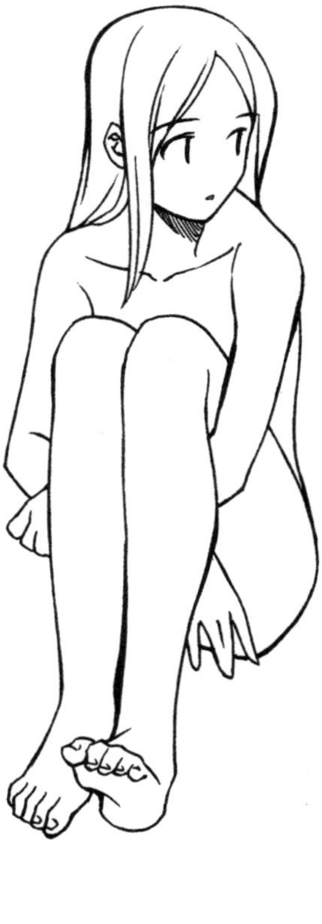

Arcing the Back/Leaning Back

The upper back contour is usually convex.

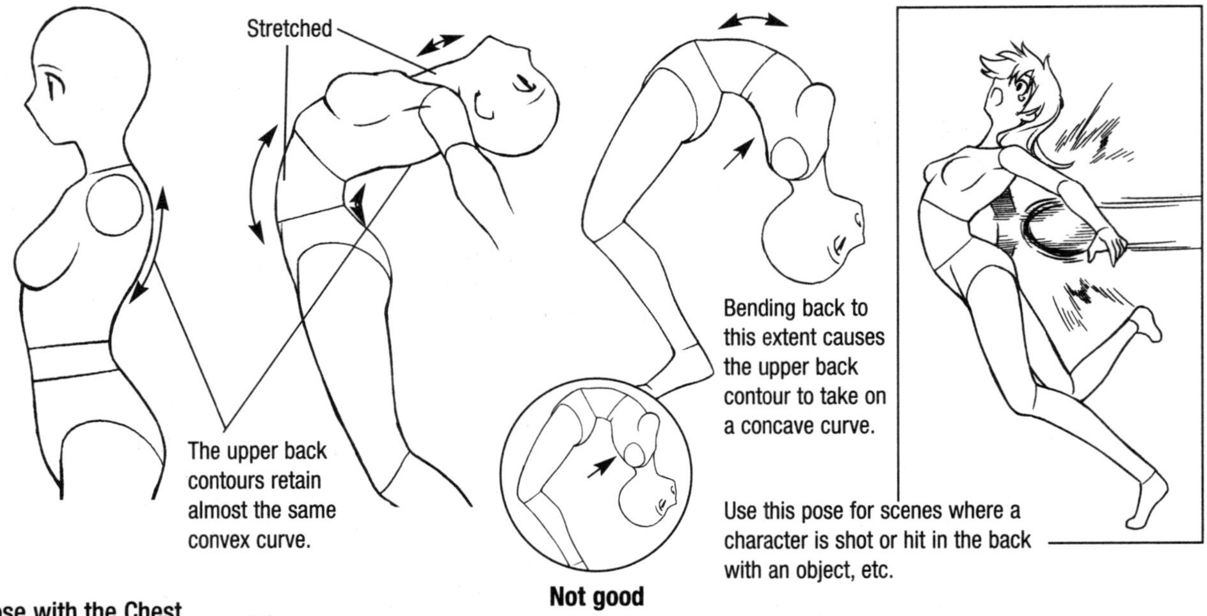

Pose with the Chest Dramatically Thrust Outward

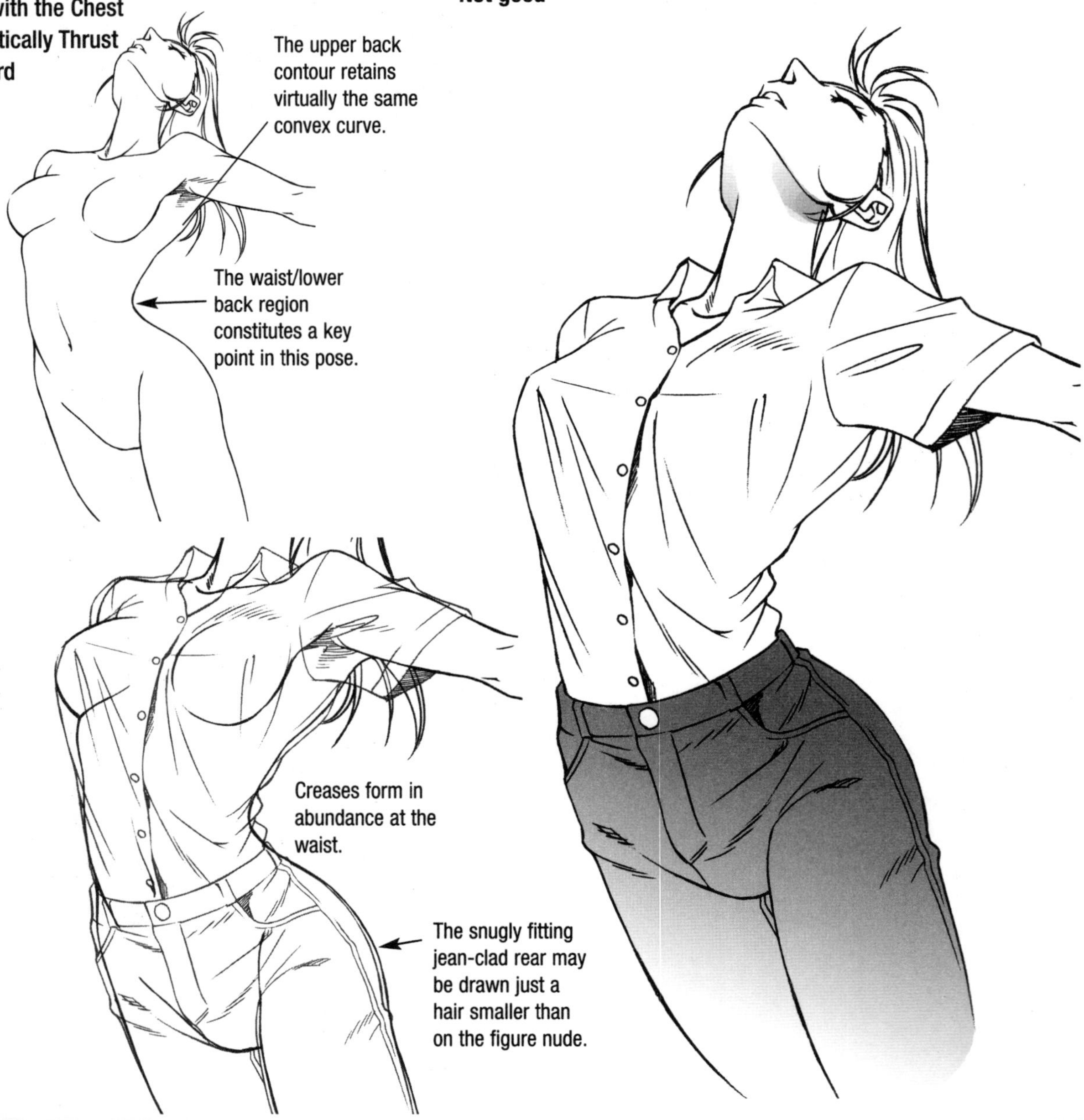

The Standard Convex Curve of the Upper Back

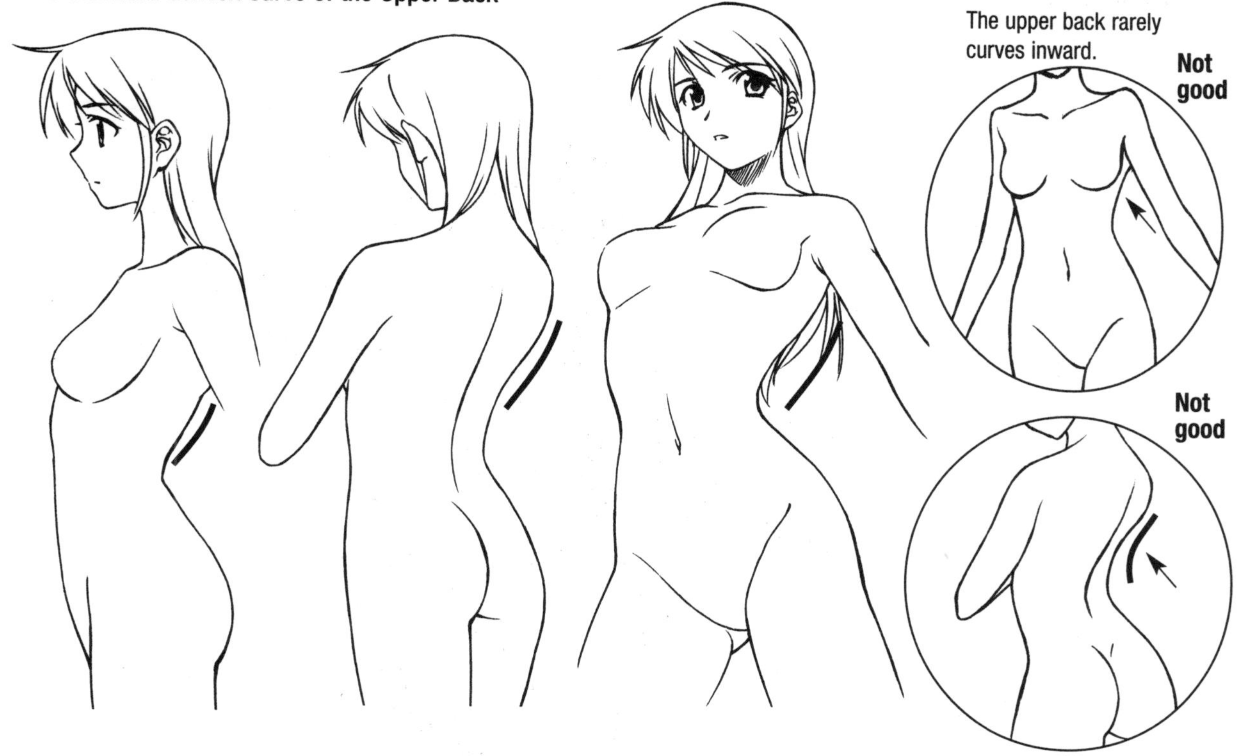

Special Cases for Drawing the Upper Back with a Convex Curve

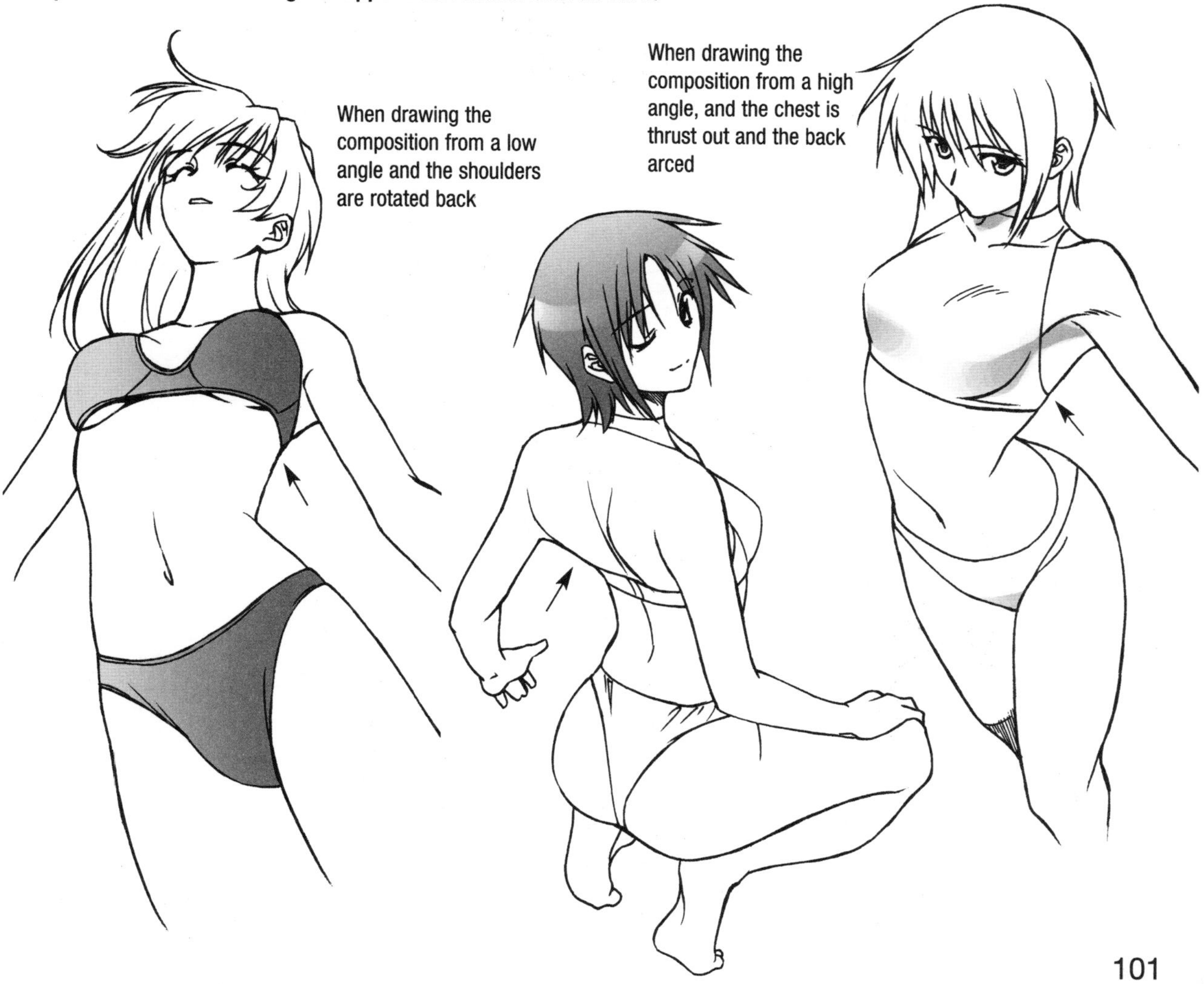

Uses of Arcing the Back 1: Cheering

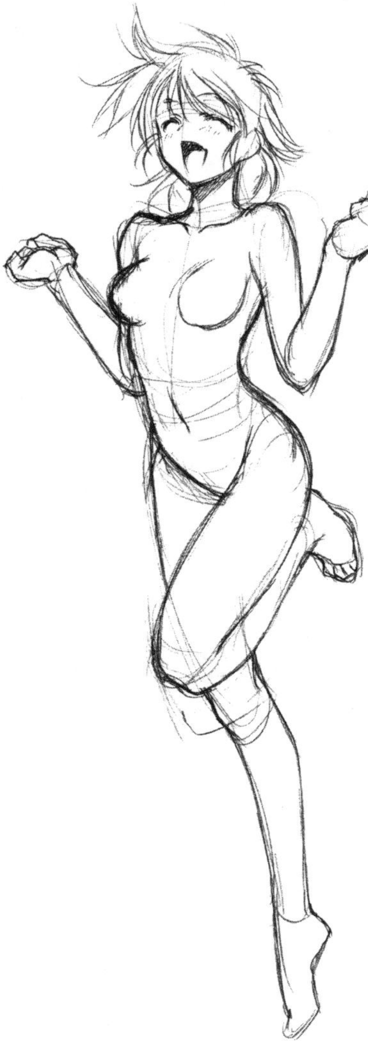

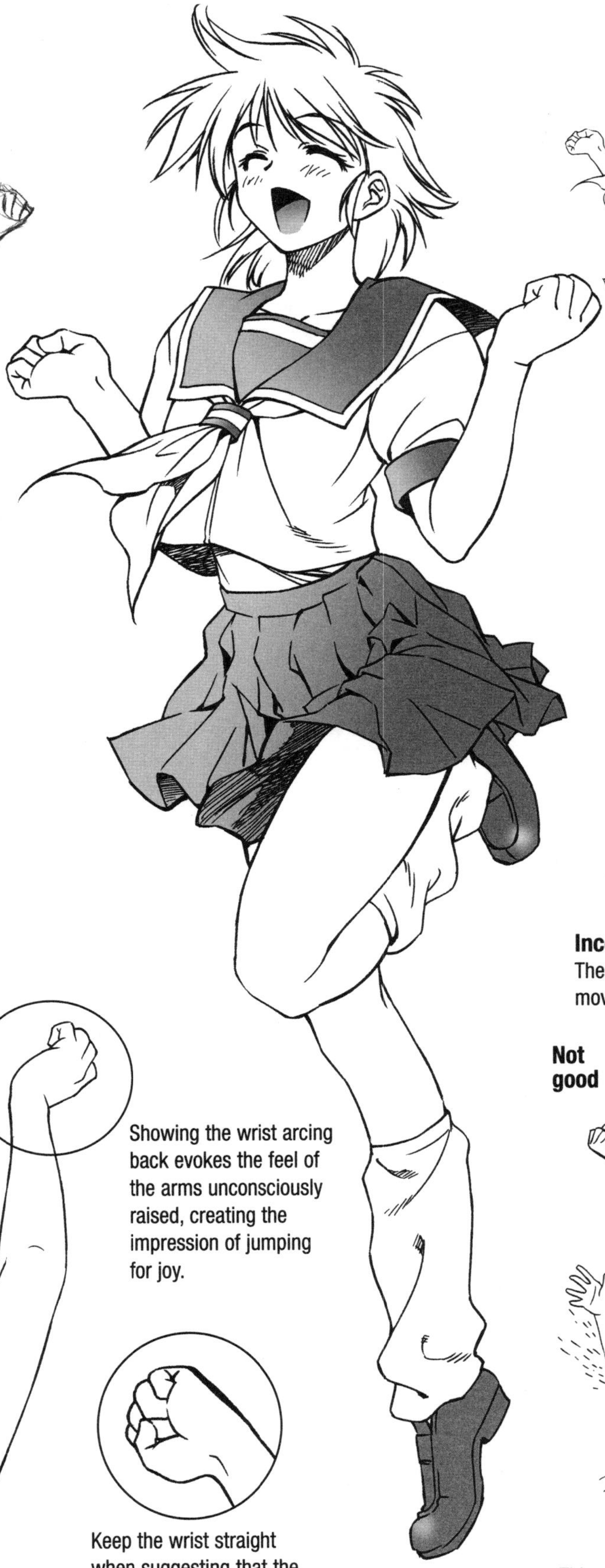

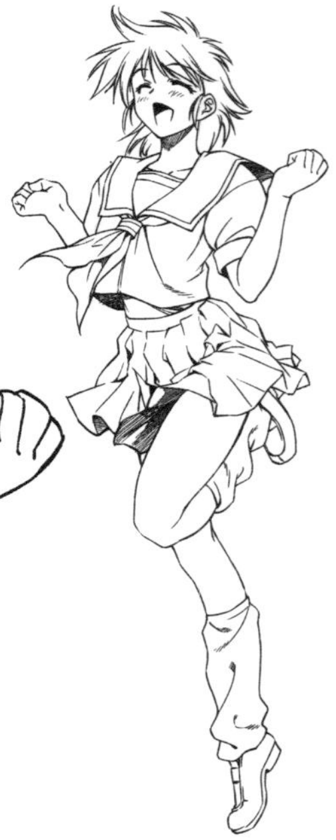

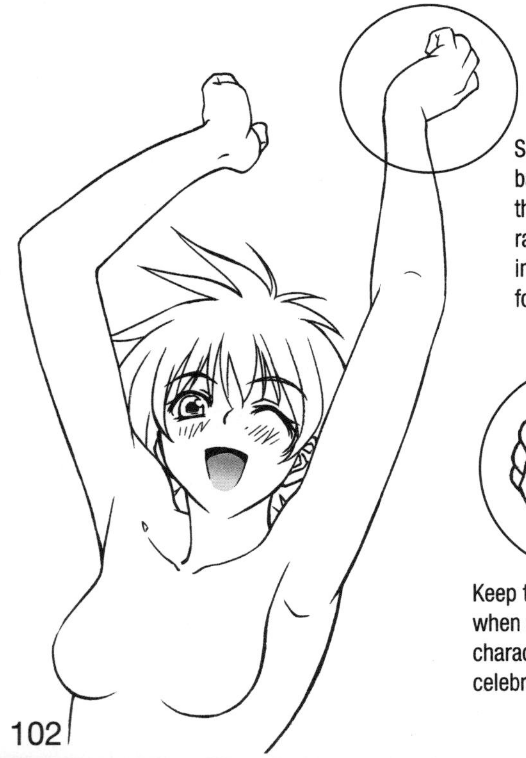

Showing the wrist arcing back evokes the feel of the arms unconsciously raised, creating the impression of jumping for joy.

Keep the wrist straight when suggesting that the character is consciously celebrating.

Incorrect
These samples lack movement.

Not good

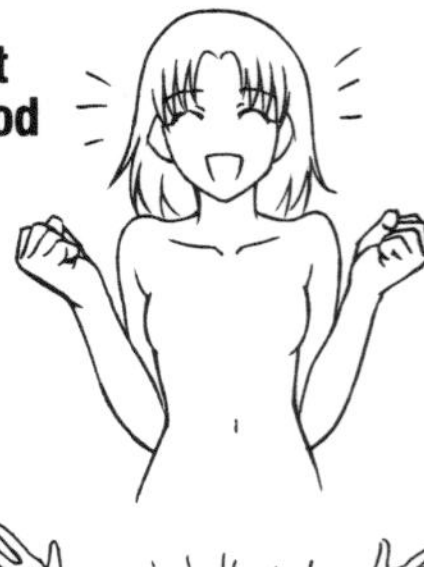

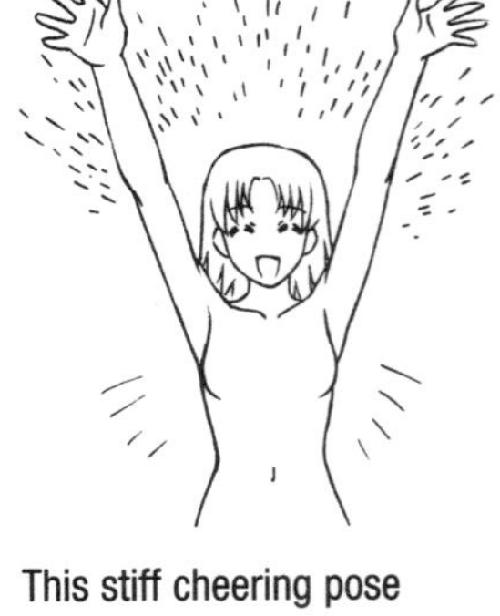

This stiff cheering pose leaves little impact on the reader.

Practical Application Samples

Tilting the head down turns this into a "yawning" or "stretching" pose.

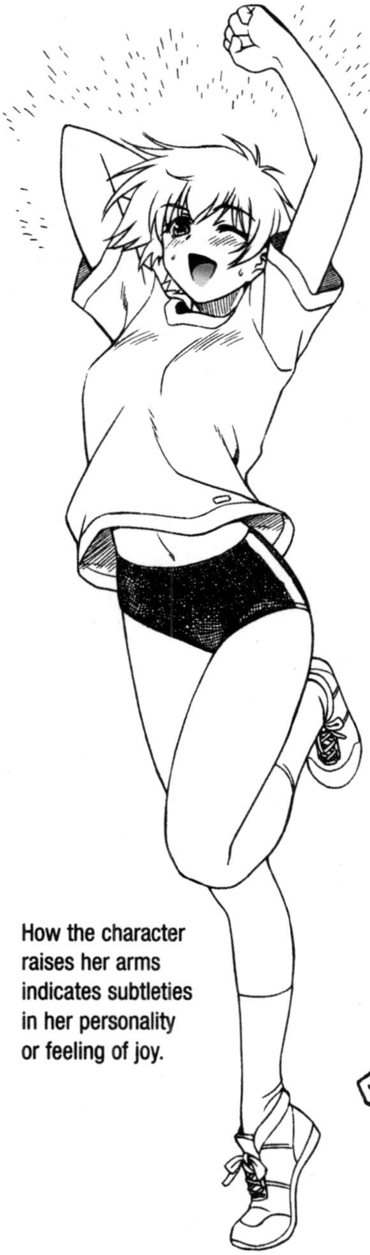

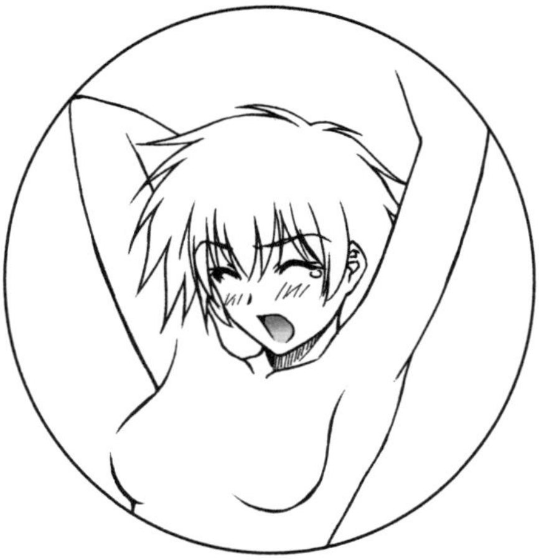

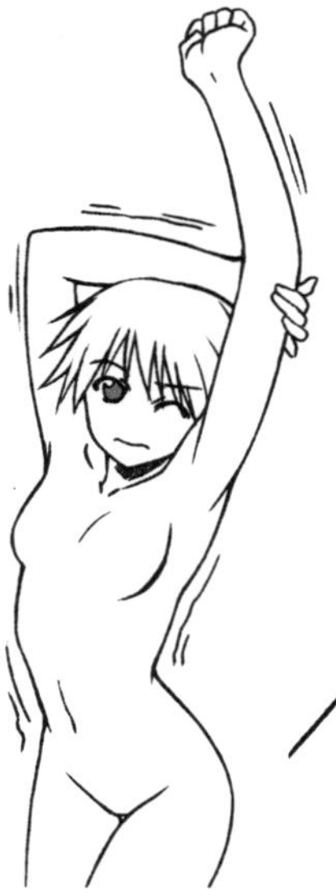

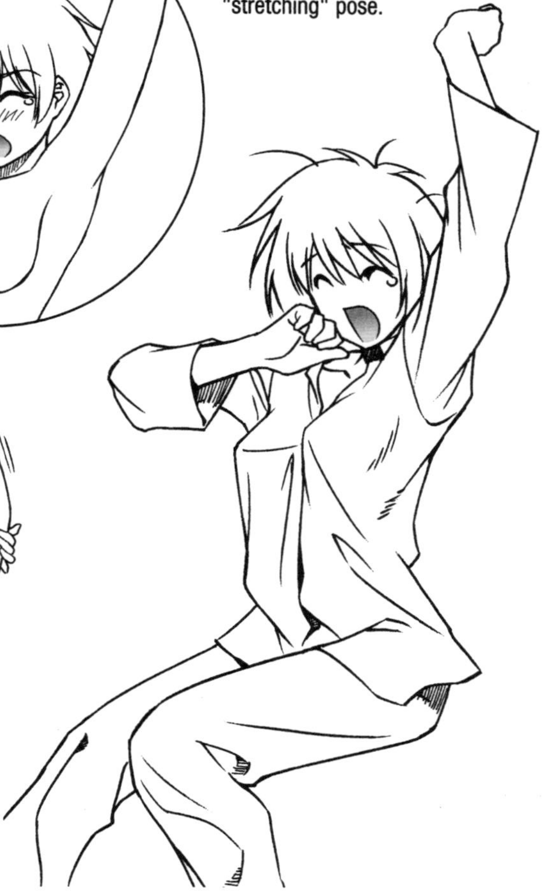

How the character raises her arms indicates subtleties in her personality or feeling of joy.

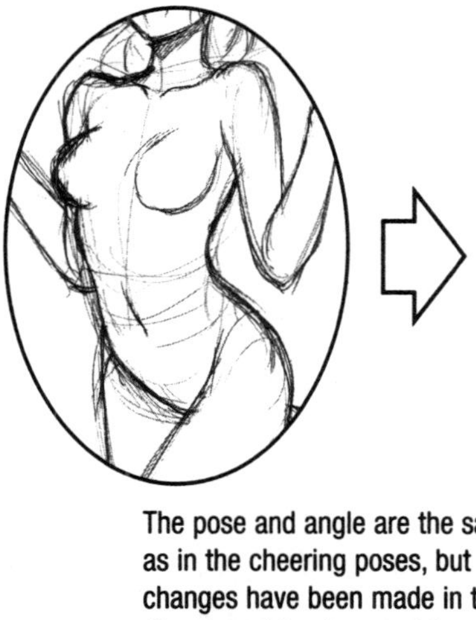

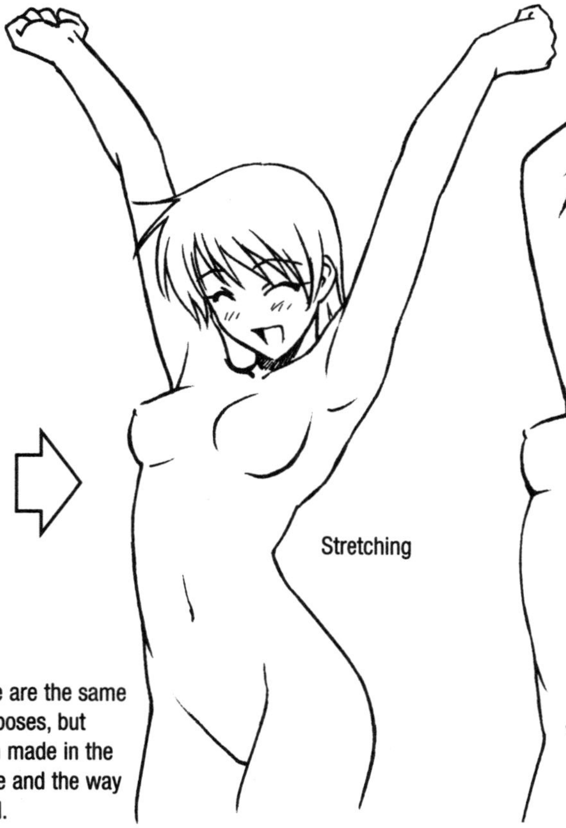

Stretching

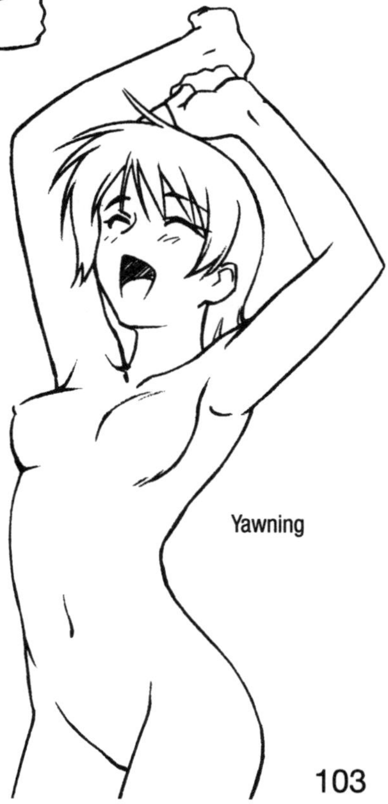

Yawning

The pose and angle are the same as in the cheering poses, but changes have been made in the direction of the face and the way the arms are raised.

Uses of Arcing the Back 2: Escaping (Unwanted Grasps, etc.)

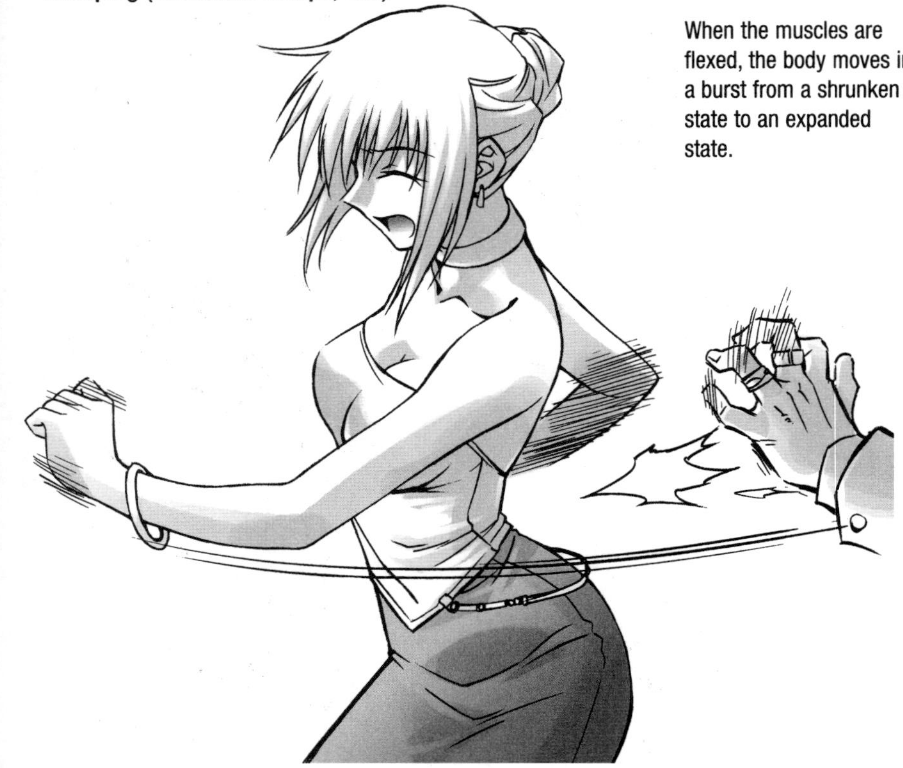

When the muscles are flexed, the body moves in a burst from a shrunken state to an expanded state.

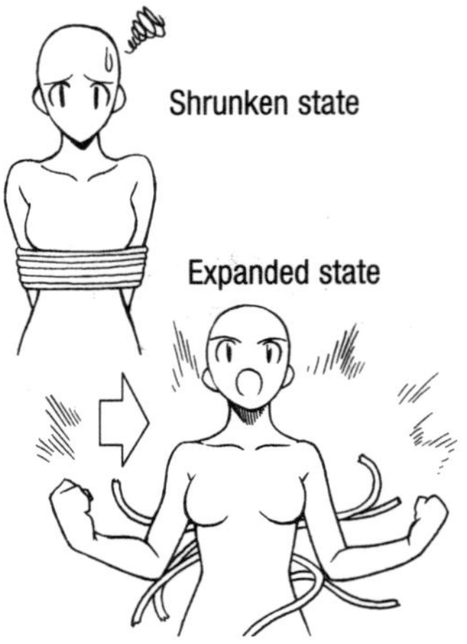

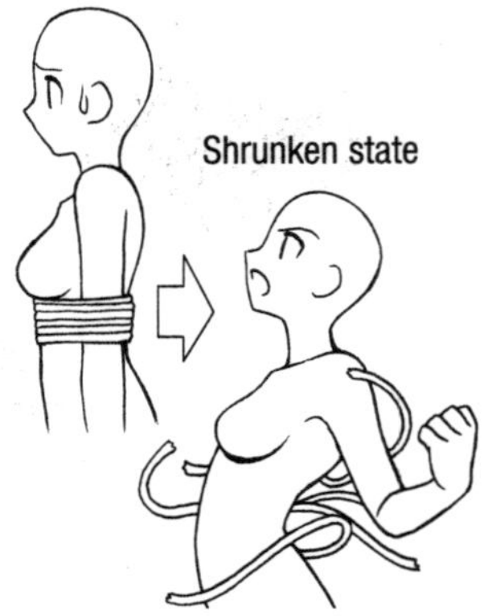

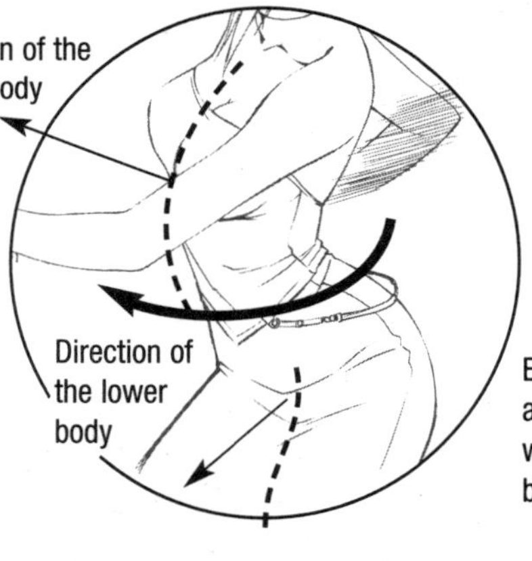

Elements of twisting are being mixed in with the arcing the back action.

A character grabbed and shaking off her assailant's grasp

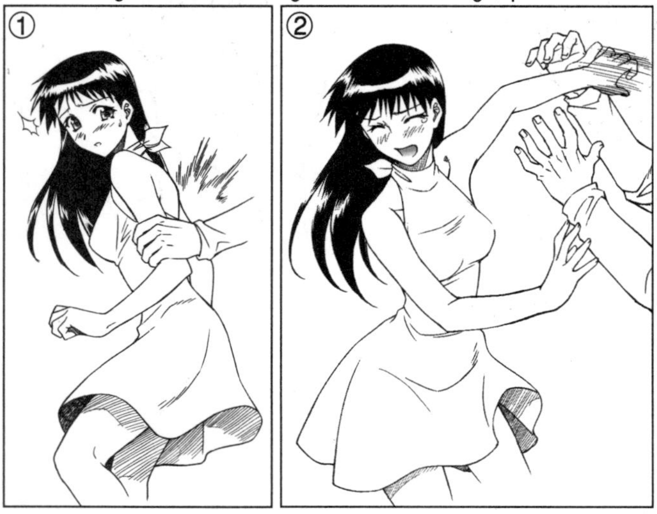

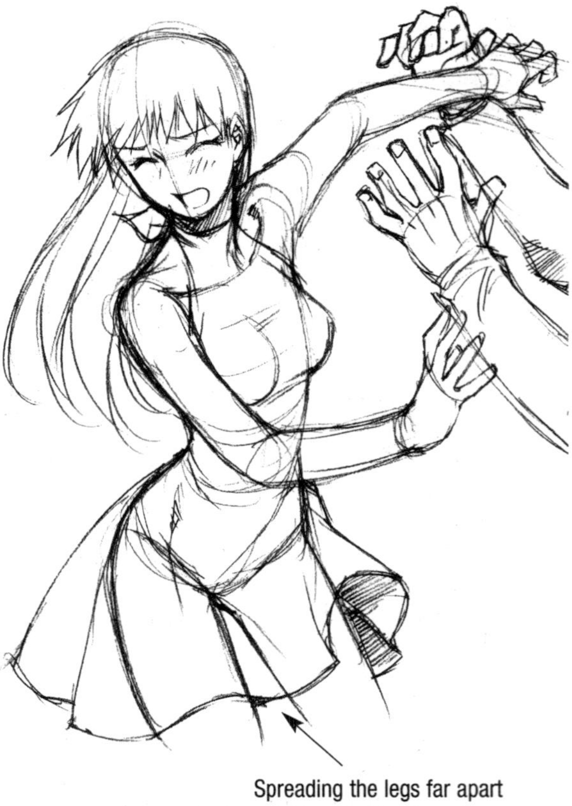

Spreading the legs far apart would make the character seem like a martial arts expert, so position them on the close side.

Uses of Arcing the Back 3:
Running/Escaping: Running Away Scenes

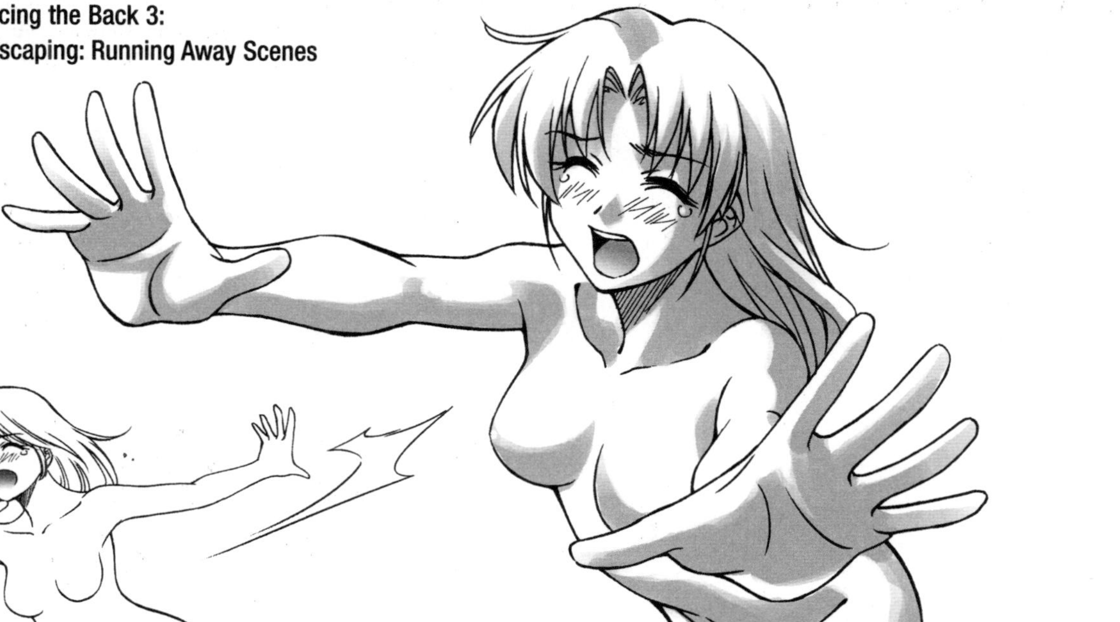

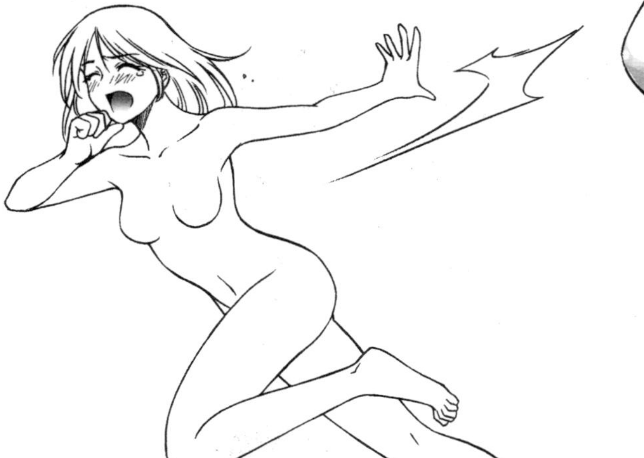

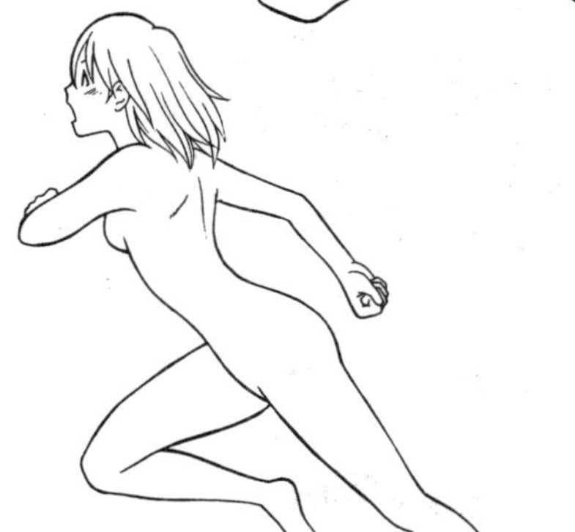

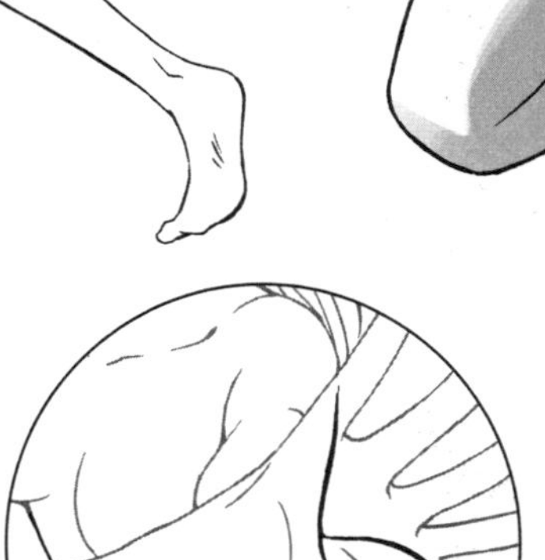

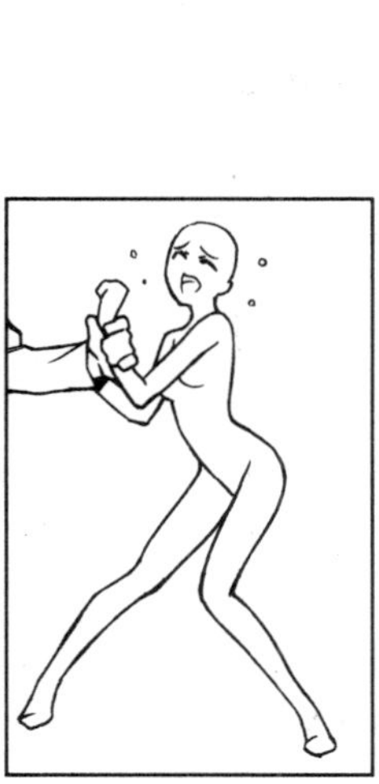

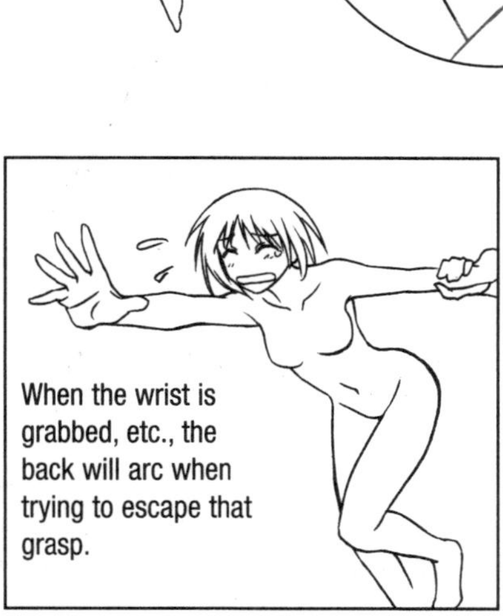

When the wrist is grabbed, etc., the back will arc when trying to escape that grasp.

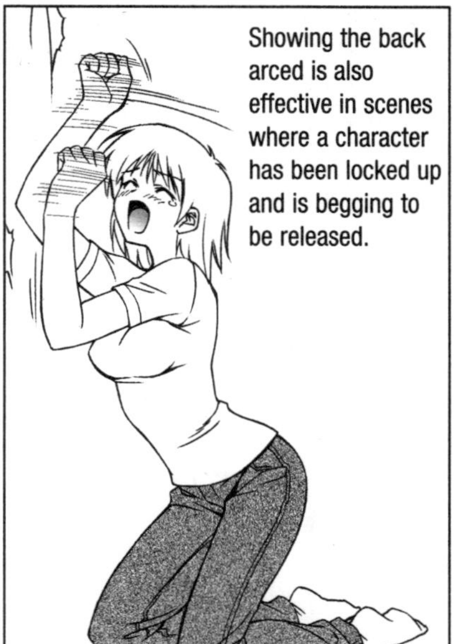

Showing the back arced is also effective in scenes where a character has been locked up and is begging to be released.

Leaning to the Side: Fashion Model Poses

These S-curve poses are affected poses the character adopts when intentionally attempting to make herself appear attractive and are, consequently, used for scenes when a character makes a first entrance to give that scene impact.

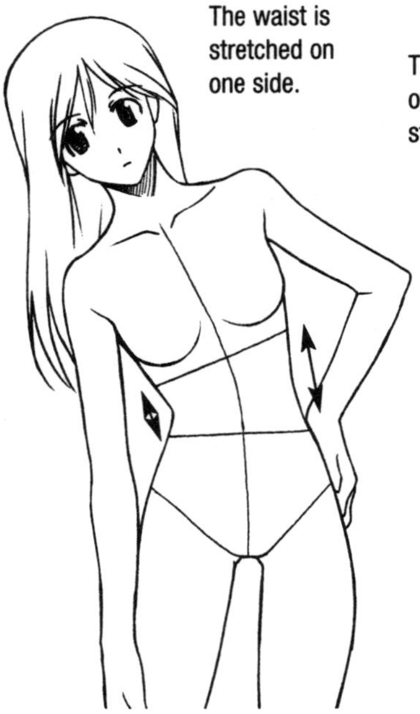

The waist is stretched on one side.

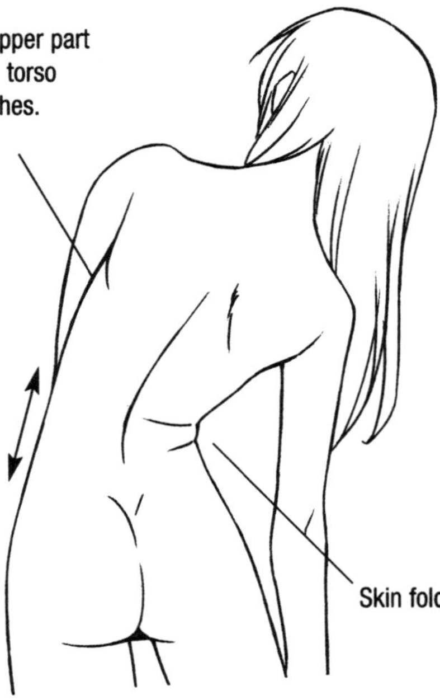

The upper part of the torso stretches.

Skin folds

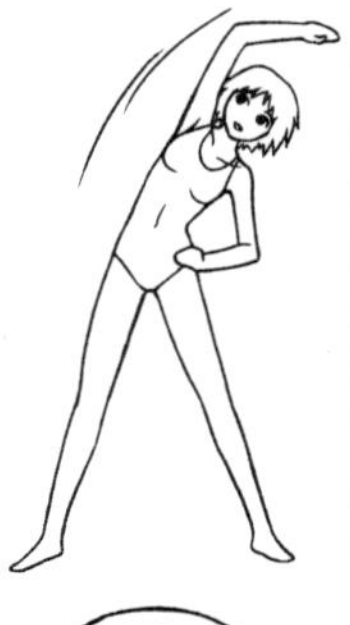

This is typically an exercise pose, and just a means of moving the body. However, it has wide applications in key compositions.

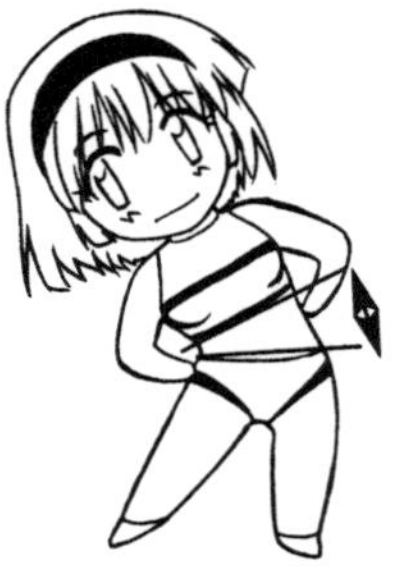

Chibi character in pose

Contrast of S-Curve Poses

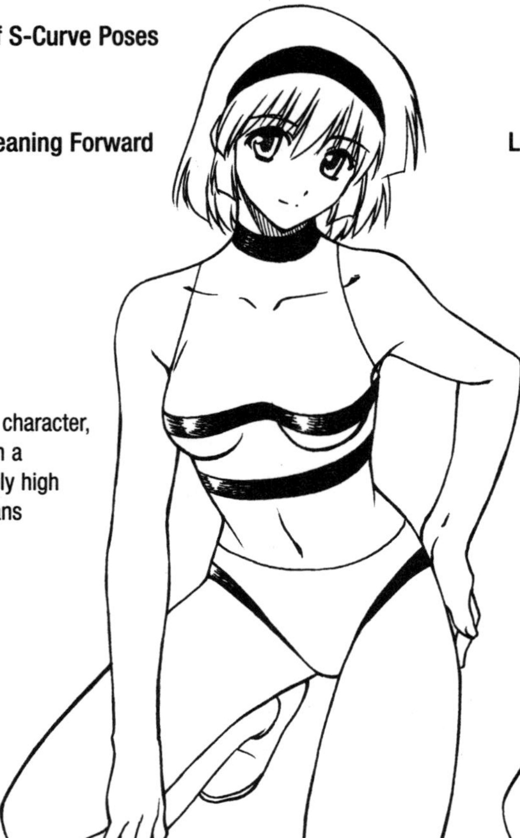

Leaning Forward

Here, the character, seen from a moderately high angle, leans forward.

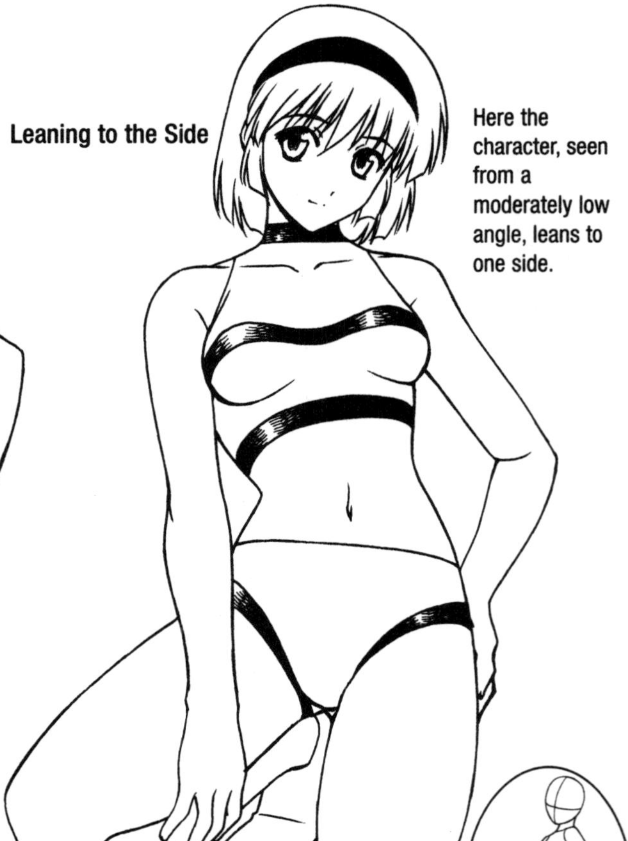

Leaning to the Side

Here the character, seen from a moderately low angle, leans to one side.

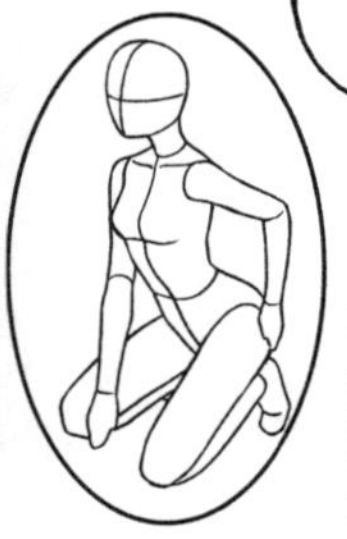

Common pose: Figure arcing the back while leaning forward

While these two S-curve poses are similar, they differ in that one leans forward, while the other, to the side.

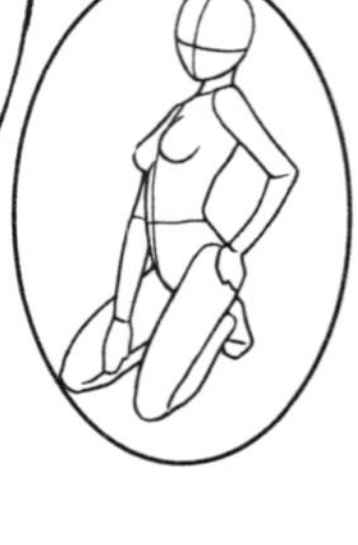

Figure arcing back toward one side

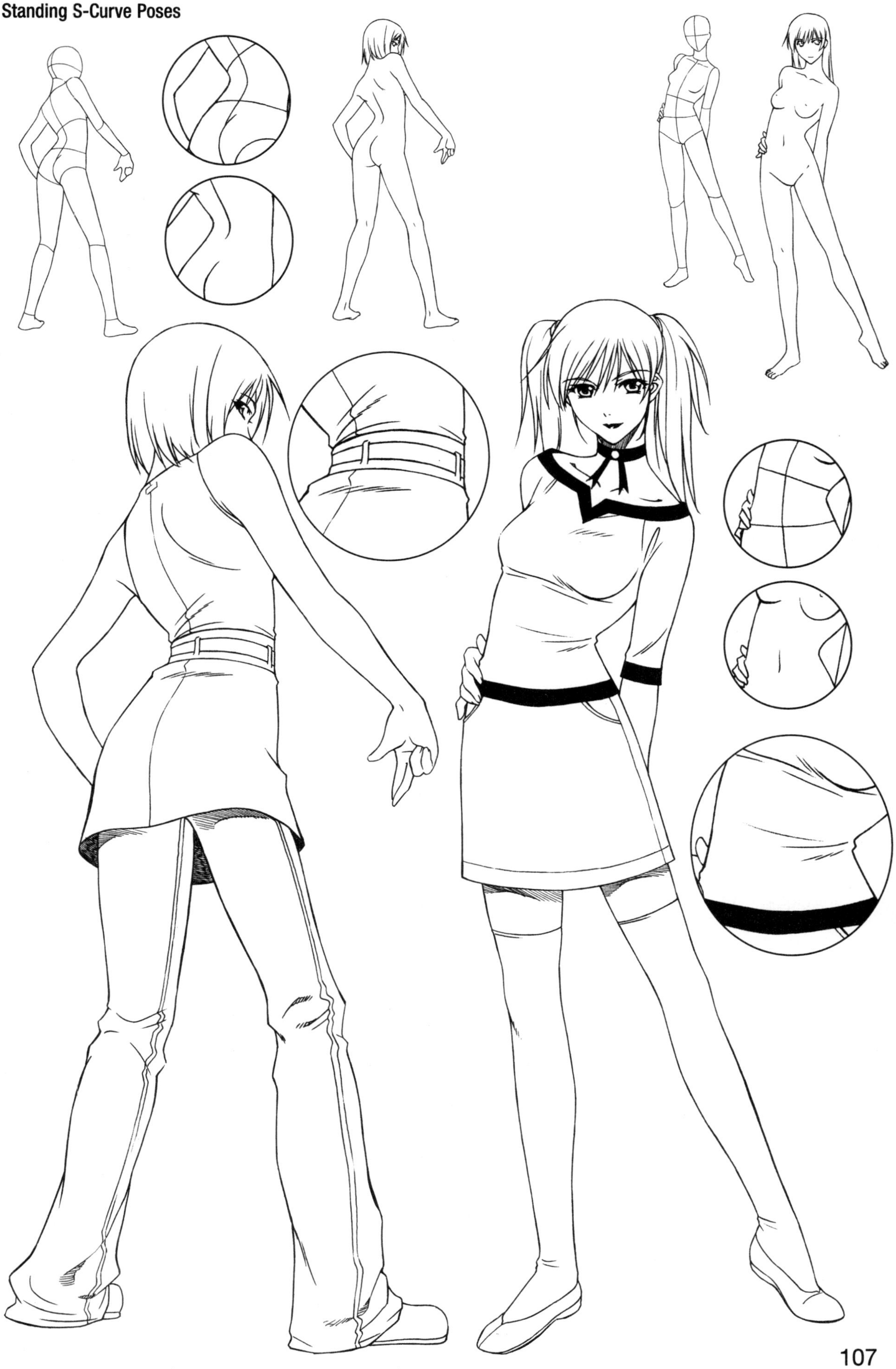

Twisting and Turning

While torsion does appear in the waist during the common act of walking, this torsion becomes important in scenes of a character running and principally in combat scenes.

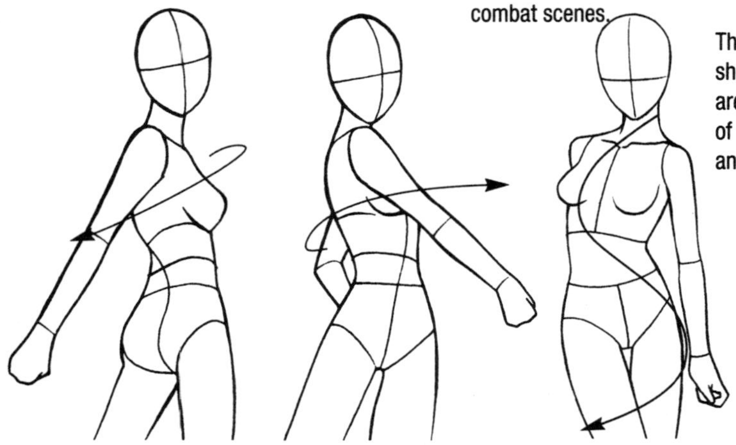

Glancing back   Establishing a stance   Walking

The fundamental aspect of showing twisting or turning are changes in the directions of the upper body and lower body.

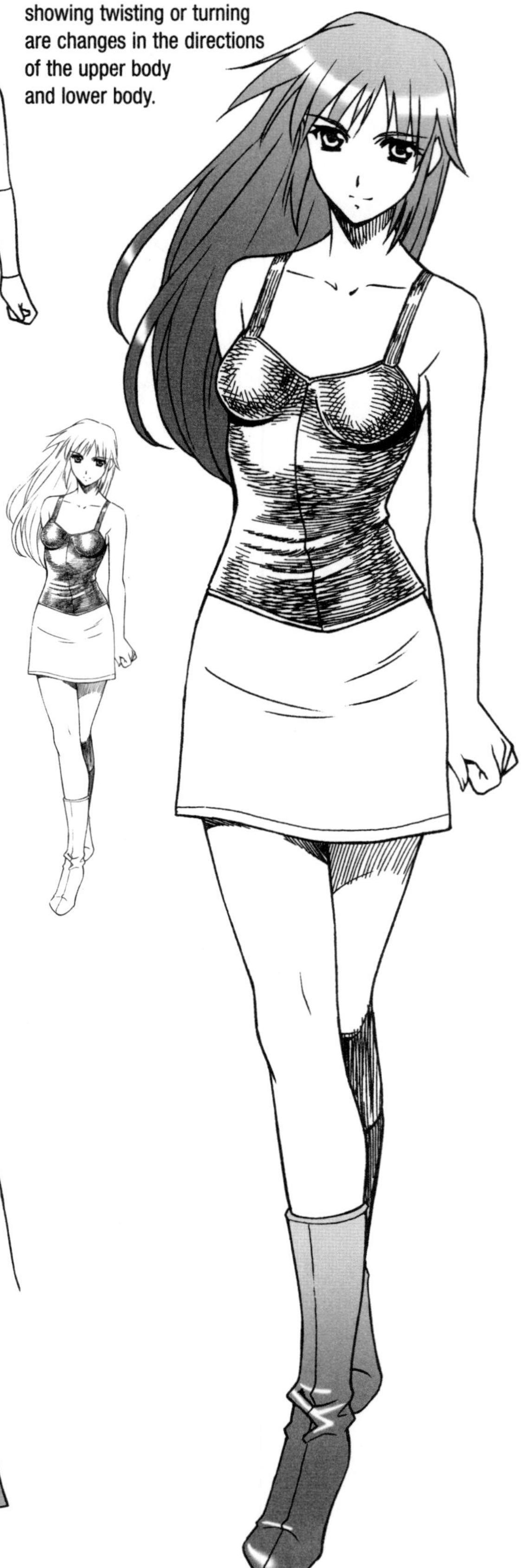

Manga-Style Stylization: Figure with Only the Chest Turning

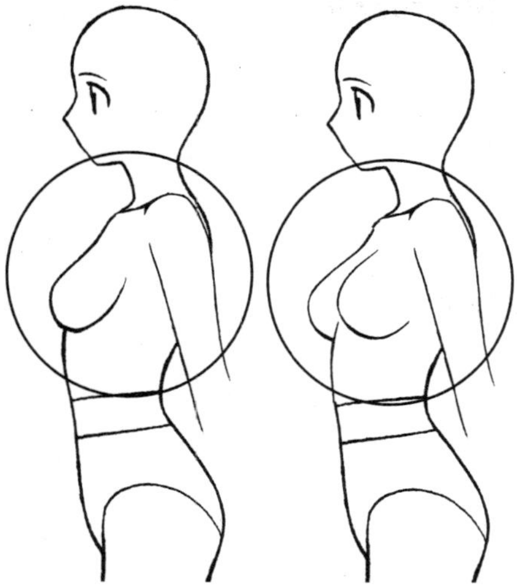

Figure in perfect profile (Normal view)

Figure with the chest turned

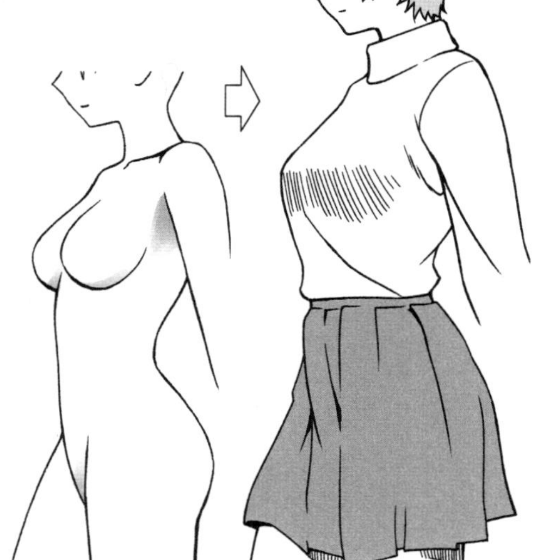

If there is no need to adhere to actual physical structure, a character may be drawn in profile, but with her chest turned slightly. This technique, unique to *manga*, enhances the character's sense of presence once she is dressed in clothing.

Contrast of Figures in S-Curve Poses and with Torsion

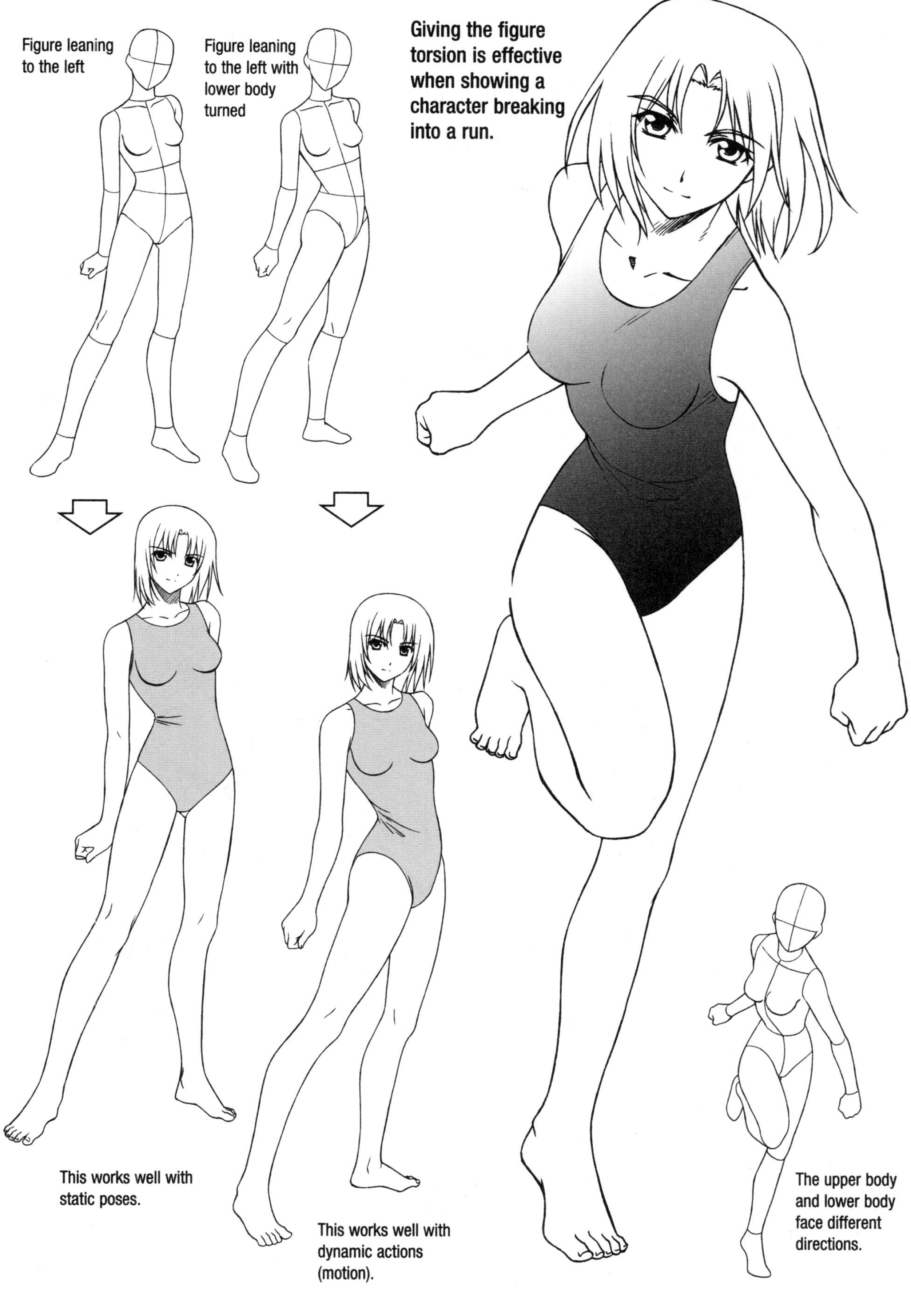

Twisting and Turning Are Key Factors in Combat Scenes: Torsion Symbolizes Combat

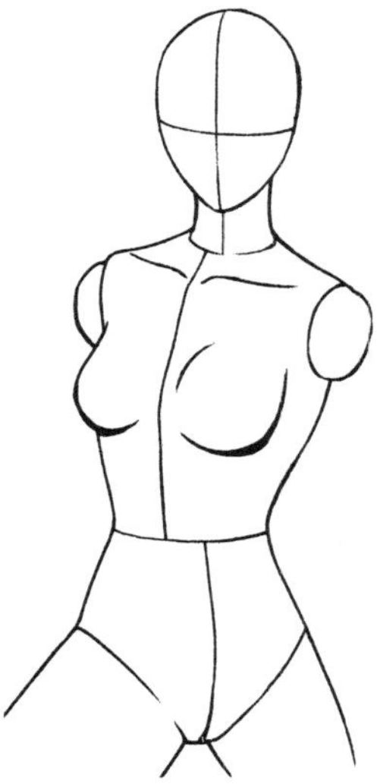

Study figure illustrating the conventional "twist."

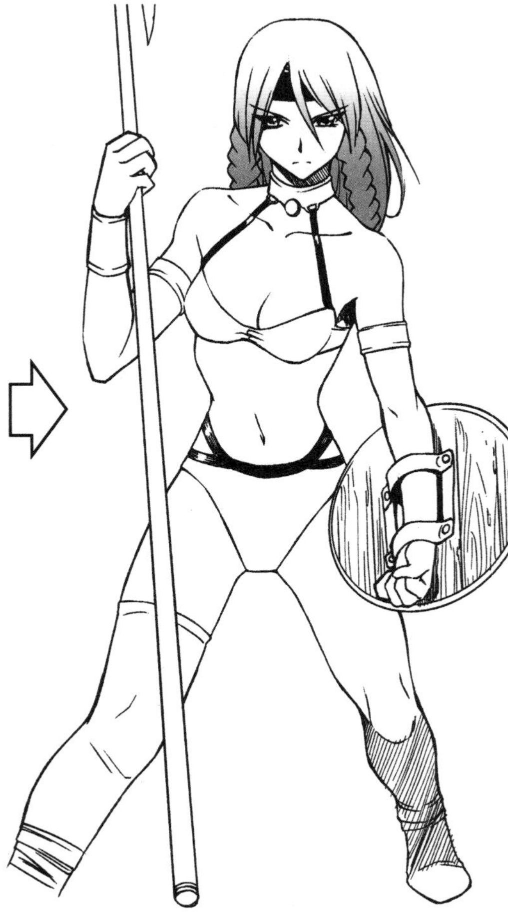

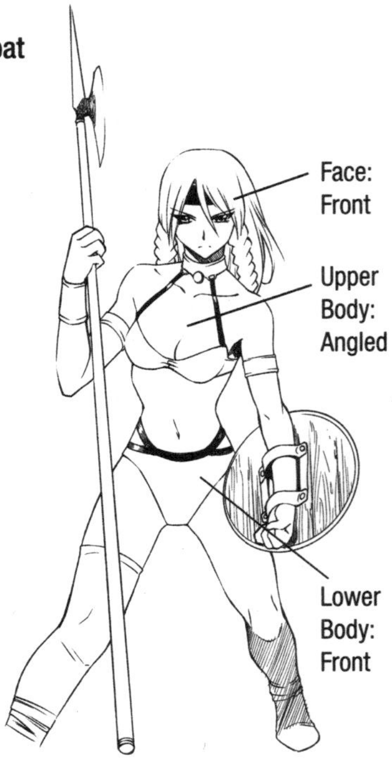

Bad example

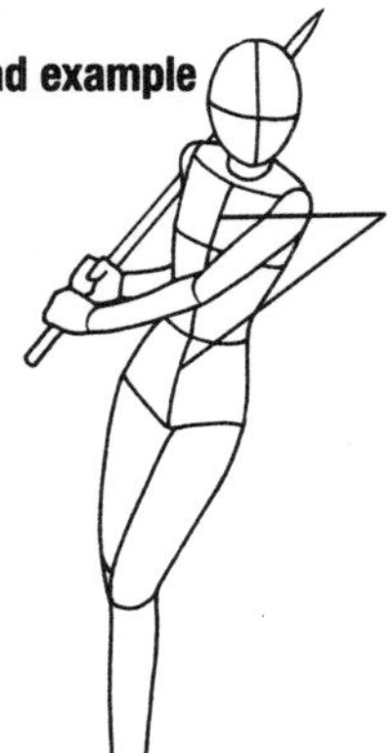

The centerline from the upper body to lower body is straight. Her backside seems to be jutting out, causing the figure to loose force.

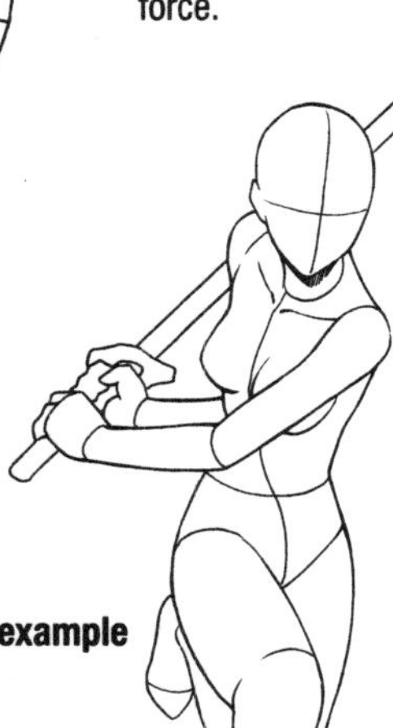

Good example

Here, the upper body and lower body face different directions, forming the centerlines into an S-curve.

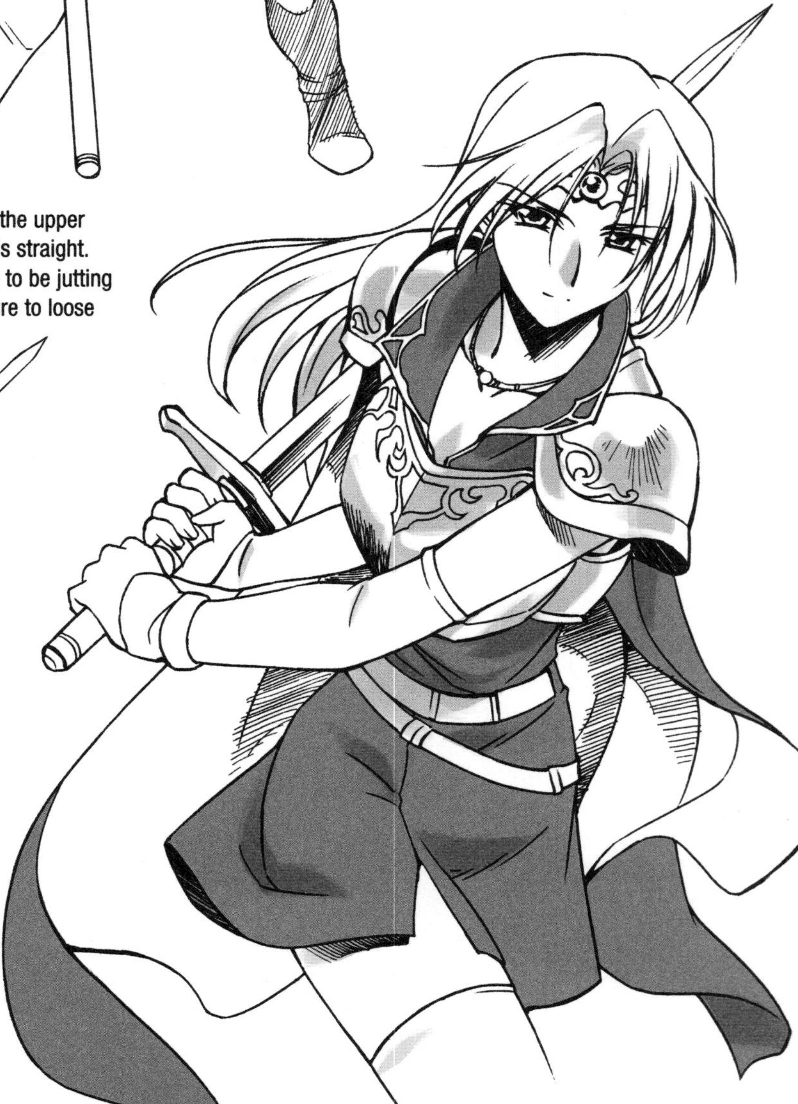

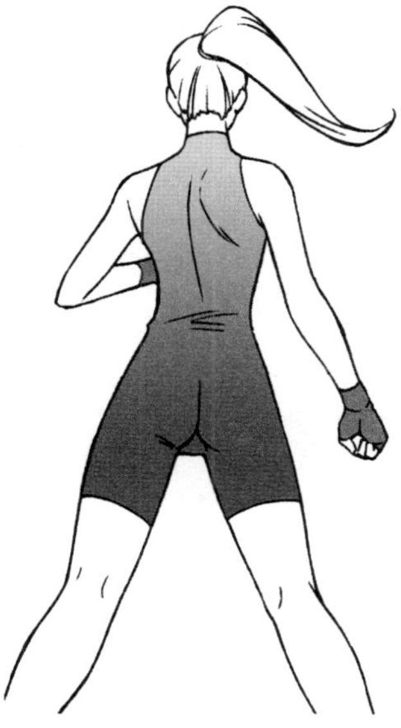

Even in a simple back view, a bit of torsion evokes the look of a combat expert.

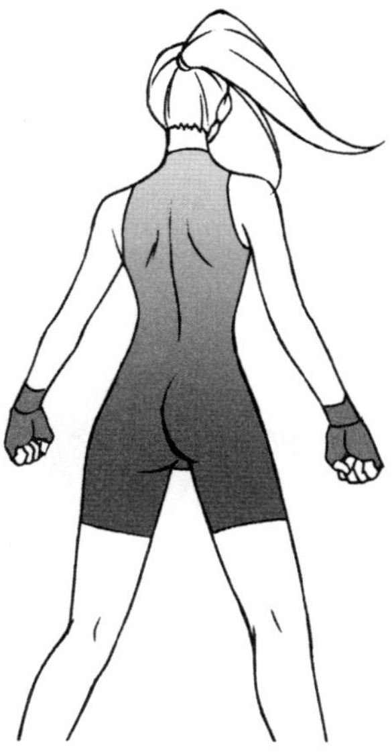

This figure has no torsion and is standing bolt upright. Now, the character appears unaccustomed to fighting.

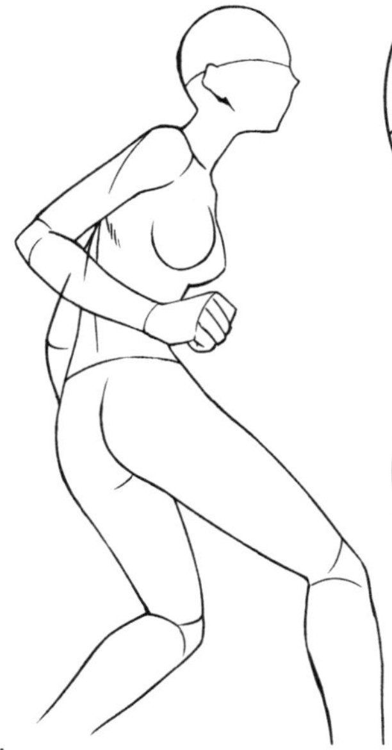

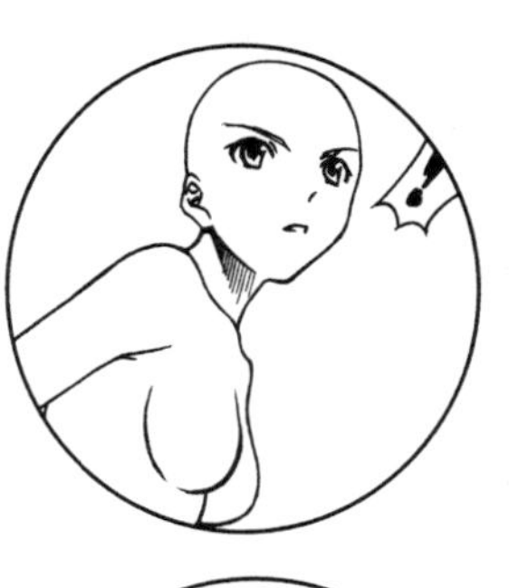

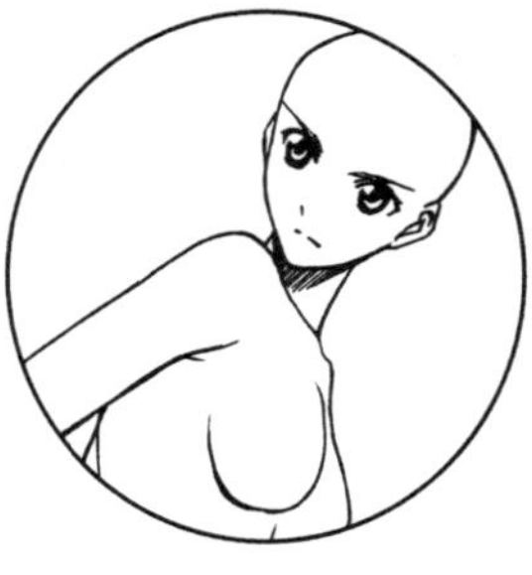

Changing the direction of the head on twisting/turning poses allows the creation of limitless new variations.

Using Diagonal Lines to Suggest Speed

Add fine, diagonal lines, symbolic of movement to enhance a dynamic composition's impact.

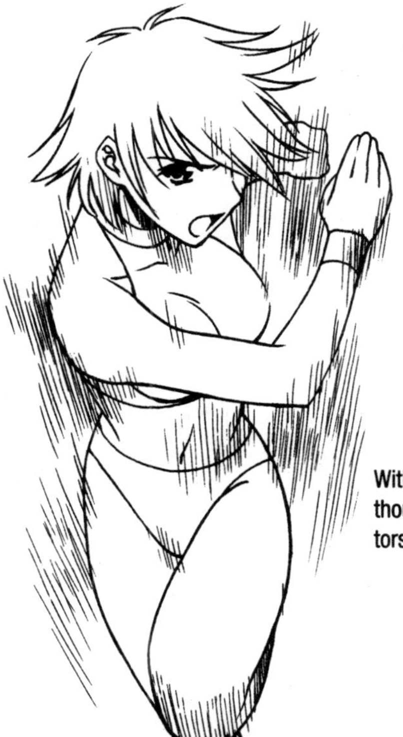

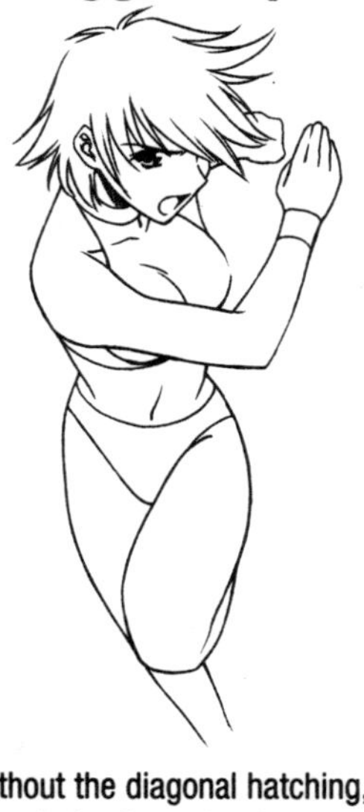

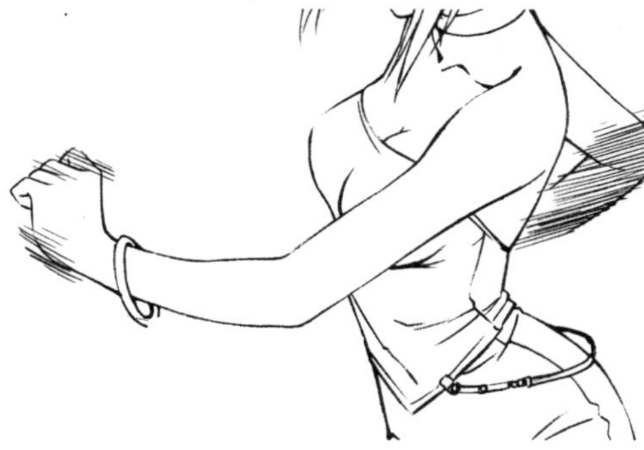

Without the diagonal hatching, even though the figure has been given torsion, it still lacks force.

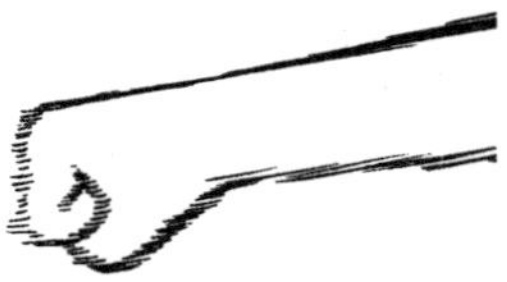

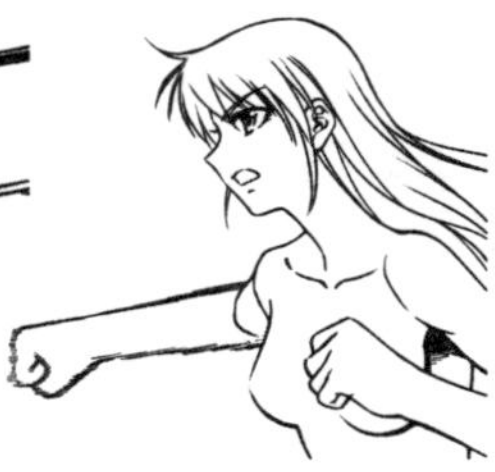

Here, the hand's contours are rendered in diagonal hatching.

Alternative Styles

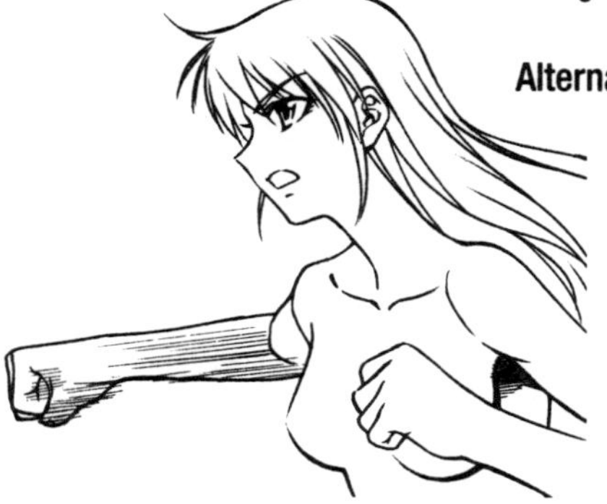

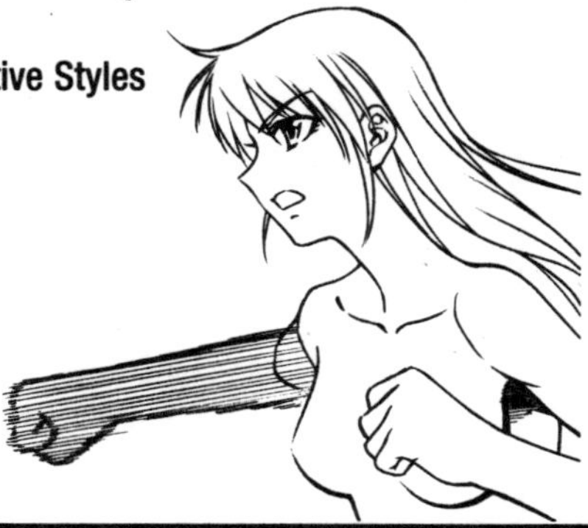

Adding the Finishing Touches to a Hot "Backward Glance" Pose with Torsion

(The Steps in Attaching Tone)

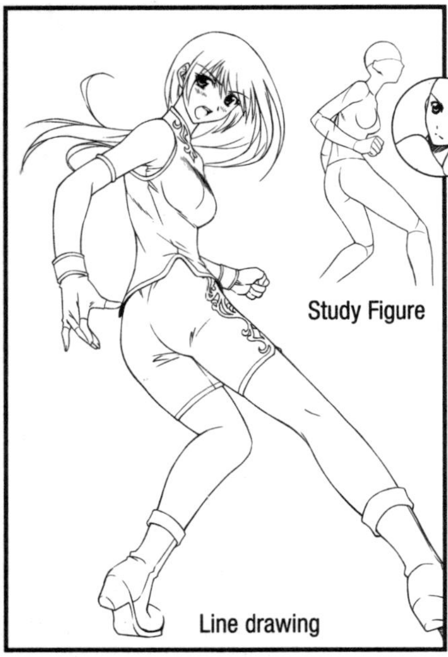

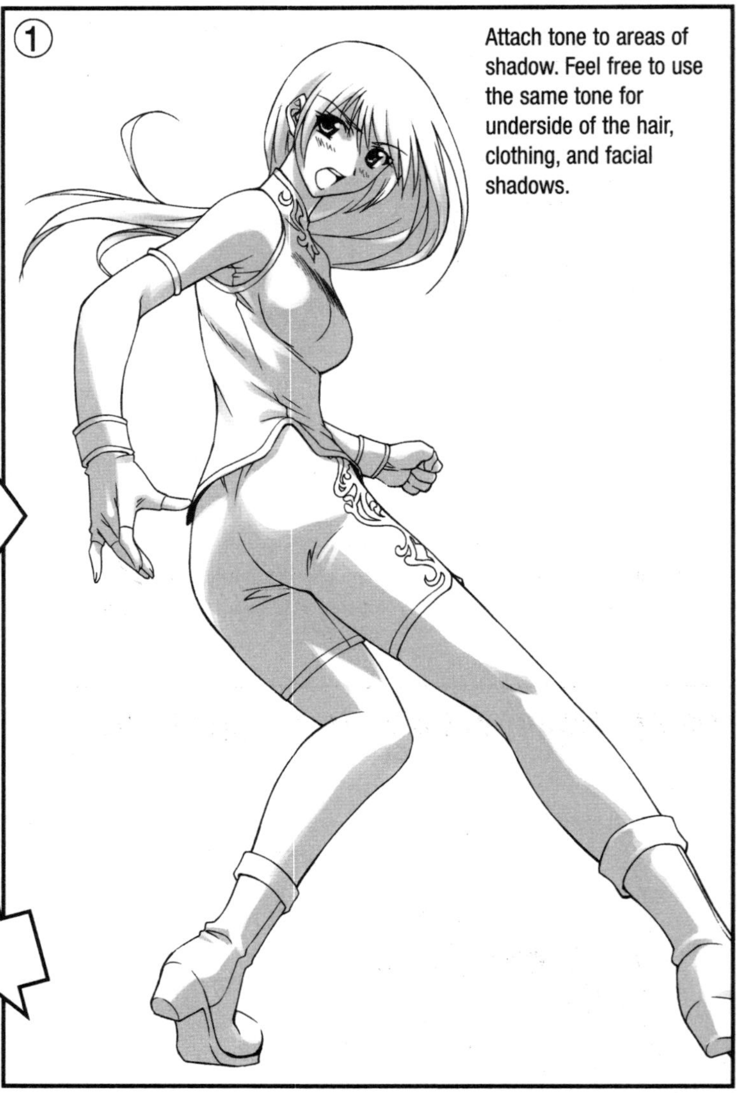

Attach tone to areas of shadow. Feel free to use the same tone for underside of the hair, clothing, and facial shadows.

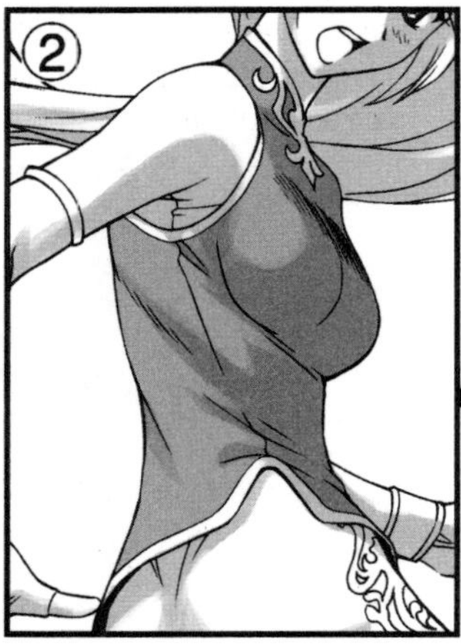

Attach 2 sheets of layered tone to the blouse. Use tone with identical line numbers to avoid a moiré effect.

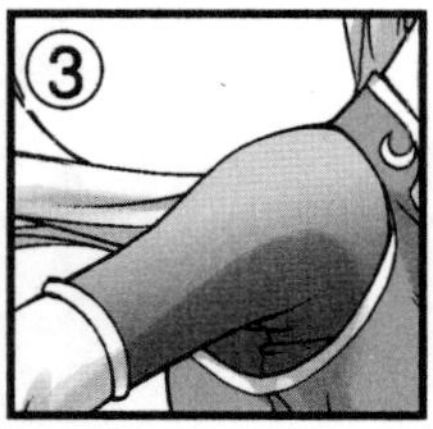

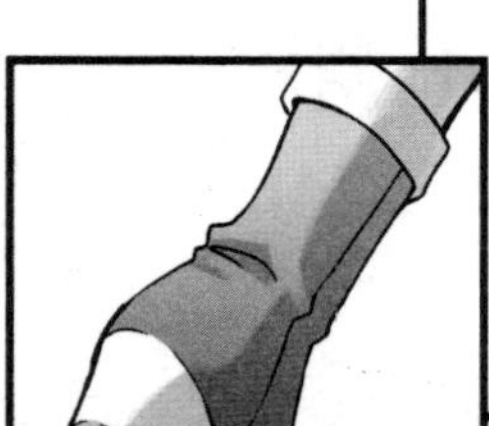

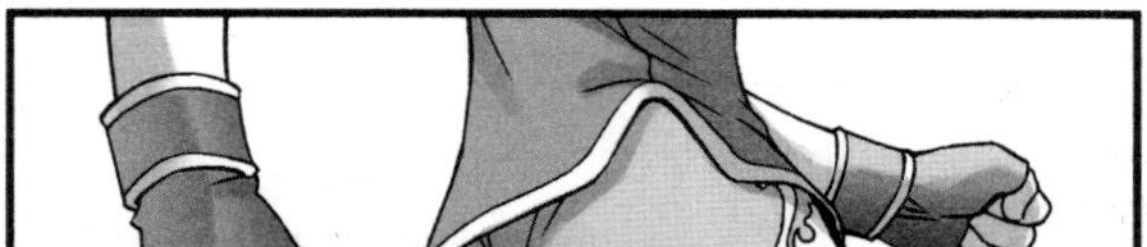

Attach a light gradation tone to the shoulders, shorts, gloves, and boots. Mixing gradation tone with regular dot tone could result in a moiré effect even if both tones have the same line number. Verify beforehand that you are using 2 compatible tones.

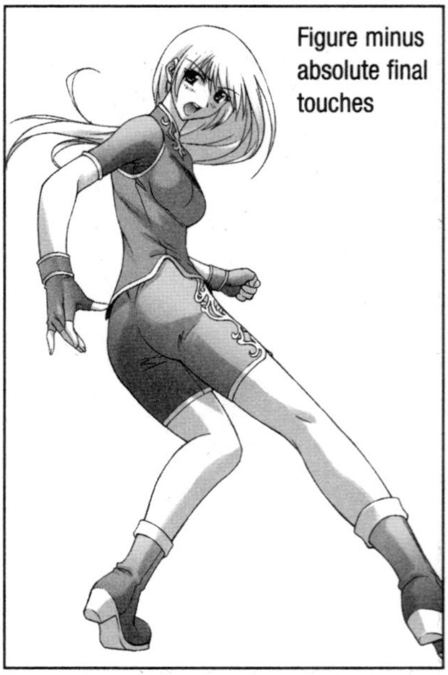

Figure minus absolute final touches

④ To finish, rub with an eraser those areas where you wish to show highlights.

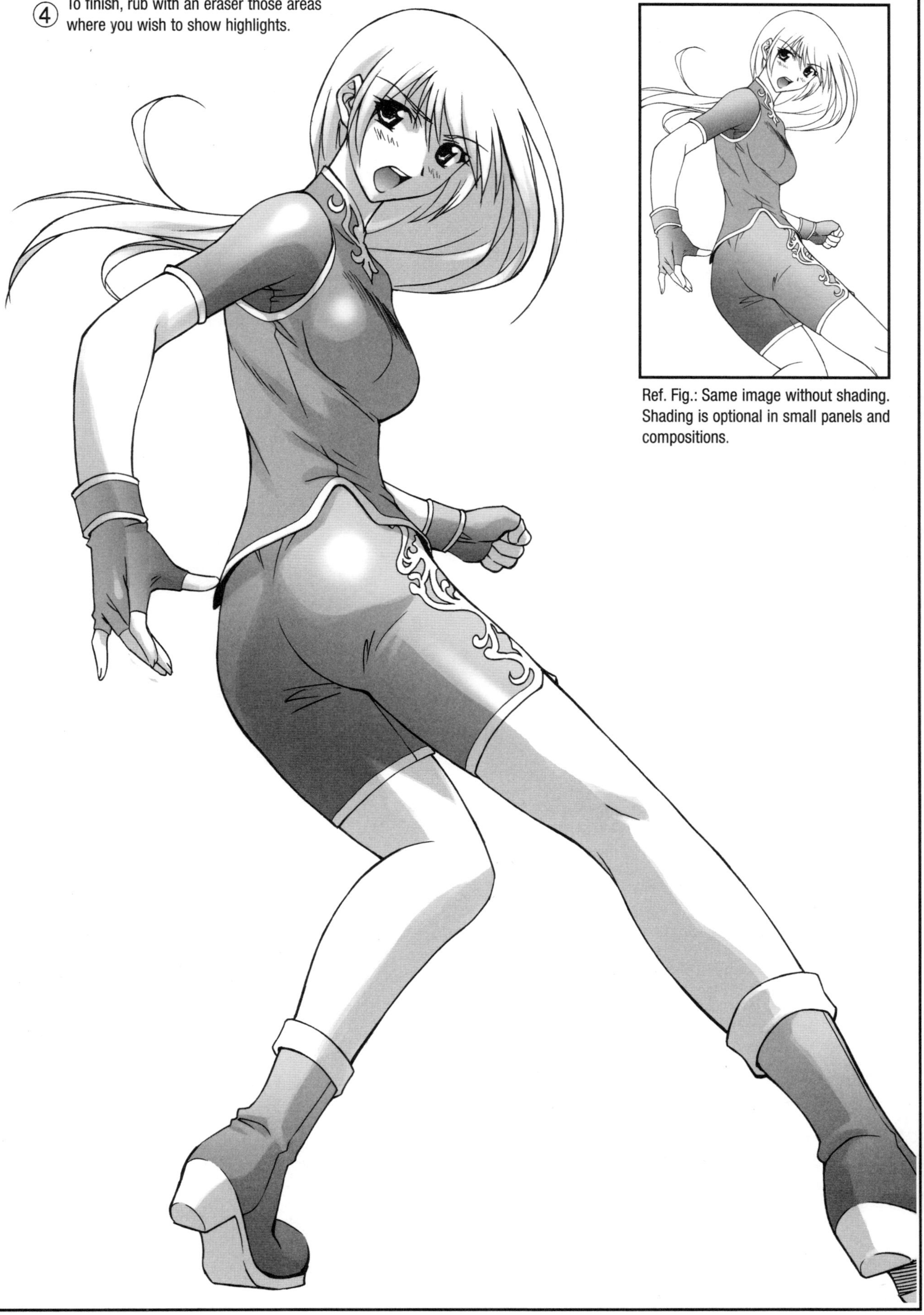

Ref. Fig.: Same image without shading. Shading is optional in small panels and compositions.

This figure was created digitally. The creation process and points of caution are the same as when attaching regular tone.

Both the figure delivering and receiving the slap have more impact with torsion at the waist.

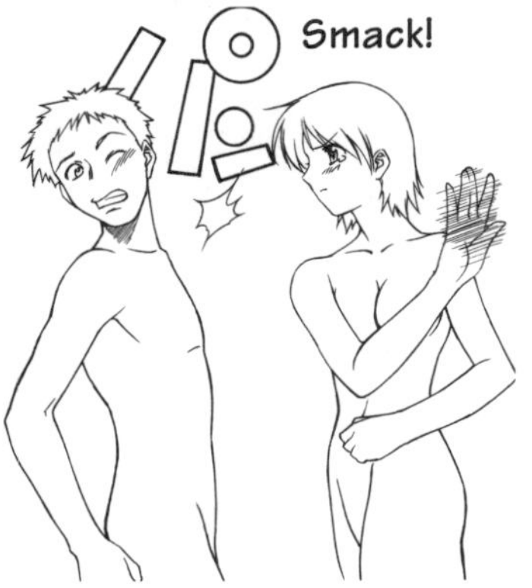

Here, both figures are drawn standing bolt upright and lack torsion at the waist.

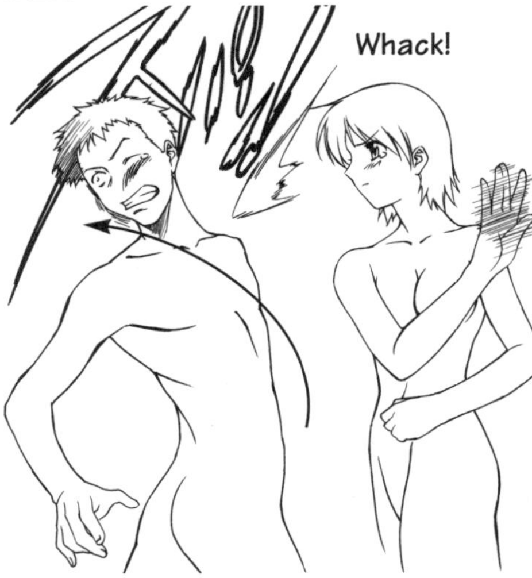

Here, the figure delivering the slap retains the same stance, but the figure receiving the slap is twisting at the waist.

Here, I take a running figure and shift the right hand to the front.

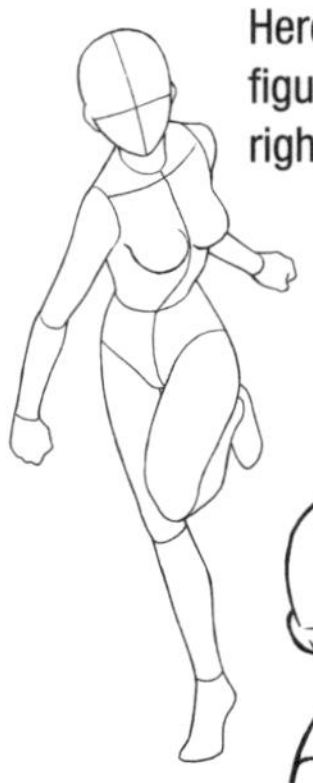

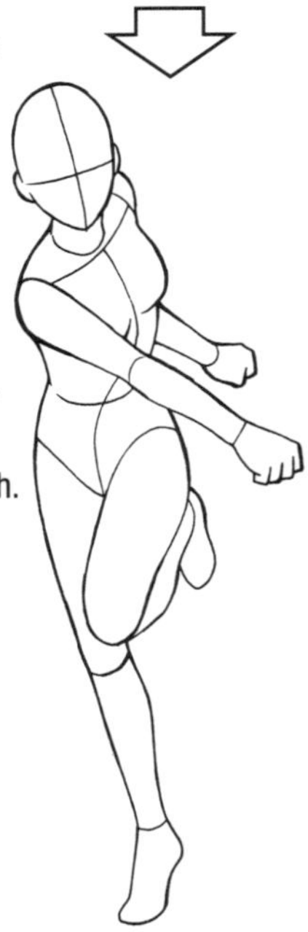

The result is a figure putting her waist into delivering a punch.

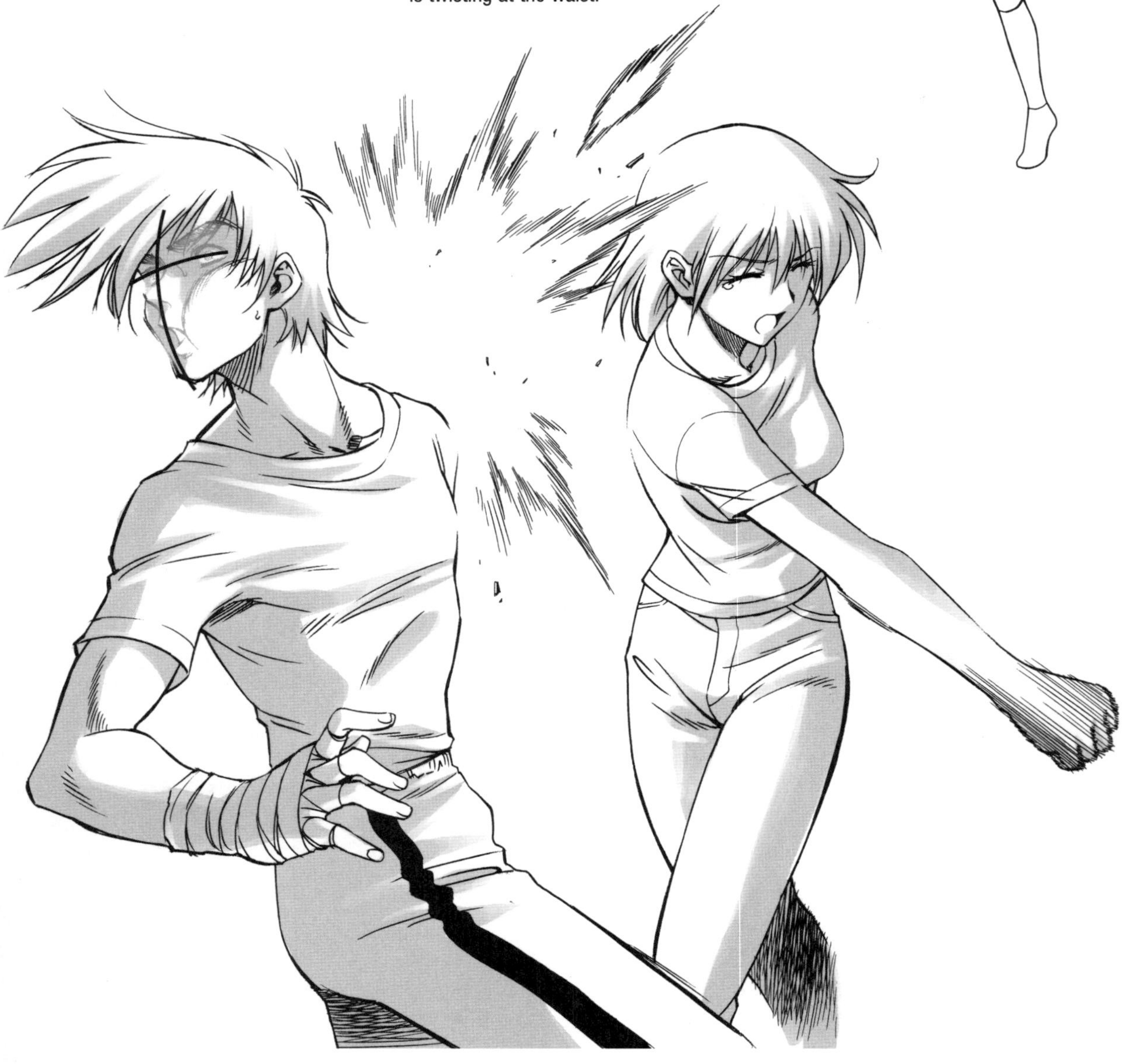

Chapter 4

More *Manga*

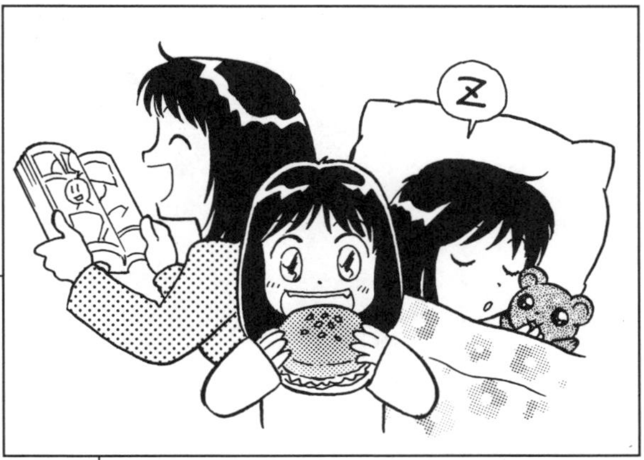

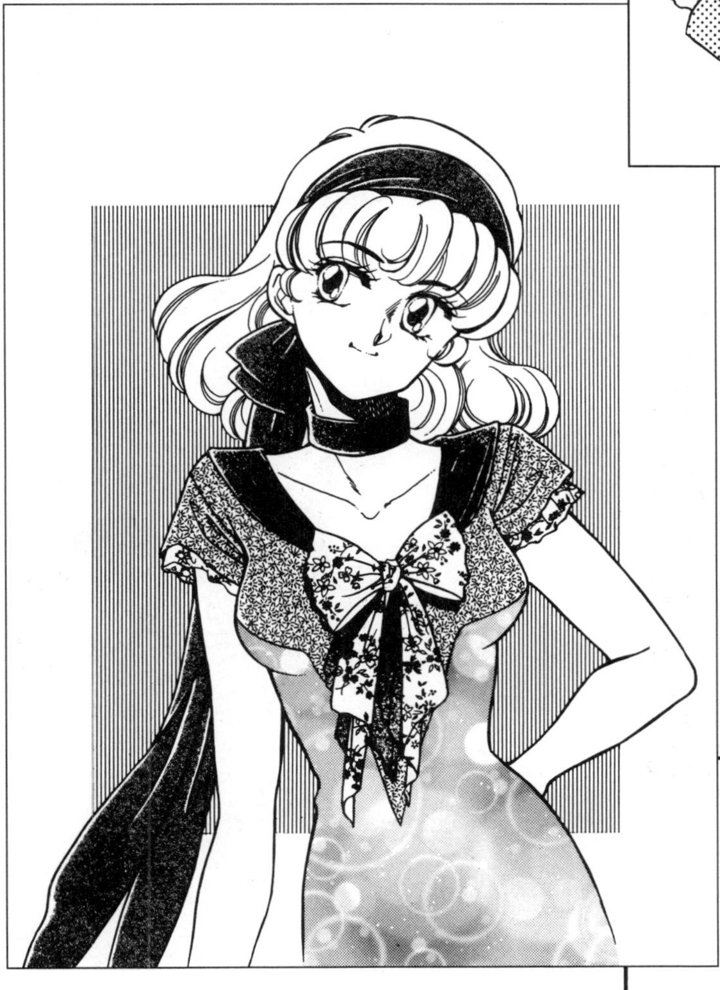

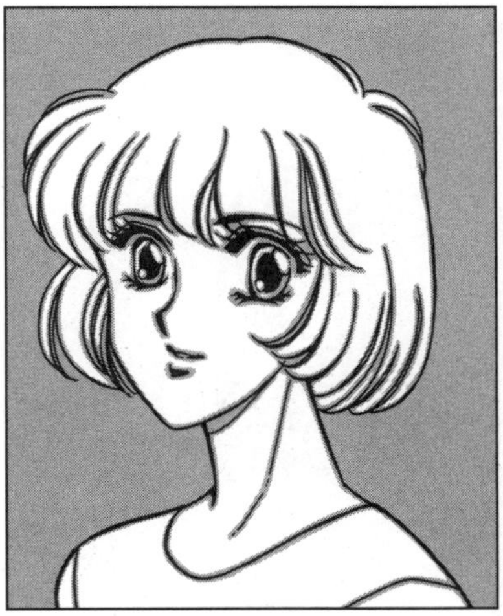

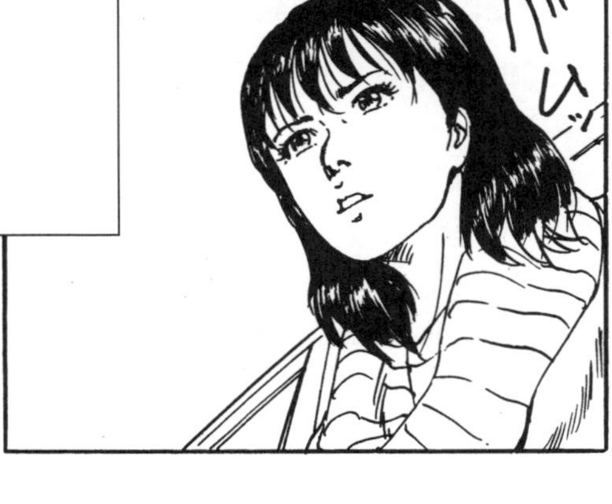

The Fundamentals of *Manga* Portrayal: Making the Composition Obvious at a Glance

4 Basic Elements

In *manga*, the reader figures out the story by seeing how the pictures flow. That is what characterizes the medium. Any dialogue or narrative text is supplementary to add to the reader's understanding. We say that in *manga*, pictures tell the story, and the significance of heightening the characters' sense of presence lies in that statement. But, let's first start with telling a story (communicating) through pictures.

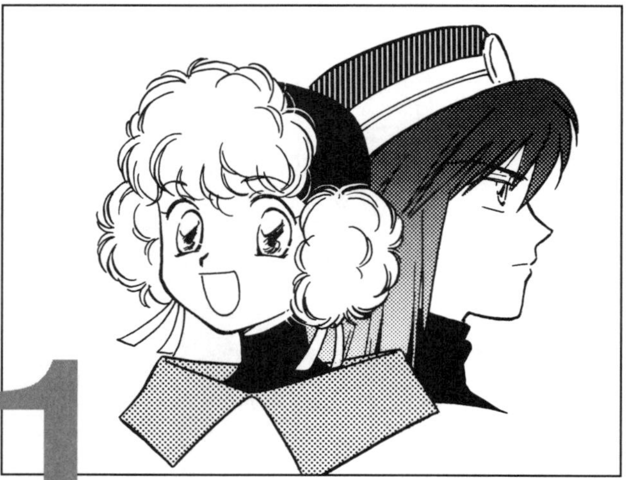

1 The Characters:

What do they look like? What are their personalities? What will they say?

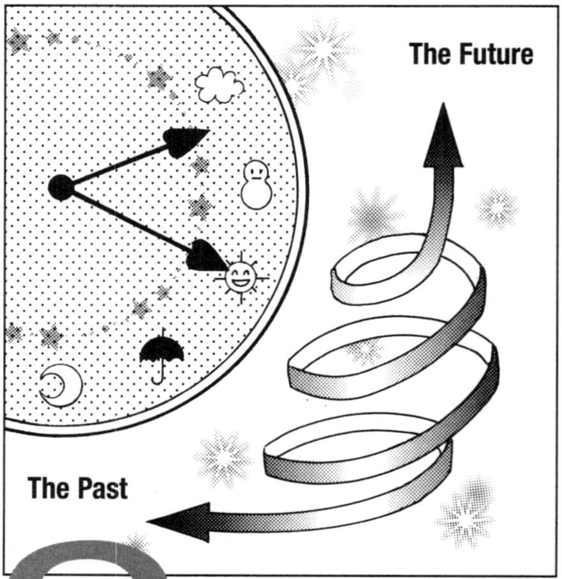

2 When (Time)

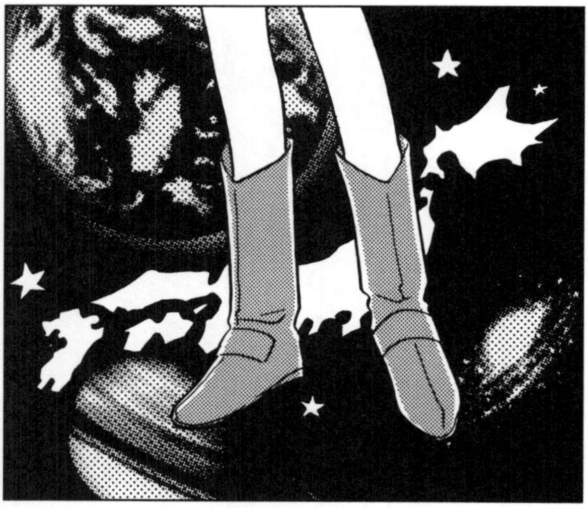

Where (Location)

3

These are the 4 points that need to be clarified in order to convey the situation to the reader and have him or her understand.

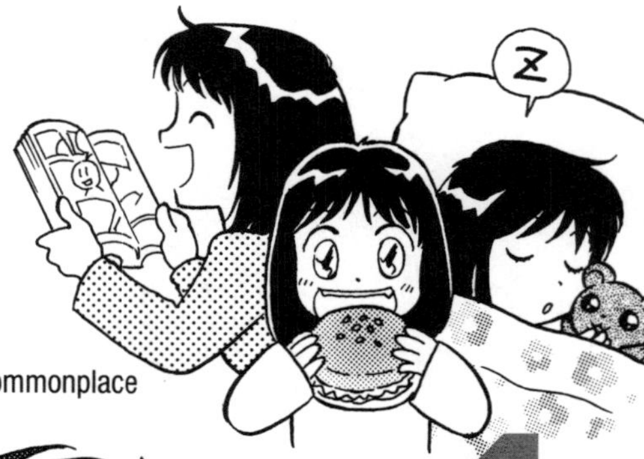

The Commonplace

4

Actions

Something done for someone's behalf

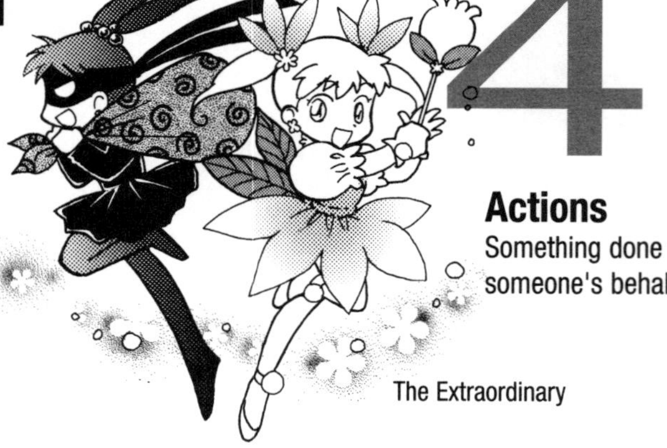

The Extraordinary

Telling a Story Visually

The key is to decide your theme—i.e. what to communicate—and what must be drawn—i.e. what information to draw.

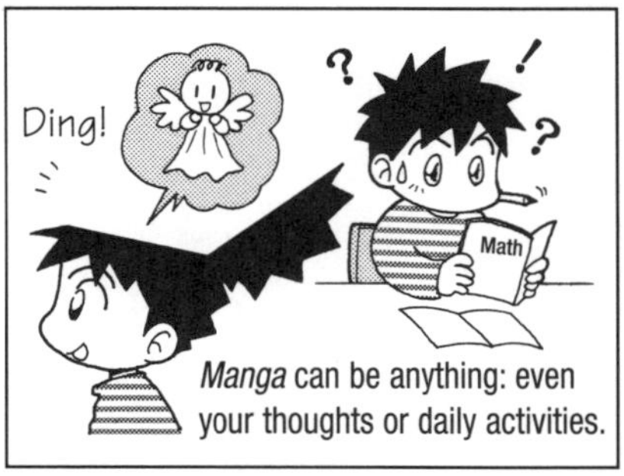

Manga can be anything: even your thoughts or daily activities.

Theme Waiting in a café

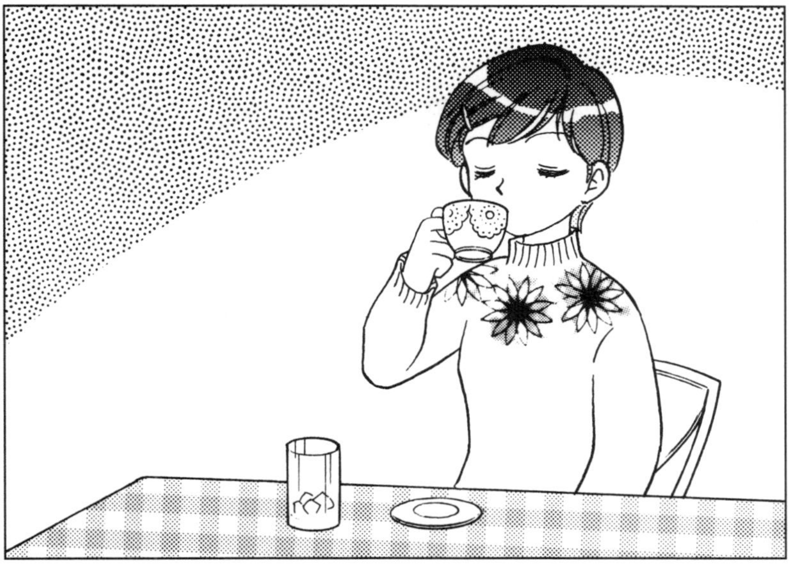

What panels will you select for your theme, "waiting in a café"?

- A character waiting
- The characters meeting
- A character waiting, and then the characters meeting

You will need to decide beforehand what types of panels you will draw. This is what it means to "decide a theme."

Bad example.:

- The setting does not necessarily look like a café.
- We have no idea what kind of person the character is.
- We are not sure what she is doing.

Good example.:

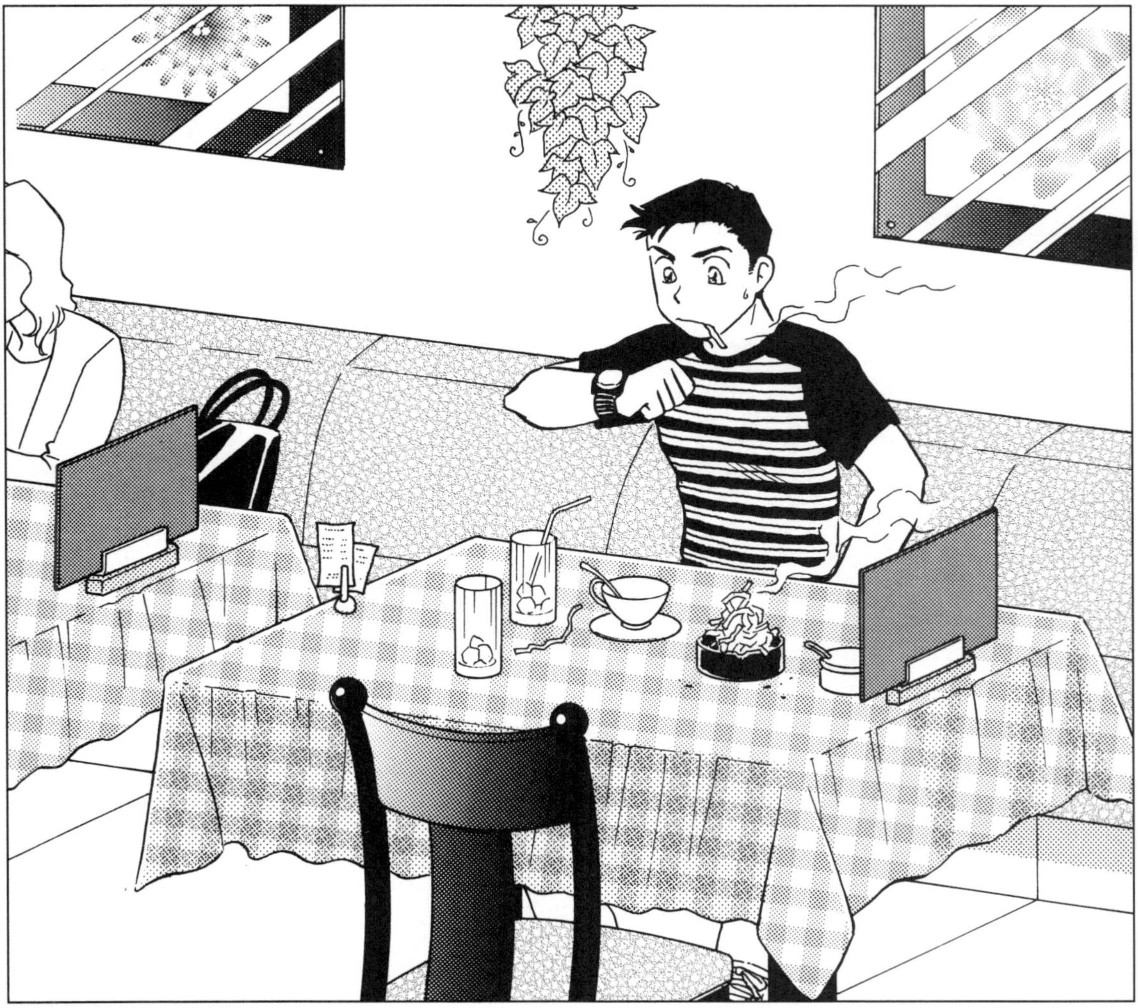

Indicators that the location is a café: a receipt, a menu, a window, etc. "Waiting" indicators: a partially read book, half drunk water. Character indicators: a cigarette dangling from the mouth, smoke drifting from cigarette butts in the ashtray. The indicators we see in the panel suggest an uncouth character type.

Panel Design (The ABC's of Page Composition)

Panel design begins with deciding what needs to be drawn. Clear panel design will lead to portraying characters with presence.

Theme: Café Rendezvous

Analysis

Main Story Points	
The 4 Elements	The Artist's Conception
The protagonist	Character: character design
During the evening	When: portrayal of evening
In a café	Where: portrayal of café
Has a rendezvous	Action: meeting, talking, etc.

"Waiting" as the Main Theme:

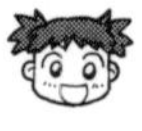
The protagonist

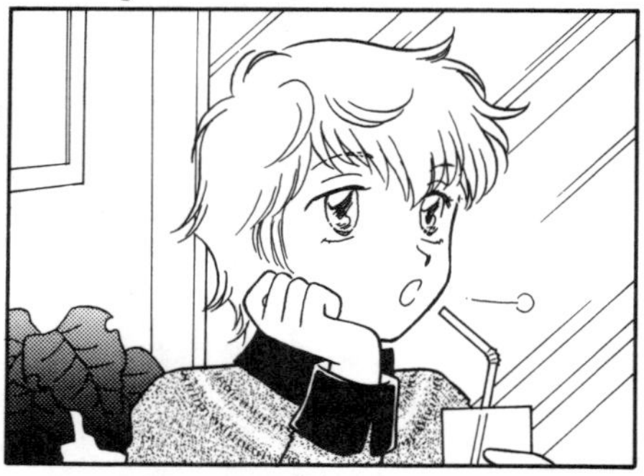

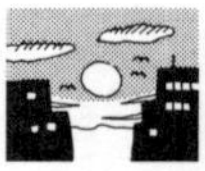
Evening

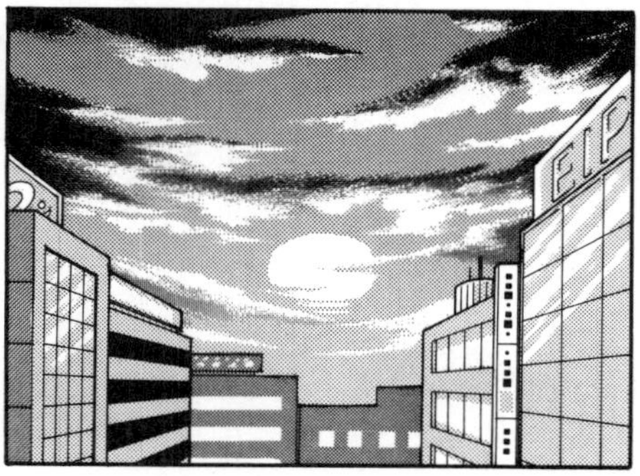

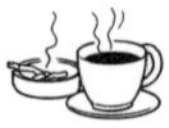
Café

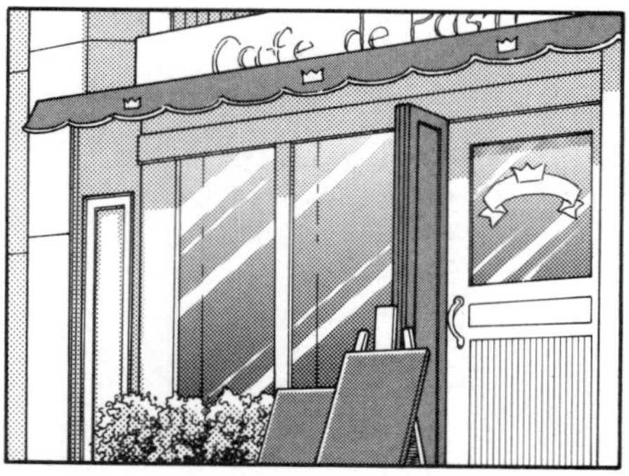

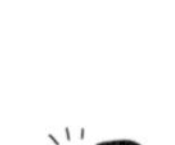

Meeting

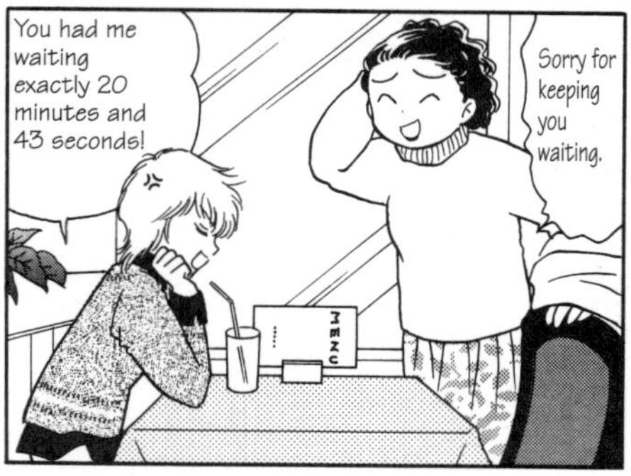

Once these 4 elements have been clarified, determine specifically the main point you wish to make.

For what purpose are you drawing a rendezvous in a café? What do you hope to communicate using this theme? You need to establish the underlying theme. Oftentimes, if you fail to clarify this point, you may find yourself unable to compose your theme, even if you try.

"Waiting," "worrying," and other acts relating to "meeting": the ways of executing the simplistic theme, "rendezvous at a café" are limitless.

The protagonist's reaction reveals her personality through "action." These 4 panels form an "incident" that illustrates the protagonist's personality.

Underlying Theme: "He's here!"

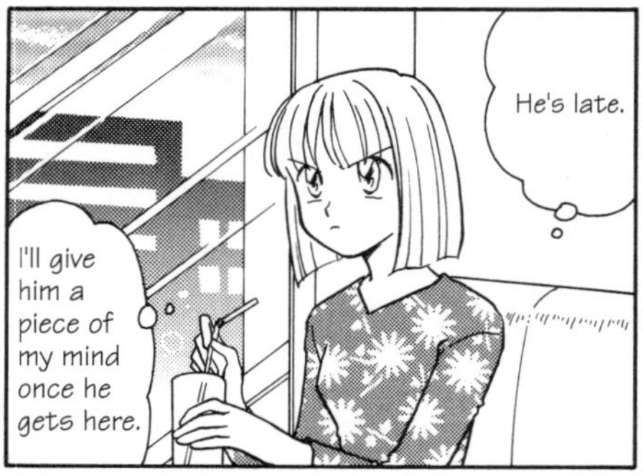

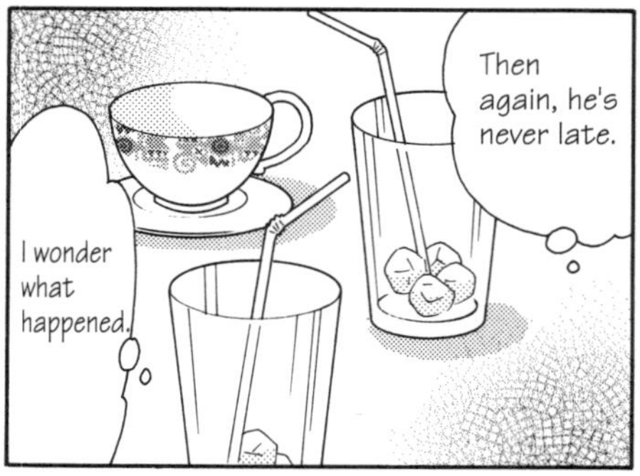

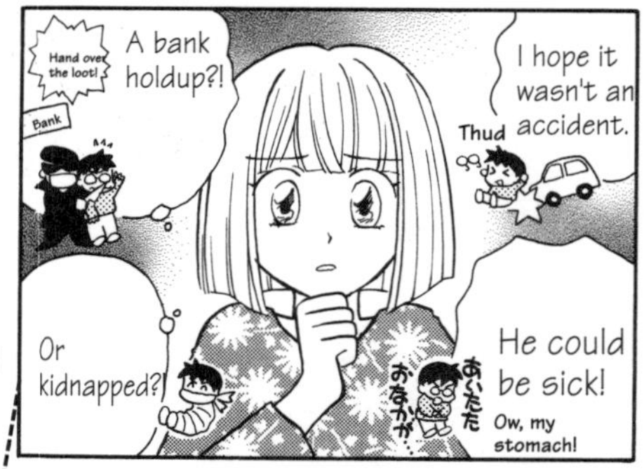

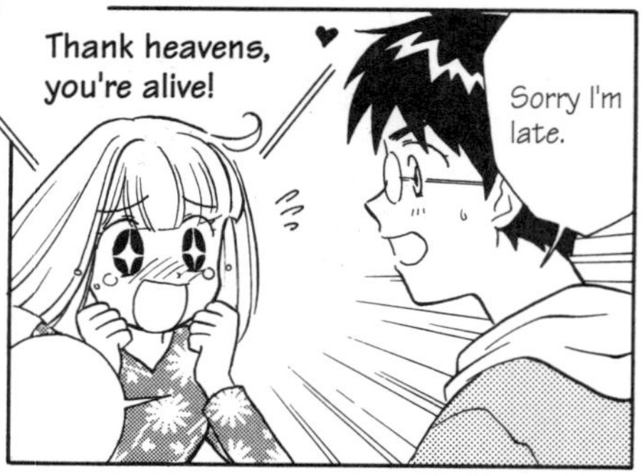

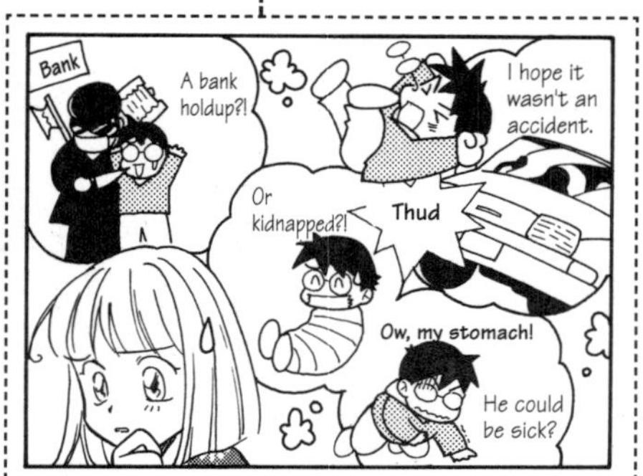

Here the third panel, where we see the protagonist's imagination let fly, is recomposed so that the visuals dominate. Now, the panel has more of a *manga* flavor, and we can tell at a glance what is taking place. However, the original panel coveys more strongly the protagonist's state of "anxiety."

Theme: Café

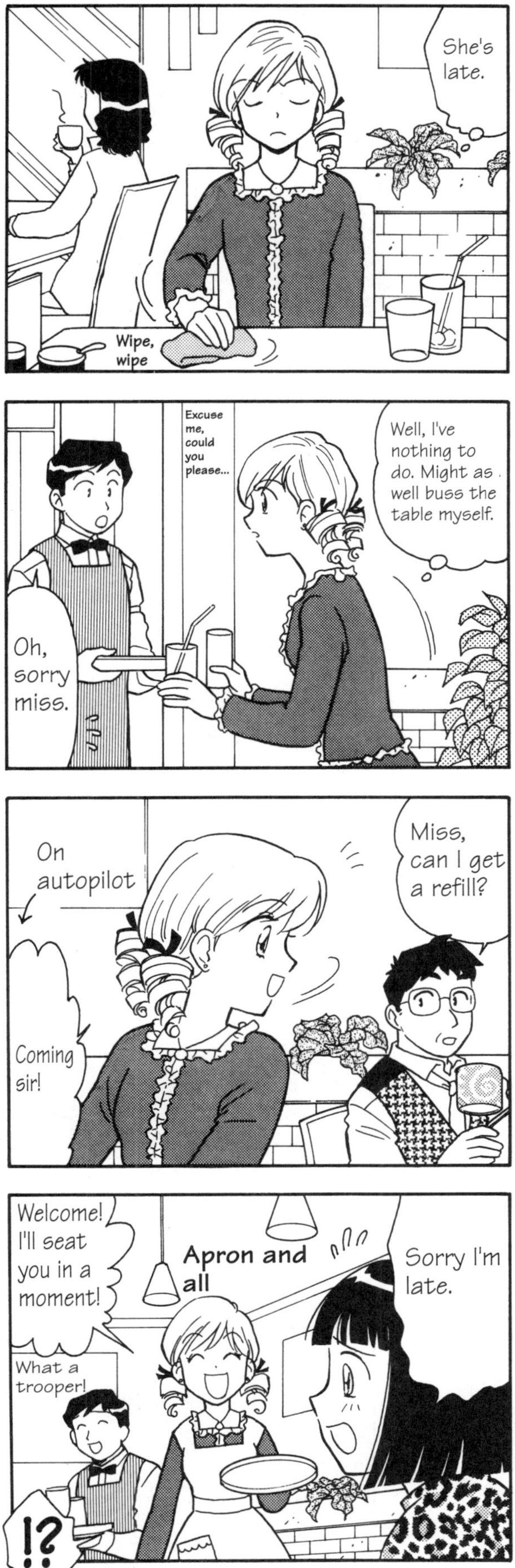

Waiting on a Friend: Character Introduction Scene

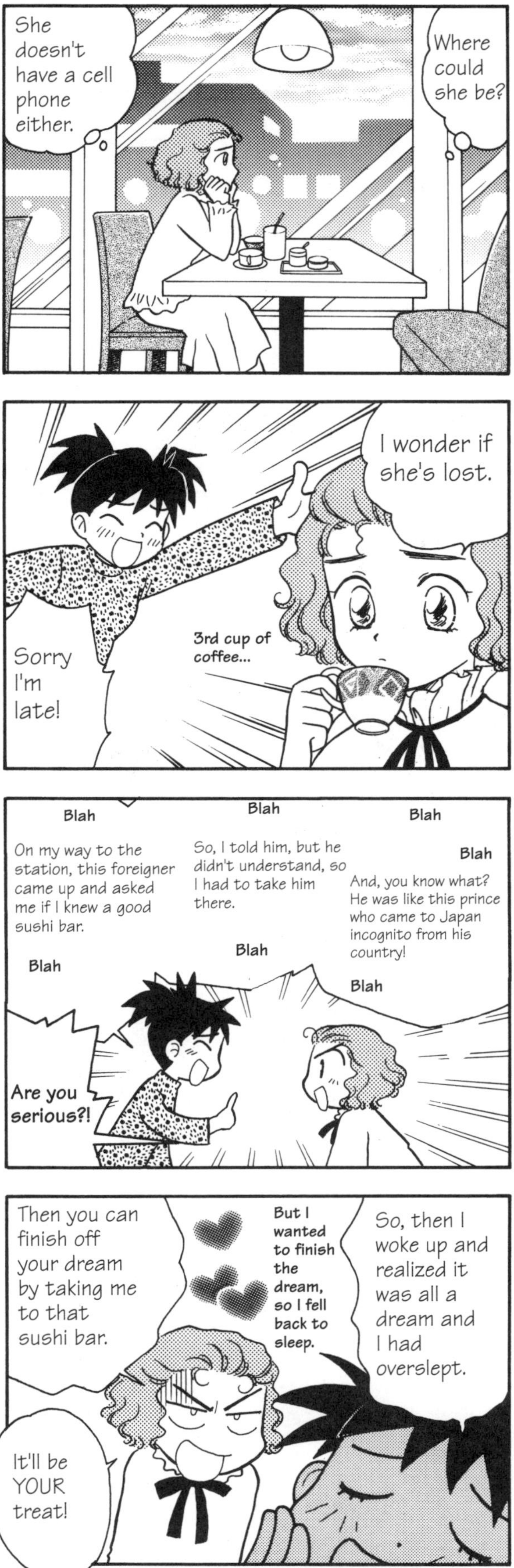

Here, the relationship between the two becomes clear immediately (explained by the scene).

Giving the Panel Design Variation

This refers to modifying the panel's size. Important panels should be made large.

Readjustment of "Waiting on a Friend": Character Introduction Scene

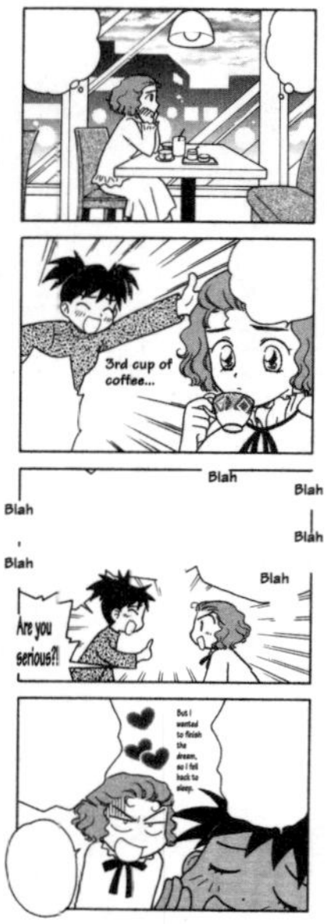

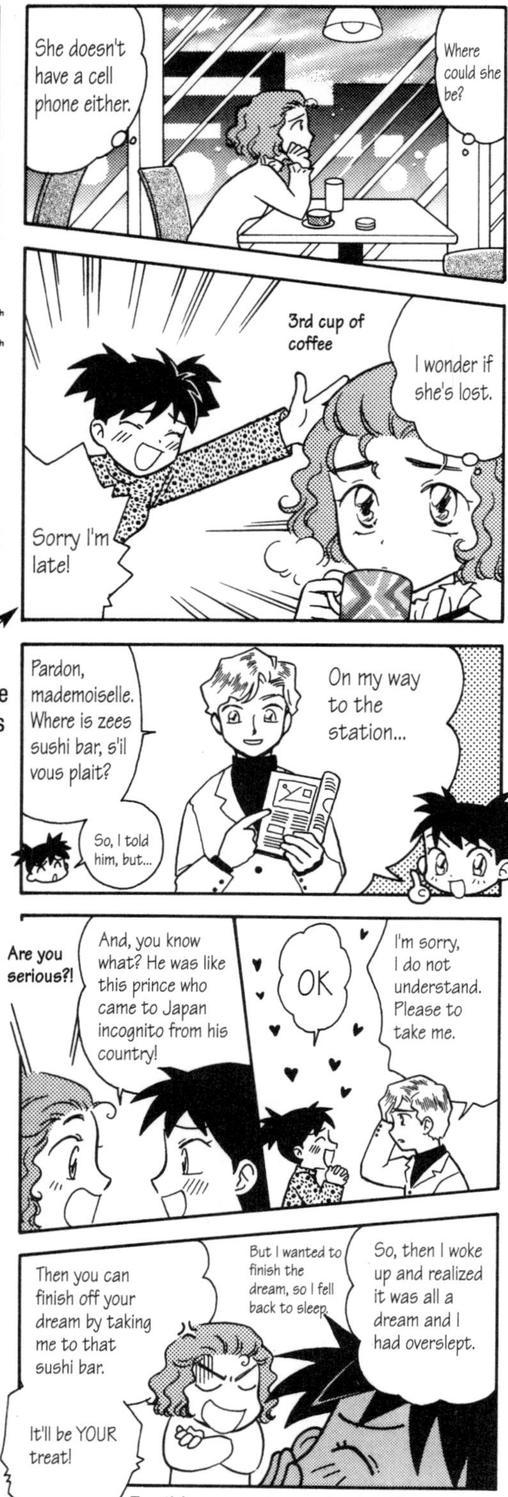

Since the idea that the friend finally arrived is the main point, her appearance panel is made the largest.

For this scene, to emphasize the character's personality, the "Thank heavens!" panel should be made larger, as shown above. To introduce the "late friend," lay out the panels as seen below. Since the fifth panel illustrating the protagonist's worrywart wanderings was drawn rather large, the first example works better within the flow.

Readjustment of "He's here!"

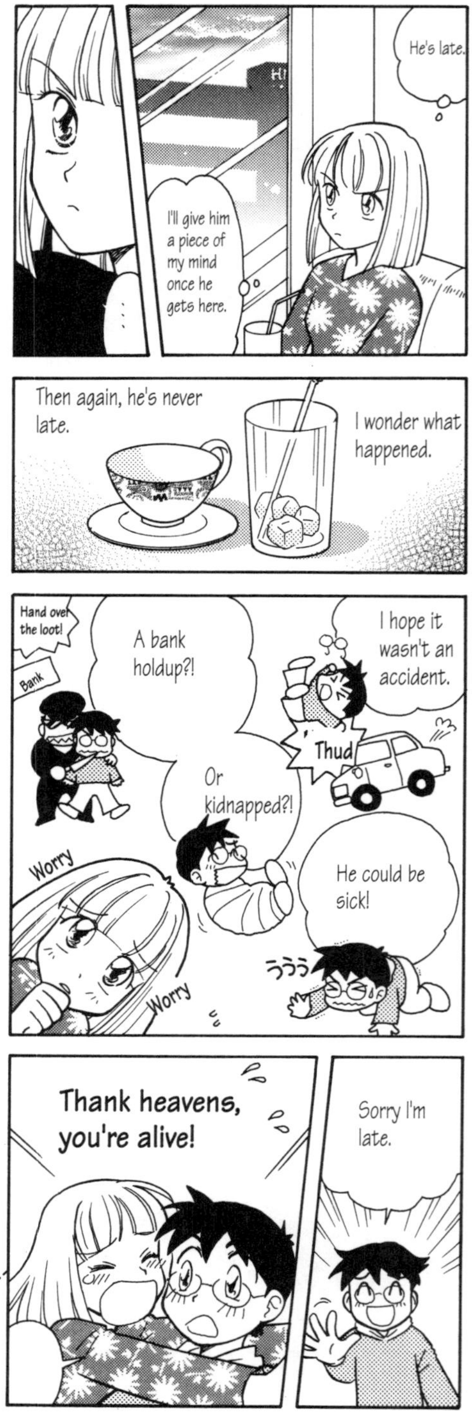

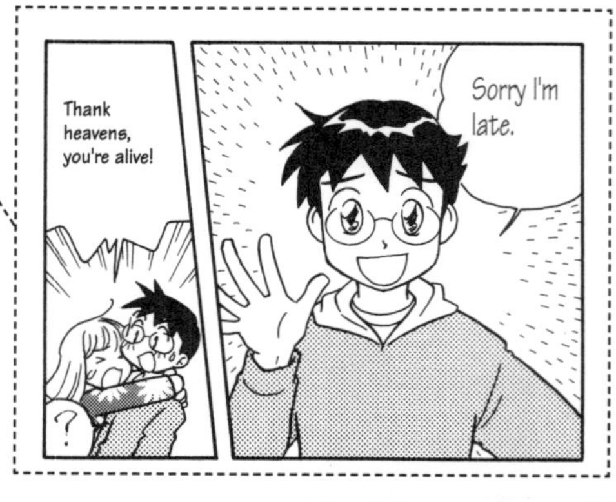

Panel Design Heightening the Boyfriend's Sense of Presence

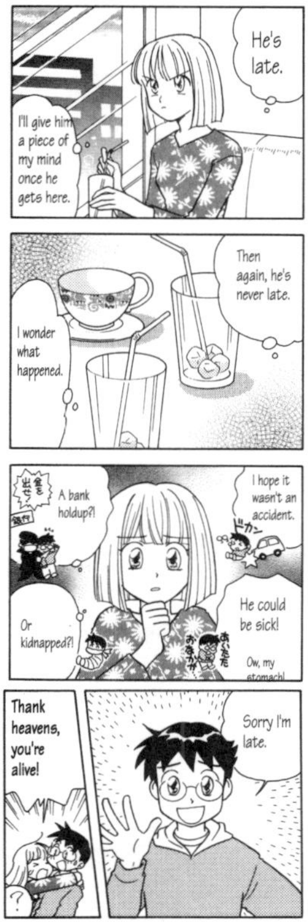

Good Example

Here, the panel design has been given variation by making the largest the panel introducing the boyfriend, who is the focus of the scene.

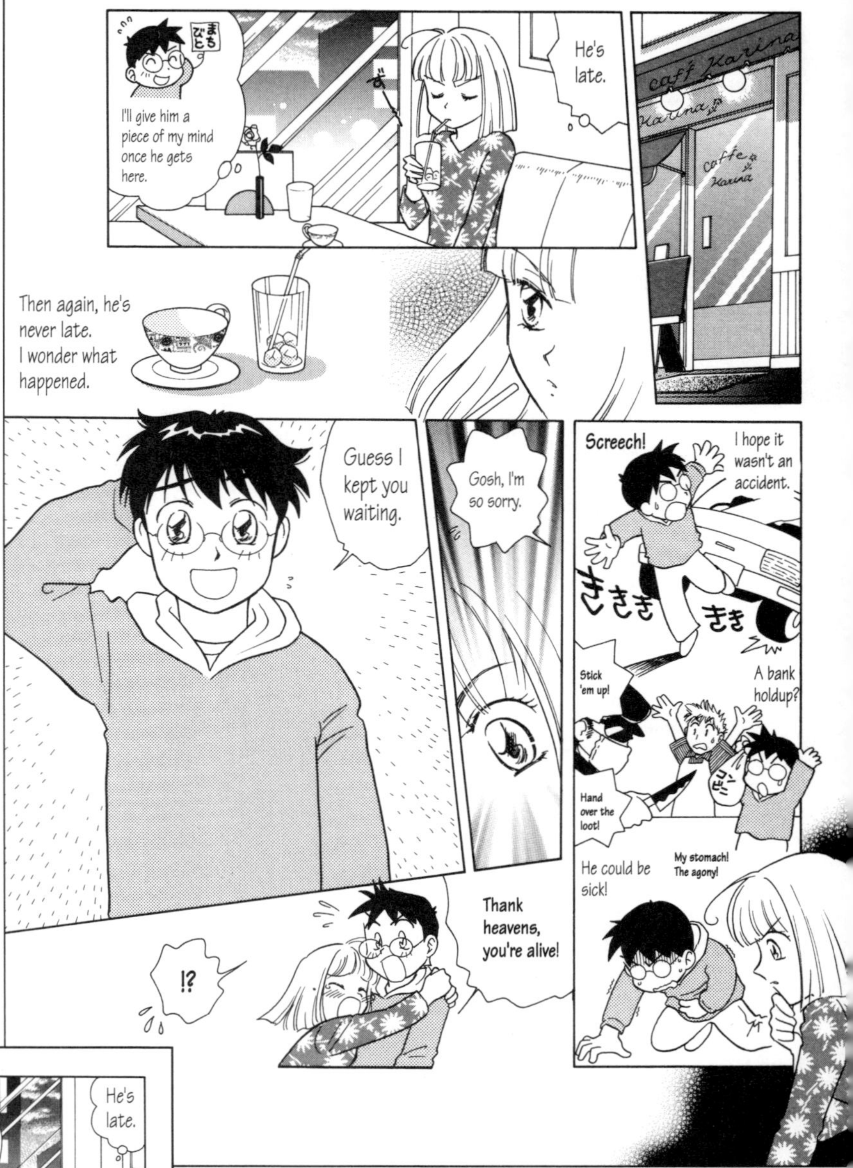

Here, each panel is viewed as equally important, and, therefore, all are drawn the same size.

Static Panel Design

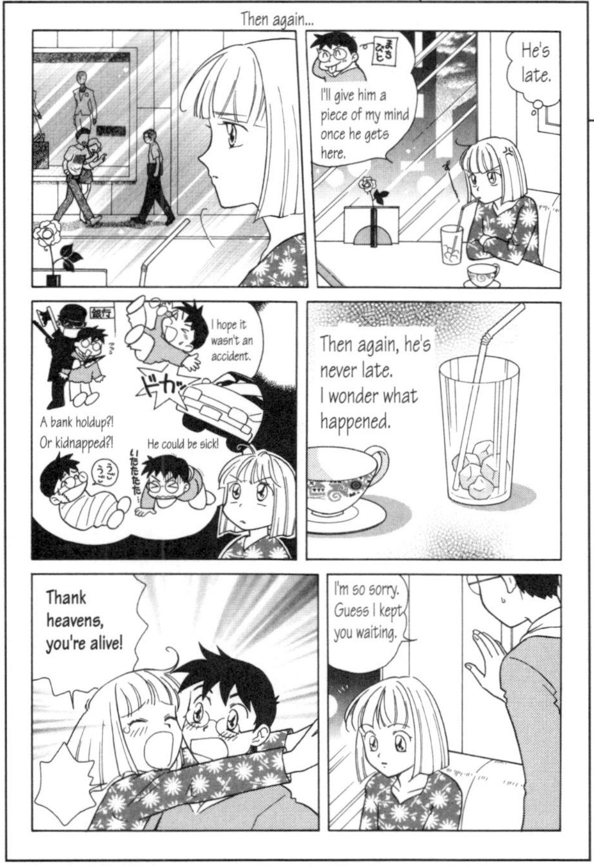

For this, I took the original 4-panel scene and redesigned the panels, making his appearance the key panel. Varying large and small panels turns this 4-panel scene into a full-fledged 1-page episode.

The same theme can appear greatly different (i.e. give the reader an entirely different impression) simply by modifying the panel design. With all panels the same size, the reader is unclear of the scene's gist.

You, the artist, must determine what point you want to make, what you want to tell to the reader, and what it is you need to communicate. Failing to do so could easily result in a monotonous panel design.

Your main point rests in the key panel. Draw your key panels the largest.

Figures and Cars: How to Draw Comfortably Scenes of Figures Getting in and out of Cars

Manga convention dictates using sound effects of car doors opening and closing to portray getting in and out of a car.

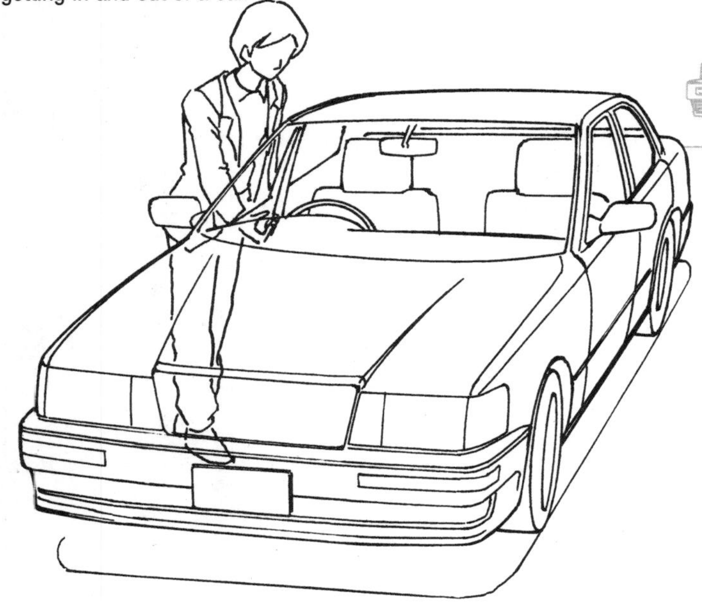

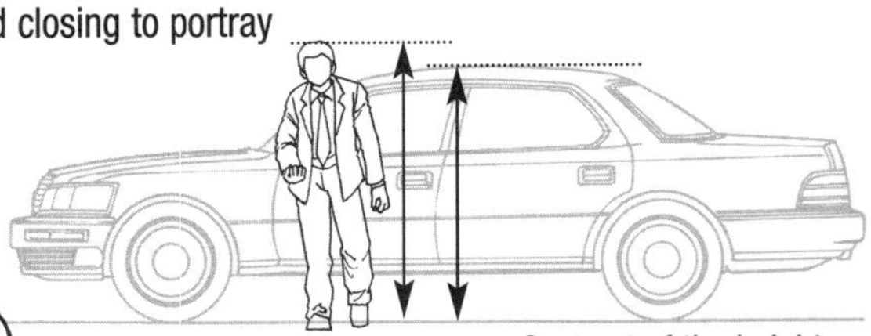

Contrast of the height of a car and a person

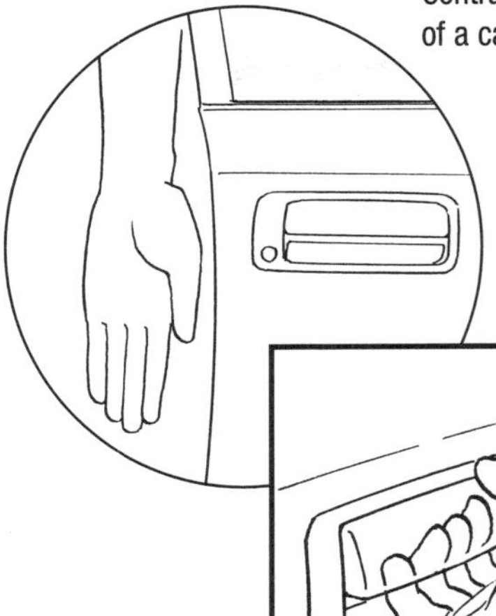

The door handle should be situated about the same level as the hand when hanging.

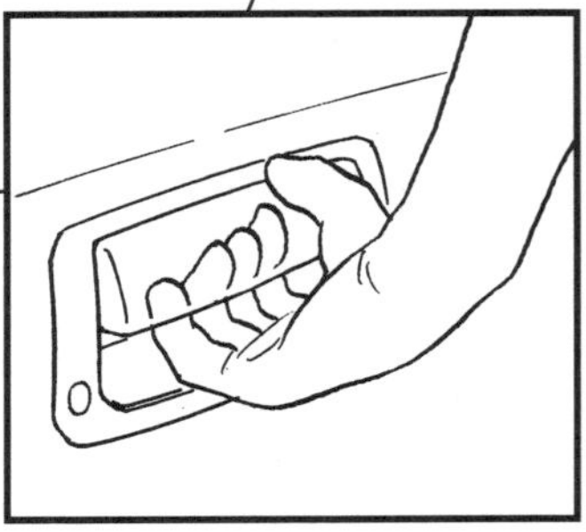

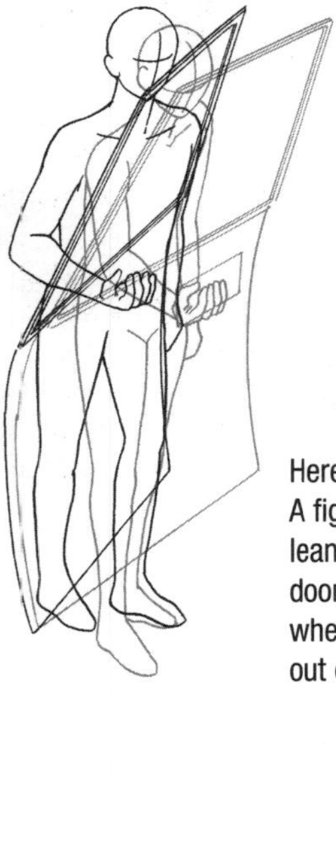

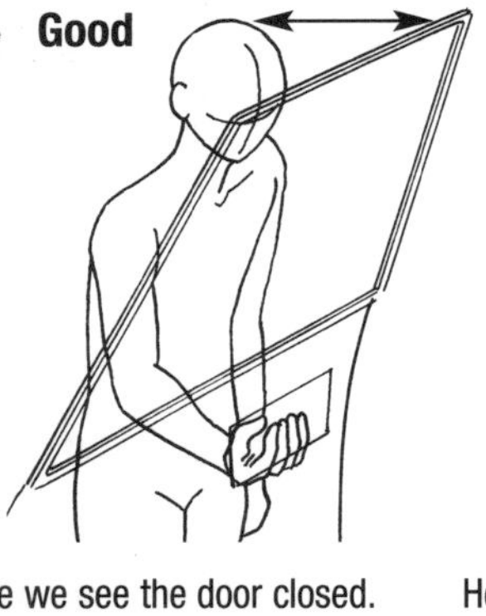

Good

Here we see the door closed. A figure assumes this forward leaning pose when opening the door (getting in the car) and when closing the door (getting out of the car).

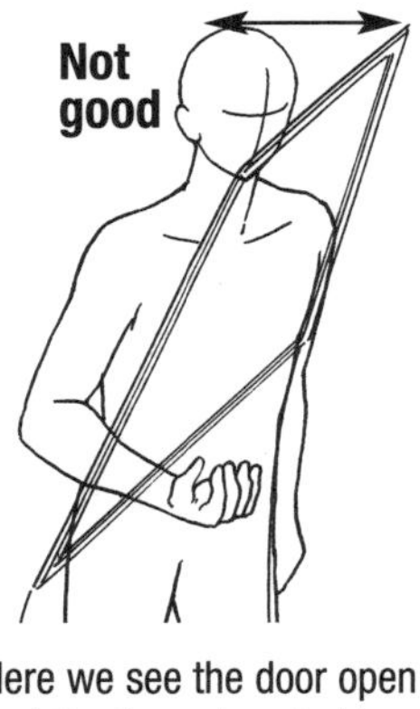

Not good

Here we see the door open and the figure in a fashion model pose. Even with the door open, the forward leaning pose would look more natural.

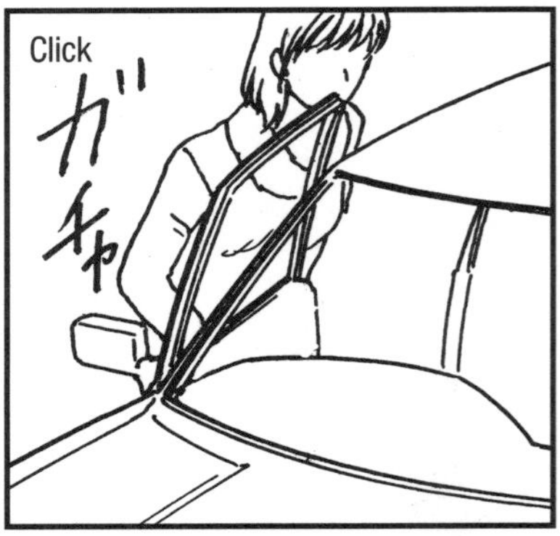

Here we see a character getting into a car. Without the sound effects, this could also be interpreted as a disembarking scene.

With the same composition, the different sound effects indicate whether the door is being opened ("click") or closed ("slam!").

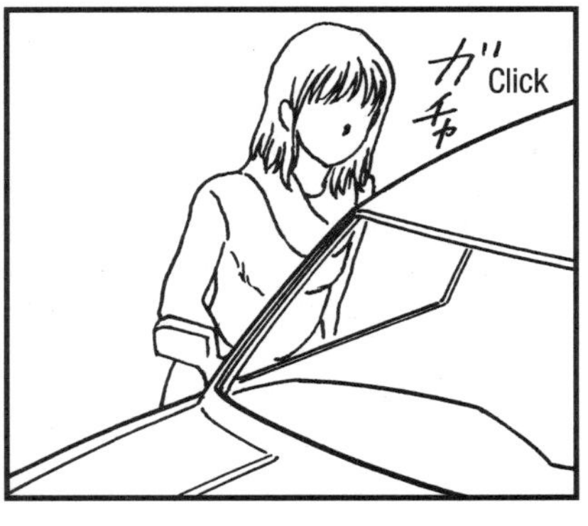

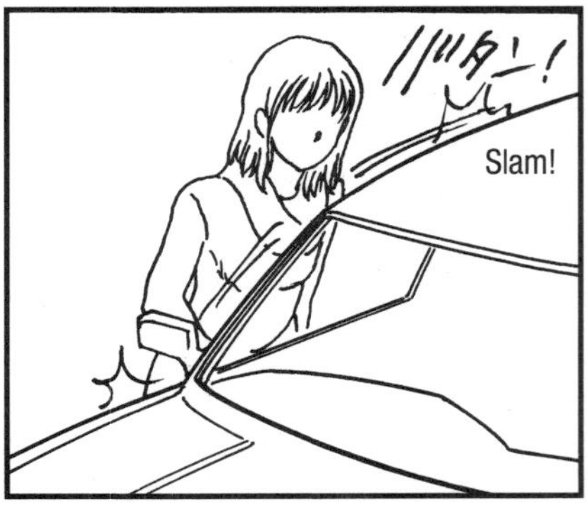

Normally, artists are limited to the page space or number of panels they can use to portray characters getting into a car. Here we have samples illustrating that minimal artwork, using few panels (1 to 2) allows you adequately to portray "getting into or out of a car." " provided that a shot of the front, side, or rear of the car has been included.

Published *Manga* Sample Scenes: Getting in and out of a Car

A side view of the car and close-up of the front windshield explain the scene.

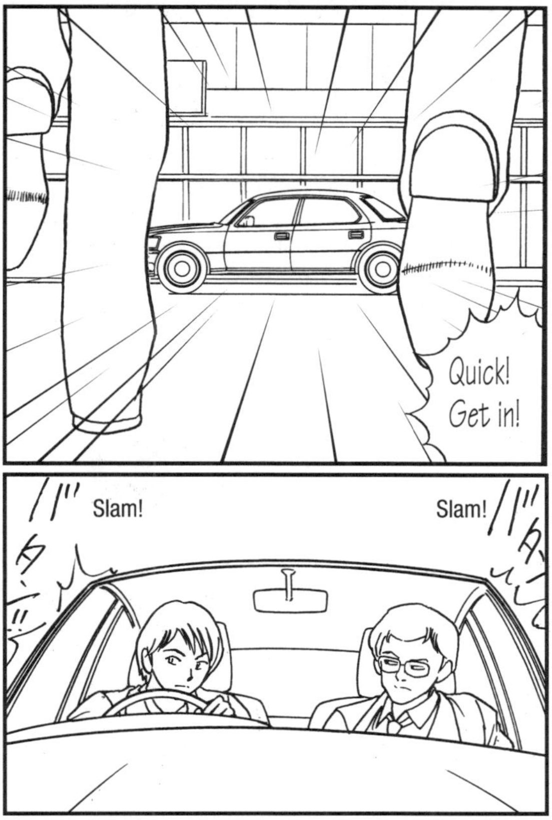

Here, a side view of the car is used, and any shot of opening the car door has been omitted. Still, we understand that the characters have gotten into the car.

Scene portrayed using a front view of a car and partial door shots

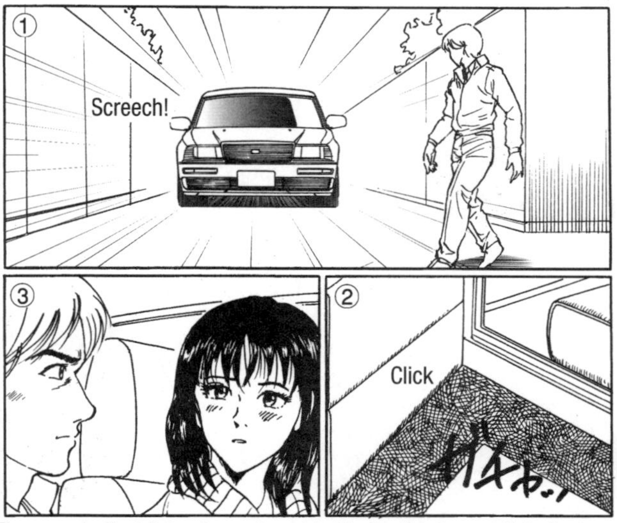

The sound effect "slam" may be added to the third panel if desired. Drawing the female character instead the male in panel 1 would have altered the scene so that she was the one boarding. Turning the vehicle into a foreign car (i.e. switching the steering wheel to the left side) would suggest that the male character is the one boarding. Alternatively, it could be that she was driving the car but turned the wheel over to him.

Here, the car is stopped, and the two riders get out. Showing the car door open in the second panel is in line with common practice in portraying scenes of getting in and out of a car.

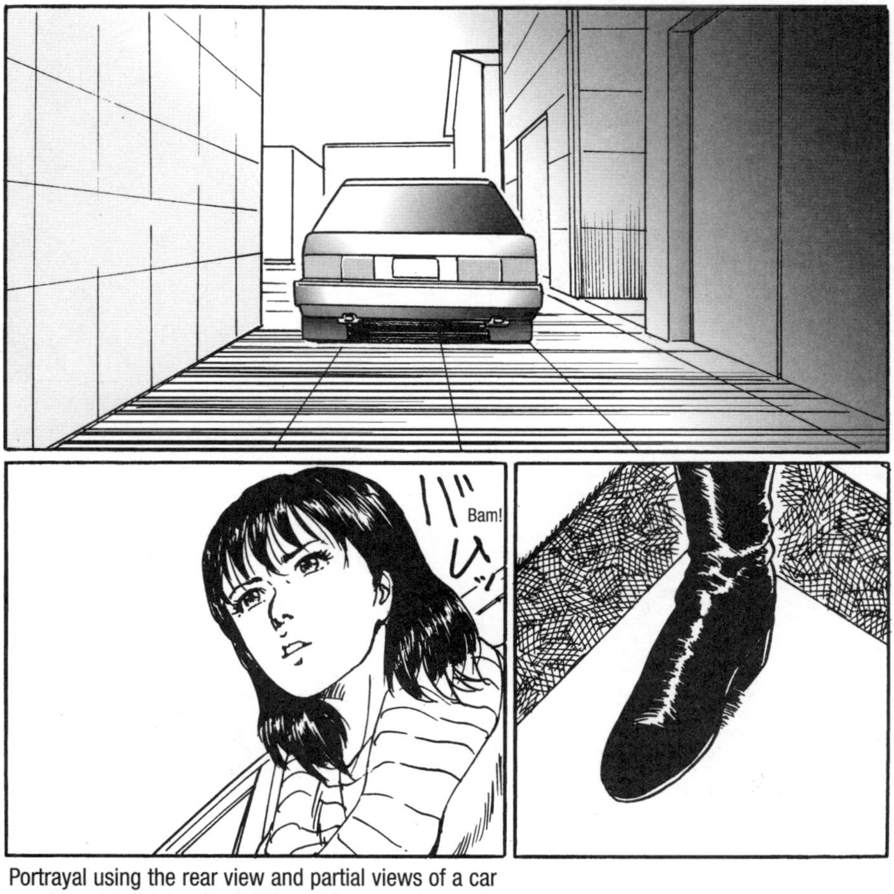

Portrayal using the rear view and partial views of a car

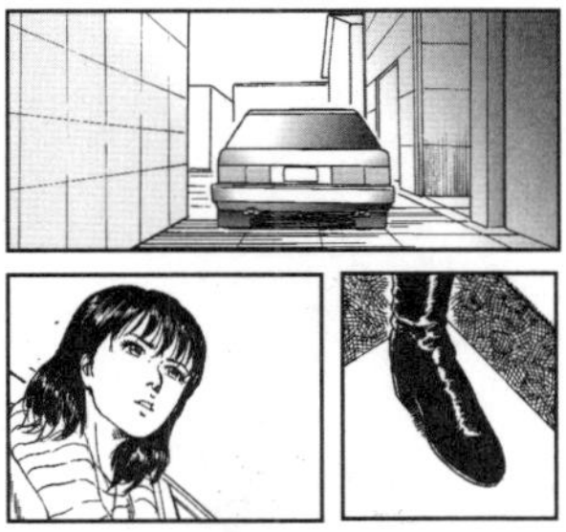

Reversing the images in the last two panels could be used to suggest that the character emerged from a rear passenger seat or that the driver had emerged and is standing still.

Special Effects That Enhance a Character's Sense of Presence

Attaching a Simple Tone as a Character Backdrop

The manner in which tone is attached as a character backdrop allows you to suggest movement by using a bit of ingenuity, thereby enhancing his or her sense of presence.

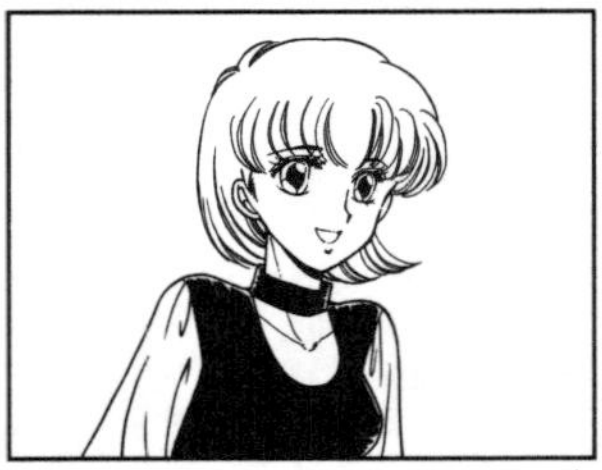

Good Example

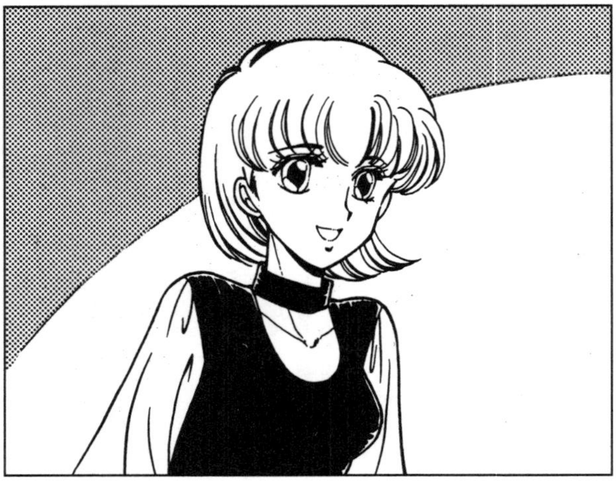

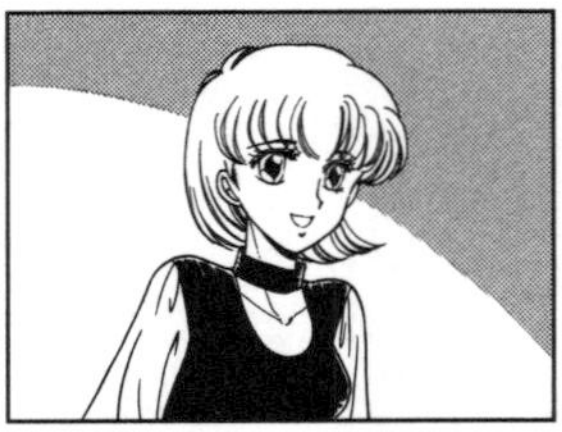

Here, the composition is open in back of the character. This creates a sinister mood, as if something might creep up from behind.

Keep the composition open in the direction the character faces.

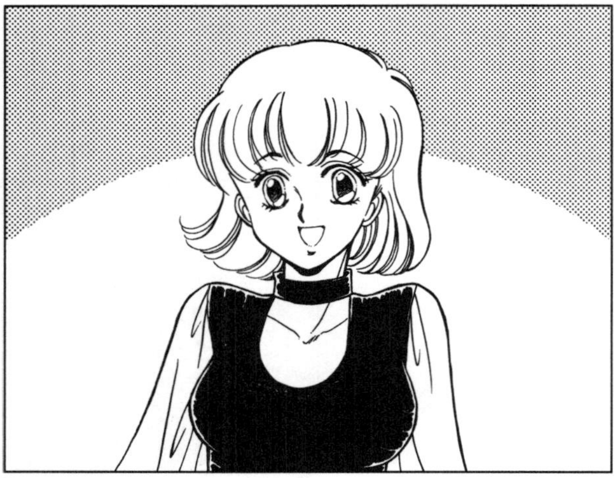

Front view tone effect

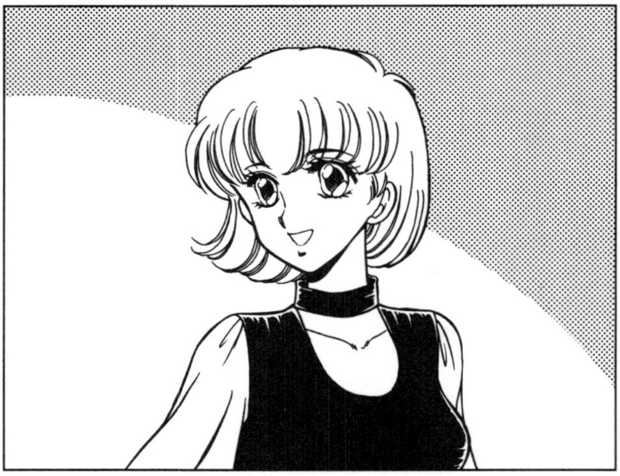

Even if the character's body is facing one direction, keep the composition open in the direction the head faces.

Alternative Styles

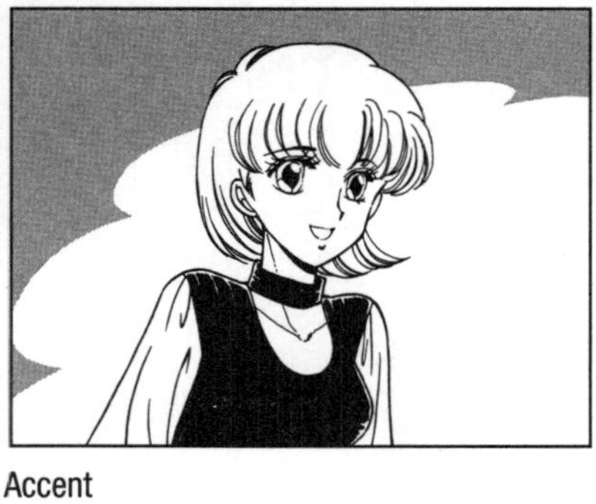

Accent

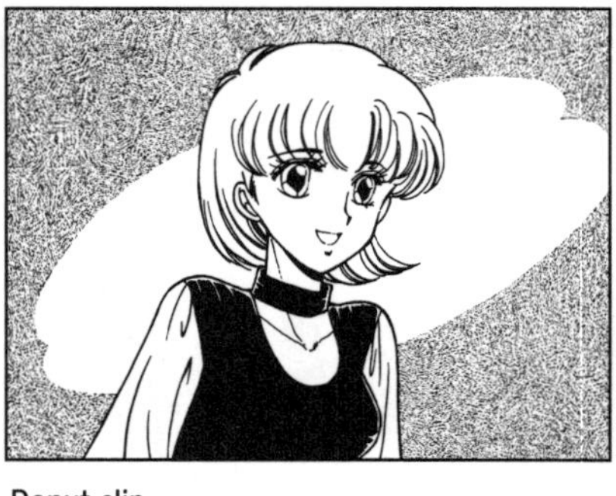

Donut clip

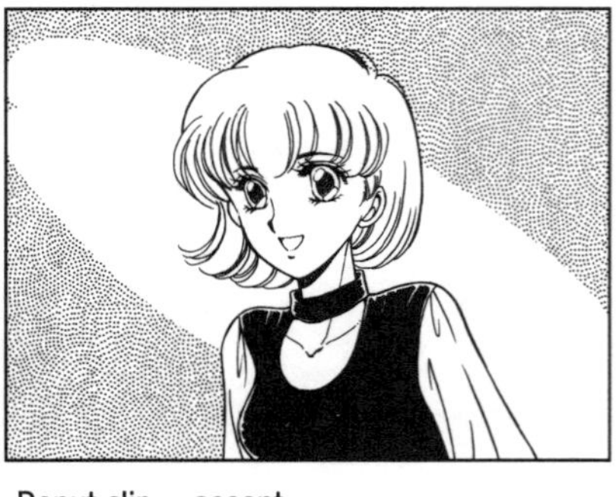

Donut clip + accent

Use a Little Creativity When Attaching Tone to a Character

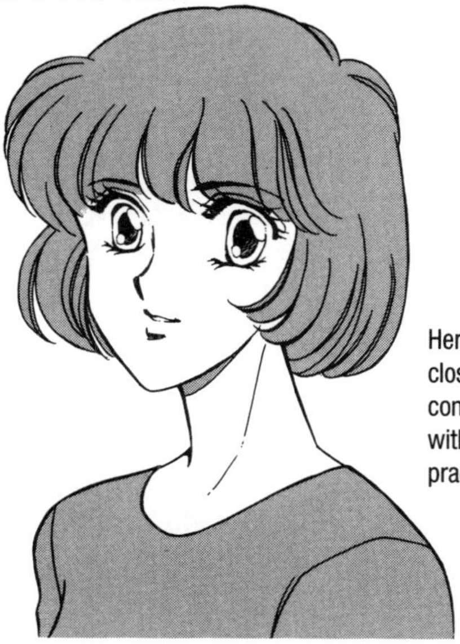

Here, the tone is cut closely along the contour lines, in line with standard practice.

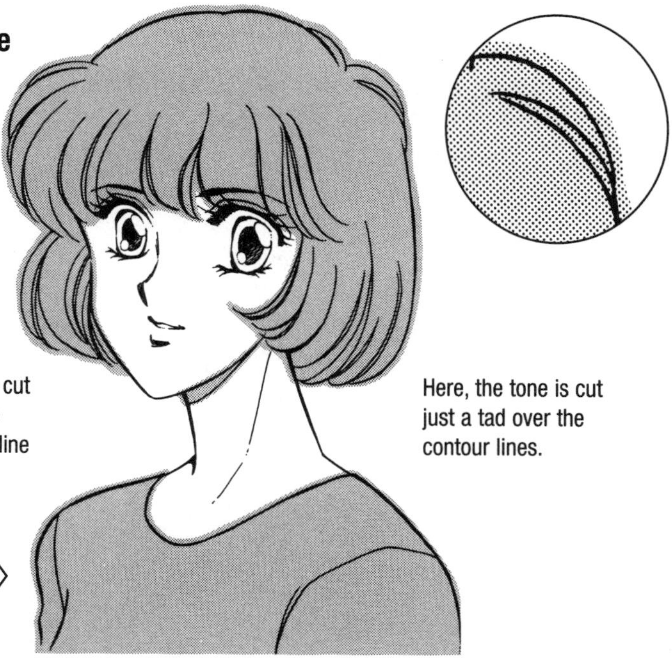

Here, the tone is cut just a tad over the contour lines.

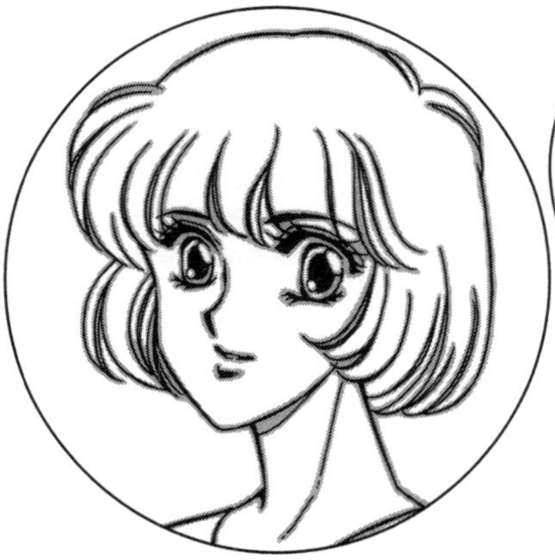

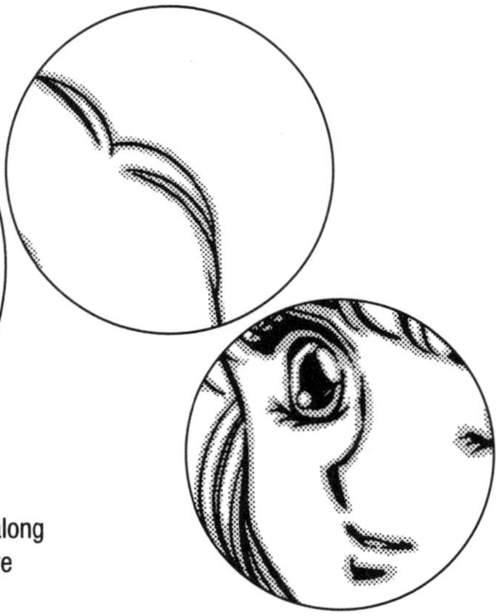

Here, even though the tone has been cut along the contour lines, it still evokes a distinctive impression.

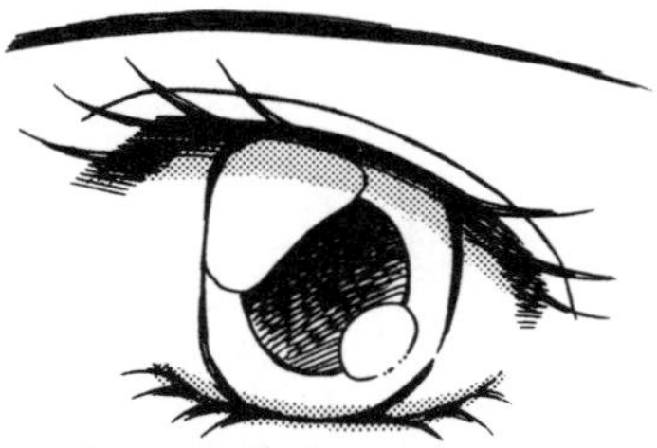

Detailed effect: Shadow falling across the iris

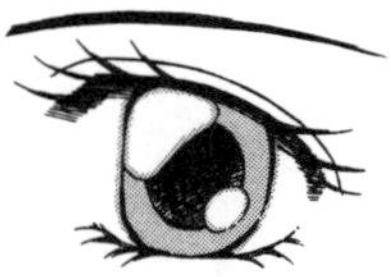

Execution suggesting brown or blue eyes

Emotional Portrayal and Tone Effects:

Create a Mood Using Backdrops of Cutout Tone

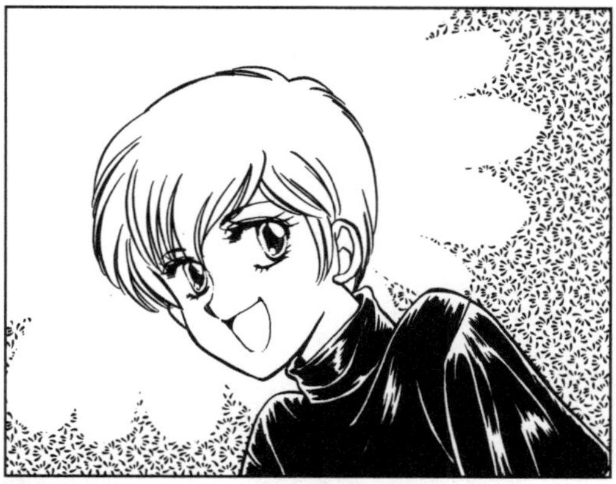

Vivaciousness/mirth

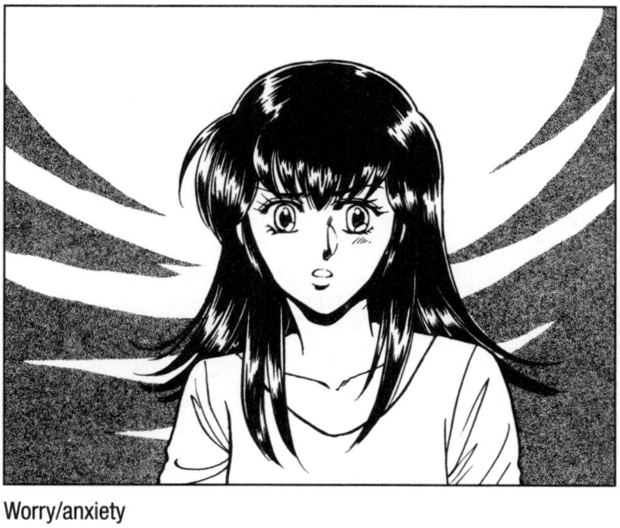

Worry/anxiety

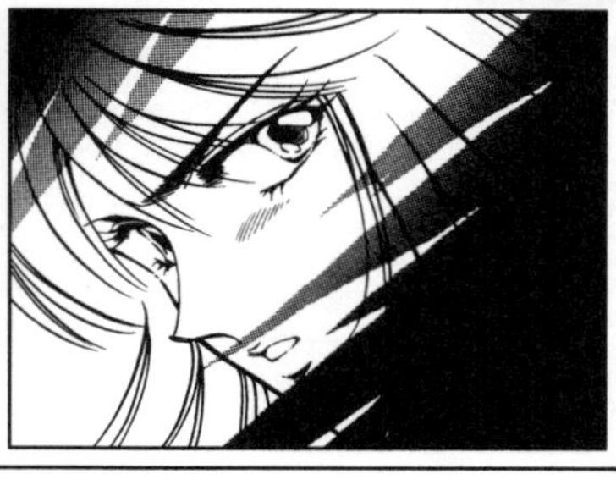

Tension/nervousness

More Tones: Composition Using Popular Tones Other than Standard Dot and Gradation

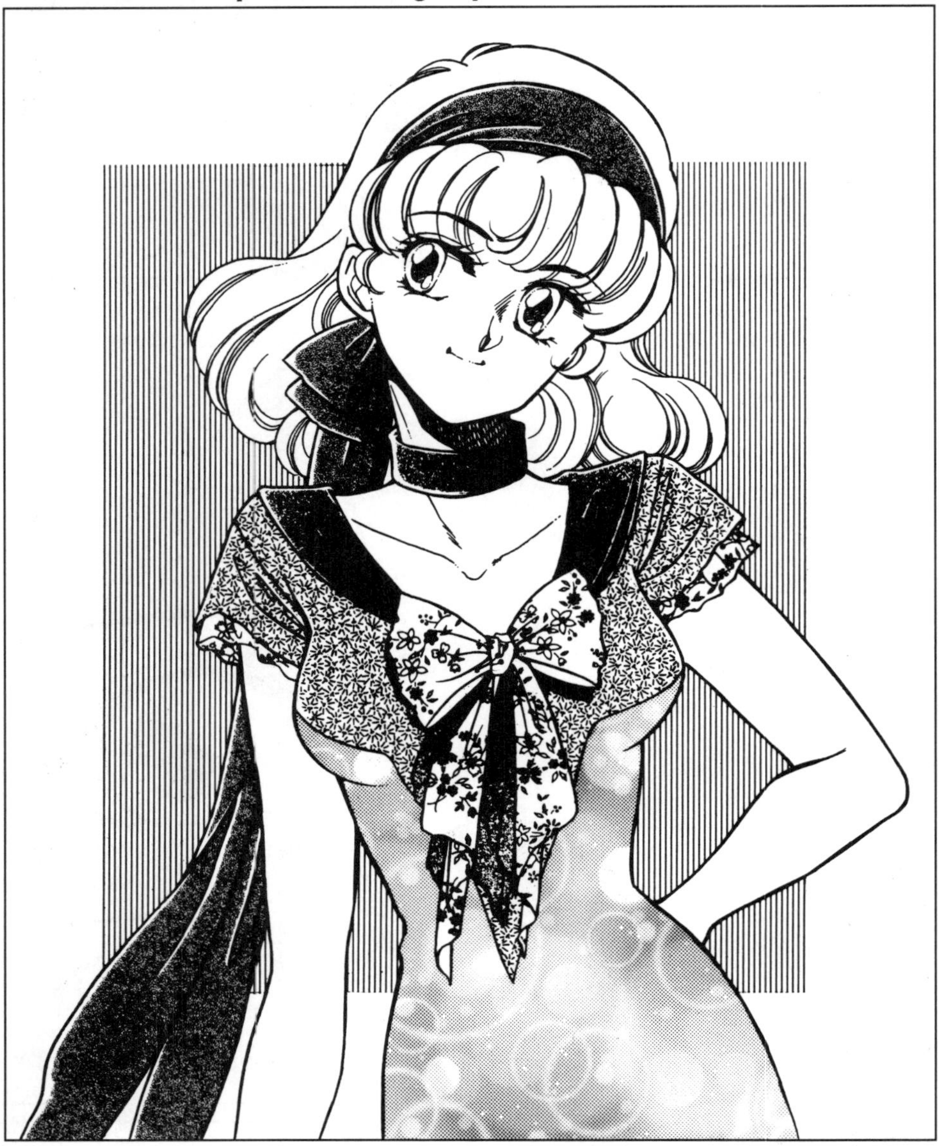

Tone comes in a myriad of patterns, the most common of which outside of dot and gradation may be roughly grouped into the following 6 categories.

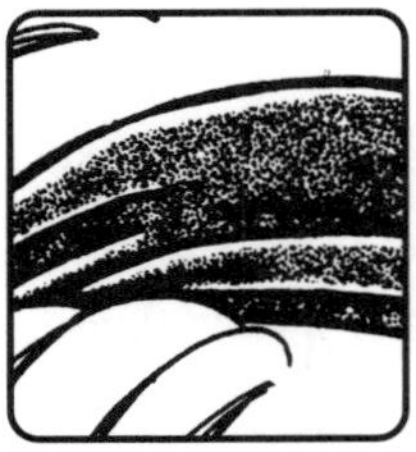

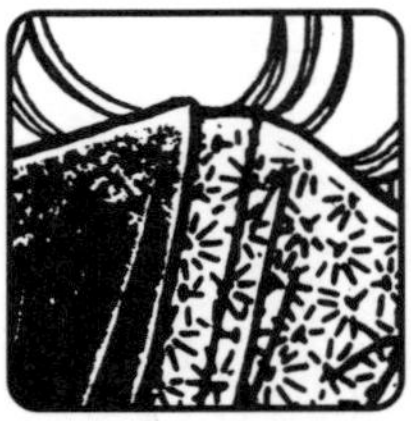

When using random dot or patterned tone, keep a slight gap between contour lines and the tone. In particular, when using motif tone for cloth patterns, having the pattern continue without interruption at, say where a dip in a ripple. etc. should occur, results in a visually awkward image. You can easily show dips in a ripple or crease by etching the tone along the crease line.

① 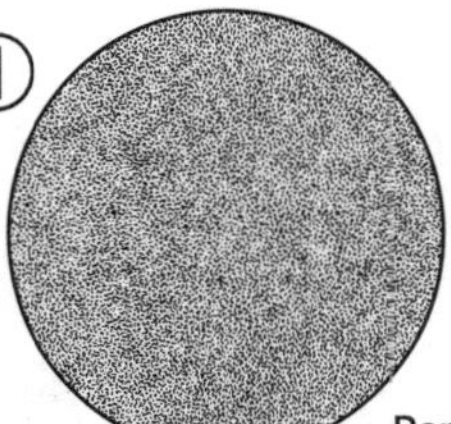
Random dot

② 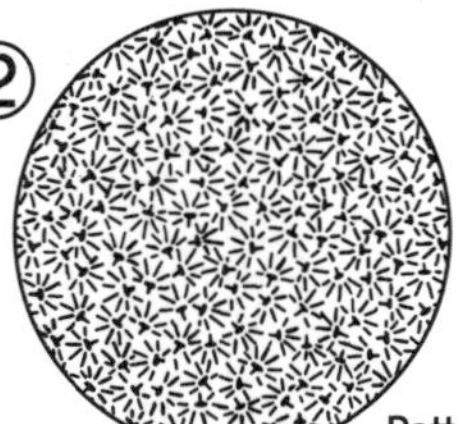
Patterned

③ 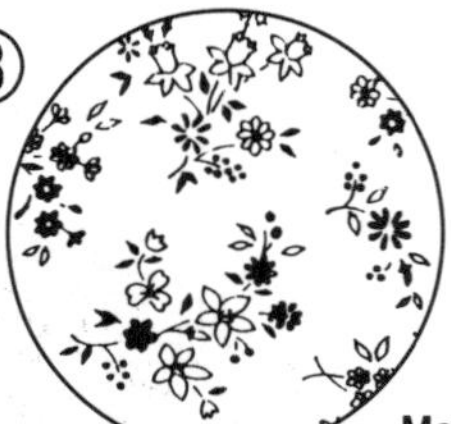
Motif

④ 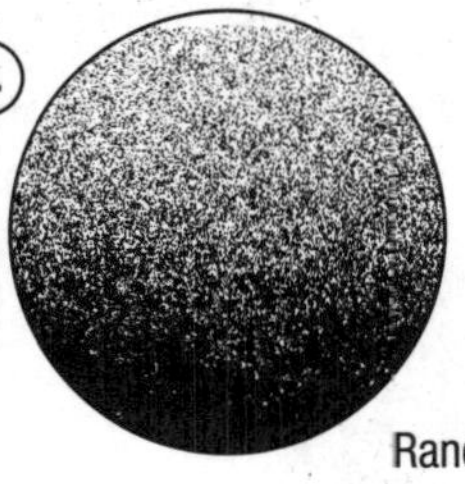
Random dot gradation

⑤ 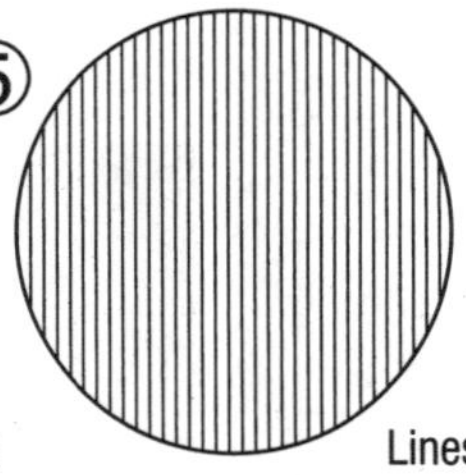
Lines

⑥ 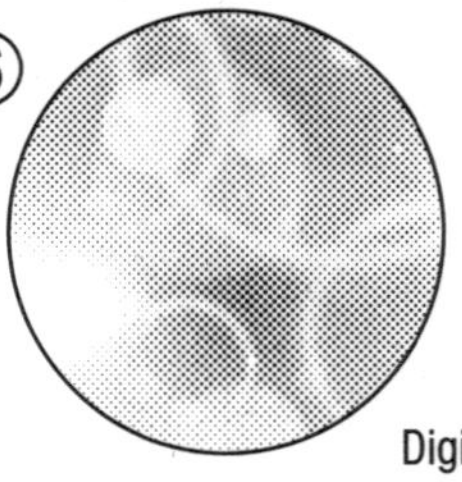
Digital Tone

Artist's Profile

Hikaru Hayashi

1961 Born in Tokyo.

1986 Graduated with a degree in the Social Sciences and Humanities from Tokyo Metropolitan University with a major in Philosophy.

1987 Received a hortative award and honorable mention for his work on Shueisha Inc.'s *Business Jump* and served as assistant to Hajime Furukawa.

1989 Worked on Shueisha's *Shukan Young Jump* while apprenticing under Noriyoshi Inoue.

1992 Published his debut work based on a true story, "*Aja Kongu Monogatari*" ["The Story of Aja Kong"] in *Bear's Club*.

1997 Founded the *manga* design and production studio, Go office. Produced illustrations for the works *Butsuzo ni ai ni iko* [on the appreciation of Buddhist sculpture] by Hiromichi Fukushima (published by Tokyo Bijutsu Inc.)

1998 Authored *How to Draw Manga: Female Characters*, *How to Draw Manga: Male Characters*, *How to Draw Manga: Couples*, and *How to Draw Manga: Illustrating Battles*.

1999 Authored *How to Draw Manga: Bishoujo around the World*, *How to Draw Manga: Bishoujo/Pretty Girls*, *How to Draw Manga: Occult and Horror*, and *How to Draw Manga: More about Pretty Glas* ; promoted, produced, and wrote the *manga* copy for Koki Ishii's *Kokuhatsu manga riken retto* (book on the wasteful spending of Japanese politicians), published by Nesco Co., Ltd.; and produced the corporate identity mascot character for Taiyo Group driving school.

2000 Authored *How to Draw Manga: Animals* ; produced and initiated the release of *Bishoujo Fighting*, a *dojinshi* (fanzine or small press comic) for pro wrestling fans under the name of Meto (a fanzine specializing in woman's wrestling and cat fight videos, published biannually when matches occur; fifth issue on sale as of 2002).

2001 Coauthored *How to Draw Manga: Martial Arts and Combat Sports*, *How to Draw Manga: Giant Robots*, and *How to Draw Manga: Costume Encyclopedia, Everyday Fashion.*

2002 Coauthored *More How to Draw Manga Vol. 1* and *How to Draw Manga: Costume Encyclopedia, Intimate Apparel*, published by Graphic-sha. Mr. Hayashi continues the planning and production of original Go Office fanzines.

Rio Yagizawa

Ms. Yagizawa was born in Tokyo on January 8. She is a Capricorn with an A blood type. She first started doodling in pencil in nursery school and made her first attempt at drawing *manga* in pen during the fifth grade. In junior high, she began to produce *doujinshi* type *manga* works with friends from upper grades and in her class.

In 1981 she debuted as an illustrator with Minori Shobo's monthly publication, *Gekkan OUT*. She acted as an illustrator, an aniparo (animation parody) and *manga* artist, an anime writer, etc., contributing illustrations to Minori Shobo's Aniparo Comics, Akita Publishing's *My Anime*, Tokuma Shoten's *Animage*, etc.

In 1986 she debuted as a full-fledged *manga* artist in Kobunsha's Comic Val. Since then, she has contributed series and single publication works to Kobusha's *Pretty*, as well as cover and page illustrations for paperback editions targeted toward young readers published by Seishinsha, Kadokawa Shoten, Shogakkan, and other publishers. She has authored 9 *manga* volumes and illustrated more than 25 paperback books.

In 1998 she began to participate on the production side with Graphic-sha and Go Office, starting with *How to Draw Manga: Couples* and continues such efforts today.

Go Office Profile

Go Office was founded in May 1997 and has been specialzing in the production of tutorial resources using *manga* and illustrations, which include publications on *How to Draw Manga* series.